# The Eudaimonic Turn

# The Eudaimonic Turn

## *Well-Being in Literary Studies*

Edited by James O. Pawelski and D. J. Moores

FAIRLEIGH DICKINSON UNIVERSITY PRESS
Madison • Teaneck

Published by Fairleigh Dickinson University Press
Copublished by The Rowman & Littlefield Publishing Group, Inc.
4501 Forbes Boulevard, Suite 200, Lanham, Maryland 20706
www.rowman.com

16 Carlisle Street, London W1D 3BT, United Kingdom



First paperback edition 2014



British Library Cataloguing in Publication Information Available

**Library of Congress Cataloging-in-Publication Data**

The hardback edition of this book was previously
catalogued by the Library of Congress as follows:

The Eudaimonic turn : well-being in literary studies / edited by James O. Pawelski and D.J. Moores.
p. cm.
Includes bibliographical references and index.
1. Peace of mind in literature. 2. Happiness in literature. 3. Well-being—Psychological aspects. 4. Books and reading—Psychological aspects. 5. Quality of life. 6. Satisfaction.
I. Pawelski, James O., 1967– II. Moores, D. J
PN56.H27E93 2013
809'.93353—dc23
2012038492

ISBN 978-1-61147-528-9 (cloth : alk. paper)
ISBN 978-1-61147-735-1 (pbk. : alk. paper)
ISBN 978-1-61147-529-6 (electronic)

For Suzie and Liam (J.O.P)

And for Tatsiana (D.J.M.)

with love and gratitude

# Contents

# Acknowledgments

This volume is the fruit of a friendship that started in the Spring of 2010, when we, the editors, met at the University of Pennsylvania's Positive Psychology Center. The initial meeting sparked several conversations, one of which involved the psychologist Marty Seligman, about the intersections of positive psychology and literature. Through these discussions, we discovered much common ground in our explorations of eudaimonia and a shared perspective on how to carry that work forward in the domain of literary studies. One of us (Pawelski) had published a book on William James and the eudaimonic aspects of epiphanic experiences. He was also preparing to teach a graduate course on the "Humanities and Human Flourishing" while leading efforts to explore connections between the science of well-being and the various disciplines in the humanities. The other (Moores) was a specialist in literature who had explored the eudaimonic aspects of transatlantic Romanticism in two previous books and had also just completed editing an anthology of ecstatic poetry. Given these interests, this volume seemed like a valuable way to explore more deeply the importance of well-being in literary studies and to bring together the work of other scholars with similar perspectives.

As we have labored to prepare this volume for publication over the past two years, we have been aided tremendously by a number of people. We would like to thank Marty Seligman, Mihaly Csikszentmihalyi, Chris Peterson, Bob Vallerand, Martha Nussbaum, Susan Wolfson, Darrin McMahon, Jerry Singerman, Ryan Niemiec, and the many others who have offered us such helpful advice and strong encouragement. Thanks to each of the authors for their insightful contributions, and especially to Adam Potkay for writing the Foreword. In addition, we would like to thank our respective universities for much-needed support for our endeavors: the University of Pennsylvania (and especially Nora Lewis and Dave Bieber, as well as the Positive Psychology Center); and Kean University (and especially James Cowen and the Ocean County College Library). We would also like to thank our students, particularly those in the Master of Applied Positive Psychology (MAPP) program at the University of Pennsylvania, including Behdad Bozorgnia and the participants in Pawelski's course on the Humanities and Human Flourishing, as well as students at Kean University who took Moores's courses on ecstatic and eudaimonic poetry. We are grateful to David Dunning, an outstanding student research assistant at the University of Pennsylvania whose insights and perspectives helped to improve this volume in fundamentally significant ways, and to Christina Walling, whose many hours of editorial labor on the text are evident throughout this book. Finally, we would like to thank those to whom this book is dedicated: Suzie and Liam for their love, support, and understanding during the long morning and weekend hours the work required; and Tatsiana for her love, encouragement, and dedication.

# Foreword

## Adam Potkay

"How will this make me a better person?" That's the question with which a high school friend of mine used to torment our senior-year English teacher, as he did his best to get us excited about a variety of great books from the *Odyssey* through *Macbeth*. The question evidently served a couple of purposes. It was, to a large degree, a challenge or accusation, with the rhetorical force of either "why should I know this?" or "this doesn't matter." Taking it in this sense, our teacher dismissed the question as a jibe at authority. But I believe the question was also, at least in small part, a genuine and ethical one: how *does* or *might* literary study make one a better or more flourishing person?

My friend's question was, in effect, my introduction to the moral potential of literature. Earlier I had only a strong sense of the pleasure of books, my life of reading beginning with Marvel Comics (Spider Man, *et alia*) in the 1960s, the so-called silver age of comics, and extending by high school through the twentieth-century American novel and into my first acquaintance with poets. The closest thing to a moral defense of reading I had heard was offered by my father when I was very small and other parents would ask him why he allowed me to read comic books (they were not yet a respectable genre): he would answer that they taught a surprising number of vocabulary-building words. The good of reading, then, pertained to the good of having a good vocabulary. It occurred to me only much later that my father meant this more as a social good than as, strictly speaking, an ethical one—though the line between the two is sometimes a fine one.

I learned many more words, as well as how to do things with words, in my college years (1978–1982). But the moral dimension of literature was then very out of fashion. I was schooled in the slipperiness of language and particularly of literary language. I memorized this dictum by Paul de Man: "Rhetoric radically suspends logic and opens up vertiginous possibilities of referential aberration."[1] I discovered the historical relativity and theoretical instability of binary oppositions, including the ethical ones of good and bad, and good and evil. What was presumed in this unsentimental education was that literary and philosophical study could make one a better person only in the sense of making one more skeptical and tough minded. And these traits greatly appealed to me. Indeed, they proved virtues, I think, insofar as they protected me from an uncritical adherence to the political pieties of much literary criticism in the later 1980s and 1990s, criticism that (in the language of the time) "interrogated" authors of the past according to their notions of race, class, gender, and empire, and very often condemned them.

After skepticism, after suspicion, there was no return to a view of literature as morally edifying in any simple way: for convenience, let's call it the Victorian way. Back in 1850, University of Pennsylvania professor Henry Reed began his *Lectures on English Literature* by addressing literature as "akin to religion, for it is a ministry of the soul, and deals not so much with what we know as with what we are, what we can do and what we can suffer, and what we may become here and hereafter."[2] Very many, perhaps most literature professors today will either smile or cringe at this unabashed statement of literature's place in a religion of humanity. I do not unqualifiedly endorse it myself, but I do find in it a useful corrective or counterweight to the anti-humanist excesses that have characterized literary studies and that have made them largely irrelevant to any but the most rarefied academic audiences—until recently.

But now we find in literary study what James Pawelski and D. J. Moores aptly call the "eudaimonic turn." This phrase requires some clarification. The ancient Greek term *eudaimonia* has traditionally been translated into English as "happiness," although scholars now prefer "(human) flourishing." Eudaimonia literally refers to the "good daemon" or "good genius" that was thought to accompany a successful or flourishing person, but Greek philosophy uses the term to refer to the sort of human flourishing that, independent of good demons, depends upon an individual's reason or choices. Eudaimonism gives reason (or at least reasonableness) pride of place over any and all competing aims and desires found in the psyche or soul; thus it defines happiness as the ability not necessarily to get what you want, but to know what you *should* want, which is the same thing as what you would want were your soul ordered properly. For Plato and the ancient Stoics, happiness often appeared a settled product or once-and-for-all achievement. However, contemporary philosophers who engage with the ancients tend to see happiness as an ongoing process of weighing conflicting desires and motives, the continuous interpretation and evaluation of a life. They may also admit into the happy life the passions (love, joy, even righteous anger), understood as a way of evaluating the world and one's place in it; some, like Charles Altieri, have argued for the noncognitive value of affect in connecting us, with more or less intensity, to life itself.[3]

But how might eudaimonism relate to literary study? Martha Nussbaum argued as long ago as 1983 that literary narrative might contribute to eudaimonistic ethics, maintaining that in the Aristotelian tradition the search for a good or happy life could not be fully guided by antecedent rules but rather must take into account the concrete experiences and particular deliberations that we find in life and literature.[4] Conversely, the study of ethics enabled me, as a literary critic, to get a handle on a moral vocabulary that is now partially lost to most of us. Thus "happiness," though now often used with reference to a subjective mental state, can and still does refer us back to eudaimonia. "Joy," as something quite distinct from happiness, may refer to an individual's passionate response to something that brings pleasure or seems a good; but it also in certain contexts retains its ancient Stoic sense, influentially reflected in the New Testament, of a calm reflective attitude toward the ultimate good. Knowing the full resonance of these words helps one make sense of many works of literature—take, for example, Elizabeth Inchbald's 1791 novel *A Simple Story,* in which the narrator remarks: "poor Matilda's sudden transports of joy, which she termed happiness, were not made for long continuance" (269). Inchbald allows for the ironic discrepancy between what Matilda *calls* her happiness, using the word incorrectly, and what the narrator would have her reader recognize as true happiness—that is, something stable, tranquil, and enduring. Jane Austen follows Inchbald in distinguishing "joy" from "happiness" in a precise way—the precision, in *Sense and Sensibility* (1811), with which "Marianne's joy was almost a degree beyond happiness" in leaving for London with Mrs. Jennings (158). Marianne's joy seems excessive; it is either alien to true happiness, or it disturbs whatever subjective happiness she has. Austen's language here remains slippery—that is the glory of literature—but in doing so, it engages us in questions of how to live.

I'd like then to revise my father's assumption about what literary reading is good for. The good of reading depends in part on developing one's vocabulary about the good or competing goods. Reading is good for finding the words and concepts that might frame our experience or enable our analysis of what we do, what we feel, and who we are. It exercises our intuitive responses to far more life experiences than any one of us is apt to have in our life outside reading. And along the way it's apt to provide some useful moral maxims. Among the maxims I picked up in my early life of reading is this one from Spider Man's inaugural story (originally in *Amazing Fantasy* #15, August 1962): what our hero comes to recognize by the comic's final frame is "that in this world, with great power there must also come—great responsibility!" When I first read this line I had very little power or responsibility, and probably a very imperfect notion of what either of these concept words even meant. But it was exciting to think that one might gain great power, whether through being bitten by a spider or in the normal course of nature. And it was bracing to think, if still only darkly, that great power didn't *just* confer great self-gratification, but that life as it ought to be led had other things in store. By engaging literary characters—be they narrative, dramatic, or lyric—we become, if not necessarily better persons, at least more expert in the forms practical excellence might take.

—Adam Potkay

College of William and Mary

## BIBLIOGRAPHY

Altieri, Charles. *The Particulars of Rapture: An Aesthetics of the Affects*. Ithaca: Cornell University Press, 2003.

Austen, Jane. *Sense and Sensibility*. Edited by R. W. Chapman. 3rd edition, Oxford: University Press, 1933.

De Man, Paul. *Allegories of Reading*. New Haven: Yale University Press, 1979.

Inchbald, Elizabeth. *A Simple Story*. Editd by J. M. S. Tompkins. Oxford: University Press, 1988.

Nussbaum, Martha C. *Love's Knowledge: Essays on Philosophy and Literature*. New York: University Press, 1990.

Reed, Henry. *Lectures on English Literature from Chaucer to Tennyson*. Philadelphia, 1855.

## NOTES

1. Paul de Man, *Allegories of Reading* (New Haven: Yale University Press, 1979), 10.
2. Henry Reed, *Lectures on English Literature from Chaucer to Tennyson* (Philadelphia, 1855), 39.
3. Charles Altieri, *The Particulars of Rapture: An Aesthetics of the Affects* (Ithaca: Cornell University Press, 2003).
4. Martha C. Nussbaum, *Love's Knowledge: Essays on Philosophy and Literature* (New York: University Press, 1990), 138-42.

# Introduction

## *What Is the Eudaimonic Turn?* and *The Eudaimonic Turn in Literary Studies*

James O. Pawelski and D. J. Moores

## WHAT IS THE EUDAIMONIC TURN?

JAMES O. PAWELSKI

Well-being is one of the most central concerns of human experience. In an uncertain world of opportunities and dangers, knowing what makes life go well is of crucial importance. Not something to be taken for granted, well-being often comes only by means of significant efforts to modify subjective experience and objective conditions to suit human needs and interests. On some occasions well-being is easily attained, but at other times it seems to require more than the available resources and skills. Even when everything has apparently been done right, well-being sometimes proves elusive, and it is not apparent what further effort is required to achieve this highly prized outcome. As a result of such frustrations and puzzlements, it is possible to lose clarity about what well-being itself might actually signify.

In spite of these difficulties with well-being, there are certainly times when it seems a fairly straightforward matter. Emotions such as gratitude, serenity, and contentment frequently carry with them a strong sense of well-being, as do more active experiences, such as achieving a long-sought goal, understanding oneself or the world in a deep new way, or becoming inspired by a significant possibility. Well-being also goes beyond subjective feelings and emotions. Objective aspects of life such as physical health, control over one's environment, relationships with others, membership in a supportive community, and meaningful work are also constitutive of well-being.

However ironic it may be, consciousness of well-being is often at its highest when it is threatened, triggering desperate attempts to find protection against its loss. When bodily integrity, possessions, or companions are in peril, all available means are marshaled to eliminate the danger—or, if the danger is overwhelming, to escape from it as expeditiously as possible. Sickness increases the perceived value of health and creates a determination to invest all available resources and expend every effort to recover it. Depression or anxiety raises the value of peace of mind and precipitates a search for pharmacological or psychotherapeutic remedies to reestablish it. Fraud highlights the value of rights and property and instigates litigation to protect the one and recover the other. Oftentimes, it seems human concern lies more with protection against the loss of well-being than with its direct enjoyment, and this imbalance is a key problem this volume is intended to address.

Daily efforts to seek out well-being and find protection against its loss consume much time and many resources. Still, they do not exhaust human interest in the subject. Occasional pauses from these concrete occupations shift attention from concrete to abstract questions about well-being. What, in general, is the best kind of life for human beings to live? In the broadest sense, what does it mean to flourish? What is the overall most worthy way to live? In short, what is the good life?

Difficult though these concrete and abstract questions about well-being may be, there is one sense in which they admit of an easy answer. It is an answer Aristotle indicates when, examining these questions in the *Nicomachean Ethics,* he points to nearly universal agreement among scholars and lay persons alike that "the good life" or "doing well" is the same thing as eudaimonia.[1] Already hundreds of years old at that point, the term *eudaimonia* signified a condition of human flourishing and carried with it connotations of a blessed life. When the Greeks thought about the kind of life in which things are going well, they agreed this was a life of eudaimonia.

This term has traditionally been rendered into English as *happiness,* a problematic translation, since the Greek word carries with it more of a sense of overall flourishing or well-being and less of a sense of the subjective and momentary experience the English term often conveys. But there are some ways in which the word *happiness* plays similar roles in the English language to those played by *eudaimonia* in Greek. People often speak of happiness as their highest goal, friends try to help each other steer toward happiness, and parents often say regardless of the occupation their children choose the most important thing is they be happy. One problem (among many) with the word *happiness,* however, is that people do not always seem to know what they mean by it, and there is no guarantee that friends all share a similar understanding of it or that children will define it in the same way as do their parents.

Similar problems arise in Greek with the word *eudaimonia.* Aristotle observes that digging beneath the surface of the widespread verbal agreement about this term quickly reveals serious complications. After connecting eudaimonia with the good life and doing well, Aristotle continues his analysis by acknowledging that "what constitutes eudaimonia is a matter of dispute."[2] In Aristotle's day, there was considerable disagreement among those who thought of eudaimonia as pleasure, wealth, honor, or virtue. Those debates did not go away but instead formed the basis of a rich conversation that has endured throughout the ensuing millennia and continues to inform academic work in a variety of disciplines today.

An analysis of this conversation in the twenty-first century reveals something striking: a meaningful turn is taking place in the discussion. Scholars across a large number of disciplines are increasingly focusing their attention on the immediate constituents of well-being, attempting to identify and investigate those aspects of the human condition widely accepted to be at the center of human flourishing. Such scholars are less concerned with the study of what can go wrong with human experience and more concerned with the study of what causes individuals to flourish and communities to thrive. These eudaimonic scholars are less interested in ideological pronouncements and entrenched positions and more interested in innovative approaches, interdisciplinary collaborations, and empirical investigations. We call this recent development in the conversation about well-being, with its focus on the interdisciplinary investigation of the best things in life, the "eudaimonic turn." Led in part by new scientific approaches to the study of human flourishing, scholars involved in this turn are asking questions about well-being in novel ways and in a variety of domains. Psychologists are developing advanced methods for measuring well-being, economists are rethinking what it means for a nation to flourish, philosophers are creating new theories of well-being, intellectual historians are reexamining historical debates from the standpoint of current perspectives, and literary theorists are taking up new themes and fresh approaches to interpretation.

This eudaimonic turn is a significant development in the investigation of well-being. The opportunities for theoretical advancement and practical improvement are considerable, especially since the eudaimonic turn is not controlled by any particular religious, political, or ideological agenda but represents a larger scientific and cultural investigation collaboratively carried out by scholars and practitioners of widely varying perspectives and methodologies. What unites them is the endeavor to study well-being by all available methods to create valuable and ever-refinable knowledge for the effective guidance of scholarly inquiries and practical applications.

The eudaimonic turn is important for well-being on the individual and global levels. The resulting knowledge is adding to our scientific understanding of persons and communities, and the practical implications of this knowledge are changing standards of practice in such applied fields as psychotherapy, education, medicine, business, and public policy. At the global level, billions of human beings live in developing economies whose policies and efforts are shaped by certain ideals of well-being and the attempt to realize those ideals for their citizens. It is imperative that these efforts be guided by accurate information about the causes and constituents of well-being. This is especially true if misguided attempts to achieve well-being could prove unsustainable across the globe and ruinous for the environment.[3]

In this introductory chapter, we will consider the eudaimonic turn in more detail, first by exploring some of the agreements and disagreements Greek and Roman writers had about what constitutes eudaimonia, then by examining various theoretical points to show what we mean—and do not mean—by this concept. We will conclude the chapter by surveying the effects of the eudaimonic turn in a number of different disciplines, focusing especially on the field of literary studies to investigate how this turn can enrich our understanding of texts and fuel a search for valuable new interpretive strategies.

### *Ancient Agreements and Disagreements about Eudaimonia*

In contemporary scholarship, the term *eudaimonia* is perhaps most frequently linked to Aristotle, since it figures prominently in his ethics. The term, however, was in use well before Aristotle's time. In his comprehensive study *Happiness: A History*, Darrin McMahon gives a rich account of the historical uses of this word, with its first extant appearance occurring in ancient Greek literature.[4] Hesiod, writing about 700 BCE, uses the word in its adjectival form, ending his *Works and Days* with the claim, "Happy [*eudaimon*] and blessed is the man who knows all this and does his work without offending the immortals, ever watching birds of omen, ever shunning transgression."[5] *Eudaimonia* is a compound word, constructed from the Greek *eu* (good) and *daimon* (god, spirit, demon). It carries with it connotations of good fortune and divinity, of what might be called blessedness. *Eudaimonia* is one of the terms Herodotus uses in the first book of his *Histories* when telling the story of Croesus. An unimaginably wealthy king of Lydia, Croesus thought his position must make him the happiest[6] man in the world. The visiting Athenian sage Solon, however, nominated for this title a commoner who had lived and died well. Upon being questioned by Croesus, Solon argued that human beings are subject to many things outside their control, including reversals of fortune, and that it is not safe to call a man happy until he is dead. For Solon, and for Herodotus, happiness is closely connected with fate, fortune, and good luck.[7]

Indeed, this view seems to be borne out in the epic poems and tragic plays that comprised so much of ancient Greek literature.[8] At every turn, protagonists are subject to reversals of fate brought about by causes beyond their control. While those who struggle against fate may be admirable, in the end they lose the struggle. In those cases where the story does turn out well, it is frequently through a *deus ex machina* intervention, once again showing that happiness is beyond human control. For these reasons, McMahon argues that "happiness at the dawn of Western history was largely a matter of chance."[9]

Beginning with Socrates, Greek philosophers took a very different opinion of human happiness. It was Socrates who applied to the study of human nature the rigorous methods earlier Greek philosophers had developed to investigate the natural world. He was the first of a number of influential philosophers to lead his life around the study, practice, and teaching of well-being. In contrast to the tragic notion of happiness present in so much Greek literature, Socrates argued that human beings have agency and that its proper use can lead to happiness. As Plato explains in his dialogues, however, the philosophical notion of happiness is very different from the sensual and hedonistic experiences the Greek writers spent so much time pursuing. Philosophical happiness turns normal conceptions of happiness upside down, as can perhaps most clearly be seen in Plato's *Symposium*.[10]

The philosophical treatment of happiness brought eudaimonia into the realm of ethics. Indeed, as Julia Annas points out, eudaimonia is the most important and central theme in all of ancient ethics.[11] In his most important ethical work, the *Nicomachean Ethics*, Aristotle takes up the discussion, arguing that eudaimonia is something that is valued for its own sake and not as a means to some other end. It is for the sake of eudaimonia, he argues, that we do everything we do. It is "the End at which all actions aim,"[12] the highest human good. As we have already seen, Aristotle observes that there is near-universal agreement that all human actions are for the sake of eudaimonia but acknowledges that there are many opinions as to what constitutes eudaimonia. He considers and rejects claims that eudaimonia consists in pleasure, honor, virtue, wealth, or a Universal Idea of the Good and argues, instead, that eudaimonia consists in human beings playing their proper function well. That proper function, he claims, is to reason, and he argues that reason is of two kinds: theoretical and practical. Eudaimonia, then, consists in the excellent use of both theoretical and practical reason. Aristotle specifies further that to be truly *eudaimon*, a person must use reason in this way for an entire life, not just one day. He also argues that some external goods are necessary for eudaimonia. Friends, wealth, and political power are sometimes needed for noble actions, he claims, and eudaimonia in full measure is not possible without good birth, satisfactory children, and personal beauty.[13]

After Aristotle's death, a number of philosophical schools were founded around different conceptions of eudaimonia. Two of the most influential were the Epicurean and the Stoic schools. The Epicureans held that eudaimonia consists in pleasure, defining pleasure largely in negative terms, in *ataraxia* (freedom from mental anguish) and *aponia* (freedom from physical pain). This negative approach rendered Epicureanism a rather conservative form of hedonism, since its proponents taught that pleasures bringing pain in their wake are to be avoided in favor of purer, if less intense, pleasures. While we may tend to think of virtue as an enemy of hedonism, the Epicureans thought of hedonism as an essential means to the achievement of the kind of pleasure they sought. In contrast to the Epicureans, the Stoics held that eudaimonia consists in virtue itself. Like the Epicureans, they described their desired state with a negative term: *apatheia*, or freedom from control by the passions. The Stoic ideal was to live in accordance with the rational soul of the universe, accepting without complaint or frustration the things that happen in one's life. The Stoics argued that eudaimonia is an internal state, completely independent of the conditions of one's life, so that a wise person can be happy even on the rack.[14]

This brief overview of some of the most important views on eudaimonia in the ancient world shows significant agreements and disagreements. The philosophers whose views we have discussed agree that eudaimonia is the final goal of life and that it is an active state over which we have at least some control. In addition, they hold that eudaimonia is not a temporary condition but rather a lifelong matter, and they contend that it is not simply subjective: thinking one is happy is not sufficient to make it so. These points must be especially emphasized when following the convention of translating eudaimonia as happiness, as we have done here, since they are points of departure between the meaning of eudaimonia and some common meanings of happiness. In spite of the agreements among them, however, these thinkers disagree sharply on some key points. Although they all agree that virtue is necessary for eudaimonia, only the Stoics (and perhaps Socrates) hold that virtue is sufficient for eudaimonia. Aristotle in particular emphasizes that it is possible to be virtuous without being happy. The connection between eudaimonia and pleasure is also a matter of contention among these thinkers, with the Epicureans claiming that pleasure is the same thing as eudaimonia, the Stoics arguing that it is unimportant for eudaimonia, and Aristotle holding that it is a byproduct of the virtuous life. Finally, there is disagreement on the role of external goods in eudaimonia, with Aristotle arguing that they are indispensable, the Stoics that they are irrelevant.

### *What Do We Mean by the Eudaimonic Turn?*

Moving from the various views on eudaimonia in the ancient world to what we mean by it in this volume, we must begin with a caveat. It is inevitable that there be considerable indeterminacy in a word used for hundreds of years in Greek literature and philosophy and then occupying a central role for thousands of years more in debates among subsequent generations of international scholars. Our intention here is not to stake out claims regarding the various historical meanings of the term or to theorize about what the word should mean. We will focus, instead, on three different meanings the word can take; meanings that, similarly, correspond to three different meanings of the term *well-being*. In its most limited sense, eudaimonia can refer to those aspects of life that are directly constitutive of well-being. In a broader sense, it can be taken to mean those aspects of life that bear in some positive or negative way on well-being, aspects philosophers sometimes refer to as prudential values. In a still broader sense, it can refer to the domain of all human values dealing with the choice-worthy life, with what is often referred to as the good life. Each of these meanings is important, but if not properly distinguished they can cause considerable confusion.

When we refer to the eudaimonic turn, we are primarily using the term *eudaimonia* in the first, most limited of these meanings. As already mentioned, eudaimonia refers to well-being or human flourishing, with its root *daimon* connecting it to divinity and giving it a connotation of blessedness. Eudaimonia refers to the things that make life most worth living and thus enable human beings to thrive. Most centrally, then, what we mean by the eudaimonic turn is an increased interest in well-being, human flourishing, and thriving. This includes things such as joy, love, tranquility, wisdom, creativity, optimism, inspiration, personal growth, positive relationships, purpose in life, life satisfaction, and play. It is important to note that we do not mean by the eudaimonic turn an absolutely precise theory to which all the scholars involved in it subscribe; rather, this term serves as a general description of a number of closely related approaches that share some key perspectives. Our aim is to clarify some of these key perspectives without forcing uniformity on the variety of rich projects that are based on some shared core values but that do not align in every detail. While these projects have much in common, there is still room—and significant need—for healthy debate.

The eudaimonic turn can perhaps best be described in terms of what psychologist Mihaly Csikszentmihalyi has referred to as a "metaphysical orientation."[15] This metaphysical orientation holds that the good things in life are just as real as the bad things. This implies that positive emotions are just as real as negative emotions and are not just the relief from or transformation of negative emotions, that mental health is just as real as mental illness and is not just the absence of psychopathology, that strengths are just as real as weaknesses, and that optimal psychological states like flow are just as real as states of anxiety and depression. The metaphysical orientation of the eudaimonic turn stops short of the more extreme metaphysical orientations toward the good suggested by philosophers throughout history. It stops short, for example, of joining Plato in orienting metaphysics around the "good beyond being;"[16] of claiming, as Augustine does—with his doctrine that evil is merely a "privation" of the good—that existence can properly be predicated only of the good;[17] or even of arguing with Leibniz that, since this is the "best of all possible worlds," it contains as much goodness as it possibly can.[18] It is important not to take the affirmation of the good or the positive as a sign of dispensing with the bad or the negative, as both false friends and false enemies of the eudaimonic turn sometimes do. False friends applaud the eudaimonic turn for the same thing for which false friends critique it: dismissing the negative. Such friends and enemies, however, are both false, since the eudaimonic turn does not imply a dismissal of the negative. Without making metaphysical claims about the negative, leading voices of the eudaimonic turn in various disciplines have pointed out that positive states and processes have all too often been ignored in the interest of attempts to repair negative conditions. This is a deceptively simple point and requires careful thought to understand its full import. Let us consider this claim and its implications more carefully by means of a thought experiment.

Imagine a neuroscientific breakthrough in which researchers develop two pills to enhance specific human mental powers. A red pill enhances the ability to fight against threats to well-being such as hunger, poverty, violence, and injustice; and a green pill enhances the ability to fight for constituents of well-being such as peace, understanding, harmony, and justice. Which pill would be of greater service to the human race?

It may seem immediately obvious that the red pill would be of more value. Given the suffering in the world today, it seems more important to end that suffering than it does to add to the pleasure of those who are not suffering. If two children are in a nursery and one is crying and the other is smiling, it seems cruel to ignore the crying child in order to try to make the smiling child laugh. If people are starving to death or killing each other in battle, it would seem irresponsible to ignore them to help well-off citizens of peaceful countries increase their enjoyment of life. A further point in favor of the red pill is the consideration that eliminating harm will allow the things we value to grow. If a child stops crying, she will be able to notice things that make her smile and laugh. When people put down their guns and stop killing each other, they will be able to invest their time and energy in improving their lives. It is hard to build schools and community centers, after all, while dodging bullets or suffering from malnutrition. Finally, it might seem that there would be much more agreement on how to put the red pill to good use. It often seems much easier to agree on what problems need to be solved than on what opportunities should be pursued. This has been played out repeatedly on various national stages when citizens of a country unite to overthrow a dictator and subsequently splinter into bitter rival factions that have a hard time agreeing on how to move the country forward.

Further consideration may point out some advantages of the green pill. First, relative advantages may arise because of problems associated with use of the red pill. There are at least some times when focusing on getting rid of harm seems to make the undesirable thing multiply. Fighting violence with violence, for example, often seems to have the effect of spreading violence. Killing terrorists seems to increase their numbers, and incarcerating criminals often has the effect of multiplying them. In these cases, the processes meant to put a stop to something actually seem to perpetuate that very thing. Second, there are many cases where use of the red pill does not obviate the need for the green pill but use of the green pill does seem to render the red pill unnecessary. Getting rid of harmful things does not necessarily result in the growth of beneficial things. Children who stop crying do not necessarily start smiling. People who stop killing each other do not necessarily turn their attention to the founding of civic institutions, the growth of social capital, and the building of economic prosperity. Getting rid of violence will not necessarily bring harmony. Yet, conversely, children who start smiling stop crying. People who turn their attention to the founding of civic institutions, the growth of social capital, and the building of economic prosperity typically stop killing each other. If people feel harmony toward each other, violence will end. It seems, then, that there are at least some cases where eliminating harmful things does not necessarily result in the growth of beneficial things, but where growing beneficial things does eliminate harmful things. Finally, beneficial things are of great value to our lives. The purpose of life must surely be broader than simply the eradication of the things that cheapen or threaten it. It is the green pill that directly addresses so many of the experiences and conditions that make life worth living. Love, joy, beauty, ecstasy, wisdom, intimacy, belongingness, understanding, and the like are among the things we value most in life. Their enhancement and enjoyment must make up at least part of the core of the good life.

Admittedly, this thought experiment has its limitations. The criteria by which certain things are determined to be beneficial and others to be harmful are simply assumed. Moreover, the beneficial and the harmful (and earlier in the text, the good and the bad and the positive and the negative) are presented as a simple dyad with no possibility indicated for something to be both or neither. Although this is problematic in ways we discuss below, it is valuable to pause before rushing to deconstruct the binary. The distinction between things deemed beneficial and things deemed harmful (and between what is perceived to be good and bad or positive and negative) has deep psychological and physiological roots. Following Kurt Lewin, psychologists often put this distinction in terms of approach and avoidance motivation. In accordance with present needs, subjects are motivated to move toward certain stimuli and embrace certain experiences and to move away from other stimuli and reject those experiences. Researchers have argued that this basic tendency for approach or avoidance is an elemental reaction of all organisms to their environment, that it is the result of automatic evaluations processes, and that there are different approach and avoidance systems in the brain.[19] On this evidence, the thought experiment may not be as far-fetched as it might have initially seemed. If there are different approach and avoidance systems in the brain, then it is at least theoretically possible to develop a way to enhance those systems. More relevant to present purposes, however, is the recognition that the experiences and results of using each of these systems are very different. The point of this thought experiment is not to argue that one pill is better than the other (humans would be lost without both approach and avoidance systems); rather, the intention is to help point out a problematic ambiguity between two different meanings of eudaimonia (and well-being).

A look at the definition of well-being in contemporary philosophical discourse can help bring this ambiguity to the fore. Daniel Haybron states this definition as follows: "The concept of well-being is a normative or evaluative concept that concerns what *benefits* a person, is in her *interest,* is *good for* her, or makes her life *go well for* her."[20] Clearly, getting what is good for a person helps life go well for that person. In light of the thought experiment above, however, there is also another question to be asked. Is it not also true that avoiding what is harmful for a person also helps life go well for that person? There seem to be two different approaches to having life go well: directly, by getting more of what is beneficial; and indirectly, by getting less of what is harmful. The term *well-being* is applied sometimes in a more limited sense to what is directly beneficial and sometimes in a broader sense to what is either directly or indirectly beneficial. A lack of clarity here can lead to problematic ambiguities in discussions of eudaimonia and well-being. Let us consider this point further.

If what is of direct benefit to a person is well-being, then what is of direct harm can be referred to as ill-being. Mitigating ill-being, of course, is an indirect way of making life better. It seems that overall well-being, then, is a function of enhancing direct well-being and mitigating ill-being. Referring to overall well-being in this way makes it possible to think of well-being as a continuum on which some people enjoy positive levels of well-being and others suffer negative levels of well-being. Thinking this way may be helpful, but it is important to keep in mind that this continuum is actually a composite of two irreducible components: the level of direct well-being and the level of ill-being. Suppose someone is asked on a psychological measure to indicate his level of overall well-being on a scale from +10 to -10. If he rates his level of well-being at a 2, this could mean a couple of different things. It could mean that he does not have much to celebrate in his life but that he has even less to complain about, so things average out to being slightly positive; or it could mean that he is under tremendous strain and pressure but that he is also enjoying significant success, so overall his well-being is slightly positive. To understand this point more clearly, it will be helpful to explore the meaning of opposites and the sense in which the terms *well-being* and *ill-being* are opposites.

A satisfactory definition of a term is one that includes everything to which a term refers and nothing to which it does not refer. In some cases, however, the domain to which a term does not refer contains the term's opposite. An opposite is a special case of what a term does not mean. It has a particular logical relation to the original term, a relation that can be called an inverse reference. Consider the term *light. Light* refers to certain types of electromagnetic waves. It is what a candle flame shines into a room at night and what makes the world visible when the sun comes up in the morning. Clearly, there is a large domain of things not referred to by the term *light.* This domain includes things like rain, squirrel, and molecule. There is, however, one item in the domain of things to which *light* does not refer that bears a special logical relation to it. Darkness is clearly not an example of light, but it has a certain logical relation to it that rain, squirrel, and molecule do not: darkness is the absence of light. Because of this relation, in which light inversely refers to darkness, we say that darkness is the opposite of light. Light and darkness are examples of what can be called existential opposites, since the relation that makes them opposites is the existence/nonexistence of the same thing. They are on a continuum, with light at one end and darkness at the other, and wherever one starts on that continuum, moving toward light necessarily means moving away from darkness and moving away from darkness necessarily means moving toward light.

Consider another set of opposites: joy and sadness. Joy and sadness are opposites in a very different sense than are light and darkness. Joy and sadness are not existential opposites, since they are not the presence and absence of the same thing. Rather, they are examples of what can be called "substantive opposites." They are each substantial, real states. They are considered opposites because of the contrasting ways we feel and behave when experiencing them. It is possible, however, to experience joy but not sadness, sadness but not joy, or neither joy nor sadness. It is even possible to experience both joy and sadness at the same time, as baseball player Kendry Morales of the Los Angeles Angels did when he hit a game-winning grand slam then finished his tour of the bases with an ill-fated celebratory leap to home plate that twisted and broke his leg. In the case of joy and sadness, then, the presence (or absence) of one does not indicate the presence (or absence) of the other, nor does an increase (or decrease) of one specify an increase (or decrease) of the other.

Coming back to the discussion of well-being, it is clear that, like joy and sadness, well-being and ill-being are substantive opposites. They are both real conditions and not simply the presence or absence of the same thing. A person can have high or low (or increasing or decreasing) levels of well-being at the same time she has high or low (or increasing or decreasing) levels of ill-being. This means attempts to increase well-being in the composite sense will have to consider both levels of direct well-being and levels of ill-being. Neither direct well-being nor composite well-being is simply the absence of ill-being, and a person's best interests are served by having both high levels of well-being and low levels of ill-being.[21]

If human flourishing requires both high levels of well-being and low levels of ill-being, where should efforts be expended and limited resources concentrated in order to maximize flourishing? Should the focus be on understanding and cultivating what is directly beneficial, or should it be on understanding and removing various obstacles to human flourishing? This is a difficult question, and it may be that no single answer can serve as a guide in all circumstances. Scholars in a wide variety of disciplines, however, argue that whatever the right ratio between the promotion of well-being and the mitigation of ill-being might be, the balance has been severely skewed toward the mitigation of ill-being. The reason the eudaimonic turn is so widespread is that there is a strong sense among these scholars that the promotion of well-being has been neglected to the point that overall levels of flourishing are suffering.[22]

To this point, we have been discussing well-being and ill-being as though they were strict dyads. There is such a tendency to conflate them, especially through a confusion between direct well-being and composite well-being, that it is important to dwell on their difference. It is also important, however, to acknowledge that they are not completely separate and to show how they are related. The intention here is not to deconstruct the binary until all difference is again lost, as that would run counter to the points made above. There are, however, three specific interrelations to be considered.

First, although well-being and ill-being are substantive opposites, there is good evidence that they are moderately negatively correlated. Researchers using the Positive and Negative Affect Schedule (PANAS) know it is possible to score high on positive emotions and low on negative emotions, low on positive emotions and high on negative emotions, high on both positive and negative emotions, or low on both positive and negative emotions. There is, however, a moderate tendency that persons high on one will be low on the other.[23] Sociologist Corey Keyes has found a similar relation when measuring overall mental health. His complete state model, described in more detail in the next section, is a composite of levels of mental flourishing (well-being) and levels of mental illness (ill-being). Here, too, it is possible to have any combination of high and low scores, but those who score high on one dimension have a moderate tendency to score low on the other.[24] Research in neuroscience has also supported this conclusion about well-being and ill-being. In one study, discussed below, researchers tested nine biomarkers to see if they behaved as distinct or mirrored characteristics and found that seven behaved as distinct characteristics and two behaved in a mirrored way.[25] That is, seven of the biomarkers behaved as substantive opposites and two as existential opposites.

The empirical results just mentioned provide good evidence that, although well-being and ill-being are substantially different, there is some real connection between them. They are moderately inversely correlated, so persons who have one at any given time are somewhat less likely to have the other at that same time. The situation becomes more complicated with the introduction of the time element to consider how the present occurrence of one effects the subsequent occurrence of the other. Interestingly, the effects are somewhat asymmetrical. On the one hand, the present occurrence of well-being predicts a lowered likelihood of ill-being in the future; that is, well-being provides a buffer against the onset of ill-being. Joy provides a buffer against sadness, optimism provides a buffer against depression, and meaning provides a buffer against despair. It is as though well-being provides a kind of "eudaimonic capital" that can be drawn on in difficult times. There is no guarantee, of course, that well-being will prevent the growth of ill-being, but it often makes that growth more difficult. On the other hand, the present occurrence of ill-being does not necessarily lead to lower levels of well-being in the future. There are occasions, in fact, where going through traumatic experiences can increase our well-being in the long run. As Nietzsche famously claimed, "What does not kill me makes me stronger."[26] Empirical research shows that, although this is not always true, it is true to a surprising degree. Many people, of course, are shattered by what does not kill them. Victims of war, violent crime, and natural disasters often suffer posttraumatic stress disorder (PTSD), with their conscious and subconscious lives forever damaged by the events they experienced. In this case, the presence of ill-being predicts lowered well-being in the future. Other people in similar circumstances are resilient and bounce back more or less to the level of well-being they had before suffering the traumatic event. Significantly, there is a third group of people who, with Nietzsche, are made stronger by what does not kill them. They experience posttraumatic growth (PTG), with the presence of ill-being leading to increased levels of well-being in the future.[27] This outcome is of special interest to eudaimonic scholars. It is important to understand how some people are able to transform difficult experiences into positive outcomes, in part to see if processes of this sort are teachable. It is also important, however, not to overemphasize the value of trauma. Not all trauma leads to growth, and not all growth comes from trauma. Empirical researchers have begun investigating postecstatic growth (PEG) to try to understand the long-term positive effects that sometimes follow moments of intense well-being,[28] and Csikszentmihalyi and his colleagues have spent decades documenting the considerable growth that can result from the positive state of flow, where one is fully immersed in an activity in which skills and challenges are matched.[29]

These considerations demonstrate that, while well-being and ill-being are substantially different, they also interact robustly. Further considerations show an even greater level of indeterminacy in these concepts. To this point, we have defined them fairly loosely in terms of what is beneficial versus what is harmful, and we have stated some examples of each. These examples, however, are not quite as straightforward as we have implied. Joy is an emotion we have classed with well-being. All things being equal, this categorization seems appropriate. But things are not always equal. There are times when joy is not an appropriate emotional response and even times when it is an indicator of a pathological condition like a psychotic break. Conversely, sadness is an emotion we have classed with ill-being. Again, this seems like an appropriate categorization—until we consider that there are certain contexts, like personal tragedies or national calamities, where sadness is a healthy response. These examples indicate that no state, quality, or process can be categorically identified with either well-being or ill-being, since the context is crucial in such a determination. The situation becomes even more complex, moreover, when we consider that even a knowledge of the context may be insufficient for making the proper identification, since there is often considerable disagreement on what counts as a healthy response. This indeterminacy is considerable and important. Failure to be aware of it can lead to a number of confusions and unfortunate consequences. It would be a mistake, however, to use this indeterminacy as a cause for abandoning the eudaimonic turn. On the contrary, the indeterminacy itself is all the more reason for a careful investigation of these matters that are so vital to human experience. The eudaimonic turn, with its multiple methods of inquiry from an array of research traditions in the humanities and sciences, is a key resource for effectively understanding and cultivating human flourishing, in spite of the indeterminacy involved. The role of the humanities, in particular, is all the more crucial since well-being is a culturally bound construct. Like the concept of health, well-being involves a number of concrete factual markers, but the way these are put together to define the term is subject to debate. Conceptions of well-being need to stick as closely as they can to the facts, but they also go beyond the facts to what we value. The eudaimonic turn, then, seeks new factual knowledge about human flourishing, but it also encourages robust discussion of cultural processes for creating the best possible constructs of well-being.

We noted at the outset of this section that there are three definitions of the term *eudaimonia* (one primary and two secondary) that are of particular importance for our present discussion. To this point, we have focused on the primary meaning of the term, on its reference to those things directly constitutive of well-being. We have discussed how direct well-being is similar to and different from ill-being and from composite well-being, and we have explored some of the resulting complexities and indeterminacies of this concept. We turn now to a (somewhat briefer) consideration of the secondary meanings of *eudaimonia*.

The first of these two secondary meanings refers to a particular domain of values. Beyond direct well-being, eudaimonia can refer generically to the overall domain of human interest in well-being and ill-being. To avoid confusion, we will refer to eudaimonia in this generic sense as "prudential value," intending by this term to refer in a general way to things that relate to how a person is doing. Enhancing direct well-being is an example of a prudential value and so is mitigating ill-being. It is important to recognize that, although scholars involved in the eudaimonic turn emphasize the significance of direct well-being and hold its enhancement to be a prudential value of great importance, they do not claim that this is the only important prudential value in life or even necessarily that it is the most important one. A researcher could very well hold that the mitigation of ill-being is more important, in general, than the promotion of well-being but also contend that the imbalanced emphasis on the former calls for a renewed focus on the latter.

Just as the eudaimonic turn does not imply the claim that direct well-being is the only prudential value or even that it is the most important of the prudential values, so it does not imply the claim that prudential values are the only human values or even that they are necessarily the most important ones. There are other important human values, as the philosopher Roger Crisp indicates when he writes that "well-being is a kind of value, sometimes called 'prudential value,' to be distinguished from, for example, aesthetic value or moral value."[30] Crisp goes on to note that what distinguishes prudential value from aesthetic or moral value is that it is good for the subject. All things being equal, joy is good for those who experience it. We may also consider a poem celebrating joy. The joy of the poem may be an aesthetic value, and it may be good for us to read about such joy, but it does not make sense for us to talk about this joy as being "good for" the poem. Perhaps more clearly and of greater importance, prudential values are very different from moral values. It may be morally good to return a stranger's wallet with the money still in it, but it is not immediately clear whether this is prudentially good, since it is not evident that this serves the finder's interests.

The relation between prudential value and moral value has long been a matter of dispute in philosophy. In the first book of Plato's *Republic*, Thrasymachus famously argues that virtue is a detriment to one's prudential interests. Plato's refutation of this position, which he puts in the mouth of Socrates, is that only a virtuous soul can flourish, a point that does not seem completely convincing. It did not, for example, persuade Immanuel Kant, who argued that there are plenty of cases where happiness and vice coexist. Kant had a variety of disagreements with the Greeks on the relation between prudential and moral values. Although he did agree with Aristotle on the importance of reason, he rejected Aristotle's claim that the ultimate aim of life is prudential. For Kant, the proper function of reason is to produce a good will, with a good will (and not happiness) being the highest human good. Without a good will, he points out, all other things, including power, riches, honor, health, general well-being, and even happiness, are corruptible. The only thing that is not corruptible, Kant claims, is a good will, and a good will makes us moral but not necessarily happy. It follows, then, that morality and not happiness must be our proper end. Kant does not, however, disparage happiness; he argues, in fact, that the good life is composed of both morality and happiness. Although a moral life does not guarantee a happy life, he concludes, it does make us worthy of happiness, and although our chief duty is to morality, we may choose happiness when it is not in conflict with duty.[31] Kant would have no quarrel with the eudaimonic turn, then, as long as moral values are prioritized over prudential ones when they are in conflict. A mere consideration of the devastation that follows when political leaders put prudential values above moral values makes Kant's stipulation seem reasonable. Placing moral values above prudential ones, however, does not render the latter unimportant. Even if they are not the only values we have, or even the most important ones, prudential values are still enormously significant for shaping our lives and the world.

The final definition of *eudaimonia* we will consider here is even broader than prudential values and refers to the entire domain of human values. It is in this sense that the term *well-being* sometimes refers to all the things we value in life. Although philosophers, as we have seen, may try to limit the use of this term to prudential considerations, common usage sometimes includes other values, such as moral values, as part of what in the broadest sense constitutes a life of well-being. In some places, even Aristotle seems to conform to this common usage. Haybron argues that there is a fundamental ambiguity in the way Aristotle uses the term *eudaimonia*. On the one hand, he defines it as "the highest of all the goods that action can achieve."[32] It is "the End at which all actions aim,"[33] the "Supreme Good,"[34] the "good life."[35] Haybron states more precisely what is meant by the good life:

> To give a theory of the good life is not to characterize some special kind of value, but simply to specify all the things that ultimately matter in life, whether they benefit the agent or not. THE GOOD LIFE functions as an umbrella concept encompassing the domain of values that matter in a person's life, and can be employed within any ethical framework.[36]

Understood in this way, eudaimonia refers to all the things we value in life, without specifying exactly what those things are. It stands for the final good, the ultimate end for which all the actions of our lives are undertaken, but it does not provide any detail as to what, specifically, should be included in that life. It is certainly helpful to have this term available, but it is also important to realize that it is, as Julia Annas puts it, "an obvious, but thin, specification of the final good."[37] Aristotle himself recognizes this when he writes, "to say however that the Supreme Good is happiness will probably appear a truism; we still require a more explicit account of what constitutes happiness."[38] His more explicit account, as we have seen, is that happiness lies in the active fulfilling of our proper function (which is to reason), and in doing it well and over a lifetime. This involves a very different use of the term *eudaimonia* than when referring to the good life. In this sense, it is not just a general term standing for some as yet unspecified set of values; rather, it is a specific theory of what it means to do and be well. For Haybron, Aristotle does not adequately distinguish these two uses of the term *eudaimonia* and thus tries to understand well-being by asking questions about the good life. As Haybron points out, however, a theory of well-being is very different from a theory of the good life. Still, we do sometimes use the term *well-being* in a very broad way to refer to a good life, and a good life seems connected to well-being in the fullest and richest sense of the term, in the sense that describes the overall best, most choice-worthy life. In this sense, eudaimonia and well-being may, indeed, be connected to the full domain of human values.

In light of this discussion of eudaimonia and well-being, we can state more precisely what we mean by the eudaimonic turn in this volume. In a broad sense, we mean a general concern with the overall question of well-being. We mean a return to the central questions of Greek ethics: How ought I to live? What should my life be like? In this broad sense, the eudaimonic turn means a return to these ancient questions, to a consideration of the full range of human values and the good life. In the contemporary context, however, this return is accompanied by new knowledge, new perspectives, and new cultural conditions that help generate new answers, fitting for our times, to these perennial questions. In a less broad sense, by the eudaimonic turn we also mean a reengagement with prudential values. We mean a focus on questions about what is in a person's best interest, what is good for a person, what benefits a person. Prudential concerns are certainly not the only things we value, but they are critically important, both for the quality of individual lives and for the overall welfare of the human race. These two meanings of the eudaimonic turn are important, but it is a more limited meaning that is primary for our purposes in this volume. In this core sense, we mean by the eudaimonic turn an emphasis on that which is directly constitutive of well-being. We mean by it the study of human flourishing in all its forms, the investigation of what it means for individuals and communities to thrive.

We will shortly take up an examination of the work carried out by scholars making the eudaimonic turn in various disciplines. Before doing so, however, it is important to make a few further theoretical observations about this turn. First, this shift in the conversation about well-being is a turn and not a revolution. Although it is true that scholars involved in the eudaimonic turn argue for an increased emphasis on what humans directly value, they are aiming, in good Greek fashion, for greater balance. Not seeking a revolution, which would simply cause an imbalance in the opposite direction, they do not advocate discarding everything outside of the eudaimonic turn. On the contrary, they understand that the interests of well-being in the composite sense would not be served by an exclusive focus on the cultivation of direct well-being and that it is important to continue to find protection from the harms and threats that vitiate human experience and destroy human life. The secondary meanings of the eudaimonic turn are especially important in this regard, since they help situate its primary meaning within the full range of prudential and nonprudential values that are important for well-being in its broadest sense.

Second, the well-being that is the focus of the eudaimonic turn is not the shallow kind of happiness that has rightly been criticized by so many careful thinkers.[39] Nietzsche was deeply critical of a kind of happiness that values comfort, ease, and security above all. He calls the person who is happy in this sense "the last man," and describes him as "the most contemptible of all things."[40] Last men are contemptible, for Nietzsche, because they avoid the hardships and challenges necessary for growth, seeing in them threats to their lives of contentment. More important than the will to happiness, Nietzsche argues, is the will to power. More important than ease through the avoidance of suffering is greatness through the affirmation of suffering and the overcoming of obstacles. Nietzsche describes the Übermensch as one who holds nothing back in the service of the will to power, who lives only for the realization of one's full potential. In the language of the eudaimonic turn, Nietzsche rejects a shallow kind of happiness in favor of a robust form of well-being. As we have already seen, posttraumatic growth is a real path toward increased well-being. It is a path the Übermensch has found, and although he no doubt focuses too exclusively on this single means of achieving well-being, his emphasis is an important reminder to avoid the temptations of lazy happiness.

Third, and related to this point, the work of the eudaimonic turn is complex, and the investigation and cultivation of well-being is difficult. In contrast to the simplistic formulas, effortless programs, and guaranteed approaches to happiness that flood the self-help market every year, the study and cultivation of direct well-being is just as serious as the investigation and mitigation of ill-being. Nothing about this study is simplistic, effortless, or guaranteed. There are no shortcuts to well-being. As we will see in the next section, it is the painstaking application of the best research methods in each field that brings real progress to the understanding of human flourishing. Each of the scholars involved in this work shares the metaphysical orientation discussed earlier that the positive is just as real as the negative. Where they differ is in the epistemological methods of inquiry they employ. The methods of investigation in empirical psychology, neuroscience, economics, philosophy, and literary studies are significantly different from each other. Part of the fascination of work in the eudaimonic turn comes from noting the range of investigations into well-being that employ various empirical, statistical, theoretical, and hermeneutical methods. Perhaps even more impressive is the multidisciplinary work that yields results beyond what can be obtained through any single method of investigation. If the work of the eudaimonic turn is to be successful, all reliable methods of inquiry will be required.

Fourth, the eudaimonic turn is concerned with both individual and collective well-being. A comprehensive understanding of human flourishing requires clarity about human thriving at the individual, relational, organizational, communal, and social levels. Although we acknowledge the importance of human thriving at all these levels, our choice is to make the complex topic of well-being more manageable for a single volume by emphasizing the flourishing of individuals. Such an emphasis seems justified by both historical and scientific reasons, as well. Historically, although the Greeks certainly had a great interest in social well-being, eudaimonia was more directly linked to individual flourishing, and social well-being was valued because of its positive effects on individuals. Similarly, scientific evidence from contemporary empirical work in psychology seems to indicate that individual factors are more important than social factors for at least some key elements of human flourishing.[41] We believe these reasons are sufficient grounds for justifying our focus in this volume, but they should not be used to exclude notions of collective flourishing from the eudaimonic turn. Considerations of social well-being are of great importance, and some of the chapters in this volume do explore the social conditions that contribute to eudaimonia, but for the most part we leave it to other scholars to develop this significant part of the eudaimonic turn.

Finally, whether or not Rousseau was right that man can be forced to be free,[42] it should be abundantly clear at the beginning of the twenty-first century that human beings cannot be forced to flourish. History is riddled with catastrophic attempts to impose certain notions of well-being onto unsuspecting masses. In some cases, those attempts were apparently well-meaning, but in many instances, they were cynical efforts to exploit large populations in the interests of a privileged class. Although no one can guarantee that any particular knowledge will never be misused, scholars making the eudaimonic turn do not force the results of their research onto others. As we discussed above, well-being in the core sense is a prudential value and not a moral value. Moral values carry with them a sense of obligation, with Kant going so far as to say that moral imperatives are categorical, not things that are contingent on our needs or desires. Whether or not he was right about this, prudential values are hypothetical imperatives, where the relation is conditional. Knowledge about what promotes well-being allows for the more effective cultivation of human flourishing, but there is no requirement that this knowledge be applied in any particular situation, especially in contexts that may involve concerns of greater importance than prudential values.

*Disciplinary Examples of the Eudaimonic Turn*

Let us move now to an examination of the role the eudaimonic turn is playing in a variety of disciplines. It is fitting to begin with psychology, since the eudaimonic turn is perhaps nowhere more visible than here, where it has resulted in the founding of a new branch of the discipline. The eudaimonic turn in psychology was catalyzed in 1998 by Martin Seligman when he was president of the American Psychological Association. In his presidential address that year, he surveyed the state of psychology and argued that, since World War II, psychology had focused largely on healing. Seligman noted that this focus had generated remarkable results: by his count, some fourteen mental disorders could be cured or at least effectively treated that could not have been so treated fifty years earlier. Seligman argued, however, that this is only part of psychology's mission. Psychology should concern itself with healing disease, but more broadly it should also concern itself with making the lives of all people better. Exclusive focus on pathology leaves out the study of flourishing individuals and thriving communities, along with the information this study might yield for fostering such individuals and such communities. This situation is particularly unfortunate, Seligman argued, since one of the most effective ways of buffering against mental illness is the cultivation of human strengths. To remedy the situation, he proposed the founding of the new field of "positive psychology."[43]

Two years later Seligman, along with Mihaly Csikszentmihalyi, coedited a special issue of the American Psychological Association's flagship journal *American Psychologist* on the topic of positive psychology. In their introduction to the issue, Seligman and Csikszentmihalyi argued that an overemphasis on the study of pathology had left psychologists largely ignorant of things like hope, wisdom, creativity, future mindedness, courage, spirituality, responsibility, and perseverance, all of which make life worth living. They defined positive psychology as a "science of positive subjective experience, positive individual traits, and positive institutions" and stated that the aim of positive psychology "is to begin to catalyze a change in the focus of psychology from preoccupation only with repairing the worst things in life to also building positive qualities." They claimed that such a science would "improve quality of life and prevent the pathologies that arise when life is barren and meaningless."[44] Since that time, research in positive psychology has burgeoned. Hundreds of millions of dollars in research grants have been awarded, journals have been founded to publish the new research, and regular conferences now take place all around the world where scholars share their latest findings. Because of this increased interest in the positive qualities of life, a number of evidence-based psychological models of well-being have been proposed or studied anew.

Although the founding of the field of positive psychology has given a huge boost to the eudaimonic turn in psychology, there was, of course, interest in psychological well-being long before 1998. Back in 1906, William James called for the founding of a new branch of psychology to study optimal human functioning,[45] and several decades later Abraham Maslow and Carl Rogers published ground-breaking work on what they called "self-actualization" and the "fully-functioning person," with Maslow actually using the term "positive psychology" to describe his approach to studying "fully-functioning and healthy human beings."[46] In 1958, Marie Jahoda published a conceptual definition of mental health, in which she identified six key elements of positive functioning: attitudes of an individual toward oneself, self-actualization, integration, autonomy, perception of reality, and environmental mastery.[47] In 1989, influenced in part by the work of Jahoda, Carol Ryff proposed a model for psychological well-being that similarly includes six dimensions: autonomy, environmental mastery, personal growth, positive relationships, purpose in life, and self-acceptance.[48] In 1984, Ed Diener proposed a very different model, which he called subjective well-being, where well-being is a composite of three factors: positive emotions, negative emotions, and life satisfaction.[49] In addition to raising the interest of psychologists in these various perspectives and models, the founding of positive psychology has also encouraged the development of new models. Seligman, for example, has recently proposed a five-factor model of human flourishing, known by its acronym PERMA, which includes positive emotions, engagement, relationships, meaning, and accomplishment.[50] Keyes has suggested a complete state model of human mental health, a model that includes independent salutogenic and pathogenic scales. For Keyes, to be truly mentally healthy is to be mentally flourishing and free of mental illness. He defines mental flourishing in terms of positive emotions, positive psychological functioning, and positive social functioning, while mental illness is measured in accordance with the *Diagnostic and Statistical Manual of Mental Disorders*.[51] Results from Keyes's research into mental flourishing and mental illness indicate it is possible for a person to have one or the other condition, or both, or neither at any given time.[52]

Just as clinical psychology has emphasized the diagnosis and treatment of mental illness, the field of medicine has focused on the diagnosis and treatment of physical illness. In spite of the World Health Organization's 1948 definition of health as "a state of complete physical, mental, and social well-being and not merely the absence of disease or infirmity,"[53] health care efforts and funding have focused almost exclusively on the mitigation or elimination of disease. Much less of an emphasis has been placed on prevention and very little on the establishment of "complete physical, mental, and social well-being." In the last few years this has begun to change, in part because of the high cost of health care and the increasing evidence that well-being can have a buffering effect against disease and infirmity. In a randomized, controlled trial, for example, researchers administered nasal drops carrying either rhinovirus or influenza to healthy volunteers and found that those with a more positive emotional style (being happy, lively, and calm) were at a lower risk of becoming infected.[54] Other studies have shown a high correlation between optimism and faster recovery from coronary artery bypass surgery,[55] as well as links between positive affect and protection against stroke in older adults.[56] One of the reasons the World Health Organization's definition of health has not been more influential is that there has been a lack of models for defining and measuring physical, mental, and social well-being. To address this problem, Seligman has proposed a conceptual framework for defining and measuring what he calls "positive health." He proposes that positive health be defined as a composite of three factors: subjective factors, including how one feels about one's health, vitality, and hardiness; biological factors, including a range of physiological and structural considerations; and functional factors, including tests of overall positive physical capacity and context-specific ecological conditions.[57]

In addition to psychology and medicine, the eudaimonic turn has made its way into the field of neuroscience. The leading figure in neuroscientific research on well-being, Richard Davidson, is the William James and Vilas Research Professor of Psychology and Psychiatry at the University of Wisconsin-Madison, where he directs the Waisman Laboratory for Brain Imaging and Behavior, the Laboratory for Affective Neuroscience, and the Center for Investigating Healthy Minds. The mission of the Center for Investigating Healthy Minds is to use neuroscience to study the positive qualities of the mind such as kindness, compassion, and focused attention.[58] Researchers study these qualities as they occur naturally across the life span. They are also interested in studying ways in which these qualities can be intentionally developed through contemplative practices, as well as the overall effects they have on outcomes such as resilience, emotion regulation, and physical health. Work by Davidson and his colleagues has yielded a number of important results, including an exploration of the neural correlates of various types of well-being (all involving greater activation of the left than the right prefrontal cortex) and suggestions for how to cultivate these various types of well-being.[59] As we noted above, Davidson and his colleagues have also investigated the biological correlates of psychological well-being and psychological ill-being and discovered robust evidence that at the biological level well-being and ill-being are not just on a bipolar continuum but rather that they have distinct biological signatures.[60] The eudaimonic turn in neuroscience has been further bolstered by a project to support innovative research programs at the intersection of neuroscience and positive psychology. Through this project, grants have been awarded to study outstanding fathers, heroically altruistic people (for example, those who donate a kidney to save the life of a stranger), the neural and genetic bases of positivity and resilience, and other topics in "positive neuroscience."[61]

In the field of economics, the eudaimonic turn is playing out in a different sort of way than in those disciplines discussed above. The debate here is not so much on how to balance out the measurement and mitigation of dysfunction as it is on how to measure the success of nations most adequately. In the 1940s, the newly formed International Monetary Fund and World Bank adopted gross national product (GNP) as the key indicator of economic growth. In the years since then, GNP—and more recently, gross domestic product (GDP)—have been the standard economic ways of measuring the overall success and well-being of a nation. Yet it is important to note that these indicators measure economic activity but not the valence of such activity. Robert Kennedy may have put it best when, on the presidential campaign trail in 1968, he said:

> Our gross national product . . . counts air pollution and cigarette advertising, and ambulances to clear our highways of carnage. It counts special locks for our doors and the jails for the people who break them. It counts the destruction of the redwood and the loss of our natural wonder in chaotic sprawl. . . .Yet the gross national product does not allow for the health of our children, the quality of their education or the joy of their play. It does not include the beauty of our poetry or the strength of our marriages, the intelligence of our public debate or the integrity of our public officials. It measures neither our wit nor our courage, neither our wisdom nor our learning, neither our compassion nor our devotion to our country, it measures everything, in short, except that which makes life worthwhile.[62]

Although GDP constitutes a valuable measure of economic activity, it does not seem to be an adequate measure for well-being or happiness. Consequently, there is increasing momentum among policy makers to supplement the GDP with other types of measures. In 2008, French President Nicholas Sarkozy created a "Commission on the Measurement of Economic Performance and Social Progress" to examine this question. Headed by economists Joseph Stiglitz and Amartya Sen, the commission recommended that quality of life issues not captured by GDP be measured and tracked. These quality of life issues include subjective well-being, capabilities, and fair allocations.[63] In 2010, British Prime Minister David Cameron announced that the UK would begin tracking national well-being, to "start measuring our progress as a country, not just by how our economy is growing, but by how our lives are improving; not just by our standard of living, but by our quality of life."[64] Some developing countries are also emphasizing the importance of quality of life as something different from economic growth. Ecuador and Bolivia have included the indigenous concept of "living well" into their constitutions, and Bhutan has been tracking its gross national happiness since 2007.

Another area in which the eudaimonic turn is at work is the field of organizational studies. Scholars in business schools have created the new field of positive organizational scholarship to study what goes right in businesses and other organizations. They have published several manifestos, including *Positive Organizational Scholarship: Foundations of a New Discipline* and *The Oxford Handbook of Positive Organizational Scholarship.* As these scholars define the field, positive organizational scholarship centers around "the study of especially positive outcomes, processes, and attributes of organizations and their members. It does not represent a single theory, but it focuses on dynamics that are typically described by words such as *excellence, thriving, flourishing, abundance, resilience,* or *virtuousness.*"[65]

In education, the eudaimonic turn is changing what goes on in classrooms around the world. In her insightful book *Happiness and Education,* published in 2003, noted American educator Nel Noddings argues that "happiness should be an aim of education, and a good education should contribute significantly to personal and collective happiness."[66] Noddings goes on to discuss various definitions of happiness, the important roles of unhappiness and suffering in life, and ways education can do a better job of making classrooms happier places and of preparing students more adequately for happier lives once they leave the classroom. Consonant with these ideas and inspired by the application of positive psychology to education, "positive education" is gaining momentum around the world. The basic premise of positive education is that well-being should be both an instrumental and a noninstrumental goal in education: instrumentally, it is an important cause of academic success; noninstrumentally, it is a proper goal of education in its own right. Studies of positive education programs in North America, Europe, and Australia, have shown improvements in students' academic performance, social skills, classroom behavior, and enjoyment of and engagement in school.[67]

The eudaimonic turn is also making its way into the humanities. As is evident from the first section of this chapter, philosophers have long had an interest in well-being, and in recent years philosophical work in this area has been on the rise. In his 1984 book *Reasons and Persons,* Derek Parfit divided theories of well-being into three categories: hedonistic, desire, and objective list theories. More recently, Dan Haybron has added two new categories to this list: authentic happiness theories and nature-fulfillment theories.[68] Hedonistic theories like Epicureanism and utilitarianism define well-being in terms of pleasure, and desire theories, favored by most economists, take well-being to be the fulfillment of desire or preference satisfaction. Authentic happiness theories emphasize life-satisfaction as a way to combine the first two sets of theories while overcoming some of their most serious objections, and objective list theories identify well-being with a specific list of goods claimed to be constitutive of well-being. The final group of theories hold that well-being is a function of the fulfillment of human nature. The most well-known of these theories is Martha Nussbaum's capabilities approach. Building on the work of Amartya Sen, Nussbaum argues that there are ten central human capabilities necessary for human flourishing: living a normal life span; bodily health; bodily integrity; being able to use the senses, the imagination, and thought; experiencing normal human emotions; development of one's capacities for practical reason; capabilities for affiliation; living with other species; play; and control over one's environment.[69] Very recently, Anna Alexandrova has argued against philosophical attempts like these that seek to arrive at the essence of well-being. She argues for a contextualist view that acknowledges that well-being means different things in various scientific and practical domains.[70]

We will not take sides in these debates here but simply point out that the nature of the work on well-being in philosophy supports the claim that the eudaimonic turn does not imply a uniformity of perspectives. Studies of intellectual history, including McMahon's work on the history of happiness discussed previously, show that there have always been multiple approaches to—and vigorous disagreements about—well-being, happiness, and the good life. This multiplicity of perspectives can be a valuable asset when studying something as complex as eudaimonia. Owen Flanagan has suggested a way to capitalize on this multiplicity of perspectives through the integration of various approaches to the study of well-being. He has coined the term "*eudaimonistic scientia*" to describe this work, which he defines as the "empirical-normative inquiry into the nature, causes, and conditions of human flourishing."[71] He calls this inquiry "eudaimonics," for short, and describes it further as providing a "framework for thinking in a unified way about philosophical psychology, moral and political philosophy, neuroethics, neuroeconomics, and positive psychology, as well as about transformative mindfulness practices that have their original home in non-theistic spiritual traditions such as Buddhism, Aristotelianism, and Stoicism."[72] In her recent book *Exploring Happiness: From Aristotle to Brain Science*, Sissela Bok argues for an even broader integration of perspectives, bringing together the methods and insights of literature, the arts, history, and philosophy with empirical methods in the natural and social sciences. In this type of inquiry, Bok argues, a range of views is essential, with no perspective discarded out of hand and with the full panoply of approaches carefully considered to yield the richest understandings of such a complex concept.[73]

Finally, the eudaimonic turn is taking place in comparative religion and theology, as well. Karen Armstrong has recently argued that the core message of each of the major world religions is compassion, which she defines as "an attitude of principled, consistent altruism."[74] Ellen Charry, a Princeton Theological Seminary theologian working within the Christian tradition, is developing what she calls a "positive theology." In her 2010 book *God and the Art of Happiness*, she examines views on happiness in the history of Christian theology and considers why there has been no well-developed doctrine of happiness in Christianity. She then attempts to develop just such a doctrine under the name "asherism," roughly the Hebrew equivalent of eudaimonia.[75]

This brief overview of the eudaimonic turn at work in these disciplines helps to clarify several important points. First, the well-developed approaches examined in these various domains are sufficiently similar to justify describing them under the single rubric of a eudaimonic turn. Second, this is serious academic work, with the scholars involved in the eudaimonic turn conducting rigorous research in accordance with the academic standards of their respective fields and with their results subject to peer review. Third, although no inquiry is completely value-neutral, the eudaimonic turn is not driven by particular ideological agendas, whether religious, political, or philosophical. Scholars making the eudaimonic turn come from a spectrum of backgrounds, perspectives, disciplines, countries, and cultures, rendering work in the eudaimonic turn interdisciplinary, multidisciplinary, and cross-cultural. Finally, although the eudaimonic turn is well under way in these disciplines, much work remains to be done in this shift toward greater balance in the long-running conversation about well-being. Investigators need to replicate key findings and push the research forward in new directions to follow up on the promising results already obtained, scholars need to integrate the work on direct approaches to well-being with other work on the mitigation of ill-being to create comprehensive models for understanding and cultivating composite well-being, and researchers need to continue to cross disciplinary boundaries to share findings, combine resources, and develop new methods of inquiry for the creation of new knowledge about human flourishing. With these general points in mind, we now shift our attention to a detailed examination of the role of the eudaimonic turn in literary studies.

## THE EUDAIMONIC TURN IN LITERARY STUDIES

D. J. MOORES

The eudaimonic turn has already begun to take place in literary studies, manifesting in three interrelated ways: (1) as a growing dissatisfaction with critique as it is commonly understood; (2) as a search for and embrace of various alternative hermeneutics; and (3) as a direct move toward the investigation of the eudaimonic aspects of human experience.

Let us deal with each of these manifestations and explore their interconnections.

To be sure, many schools of literary theory—particularly feminism, Marxism, postcolonial studies, race theory, queer theory, and others—are in a *general* sense concerned with well-being. Identity politics and multiculturalism represent a deep interest in and struggle for the eudaimonia of the various groups whose interests critics attempt to advance in their scholarly work. The problem here is that the concern for well-being manifests, at least in much literary discourse, as a preoccupation with its absence; in other words, it is really a concern with ill-being. Critics operating in this vein typically, though not exclusively, use a "hermeneutics of suspicion," a phrase famously coined by Paul Ricouer, who cited Marx, Nietzsche, and Freud as the masters of modern suspicious critique.[76] So often in such discussions, the focus is either on the discernment of a social problem the text illuminates or a demystification of a given author, whose texts and contexts can be shown, through the use of a suspicious reading strategy, to be complicit in forces that antagonize people and thus obstruct their eudaimonia. As an interpretive strategy, suspicion can be highly productive, particularly when one's task is to identify what is wrong with a text or an author's treatment of a subject or a social condition the text illuminates or obscures. But what about texts in which positive configurations of eudaimonia, such as love, joy, or serenity, are present? The question points to the shortcomings of suspiciously reading against the grain in order to demystify, that is, to uncover the covert means by which a text presents and/or obscures various ideological and/or psychological illusions. Suspicion, as it is generally used, so often proves incapable of shedding productive light on eudaimonia.

Although the suspicion model has left a rich legacy in the form of critical theory and its myriad approaches to texts, it is problematic because a suspicious eye forever on the lookout for diseased psychodynamics and/or participation in undesirable ideologies, such as racism, sexism, neuroses, false consciousness, heterosexism, patriarchy, imperialism, and the like, often only enables us to see what is wrong, not what is right and preferable, in a text or character. Such a perspective falls short when the interpretive moment calls for a "hermeneutics of affirmation," another phrase Ricouer coined.[77] The critical record clearly shows we are often, though by no means always, stymied when a given author casts human experience in a eudaimonic light. In such circumstances the hermeneutics of suspicion often compels scholars to interpret eudaimonia as psychological disease or bad politics.

A case in point is Wordsworth's "Tintern Abbey," which critics have rendered suspect for various reasons: (1) Dorothy's voice is mute, a silence that betokens the subjugation of women in the nineteenth century. (2) The poet turns his back on social ills, the French Revolution, and other problems of history in a head-in-the-sand retreat to conservatism. (3)

Nature is not actual nature but an imaginative creation of it used merely as a backdrop against which he paints an all-too-human portrait. (4) This portrait is of himself no less, for his version of the sublime is an egotistical one, as Keats famously called it. (5) His self-preoccupation shows an underlying narcissism that callously ignores the oppressed and the poor who suffer. (6) His strong sense of individualism is a quintessential example of bourgeois false consciousness and the impossible desire to divorce oneself from culture and the real determinants of human subjectivity—economics and class. (7) The "blessed mood" he reports is a naïve illusion intended to protect a fragile, underdeveloped ego in need of resolution of various psycho-sexual neuroses. (8) The "one life" he sees among all disparate entities is similarly an illusion, a manifestation of a fixation at Lacan's mirror stage of development in which the child projects a false sense of unity onto external entities in a quest to fill his or her lack. He yearns for a wholeness he will never achieve. (9) The poet's certainty about being able to "see into the life of things" is wholly undermined by his admission that it all might be "but a vain belief," clearly the thread that, when pulled, unravels the entire construction, at the heart of which is self-doubt and anxiety. His certainty and faith belie his anxieties and uncertainties.

Using a number of different methodologies, a eudaimonic critic might challenge such readings by pointing to several markers of well-being in the poem. Wordsworth's blessed moods exert significant, eudaimonic effects, all of which are interrelated. These include the following: (1) compassion for his fellow human beings; (2) the ability to discern a deep, underlying connection among all things, or a kind of integrated consciousness in which he nonrationally intuits the presence of a connective cosmic force; (3) a heightened eco-awareness in which he sacralizes the entire green earth; (4) an internalization of natural energies from which he takes his elevated moral cue and consequently lives rightly and well; (5) the ability to overcome the mundane and the petty by continually maintaining a healthy sense of optimism and cultivating gratitude for life's many blessings; (6) a highly refined and fully developed mind rich in beautiful treasures and empowered by the forces of the imagination; (7) a deep, healthy sense of wonder about the mysteries of human existence; and (8) the clarity necessary to value the most important element in human existence—love. To read the poem suspiciously may yield interesting insights, but generally such readings have caused scholars to ignore the poem's eudaimonic elements.

For such reasons, there is in literary studies an increasing disenchantment with the hermeneutics of suspicion. While the suspicion model has proven invaluable in critical discourse, it clearly has limitations. Although some expressions of happiness can be manifestations of underlying anxieties and neuroses, there are also types of happiness that authentically embody eudaimonia.

Let us not overstate the case. Only a reactionary would decry the many insights that have resulted from the critique of ideology and diseased psychodynamics in literary studies. Where would the discipline be without the depth of the psychological tradition, which has enabled scholars to question the manifest, to subvert the primacy of the ego, and to explore the mysterious depths of the unconscious? Where would the discipline be without the critique of power and ideology, which have been shown to circulate in all discourses, indeed all language? Without such critical tools, literary scholars would likely be innocent, even naïve, readers who lack the perceptual insight to be able to question and read against the grain.

Still, it is also important to stress that suspicious reading is one possibility among others, not the absolute ground of critical being, a point Eve Sedgwick argued in a challenge to "paranoid" reading strategies that call for the use of suspicion and demystification to read latent realities beneath the surface of manifest superficialities and illusions. The image of paranoid reading is in many ways appropriate, because paranoia causes us to suspect wrongly, to be wary and even fearful of an object that wills us no harm. It is difficult to see the good qualities of someone we suspect is a murderer, and our suspicion will likely cause us to see in such a person only traits that are consistent with murdering, even if he or she is innocent. To be sure, authors are often complicit in the ideologies that circulate in the historical moments in which they write, and they are often tortured souls whose psychological maladies in some ways inform their imaginative work. By no means, however, is authorial genius *reducible* to disease or bad politics. This is a common critical practice, nevertheless, in literary discourse over the last forty years. The suspicion model is useful when it enables scholars to read ideology or psychodynamics beneath the surface of a text, but such an interpretive framework often leaves unexplored other important textual dimensions. As Sedgwick argues, suspicion has become "widely understood as a mandatory injunction rather than a possibility among other possibilities."[78] An influential Queer theorist who engaged in her own share of suspicious reading, Sedgwick did not crudely call for an end to all suspicious reading strategies. Her point, rather, was that suspicion has limitations that prove unproductive when we are trying to adopt other epistemological positions, particularly those involving what she calls "reparative" interpretations—or what we are referring to here as eudaimonic readings—that have been marginalized by the suspicion model because they cause readers to see value in the text and derive "sustenance" from it.[79]

Other scholars share the view, having intuited the need for a correction by similarly setting their sights on alternative hermeneutic frameworks. In an interesting discussion of why critique has faltered in academic discourse, Bruno Latour questions the excessive distrust that has come to be synonymous with critical reading, which is now tantamount to positioning oneself above the text, its truth/power, and other various "illusions." Like Sedgwick, Latour does not call for a complete reversal of course. An influential social theorist who spent much of his career using suspicion to deconstruct the "factual" illusions of science, Latour nevertheless calls into question the suspicious form of critique in which the attempt to demystify becomes a totalizing notion excluding all other hermeneutic possibilities. In spite of his own deconstructive work, he argues for the adoption of a new form of critique to supplement suspicion, one that will "associate the word criticism," which, he claims, has gone stale, "with a whole new set of positive metaphors, gestures, attitudes, knee-jerk reactions, [and] habits of thought." He advocates focusing less on demystifying "matters of fact" than on exploring, with the same level of sophistication, "matters of concern."[80] By implication, he too is calling for a hermeneutics of affirmation, a eudaimonic turn.

Demystification can open new interpretive doors, but it can also be paralyzing and prevent an understanding of anything outside of its purview, a point Rita Felski explores in two recent articles.[81] To become a "critical reader" in the current atmosphere in literary studies, as she observes, "means moving from attachment [to an author or text] to detachment and indeed to disenchantment."[82] However problematic it may be, suspicion too often causes readers to destroy valuable (positive) affective responses to texts and impels them to (mis)interpret eudaimonic experience in a negative light. It causes readers to question and /or elide the value of love, meaning and purpose, character strengths and virtues, the exquisite joys of beauty, and other aspects of well-being. It causes readers who look to literature as a source of wisdom and insight to dominate and subordinate texts by demonstrating that textual illusions, such as happiness, joy, connections to nature, and the like, quickly evaporate when exposed to the heat of various critical methodologies. The result is an interpretive paradigm in which anything other than suspicion becomes the antonym of informed, sophisticated reading. But surely it is possible to read affirmatively and to derive sustenance from a text while doing so in highly complex ways. Reading affirmatively, or eudaimonically, to be more precise, is not simple-minded reading. To the contrary, it can be just as complex, if not more so, than reading suspiciously.

In response to such excesses, there is now a growing disenchantment with disenchantment. Scholars are seeking alternatives in their rejection of the suspicion model, the origins of which Ricouer located in Cartesian thought but which Felski locates, perhaps more accurately, in the medieval era and its atmosphere of sniffing out heresy. Just as the excesses of the Inquisition eventually exhausted themselves, so is there now in literary studies "a dawning sense . . . that a shape of thought has grown old," as Felski observes in her manifesto, *Uses of Literature*. Ideas that once seemed radical and even "revelatory," such as the decentered subject and the social construction of reality, "have dwindled into shopworn slogans."[83] In the current posttheory age, such suspicious reading, "[a] style of interpretation that once seemed entirely self-evident and self-explanatory, now finds itself squirming under the spotlight."[84] Admittedly, the questioning of suspicion is complicit in the project of suspicion itself. As she acknowledges, "the doubting of doubt underscores the critic's entrapment within a suspicious sensibility and the mentality of critique, as she finds herself caught in an infinite regress of skeptical questioning." No objection to suspicion, in other words, "can entirely escape the snarls of this contradiction."[85] Such complicity, however, poses no real barrier to the new turn. One of the greatest insights to come out of theory is that in some ways readers and writers are always implicated in the positions they refute, but by no means does such a truth need to result in an abandonment of the search for newer, more productive, and thus more relevant critical theories and practices.

Indeed, the opposite is true, for the search seems to be intensifying in productive ways. Heather Love, for instance, has called into question the "depth" in "depth hermeneutics," which has been (mis)understood as the suspicious discernment of neuroses, false consciousness, and other manifestations of "objectionable" psychodynamics and ideologies. According to Love, critics are increasingly locating such depth in a eudaimonic dimension that attributes "life, richness, warmth, and voice to texts." Love's essay is not a manifesto but rather a description of the changes taking place in the field. As she observes, "it is this hermeneutics of recognition and empathy—originally sacred and now grounded in an unacknowledged but powerful humanism—that defines literary studies, even in an age of suspicion."[86]

Stephen Best and Sharon Marcus also offer an alternative in what they call "surface reading," by which they mean subtextually reading with the grain to discern what the text implies rather than what it obscures. In their rejection of "symptomatic" reading, an interpretive strategy that seeks to disclose "the absent cause that structures the texts inclusions and exclusions,"[87] Best and Marcus offer "literal" reading, which is by no means tantamount to superficial analysis, as many scholars believe. To the contrary, it involves significant subtextual exploration. As the editors of a special issue of *Representations*, Best and Marcus point to the myriad, sophisticated loci implicated in reading on the "surface." These include the surface as materiality; as the intricate verbal structure of literary language; as affective and ethical stance; as a practice of critical description; as the location of patterns that exist within and across texts; and as literal meaning, among others.[88] Such reading offers a plethora of possibilities and holds up the promise of a transformation in literary studies. As Best and Marcus conclude in their introduction to the issue, ". . . the moments that arrest us in texts need not be considered symptoms, whose true cause exists on another plane of reality, but can themselves indicate important and overlooked truths."[89] The august scholars associated with surface reading (and who thus appear in the special issue) include Christopher Nealon, Margaret Cohen, Mary Thomas Crane, Anne Anlin Cheng, and Leah Price.

In this dissatisfaction with suspicion and the embrace of alternatives, what seems to be making its way into critical consciousness is an intuitive understanding that the question of well-being, at least in its positive form and not merely as the condemnation of its absence, has been woefully neglected. At some level, the aforementioned scholars seem to know that the silent other in suspicious reading, to use an image from suspicious hermeneutics itself, is the possibility of being well. To be sure, we do not mean to oversimplify the picture by reducing all rejections of suspicion to a desire to explore eudaimonia, for each of the aforementioned reading strategies is different and is thus indicative of the rich diversity of possibilities that await literary scholars. We are pointing out, however, that in all of these strategies there seems to be a tacit understanding and even a desire to retrieve the question of well-being by moving beyond the mere consciousness and condemnation of its absence. The language such scholars use surely implies as much. Phrases such as "reparative reading," "deriving sustenance from texts," dealing with "matters of concern," seeing the "life, richness, and warmth of a text," uncovering "important and overlooked truths," and "adopting affective and ethical stances"—all of this clearly suggests a eudaimonic turn is transforming literary discourse.

For all of these newer interpretive strategies, the eudaimonic turn is less of a methodological transformation than it is a shift in focus to a neglected topic. Such a shift can be seen in a developing conversation that seems to be reaching a critical mass. The discussion of well-being in literary studies is not always named as such, and sometimes scholars deal with the subject only by implication, but in the last decade the subject of eudaimonia has begun to move to the forefront of literary discourse. In highly interesting ways, critics have begun to engage in "reparative" readings, particularly those involving a central matter of human concern (at least to human beings)—human well-being. Some have even begun to write about joy, love, wonder, ecstasy, and other complex configurations of eudaimonia. These new lines of inquiry into eudaimonia point to the limitations of solely reading against the grain and the desire to push beyond the conceptual straitjacket of suspicion. They also serve as compelling indications of a turn towards the investigation of positive aspects of human experience that significantly factor in the construct of well-being. Let us briefly review some of these.

In *The Story of Joy*, a selection of which is reprinted in the current volume (see chapter 11), Adam Potkay traces the changing configurations and social constructions of joy from the Bible through late Romanticism. Given its widespread, enthusiastic embrace, Potkay's study in some ways is the most influential text to date in the eudaimonic turn in literary studies. In a sophisticated refutation of the suspicion model, Potkay sees eudaimonic value in conceptions of joy, and he does not dismiss the emotion as a naïve illusion, as so many critics have done. Still, he is highly aware of its constructed nature, as his complex cultural history demonstrates. In a similar study Vivasvan Soni also questions modern conceptions of happiness in his work, *Mourning Happiness*. Soni insightfully discerns the impoverished nature of the modern version of happiness, the origins of which he locates in the eighteenth century. Such an understanding of happiness, which reemerged in secular political discourse during the Enlightenment, is a pale imitation of ancient conceptions because it has become "hopelessly and inescapably private," as he observes. The result is "a shift from a classical republicanism and its politics of happiness to a modern liberalism and its politics of freedom," the implications of which imply "a radical impoverishment in the horizon of our political possibilities."[90] Soni supports his claim in a wide ranging analysis of eighteenth-century literary texts, particularly the sentimental novel, a genre in which happiness, as he shows, is stripped of its (important) ethical and political dimensions.

Other scholars have focused more specifically on the importance of affect, a subject badly mistreated and/or neglected in suspicion-governed hermeneutics. In *The Vehement Passions*, for instance, Philip Fisher questions the Western construct of "dispassionate knowledge," arguing that affects, particularly strong passions such as love, righteous anger, and others, are essential not only to knowing the world (and thus being able to change it) but also to self-knowledge, and, by implication, to being well. Another one of Fisher's works, *Wonder, the Rainbow, and the Aesthetics of Rare Experiences*, is a complex examination of emotions, particularly positive emotions such as wonder and related states of being, as well as the general importance of these in literary studies. Charles Altieri, a contributor to the current volume (see Chapter 1), cogently elucidates the complexities of an aesthetics of affect in his important study, *The Particulars of Rapture*. Such an aesthetics is implicated in the question of well-being, as he argues, in that it results in "a means of elaborating how there may be profoundly incommensurable perspectives on values that are nonetheless all necessary if we are to realize various aspects of our human potential."[91]

Such studies of affect are not unrelated to the interesting work of several scholars of religion and literature, the implications of which suggest the importance of spirituality as a eudaimonic determinant of human experience. Recent examples include: *Nineteenth-Century Religion and Literature*[92] by Mark Knight and Emma Mason (a contributor to the current volume), *Romanticism and Transcendence: Wordsworth, Coleridge and the Religious Imagination*[93] by the late Robert Barth, and *Mystical Discourse in Wordsworth and Whitman* by D. J. Moores.[94] Such volumes, among many others, represent the work scholars are doing in rendering credible the religious question in literary studies. Regardless of its problems of dogma and metaphysical groundlessness, religion is an important (often eudaimonic) determinant of human subjectivity, and literary scholars have recently begun to challenge the tendency to dismiss it as illusory in many examinations of religious ideas. The topic is a central concern in so many of the texts deemed worthy of continued investigation. No doubt, religion can be seen to function as the "opiate of the masses," and often it does so. But it can also facilitate agency and empowerment, a point David Bordelon explores in Chapter 8 of this volume. Religion in this sense is important to writers and readers because it can serve as the means by which one attains well-being.

The aforementioned works are fairly recent examples of the eudaimonic turn, but examinations of well-being and its myriad implications are by no means new in the discipline. In her own course on literary theory, Felski teaches, in addition to the practitioners of the suspicion model, other older, alternative perspectives whose proponents run against the grain of a reading strategy solely focused on demystification. Among those she cites are Stephen Greenblatt on wonder,[95] Susan Sontag on interpretation,[96] Charles Bernstein on absorption and literary texts,[97] and Elizabeth Long on reading as collective action.[98]

And there are others. Published in 1991, Jonathan Bate's ecocritical study of Wordsworth, *Romantic Ecology*,[99] was one of the first refutations of suspicion-governed, new historicist reductions of what is valuable and sustaining in the great poet's verse. While many, though by no means all, new historicists have reduced Wordsworth's orientation toward the natural world to bourgeois ideology, Bate sees much value in Wordsworthian conceptions of nature. In rejecting the suspicion model, he argues that the "critic's purposes can be those of the writer's,"[100] even in, and perhaps especially so, a sophisticated reading. Don Bialostoky's Bakhtinian refutation of what he implies is bad Bakhtinian reading of Wordsworth's poetry is also an excellent example of the desire to push beyond the limits of suspicion and to engage in reparative reading of a matter of concern. In his study of Wordsworth, Bialostoky rejects Bakhtinian readings that level all concerns to "social inequality" and produce "an effect of alienation that demoralizes our professional identities without reconstituting them."[101] In lieu of suspicion he offers a Bakhtinian hermeneutics that allows one to see eudaimonic value in Wordsworth while also deeply reading the poet's dialogic subtext. In *Poetic Justice* Martha Nussbaum also rejects suspicion while still operating in a sophisticated critical framework, in this case a multicultural and feminist perspective. In her study of the realist novel, Nussbaum demonstrates the ways in which a literary genre and the sympathetic identifications it inspires significantly and eudaimonically inform legal reasoning.[102] In *Love's Knowledge* Nussbaum explores the relationship between ethical knowledge and literary form, the implication of which is that moral philosophy has much to learn from literature. As she argues, however, such insights are only possible in a hermeneutics that allows one to see value in literary forms and the eudaimonic experiences they so often configure.[103]

Nussbaum's studies of the connections between moral philosophy and literature represent some of the earliest examples of the ethical turn that Marjorie Garber[104] and others observed occurring at the end of the twentieth century. One of the many works to come out of this ethical turn is *The Committed Word: Literature and Public Values* by James Engell, also a contributor to this volume (see Chapter 2). Here, Engell makes a compelling case for the eudaimonic value of literary study, not for the purposes of challenging Western ideologies but to foster well-being in the form of a heightened consciousness of ethics and social engagement, as well as in a clearer discernment of the values, objectionable or constructive, that govern our lives.

In some ways this ethical turn is an early precursor to the eudaimonic turn. With its focus on the alterity of texts and the quasi-religious nature of literariness, the ethical turn has resulted, at least among the ethically minded critics involved, in a "new celebration of literature," as Dorothy Hale calls it.[105] Still, ethical discussions are not without their problems. Heather Love points out that ethical literary criticism is a strange mix of bedfellows, since many, though by no means all, of its proponents profess antihumanist/poststructuralist affinities while tacitly advancing humanist values.[106] Felsi also questions such ethical reading practices because they are in some ways still complicit in the hermeneutics of suspicion in that the text often does the demystifying for us. In these Levinas-inspired readings, as she puts it, "we do not need to be suspicious of the text . . . because it is already doing the work of suspicion for us, because it is engaged in the negative work of subverting the self-evident, challenging the commonplace, relentlessly questioning idées fixes and idées reçus."[107] An exception to Felski's observation, and there are many, is Adam Potkay's recent study, *Wordsworth's Ethics*. Here, Potkay does not see Wordsworth using suspicion in any way, and he takes at face value the poet's desire to help his readers "to flourish" through ethical engagement. As Potkay puts it, "Wordsworth's poems examine our obligations to others, and invite us to participate imaginatively in the joys proper to all modes of being."[108]

Still, Felski's point is well taken. Notwithstanding Potkay's affirmative, eudaimonic reading, as well as those of several others, ethical critics are often complicit in some of the paralyzing positions that characterize poststructuralist thought, such as extreme anti-essentialism and the reduction of human experience to language. While ethical criticism is one of the many tributaries flowing into the eudaimonic stream now beginning to wend its way through literary studies, there is a difference between the two turns: Many ethical critics have held on to the older suspicion model while also professing, at least explicitly and consciously, their affinities with several problematic, antihumanist positions; eudaimonic critics, by contrast, have rejected suspicion in a "neo-humanist" approach that embraces some of the ideas of poststructuralism while also addressing and embracing a central humanist concern—human well-being. By this definition, a scholar such as Potkay, though he may not consciously self-identify in such a way, is less of an ethical critic than he is a eudaimonic one. This support of humanism is by no means a reactionary retreat to the older humanism, however, as eudaimonic critics seem to be highly aware of the problems associated with notions of a fixed, transcendent self that preexists the temporal, cultural, linguistic, and ideological matrixes in which human beings live. The eudaimonic turn represents a conscious embrace of some of the humanist principles so many poststructuralist ethical critics find distressing but within a context of seeing much value in previous critiques of the power dynamics in all discourses and the ideological nature of textuality.

For many years, the resistance to suspicion and the desire to explore questions of human well-being have thus coexisted alongside the *dominant* tendency to demystify texts. During the 1970s, 1980s and 1990s, the loudest voices spoke for suspicion, but also present in many areas of literary study were critics who refused to reduce literature to pathology or patriarchy or some kind of psychological or discursive illusion. The recent eudaimonic turn represents a full boiling of what has been simmering for at least four decades. It is also the most forceful and potentially productive challenge to the older hermeneutic model. The turn toward affirmative reading and the investigation of the relationship between literary forms and eudaimonia is already happening, and the consequences seem to be enriching literary studies in myriad ways.

## *The Matter of Form*

So what are the implications of the eudaimonic turn as they relate to literary forms? Will the turn entail a privileging of "Pollyanna" stories? Will it cheapen aesthetic taste and call for an overly idealized, cloyingly sentimental, positive literature? The simplest answer to these questions is that it has neither done so in the past, nor will it do so in the future. No doubt, as critics have already begun to do, it will be necessary to reevaluate texts depicting peak states of being, positive traits, and emotions conducive to well-being, all of which are complex elements in need of a complex theoretical framework. The eudaimonic turn, however, will not result in the simple categorization of literature as being either positive or negative; it will not degenerate into a simple-minded (and neurotic) privileging of the former and an elision of the latter. To the contrary, the turn has already provoked sophisticated discussions of eudaimonia in many of its permutations, and it will likely continue to do so. The eudaimonic turn is thus topically concerned with texts depicting suffering, oppression, marginalization, injustice, and even tragedy, the potential result of which is beneficial transformation not in spite of but because of hardship. Nor does it elide truly dark works depicting detrimental suffering, injustice, and/or disease with no accompanying beneficial transformation, for the eudaimonic turn follows a trajectory through tragedy, the aesthetic response to which is (arguably) beneficial for a number of complex reasons. So let us turn, then, to a discussion of the implications of the eudaimonic turn as it applies to literary forms.

### *The Literature of Well-Being*

There is a pervasive assumption in the discipline that it is not literary unless it is dark. If it is sunny or inspiring, according to this canon, it is not complex enough to warrant a serious literary analysis. The question remains, however, whether such an idea is supportable. While it is well-founded, it can also, driven to an extreme, reductively overlook complexity. A case in point is the reception of Walt Whitman in the early twentieth century, a period in which the New Critics and other arbiters of taste, such as Ezra Pound and T.S Eliot, found highly distressing Whitman's sky-blue optimism and his privileging of eudaimonic psychological states. No doubt, Pound, Eliot, and the New Critics esteemed Whitman's verse, but they did so in a context of ideas significantly informed by the pessimistic, modernist milieu in which they wrote. Whitman's complexity, nevertheless, cannot be understood without some kind of appeal to the sense of well-being found in his poetry, poetics, and prose, as several scholars have demonstrated.

The work of Emily Dickinson represents another challenge to the idea that eudaimonic literature is simple and lacks complexity. Dickinson undoubtedly wrote about the negative aspects of human existence, but she also wrote *hundreds* of poems on topics such as the value of beauty, the life-affirming properties of nature, the mysteries of love, the raptures of positive affect, and the positive growth that results from certain types of suffering. Such poems evidence considerable artistry and sophistication, and they serve to illustrate that her complexity as a writer extends over the full range of her poetry, not just over her despairing verse. She is as much of a poet of well-being as she is of despair. Dickinson's critical stereotype as a despairing poet who lost faith in traditional conceptions of God and thus cynically ruminated in her Amherst room on the bitterness and pointlessness of life's tragedies is the result, once again, of early twentieth-century negativity bias. Her first critics immediately recognized her poems of despair, and they established an interpretive paradigm that privileged the negative and ignored the question of well-being.[109] This early reception of Emily Dickinson was informed by the negativity bias of modernity, and it produced a skewed image of her oeuvre.

Such an aesthetic that privileges the negative at the expense of the question of well-being is thus neither productive nor supportable.

Still, it is important to acknowledge the dangers of overstating the case. Notwithstanding Shakespearean comedies, certain satires, and other notable literary exceptions, most happy, lighthearted stories are generally considered to be intellectually lightweight because they lack the seriousness of actual life, which often ends unhappily after considerable privation. The tidy resolutions and cheap sentimentality frequently found in simple stories belie the complexities of real life and real emotion, both of which are perhaps far more chaotic than their depictions in pleasant little fictions would suggest. The distaste for poorly done, happy stories is well-founded, as there is often considerably more wisdom and artistry in "darker" narratives.

The problem with privileging dark narratives, however, lies in misrepresentation, for they do not fully represent the human experience, which is also characterized by love, friendship, happiness, fulfillment, healing, growth, beneficial transformation through hardship and suffering, and a host of other eudaimonic experiences. To elevate "dark" narratives, by which we mean stories that depict suffering and/or end tragically, to high literary status, and to marginalize all narratives depicting happiness runs the risk of fetishizing suffering and thus clouding one's assessment of actual life. Such an aesthetic indoctrinates readers with the metaphysical assumption that life is fundamentally negative, when such an idea ultimately cannot be proven any more convincingly than can the belief that life is fundamentally positive.

Such assumptions came to the surface at a recent conference in which scholars were debating the ending of Lynne Nottage's Pulitzer Prize-winning play *Ruined*, a narrative depicting a female character who is traumatized by rape but ultimately heals herself through the transformative properties of love. Some scholars in the breakout room found the ending a bit sentimental, but others pointed out that sometimes victims of trauma do in fact heal themselves through love. In this case, what seemed to guide the criticism of the ending as being sentimental was the unsupportable leap that because life sometimes ends badly, so must all literary works, if they are worthy of our esteem. A discussion of the "positive" ending revealed the play to be complex, and perhaps even more so, because the character was able to transcend her victimhood and exercise a greater degree of agency.

The eudaimonic turn in literary studies has resulted in a recognition of the need to reexamine countless similar works that end happily but whose resolutions result in a significantly more complex character. It has not called for an embrace of all cheap, sentimental narratives that privilege the positive and neurotically avoid the unpleasant. Cheap, sentimental trash will always be tawdry and sickening. The eudaimonic turn, rather, implies a reassessment of *complex* narratives such as *Ruined* and others that shed light on the construct of well-being in some way. Because love and joy are just as mysterious and labyrinthine as are anguish and despair, literary scholars are justified (and even obligated) to cultivate an aesthetic taste for both sides of human experience.

Non-narrative forms of literature, such as lyrics and other poetic genres, offer a treasury of positive affective states to explore in discussions of well-being. Poems about love, rapture, and happiness are ubiquitous in the world's literary canons, and they represent a rich opportunity to discuss complex texts that configure peak states of being, beneficial emotions, relatedness to others, connections to nature and the cosmos, and other eudaimonic aspects of the human experience. The world's literary corpuses are steeped in such poems. The ecstatic poetic tradition, in particular, is a potentially interesting subject of scholarly inquiries into well-being. Cutting across temporal and spatial boundaries, the ecstatic poetic tradition shows human beings at their best moments, or "the soul at the white heat," to use Emily Dickinson's famous line. *Wild Poets of Ecstasy: An Anthology of Ecstatic Verse*[110] clearly represents this tradition in its selection of poets from several diverse literary corpuses, including Indian Bhakti poets, Sufis, Christian mystics, Greek lyric poets, Romantics, and several dozen other secular writers. *Human Flourishing: An Anthology of Eudaimonic Poetry*[111] is similarly focused, but it is more broadly representative of poems that suggest well-being in its myriad manifestations. Such poetry demonstrates that the literature of well-being, written by some of the world's greatest writers, can be deeply complex and intellectually stimulating.

Thoughtful nonacademics seem to have discerned such complexity, for the best-selling poet in America is Rumi, a thirteenth-century Sufi writer whose highly sophisticated, ecstatic verse speaks to the universal desire to be well. While Pulitzer Prize-winning poets are considered successful if they sell 10,000 volumes, various translations of Rumi's verse have sold in the millions in recent years. At the global level, there is also a recognition of the value and complexity of poetry configuring eudaimonic psychological states: UNESCO's designation of 2007 as the year of Rumi was not only an acknowledgment of the 800th anniversary of a great poet's birthday but also a means by which the West and Islam might achieve some kind of cultural rapprochement, for Rumi's poetry transcends ideological borders in its celebration of love and other important eudaimonic states.

To be sure, scholars have written about the poetry of love and happiness for centuries, and we do not mean to imply that literary studies has entirely neglected such verse. In the field of Romanticism, for instance, the view of Romantic poets as agents of positive, transformative healing has persisted well into the twenty-first century alongside a more cynical perspective in which they are faulted for masking their complicity in various undesirable discourses.[112] Scholars who analyze eudaimonic experience in various configurations also exist in many other areas of literary study. The point is that in the discipline the *dominant* tendency is a refusal to be "mystified" by such poetry, which scholars too often interpret in terms of psychopathology or bad politics.

This denigration of the lyrical has deep roots and represents a longstanding tradition in Western literary theory. While early Greek poetry in Orphic, lyrical, dithyrambic, and rhapsodic forms was highly affective and ecstatic, later thinkers devalued such verse genres and established an interpretive paradigm the legacy of which persists today. The Greek devaluation of the lyric, a complex subject Nietzsche famously lamented in *The Birth of Tragedy*, is seen clearly in Plato's exclusion of poets from his Republic and in Aristotle's almost complete neglect of the poetic form in his *Poetics*. These negative Greek attitudes toward poetry, informed as they are by the privileging of reason over the madness of emotion, influenced not only the Romans, who also devalued the lyric, but also most of the other Hellenized, European traditions. Despite that the lyric was initially favored among the ancient Greeks (as well as many nonwestern cultures across the globe), the form did not regain its ancient credibility in the West until the Romantics elevated it to new heights. The lyric enjoyed this newly won prominence until the recent resurgence of a centuries-old distrust of the form in new historicism, Marxism, and poststructuralism. Mikhail Bakhtin's view of the lyric captures the neo-Marxist, cultural materialist, and new historicist denigration of the genre. Bakhtin faulted the writing of non-narrative poetry "because the process closes itself off to the palimpsest of the external; it denies history and its heteroglossic superfluity of meaning." In his view, poetry is "in flight from history and the real."[113] The form, he argued, "is defined by a willful and permanent forgetting, an active refusal to allow the whole to be seen, and that part of the whole which is lost is the interaction of the world and the object over time, which has produced layers of supplementary or contradictory meaning."[114] The genre has also suffered at the hands of poststructuralists, who so often refuse the call to well-being that eudaimonic poetry voices and instead torture unintended meanings out of texts by lifting them out of their contexts, pathologizing them, and reading them as covert manifestations of dead, white, male values or examples of linguistic incommunicability and the inherent emptiness of language. No doubt, there are critics who champion the value of the lyric. For instance, Ryan Cull[115] and Nouri Gana,[116] each in different ways, have recently defended the value of the lyric on ethical grounds. The point is that the dominant tendency in the last forty years has been to denigrate the form because of its ahistorical, atemporal nature.

The eudaimonic turn in literary studies has promtped a serious, sustained reevaluation of such conceptions of poetry, not in terms of seeking their elimination but by taking them to task for their excesses and thus making possible new interpretations in relation to the discourse of well-being. Several scholars have already challenged such notions, and no doubt the new generation of young scholars will continue to do so.

*The Literature of Suffering and Growth*

Unlike lyrics, narratives are generally focused on conflict, without which there is little reader interest. Few sophisticated readers want to read a story about a nice guy who leads a good life and then dies happily as his surviving family members conclude that he was a wonderful human being who cultivated all of his potentials for the betterment of himself, his loved ones, and society. But a story about a man—say, Willy Loman—who fails to cultivate his potentials, violates his own internal calling, lives a warped dream of happiness that causes his own and his family's suffering, and dies a tragic death as a result of his misguided ideas, is immensely absorbing. The former may be an illustration of human well-being, but it is not nearly as compelling as the latter because it lacks the essential conflict so necessary in interesting narratives. Simply because narratives are conflict based, however, does not mean they are "negative" and have nothing to do with well-being. Good narratives, even dark tragedies, rather frequently depict characters who grow in positive ways, as in the case of Biff Loman, whose insight in response to his father's tragic suicide signifies a highly beneficial transformation. Even Stephen Crane, a pessimistic naturalist who often depicted human beings as victims whose fate is determined by forces outside of themselves, seemed to recognize such value in hardship and suffering. In "The Open Boat," for instance, one of Crane's characters realizes that, despite having lost several comrades in a sunken ship and rowing to near exhaustion for several days on a cruelly indifferent sea, the tragedy "was the best experience of his life." The concept of well-being includes not only love and happiness but also negative or adverse circumstances that can, in the right circumstances, result in eudaimonic growth and transformation.

In contrast to Abraham Maslow's "peak experiences," which are highly eudaimonic, psychologists have also recognized what have been called "abyss experiences," in which people by no means bask in the warm glow of ecstasy but actually suffer from trauma or an encounter with death. Such experiences often result in negative effects such as posttraumatic stress disorder (PTSD). As researchers have come to recognize, however, they can also cause psychological growth in the form of a rearrangement of priorities toward less materialistic pursuits and the alignment of values with "kindness, justice, gratitude, hope, integrity, and simple pleasure."[117] This kind of "posttraumatic growth" (PTG),[118] as it is called, is more likely to result among optimists than pessimists,[119] and it is more likely to occur if the adverse experience occurs no later than in early adulthood and to the right degree.[120] It is by no means, however, a naïve coping mechanism born out of a neurotic attempt to make sense of senseless suffering. To the contrary, PTG is "accompanied by transformative life changes that appear to go beyond illusion," and it is better understood as "an outcome rather than a coping mechanism."[121] Linley and Joseph thus call PTG the "apotheosis of positive psychology," because it "represents the psychological well-being that positive psychology aspires to, but within a context of suffering and adversity that debunks any criticism of . . . . 'Pollyanna' theorizing."[122] Scholars contributing to discussions of well-being are by no means focused only on sweetness and light. To the contrary, there is widespread recognition in such discussions that to live the good life is to suffer but also to gain wisdom and character strength from it. A scrap of paper found in a Nazi death camp speaks to the point:

> O Lord
> Remember not only the men and women of good will,
> But all those of ill will.
> But do not remember all the suffering
> They have inflicted upon us;
> Remember the fruits we have bought
> Thanks to this suffering—
> Our comradeship, our loyalty, our humility,
> Our courage, our generosity, the greatness of heart
> Which has grown out of all this;
> And when they come to judgment,
> Let all the fruits we have borne
> Be their forgiveness.[123]

Whoever wrote the prayer clearly has a saint's capacity for forgiveness and also the insightful discernment to recognize the virtues of his or her own horrifying, adverse experiences. Suffering can make well-being possible.

The eudaimonic turn in literary studies has thus shifted focus to such moments when a character displays a commendable trait in the face of hardship, experiences an insight or epiphany that results from suffering, or grows in significant ways as a result of tragedy or some other adverse event. This approach can apply as much to narratives as it can to lyrics and other poems in which a speaker is conflicted but made the better for it in some way. In Whitman's elegies, such as "When Lilacs Last in the Dooryard Bloomed" and "Out of the Cradle Endlessly Rocking," the speakers find ecstasy and poetic inspiration in suffering, sorrow, and death. There are perhaps thousands of such poems and narratives configuring conflict and suffering as sources of eudaimonic transformation. No doubt, human beings are sometimes crushed by horrific circumstances, but there are also times when harsh experiences serve as catalysts of positive growth, however "negative" they may seem to be. With its joys and sorrows, this human life, as John Keats famously said, is a "vale of soul making."[124]

*Tragedy and Dark Literature*

Not all narratives offer a positive redemption of a given character. Many, in fact, portray human beings as victims who suffer greatly and whose suffering seems to have no meaning and provides no beneficial growth. Many lyrics are expressive of woe and anguish. Films such as *No Country for Old Men* or novels such as *The Sheltering Sky* offer no form of character growth, and their conclusions do not leave us feeling inspired. To the contrary, they often leave us profoundly disturbed because they can violently shake a naïve belief in the essential benevolence of the universe. Like many similar narratives, both end rather tragically with good people suffering and evil people going unpunished for reprehensible deeds. Yet, to many sophisticated readers, such poems and stories are inherently valuable and delightful, not only aesthetically, a point we shall discuss momentarily, but also didactically in that they convey useful insights. However horrible it sounds, there might be eudaimonic value in observing human suffering. Let us explain.

The negative emotions aroused from reading a horrible tragedy or a "dark" poem might serve as a kind of affective exercise in which we experience powerful, negative feelings but in a manageable way. Because of the aesthetic distance between us and the suffering character—whom we do not really know, despite our sympathetic identifications with him or her—we are able to experience what it is like to suffer but not overwhelmingly so, the result of which is that we are better prepared for our own inevitable hardships and tragedies when they strike. Of course, we will not likely view our own suffering aesthetically—the avalanche looks far more beautiful at a safe distance than it does directly under it—but we will, nevertheless, be able to deal with hardship more effectively with strength and courage if we have previously experienced vicarious suffering. One way to explain the eudaimonic value of reading a tragic story or a despairing poem, then, is to liken it to ingesting an attenuated virus that trains our immune system to fend off similar but stronger infectious agents at a later date. Although the character may suffer immensely or die a horrible death, the responding reader experiences something like PTG and is strengthened by the character's trauma. This might account, at least in part, for why so many people take immense delight in sad songs and depictions of suffering. Another possibility, suggested by Erin Lafford and Emma Mason in chapter three of this volume, is that some literary forms do not simply steep us in sadness but actually train us in ways to deal with it. Still another possibility is "downward social comparison," a theory first proposed by Leon Festinger, whose studies showed that comparison to others who are less fortunate causes us to look on our own circumstances in a positive light, even if they are difficult or tragic.[125] There is eudaimonic value, according to this argument, in observing suffering as it is depicted in the arts. Let us explore the point further.

The negative emotions aroused by tragic and/or "negative" works can also stimulate positive affect. In Aristotle's famous conception, tragedy results in a purging of the emotions through catharsis. In Chapter 4 of this volume John Briggs explores the concept of catharsis as it relates to well-being, so we will not encroach on the discussion here other than to point to the eudaimonic value of catharsis as a means by which undesirable affective states are expunged. Tragedy, according to Aristotle, not only helps one to overcome negative affect; it also inspires a universally valued character virtue—compassion. Beyond the intuitive understanding that compassion is conducive to the survival of the human species, there is also current neurological research demonstrating the value of responding compassionately to tragedies and other depictions of suffering: according to neurologists, feeling empathy is one of the most sophisticated functions in the human brain, as Gerald Hüther and others have observed.[126] Reading literature that inspires compassion can help the brain become more efficient at one of its most complex processes. It can similarly result in a reassessment or reinforcement of one's values, a decision to undertake a constructive change, a desire to love more honestly and openly, a confrontation with fear, and the like. If we read of a character who chooses wrongly or acts reprehensibly or unjustly and then suffers for it, our own sense of morality and justice are strengthened. Here, too, tragedy and suffering can result in eudaimonic outcomes for the reader, such as greater resiliency, affirmation of priorities, and inspiration to act in more beneficial ways—all of which enable him or her to flourish, not in spite of but precisely because of the "negative" narrative or lyric that seems to offer no positive redemption.

To be sure, a valid objection here is that we are imposing an overly moral or didactic conception of the reading process on responding to dark or tragic literature. In one sense this is true. Absent from the foregoing discussion is any mention of the delights and pleasures of form—the art for art's sake conception of aesthetics, which says that moral content is irrelevant, and that art is inherently valuable not for its didactic function but simply because it is beautiful. Many literary scholars who subscribe to such a perspective would almost surely object to the idea that literature can serve the end of well-being, insisting on the amoral nature of form, the intricacies and delights of which account for the power of art. The aesthetic effect of Emily Dickinson's poem "Because I could not stop for Death," for instance, lies not in any kind of moral imperative it inculcates through content but in how the poet succeeds in making death seem to be seductive in personifying the abstraction as a chivalrous male suitor whose polite manners and enticing allure belie why he is courting the speaker, that is, to escort her across the threshold of life into the grave. The poem, despite its amorality, is an utterly beautiful work of art whose subtleties bespeak the value of form over content and thus support the art for art's sake argument. In this sense, a privileging of form is the key element in assessing *Uncle Tom's Cabin* to be a compelling but poorly written story, or, by contrast, viewing Robert Graves's "Down, Wanton, Down" as a skillfully written poem about a trivial subject matter (an erection). It is possible to render an important subject matter badly, just as it is possible to render an insignificant subject with skill. Here, form determines aesthetic merit.

In another sense, however, such a perspective is problematic because it implies an unworkable separation of form and content, a point Emma Mason and others have argued in new formalist readings inspired by Susan Wolfson's landmark work, *Formal Charges*.[127] It also assumes an impossible disjunction between the reader and the text, a point reader response scholars have compellingly argued. In the case of Graves's poem, the reader's realization of the discrepancy between the skillful use of language and the sexual content accounts for the totality of the aesthetic effect, not just form alone. In reveling in the formal intricacies of Dickinson's poem, an insightful reader inevitably realizes that the poet's achievement lies in neither form nor content but in their interrelationship. Dickinson makes a compelling subject—death—seem to be seductive. Without the content, the form is empty. The responding reader might also have the realization that he or she has been duped, however fleetingly, into accepting the beauty and allure of death, the discrepancy between which, when realized, provokes thoughts of one's own mortality, a serious subject itself inextricably linked to questions of values, ethics, morality, and even well-being. It is nearly impossible for a thinking person to ponder death and not be nagged by the question: "Have I lived well?"

The reader response theorist, Norman Holland, has compellingly argued that it is impossible to escape one's psychological bias in responding to the form and content of a work of literature. According to Holland, works of literature (and other art forms) activate our psychological defense mechanisms and call our various neuroses into play.[128] Although this theory embodies the important truth that psychologically neutral reading is impossible, its Freudian framework is questionable. While it may be true that we cannot read outside of our psychological filters, not every reader is neurotic. To put it another way, it may also be possible to engage works of art and other people without defense mechanisms, as in intimacy, which, in its healthiest forms, has nothing to do with psychological illness and actually serves to cure neuroses. The response called into play by reading a work of literature may be a healthy one linked to the impulse to flourish. So it is possible to reject Holland's Freudian interpretive paradigm but accept his valuable insight that neutral reading divorced from one's psychodynamics—the type of reading implied by the art for art's sake position—is an utter impossibility. Reading a work of literature can call one's defenses and neuroses into play, but it can also activate the psychological processes involved in psychological health and well-being, a function served not only by reading eudaimonic literature such as inspiring stories and lyrics about love and ecstasy but also tragedies and lyrics in which characters grow and also those in which they do not.

Even if one rejects the aforementioned ideas and insists that form is separable from content—and we acknowledge giving short shrift to a complex subject on which many sophisticated thinkers have written dense treatises—reading a tragic narrative with the sole (amoral) intention of reveling in its formal delights can still result in a eudaimonic outcome in that it can induce what has been variously called an ecstasy, a peak experience, or a state of flow. Previous researchers have attested to the value of such states. Marghanita Laski, one of the first social scientists to study ecstatic states, observed that appreciating art or responding to beauty is a frequent domain of experience in which such ecstasies occur.[129] As she demonstrated, responding to beauty, however it is defined, can induce a state of rapture that leaves the individual beneficially transformed, for ecstasies of many varieties result in several eudaimonic changes, such as a more complex sense of self, a rejection of values not conducive to happiness, and the embrace of beliefs and activities that facilitate well-being. Maslow conceived of a whole theory around such a concept. At the top of his famous hierarchy of needs is self-actualization, a state of being facilitated by peak experiences of several varieties, among which are what he called aesthetic peak experiences, or moments of consciousness transformation resulting from the rapture one experiences in response to beauty. More recently, Mihalyi Csikszentmihalyi, a founding figure in positive psychology, has articulated and quantified a theory of states of optimal experience that can be used to support the claim that responding to beauty, even in the form of taking immense delight in a formally intricate tragedy offering no positive affirmations or inspirations, can be highly beneficial. Csikszentmihalyi calls such states of being "flow," [130] because so many of his subjects used the term to describe their moments of optimal experience. It is possible that the state of flow induced by reading a tragedy can serve to keep us locked in negativity, but it is also possible that we can emerge from a period of flow, induced by viewing or reading a complex tragedy, with a more complex sense of self. Many people who read tragic stories and see tragic dramas often claim such an experience of heightened self-knowledge after being absorbed (that is, locked in a state of flow), by them. Perhaps this is one reason why literary theorists and scholars have privileged tragedy, the response to which is so deeply affective and, as we are suggesting, instructive.

No doubt, there are dangers in festishizing and aestheticizing tragedy, for exposure to too much artistic tragedy might reinforce negativity bias and thus be a hindrance to well-being. Watching or reading tragedy, *if that is all we do*, could potentially train us in tragedy at deep, neurological levels. To fetishize the tragic and to elevate it to the highest canonical status, as many literary scholars have done, is a kind of absolutism that drives a given truth to a fundamental extreme and renders it unworkable. Tragedy is instructive, but to teach solely by negative example, as most good teachers know, is poor instruction. In teaching solely by negative example, such teachers offer no positive modeling on what to do correctly and thus unwittingly undermine themselves by reinforcing (and teaching) the wrong things they are trying prevent their students from doing. Students need negative examples, but students also need to be encouraged when they achieve mastery in a given skill. Violinists do not ever reach world class levels if they are only ever taught what they are doing improperly. Such an idea does not negate the value of tragedy, which might be beneficial for the reasons we have stated and perhaps many more. It is reasonable to assume, nevertheless, that *too much* artistic tragedy can give us an imbalanced view of life and teach us to view the world through a tragic lens, perhaps even causing us to create tragic outcomes through self-fulfilling prophesies or at the least fostering what psychologists have called "learned helplessness."[131]

To be sure, it is entirely possible that tragedy is the one genre exempt from discussions of eudaimonia in literature, as there is no statistically supported evidence to support that it helps readers to be well. Still, a eudaimonic conceptual framework that does not allow for discussions of tragedy risks being oversimplified in its privileging of the positive. The genre of tragedy can be beneficial, provided one is also exposed to other literary forms that offer positive examples of how to live well. We need dramas about darkness and suffering, as well as those in which human beings grow through facing adversity, but we also need inspiring narratives and poems about love and gratitude. All, we suggest, have something eudaimonic to teach us.

The eudaimonic turn in literary studies, then, entails not only a reassessment of positive and inspiring literature in its narrative and poetic forms but also conflict based narratives or poems in which a character or speaker experiences a beneficial transformation because of his or her struggle, as well as tragic works offering no positive character transformations but exerting a powerful, beneficial impact on the reader's psyche. A eudaimonic turn that does not account for *all* forms of literature carries with it the risk of cheapening the complexities of literary forms by forcing them to adhere to simplistic aesthetic standards in the name of a positive value agenda. As John Keats famously said, "We distrust literature which has a palpable design upon us." The eudaimonic turn in literary studies should not be prescriptive and proscriptive by imposing a "positive" ideology on literature. Such an approach degenerates into the equivalent of the Marxist call in the late nineteenth and early twentieth centuries for social realism, as well as other such examples of the use of literature for ideological ends.

The following studies represent a topical reassessment of various works of literature without degenerating into a one-sided privileging of any particular type of literature. The question of well-being, as the essays demonstrate, factors in the study of all types of literature and the critical approaches used to study them. Let us briefly survey each one.

## OVERVIEW

In chapter 1, Charles Altieri makes a compelling case for why Nietzsche is necessary for a positive account of modernism in the arts. He explores the contrast between Rancière and Nietzsche in an evaluation of theoretical models used for appreciating what is distinctive and powerful, that is, what is *valuable*, about modernist American poetry. Altieri claims that Jacques Rancière offers an important perspective on nineteenth century aesthetics in a shift that serves as the ultimate foundations of modernism in all the arts. But this model, which characterizes the contrasts between a regime of representation and one shaped by the primacy of relations among sensations, proves insufficient for orienting oneself to poetry because it does not seek out statements about intentions and so cannot make articulate the level of purposes and challenges that drive this work. In fact, while Rancière is a superb critic of those who impose the moral and the political onto the aesthetic, his own refusal to talk about values, as Altieri puts it, "replicates a void in which those discourses will always rush." So Altieri goes the other way. He shows how Nietzsche provides a necessary model of value that can accompany Rancière's theoretical observations and at the same time account for what was a focal point for the shaping of artists' intentions. By specifying Rancière's basic picture of what becomes modernism, Altieri demonstrates, by contrast, why Nietzsche is fundamental to the picture if one is to talk about the arts in terms of positive values that are capable of resisting appeals to the political and the moral. Altieri is less concerned with Nietzsche's general ideas about the world than he is with the possible force for modernist painters and writers of the philosopher's claims about the possible roles art can take up as a means of transforming cultural life and facilitating human well-being without degenerating into the imposition of a moral and/or ideological agenda.

In chapter 2, James Engell discusses the (relatively) neglected concept of well-being in the study of Thoreau. Engell analyzes Thoreau's preoccupation with the healing properties of the natural world. Unlike the "transcendentalist metaphysicians" who simply see the transcendent divine in nature, Thoreau, as Engell demonstrates, is a transcendentalist *phy*sician who calls us to a pragmatic healing and insight, both of which interpret nature and diagnose our felt experience of it in a way that reorients how we conceive of our relationship to it. Thoreau does so in a way that brings us to greater health both conceptually and experientially. The image of natural healing in Thoreau's writing is not merely a Romantic trope; it is a lived experience replicated across time and culture. The "tonic" of nature is a symbol in the Coleridgean sense, that is, it *is* itself even as it *also* represents a greater whole. Living nature is only known and experienced by us fully as human beings when we do so through self-conscious, inner examination, through a transcendental and an empirical reckoning. As Engell concludes, "Thoreau teaches us that there is a heaven, and it is on Earth, an Elysium, a paradise, with wood ticks and rattlesnakes. It's Eden, so we may learn to be better gardeners, for heaven is under our daily cultivation, as is our health, from Penobscot Mountain even to the summit of Ktaadn."

Another focus on the healing properties of nature is found in chapter 3, written by Erin Lafford and Emma Mason. This essay is an exploration of the medicinal effects of poetic rhythm in John Clare's tree elegies. For Clare, the gradual destruction of the natural environment was a moment of deep, personal human mourning because of his self-proclaimed "friendship" with particular spots he encountered on routine daily walks. Despite what he calls the "withering" of this landscape in his natural history prose, Clare related to trees as structures of dependability and health, hearing "feathered rhymes" in their branches. Lafford and Mason argue that feathered rhymes, a sound-image of protection, softness, and controlled movement, underline the slow, patient and gentle rhythms of Clare's tree elegies ("Langley Bush," "To a Fallen Elm," "The Mores," and "The Lament of Swordy Well") to create a meter capable of aurally guiding the reader through the experience of mourning, loss, and healing. The authors also suggest that this meter is "arborescent," a term derided by poststructuralists (notably Deleuze and Guattari) as linear, vertical, and monolithic when compared to the multiplicities of thought represented by the "rhizome." In Clare's poetry, however, the tree provides a point of direction, structured wandering and patient observation, and it thus functions as a map to which readers can communally turn as a way to listen together, just as Clare hears the natural world in an immediate way through affection and attention. Clare's tree rhythms are thus healing and medicinal: the reader will necessarily "fall" as he or she works through the rhythms of these elegies (reverberating as they do with moments of sadness and grief) only to be pulled back up into emotional health by their tonal and metrical stability.

In chapter 4, John Briggs tackles the knotty problem of literary catharsis. In the last half of the twentieth century, therapeutic uses of catharsis have grown in popularity as academic interest in literary catharsis has waned. Our understandings of human happiness and human flourishing, and their possible relation to literary catharsis, have thus been affected and, as Briggs claims, impaired. Post-Freudian and postmodern understandings of social relations and the psyche have tended to reduce catharsis to physical or psycho-physical release, and they often have done so to cast doubt upon the value of catharsis for cultural and personal cures of lasting consequence. Using some of the suggestive findings of medicine, early Freudian theory, and contemporary treatment of PTSD, Briggs opens up a line of inquiry that reconsiders the phenomenon of literary catharsis. He does so in an analysis of two pivotal, Elizabethan works of literature—*The Spanish Tragedy* and *Hamlet*—in search of an understanding of the meaning and function of catharsis in these paradigmatic revenge tragedies. His study is an induction of some of the most important factors affecting these famous literary treatments of the destructive yet all-too-human motive of revenge. As he shows, the playwrights' use of distance, identification, ordeal, and reflection—separately and in their artistic interaction—reveals some of the richness of traditional understandings of catharsis and the human psyche's curative encounter with powerfully affective works of literature.

In chapter 5, Michael West analyzes well-being in terms of the image of walking. Supposedly exemplified by Poe, popularized by Baudelaire, and Marxized by Walter Benjamin, the concept of the flâneur as a gentlemanly detached stroller in the city is often invoked to describe the ambivalent response of nineteenth-century writers to increasing urbanization. But how useful is it in explaining the various rituals of walking cultivated by writers in the American Renaissance? West answers the question negatively by demonstrating the salubrious quality of the construct of walking as it appears in mid-nineteenth-century American Romanticism. In his refutation of such a neo-Marxist interpretive paradigm, West demonstrates that America's pastoral imagination inhibited the emergence of literary conventions for ritualized urban spectatorship, the likes of which were found in the European tradition. In other words, he elucidates the inapplicability of Benjamin's concept, which, he argues, is of limited utility in analyzing the styles of sauntering celebrated by American Romantic authors, whose characters' sojourns were (on a psychological level) attempts to actualize well-being.

Paola Baseotto similarly discusses the concept of healing in chapter 6. In this essay, Baseotto examines the work of Edmund Spenser, particularly *The Faerie Queene*, which offers a rich gallery of portraits of characters displaying marks of physical and/or psychological pathologies following various kinds of suffering. Some characters actively enact healing strategies while others choose immurement in chronic suffering. Spenser's text emphasizes the motive of waste and the futility of a life devoid of meaning and purpose. By laying stress on the consequences of immurement in the condition of sufferer on the psychological and physiological balance of individuals, as well as on their willingness to play an active role within their communities, his narrative sometimes functions as a negative form of persuasion on the importance of well-being. Still, as Baseotto observes, the moral, emotional, and spiritual torpor, as well as the morbid desire to grieve that characterizes some Spenserian characters, are incompatible with the overall moral and political purposes that decide his rhetorical strategies. Spenser's heroes are those who, when faced with disease or the hardship of life, hold on to the perspectives of faith and the rule of reason. By reintegrating themselves in the mainstream of life and resuming their private, spiritual, social and political duties, they develop and maintain a fully human identity. Baseotto's principal purpose is to demonstrate, given Spenser's pervasive and distinctive emphasis on duty, active engagement, and self-fulfilment, the centrality of ideas of well-being throughout his canon.

In chapter 7, Amanpal Garcha takes up the question of agency. He analyzes how nineteenth-century British novels represent human freedom, which he defines as the degree to which a human subject is able to make choices about her interactions with other people and things, act on those choices, and feel as if the outcomes of those actions express her desires and intentions. Garcha briefly contextualizes the model of freedom that Trollope's fiction so often uses—freedom as self-determination—within the history of political liberalism, which seeks to preserve subjects' capacity for choosing their own "pursuit of happiness" with minimal interference from the state. He also relates this model to the basic operations of capitalism, which depend on buyers' and sellers' acts of choice as they pursue self-interest in the marketplace, and to recent psychological research that suggests individual happiness depends on the ability to choose among different courses of actions. Yet Trollope's depictions of decision making and freedom are representative not just of the individual-centered, liberatory ideals that inform the discourses of liberalism, capitalism, and (some strains of) psychology, but also of the problems—of regret, procrastination, anxiety, confusion, and helplessness—that such freedom routinely creates among subjects in modern Western cultures. Garcha focuses primarily on Trollope's depiction of the experience of relatively open decision making, for the novelist shows this experience as productive of feelings of paralyzing dissatisfaction. In taking seriously the idea that choice can produce unhappiness rather than a contented sense of freedom, the essay questions the assumptions about self-determination and happiness that seem to underlie literary scholars' championing of open-ended or unstructured experiences. The conclusions of psychologist Barry Schwartz, along with those of other researchers, suggest that critics' equation of openness, freedom, and individual happiness is simplistic: as Trollope shows and Schwartz suggests, an individual's sense of the openness of his or her options does not necessarily produce a sense of contentment or meaningful self-determination. The process of decision making itself can be torturous and deeply unsatisfying, and having a variety of possible avenues open can make one experience a state that Schwartz provocatively calls "the tyranny of freedom." This "tyranny," moreover, has much to do with the rise of the capitalist marketplace, in which a plethora of choices seduces consumers to find happiness *only* in the market's variety and in capitalism's promises of future contentment.

David Bordelon also examines the questions of happiness and agency in chapter 8. As he demonstrates, religion in nineteenth-century America, according to the accepted narrative, acted as a controlling force, consigning women to a limited role in society. Part of the social and cultural network that constrained women to the private sphere, religion was the central tenet in the cult of domesticity. As evidence of this view, modern critics point to the popularity of domestic fiction, which, with its depiction of pious heroines, fervid protestations of Christian belief, and subjugation of women, acted as a cultural correlative of a restrictive social phenomenon. But shifting the interpretative prism from a modern, pathological reading of religion to its contemporary, eudaimonic reception calls this narrative into question. Indeed, one of the most popular works of American domestic fiction, Augusta Jane Evans's 1866 novel *St. Elmo* challenges the view of religion as a conservative and coercive force. Diaries, reviews, letters, and essays from the period document that for many nineteenth-century readers, *St. Elmo*'s religious imagery did not amount to an opiate for the reading masses. Instead, interpreting the novel through a historical framework reveals how religion provided cultural "cover" for a decidedly progressive, liberal agenda to educate women. To illustrate this, Bordelon moves from a brief historical overview of the conflict between religion and the intellect in nineteenth-century America to an explication of the novel's marriage of these ideals. In doing so, he shows that instead of poisoning women's cognitive faculties, religion made erudition safe for domestic consumption.

Like Bordelon, Daniel O'Day explores the question of the role of religious ideas as a determinant of life and literature in chapter 9. In a complex, new formal analysis of Milton's companion poems, "L'Allegro" and "Il Penseroso," O'Day argues for the necessity of melancholy as a component of religious ecstasy. While "L'Allegro" captures the pleasures of "mirth and youthful jollity," "Il Penseroso" extols melancholy as a (nonetheless) highly positive condition, which, if he could achieve it, would manifest itself in religious as well as creative ecstasies. The close formal connections between the two poems, as seen in diction, tropes, and symbols, are complemented by the movement in linear progression from "L'Allegro's" opening lines, where lightheartedness, singing, and country pleasures are introduced as antidotes to the bleaker forms of melancholy. Then, at the beginning of "Il Penseroso," melancholy of the more positive kind supplants frivolity, building up to the concluding lines of the sequence, in which the poet, who describes this linear movement as the path he wishes to follow, imagines himself in creative solitude, in tune with heavenly harmonies. The structural irony underlying this progression, is that it harks back in distinctly circular fashion to the opening lines of "L'Allegro" and the bleaker form of melancholy, which, to seventeenth-century readers of Robert Burton's *The Anatomy of Melancholy*, was unavoidably related to the happier, more constructive kind. The melancholy Milton hopes to achieve is thus suggestive of well-being primarily because it readily acknowledges and *embodies* bleakness and mirth, not just because it has outgrown them. Milton's acceptance of this connection leads him to a clearer understanding of the human condition. But it also lays the foundation for what he humbly envisions as his life's work—something *like* religious prophecy as manifested in the music of poetry, both of which, for Milton, signified, and even catalyzed, human well-being.

Just as Bordelon and O'Day turn the dismissal of religion on its head, so does Christine E. Kephart, in chapter 10, upset conventional wisdom by challenging notions of happiness in a discussion of two icons of American thought: Willa Cather and William James. Her essay is a sophisticated discussion of a modern American novelist who resisted suspicion while remaining modern in narrative approach and theory and a philosopher whose ideas continue to impact theories of well-being. Kephart specifically argues that Cather's short story "Neighbor Rosicky" incorporates concepts of happiness derived from James's influential philosophies in *Varieties of Religious Experience* and *Pragmatism*, including the conversion of the twice-born sick soul and the theory of pragmatism. Kephart explores how Cather paints in the fictional Rosicky the portrait of a Jamesian pragmatist and converted soul whose story conveys an understanding of the sometimes complex ways one comes to a life of well-being. Rosicky is thus associated with James's image of Tolstoy and with Christian and nature imagery, like trees and roots. He is a character developed with real human qualities, as symbolized by Cather's focus on his hands and eyes, two features indicating his action-oriented pragmatism, and how he spends his time, after finding his own way to flourishing, caring for the wellness of others in his community. In building a narrative about the constructs of well-being, Cather challenges her readers to examine the narrative arrangement of their own lives and the principles by which considered action and decision may work toward the thoughtful structuring of a life of happiness and contentment. In looking back to William James for her modern-era story, Cather conveys her own very real understanding that questions about what comprises happiness and how to accomplish it are indeed, as Aristotle also claimed, the primary questions of a person's life in any era.

In the final chapter, Adam Potkay traces the history of the construct of joy as it was received (and abused) in twentieth-century discourse. As he argues, the post–WWI literary mood "may be described in a number of ways, but joyful is not one of them." Reprinted from the award-winning, influential work, *The Story of Joy: From the Bible through Late Romanticism,* this chapter follows the trajectory of joy through various permutations and manifestations in twentieth-century literature and popular culture. In a brilliant critique Potkay accounts for why happiness and joy are considered an embarrassment by many academics, but he concludes the essay with a compelling peroration on why joy still matters, despite its degeneration in political, cultural, and economic discourse. The story of joy, as he concludes, "turns deprivation into a prelude to restoration, frustration into an occasion for fulfillment. As long as we judge loss, limits, and extinctions to be evils, we will never, at least in the stories we tell ourselves, be without joy."

Such studies are thus intended to bolster the burgeoning critical framework in the fields of English, comparative literature, and cultural studies by stimulating discussions of well-being in the "posttheory" moment. The volume consists of several examinations of literary and theoretical configurations of the following determinants of human subjectivity and the role these play in facilitating well-being: values, race, ethics/morality, aesthetics, class, ideology, culture, economics, language, gender, spirituality, sexuality, nature, and the body. Many of the authors compellingly refute negativity bias and pathologized interpretations of *salutogenic,* or health-engendering, experiences or conceptual models as they appear in literary texts or critical theories. Some authors examine the eudaimonic outcomes of suffering, marginalization, hybridity, oppression, and/or tragedy, while others analyze the positive effects of positive affect. Still others analyze the aesthetic response and/or the reading process in inquiries into the role of language use and its impact on well-being, or they explore the complexities of strength, resilience, and other positive character traits in the face of struggle, suffering, and "othering."

The eudaimonic turn in literary studies represents a critical turn of the critical wheel. We hope the following studies further stimulate the fruitful discussions already taking place in the discipline and give scholars a more coherent forum for the exploration of the rich complexities of human well-being and their relationship to literature.

## BIBLIOGRAPHY

Alexandrova, Anna. "Doing Well in the Circumstances." *Journal of Moral Philosophy* (forthcoming).

Altieri, Charles. *The Particulars of Rapture: An Aesthetics of the Affects.* Ithaca, NY: Cornell University Press, 2003.

American Psychiatric Association. *Diagnostic and Statistical Manual of Mental Disorders, Fourth Edition.* Washington, DC: American Psychiatric Association, 1994.

Annas, Julia. *The Morality of Happiness.* New York: Oxford University Press, 1993.

Aristotle. *Nicomachean Ethics*. Translated by H. Rackham. Cambridge: Harvard University Press, 1926.
Armstrong, Karen. *Twelve Steps to a Compassionate Life*. New York: Alfred A. Knopf, 2011.
Augustine. *Enchiridion on Faith, Hope, and Love*. Translated by Thomas S. Hibbs. Washington, D.C.: Regnery Publishing, 1961.
Bakhtin, M. M. and P. N. Medvedev. *The Formal Method in Literary Scholarship*. Translated by A. J. Wehrle. Baltimore, MD: Johns Hopkins University Press, 1978.
Barth, Robert. *Romanticism and Transcendence: Wordsworth, Coleridge and the Religious Imagination*. Columbia, MS: University of Missouri Press, 2003.
Bate, Jonathan. *Romantic Ecology: Wordsworth and the Environmental Tradition*. New York: Routledge, 1991.
Bernstein, Charles. *A Poetics*. Cambridge: Harvard University Press, 1992.
Best, Stephen and Sharon Marcus, eds. "The Way I Read Now." *Representations* 108 (2009): 1–21.
Bialostosky, Don. *Wordsworth, Dialogics, and the Practice of Criticism*. New York: Cambridge University Press, 1992.
Bok, Sissela. *Exploring Happiness: From Aristotle to Brain Science*. New Haven: Yale University Press, 2010.
Cameron, David. "Prime Minister Speech on Wellbeing: A Transcript of a Speech Given by the Prime Minister." Keynote Address. November 25, 2010. Retrieved February 17, 2012. http://www.number10.gov.uk/ news/pm-speech-on-well-being/.
Cameron, Kim. S., et al. "Foundations of Positive Organizational Scholarship." In *Positive Organizational Scholarship: Foundations of a New Discipline*, 3–13. San Francisco: Berret-Koehler Publishers, 2003.
Charry, Ellen. *God and the Art of Happiness*. Grand Rapids, MI: William B. Eerdmans Publishing Company, 2010.
Cicero. *On Moral Ends*. Edited by Julia Annas. Cambridge: Cambridge University Press, 2001.
Cohen, Sheldon, et al. "Positive Emotional Style Predicts Resistance to Illness after Experimental Exposure to Rhinovirus or Influenza A Virus." *Psychosomatic Medicine* 68, no. 6 (2006): 809–15.
Crisp, Roger. "Well-being." *The Stanford Encyclopedia of Philosophy*. Edited by Edward N. Zalta. 2008. Retrieved February 17, 2012. http://plato.stanford.edu/archives/ win2008 /entries/well-being/.
Csikszentmihalyi, Mihaly. *Flow: The Psychology of Optimal Experience*. New York: Harper & Row, 1990.
———. "Opening Remarks." Presentation at the First International Positive Psychology Summit, Washington, D.C., October 3–6, 2002.
Cull, Ryan. "Beyond the Cheated Eye: Dickinson's Lyric Sociality." *Nineteenth-Century Literature* 65 (2010): 38–64.
Diener, Ed. "Subjective Well-Being." *Psychological Bulletin* 95, no. 3 (1984): 542–75.
Elliot, A. J. and M. V. Covington. "Approach and Avoidance Motivation." *Educational Psychology Review* 13, no. 2 (2001): 73–92.
Engell, James. *The Committed Word: Literature and Public Values*. University Park, PA: Pennsylvania University Press, 1999.
Farland, Maria Magdalena. "'That Tritest/Brightest Truth': Emily Dickinson's Anti-Sentimentality." *Nineteenth-Century Literature* 53, no. 3 (1998): 3674–89.
Felski, Rita. "After Suspicion." *Profession* (2009): 28–35.
———. "Suspicious Minds." *Poetics Today* 32, no. 2 (2010): 215–34.
———. *Uses of Literature*. Oxford: Blackwell, 2008.
Festinger, Leon. "A Theory of Social Comparison Processes." *Human Relations* 7, no. 2 (1954): 117–40.
Fisher, Philip. *Wonder, the Rainbow, and the Aesthetics of Rare Experiences*. Cambridge, MA: Harvard University Press, 2003.
———. *The Vehement Passions*. Princeton, NJ: Princeton University Press, 2002.

Flanagan, Owen. *The Really Hard Problem: Meaning in a Material World*. Cambridge, MA: MIT Press, 2007.
Frankl, Victor. *Man's Search for Meaning*. New York: Pocket, 1997.
Gable, Shelly L. and Jonathan Haidt. "What (and Why) Is Positive Psychology?" *Review of General Psychology* 9, no. 2 (2005): 103–10.
Gana, Nouri. "War, Poetry, Mourning: Darwish, Adonis, Iraq." *Public Culture* 22 (2010): 33–65.
Garber, Marjorie. *Academic Instincts*. Princeton: Princeton University Press, 2001.
Greenblatt, Stephen. "Resonance and Wonder." In *Exhibiting Cultures: The Poetics and Politics of Museum Display*, edited by Ivan Karp and Stephen D. Levine, 42–56. Washington: Smithsonian Institute, 1991.
Haidt, Jonathan. *The Happiness Hypothesis: Finding Modern Truth in Ancient Happiness*. New York: Basic Books, 2006.
Hale, Dorothy. "Aesthetics and the New Ethics: Theorizing the Novel in the Twenty-First Century." *PMLA* 124, no. 3 (2009): 898.
Haney, David P. "Recent Work in Romanticism and Religion: From Witness to Critique." *Christianity and Literature* 54 (2005): 265–82.
Haybron, Daniel M. *The Pursuit of Unhappiness: The Elusive Psychology of Well-Being*. New York: Oxford University Press, 2008.
Hesiod. *Works and Days*. In *Hesiod: Theogony, Works and Days, Shield*. Translated by Apostolos N. Athanassakis. Baltimore: Johns Hopkins University Press, 1983.
Holland, Norman. *Literature and the Brain*. Gainesville, FL: PsyArt Foundation, 2009.
Hughes, Julie Lund. "The Role of Happiness in Kant's Ethics." *Aporia* 14, no. 1 (2004): 61–72.
Hüther, Gerard. *The Compassionate Brain: How Empathy Creates Intelligence*. Boston: Shambhala, 2006.
Ivanhoe, Philip J. "Happiness in Early Chinese Thought." In *Oxford Handbook of Happiness*. Oxford: Oxford University Press, forthcoming.
Jahoda, Marie. *Current Concepts of Positive Mental Health*. New York: Basic Books, 1958.
Kant, Immanuel. *Foundations of the Metaphysics of Morals*. Translated by Lewis White Beck. New York: Macmillan, 1985.
Kennedy, Robert. "Remarks of Robert F. Kennedy." University of Kansas. March 18, 1968. Retrieved February 17, 2012. www.jfklibrary.org/Research/Ready-Reference/RFK-Speeches/Remarks-of-Robert-F-Kennedy-at-the-University-of-Kansas-March-18-1968.aspx.
Keyes, Corey L.M. "Promoting and Protecting Mental Health as Flourishing: A Complementary Strategy for Improving National Mental Health." *American Psychologist* 62, no. 2 (2007): 95–108.
Knight, Mark and Emma Mason. *Nineteenth-Century R eligion and Literature*. Oxford: Oxford University Press, 2006.
Laski, Marghanita. *Ecstasy in Secular and Religious Experiences*. Los Angeles: Tarcher, 1961.
Latour, Bruno. "Why Has Critique Run Out of Steam? From Matters of Fact to Matters of Concern." *Critical Inquiry* 30, no. 2 (2004): 225–48.
Leibniz, Gottfried Wilhelm. *Theodicy: Essays on the Goodness of God, the Freedom of Man and the Origin of Evil*. Translated by E. M. Huggard. New Haven: Yale University Press, 1952.
Linley, P. Alex and Stephen Joseph. "Toward a Theoretical Foundation for Positive Psychology in Practice." In *Positive Psychology in Practice*, edited by P. Alex Linley and Stephen Joseph, 715–25. Hoboken, NJ: Wiley, 2004.
Long, Elizabeth. "Textual Interpretation as Collective Action." In *The Ethnography of Reading*, edited by Jonathan Boyarin, 180–211. Los Angeles: University of California Press, 1993.
Love, Heather. "Close but not Deep: Literary Ethics and the Descriptive Turn." *New Literary History* 41, no. 2 (2010): 371–92.

Lyubomirsky, Sonia, Kennon M. Sheldon, and David Schkade. "Pursuing Happiness: The Architecture of Sustainable Change." *Review of General Psychology* 9, no. 2 (2005): 111–31.

Maslow, Abraham. *Toward a Psychology of Being*. New York: John Wiley & Sons, 1968.

McMahon, Darrin M. *Happiness: A History*. New York: Grove Press, 2006.

Moores, D. J. *Mystical Discourse in Wordsworth and Whitman: A Transatlantic Bridge*. Dudley, MA: Peeters, 2006.

Nietzsche, Friedrich. "Twilight of the Idols." In *Twilight of the Idols and The Anti-Christ*. Translated by R. J. Hollingdale, 29–122. London: Penguin Books, 1990.

———. *Thus Spake Zarathustra*. Translated by A. Tille. London: J. M. Dent & Sons, 1958.

Noddings, Nel. *Happiness and Education*. Cambridge: Cambridge University Press, 2003.

Nussbaum, Martha C. *Love's Knowledge: Essays on Philosophy and Literature*. New York: Oxford University Press, 1992.

———. *Frontiers of Justice: Disability, Nationality, Species Membership*. Cambridge: Belknap Press, 2006.

———. *Poetic Justice*. Boston: Beacon Press, 1997.

Ostir, Glenn V., et al. "The Association between Emotional Well-Being and the Incidence of Stroke in Older Adults." *Psychosomatic Medicine* 63, no. 2 (2001): 210–15.

Parfit, Derek. *Reasons and Persons*. New York: Oxford University Press, 1984.

Pawelski, James O. "Beyond Healthy-Mindedness: William James and the Science of Well-Being." *William James Studies* (forthcoming).

———. "Happiness and Its Opposites." In *Oxford Handbook of Happiness*. Oxford: Oxford University Press, forthcoming.

Peterson, Christopher, Steven Maier, and Martin E.P. Seligman. *Learned Helplessness: A Theory for the Age of Personal Control*. New York: Oxford University Press, 1995.

Plato. "The Republic." In *The Dialogues of Plato*. translated by B. Jowett, 589–879. New York: Random House, 1892.

———. "Symposium." In *The Dialogues of Plato*. translated by B. Jowett, 299–345. New York: Random House, 1892.

Potkay, Adam. *Wordsworth's Ethics*. Baltimore: Johns Hopkins University Press, 2012.

———. *The Story of Joy: From the Bible through Late Romanticism*. New York: Cambridge University Press, 2007.

Ricoeur, Paul. *Freud and Philosophy: An Essay on Interpretation*. New Haven, CT: Yale University Press, 1970.

Roepke, Ann Marie. "Elevation as an Opportunity for Growth." Part of a symposium presentation entitled "Elevating Experiences: Research on Moral Evaluation, Awe, and Transcendence." The Second World Congress on Positive Psychology, Philadelphia, PA, July 26, 2011.

Rogers, Carl. *On Becoming a Person: A Therapist's View of Psychotherapy*. Boston: Houghton Mifflin, 1961.

Rollins, H.E., ed. *Letters of John Keats: Vol. 2, 1819-1821*. New York: Cambridge University Press, 2012.

Rousseau, Jean-Jacques. *The Social Contract*. Translated by Willmoore Kendall. Chicago: Henry Regnery, 1954.

Ryff, Carol E. "Beyond Ponce de Leon and Life Satisfaction: New Directions in the Quest for Successful Aging." *International Journal of Behavioral Development* 12, no. 1 (1989): 35–55.

Ryff, Carol E., et al. "Psychological Well-Being and Ill-Being: Do They Have a Distinct or Mirrored Biological Correlates?" In *Psychotherapy and Psychosomatics* 75, no. 2 (2006): 85–95.

Scheier, Michael F., et al. "Dispositional Optimism and Recovery from Coronary Artery Bypass Surgery: The Beneficial Effects on Positive Physical and Psychological Well-Being." *Journal of Personality and Social Psychology* 57, no. 6 (1989): 1024–40.

Sedgwick, Eve Kosofsky. "Paranoid Reading and Reparative Reading: or, You're so Paranoid, You Probably Think This Introduction Is about You." In *Novel Gazing:*

*Queer Readings in Fiction*, edited by Eve Kosofsky Sedgwick, 1–37. Durham, NC: Duke University Press, 1997.

Seligman, Martin. *Authentic Happiness: Using the New Positive Psychology to Realize your Potential for Lasting Fulfillment*. New York: The Free Press, 2002.

———. "President's Address." The APA 1998 Annual Report, appearing in the August, 1999 *American Psychologist*. Retrieved February 17, 2012. http://www.ppc.sas.upenn.edu /aparep98.htm.

———. *Flourish: A Visionary New Understanding of Happiness and Well-Being*. New York: The Free Press, 2011.

———. "Positive Health." *Applied Psychology* 57, no. 1 (2008): 3–18.

Seligman, Martin and Mihaly Csikszentmihalyi. "Positive Psychology: An Introduction." *American Psychologist* 55, no. 1 (2000): 5–14.

Soni, Vivasvan. *Mourning Happiness*. Ithaca, NY: Cornell University Press, 2010.

Sontag, Susan. *"Against Interpretation" and Other Essays*. New York: Farrar, 1966.

Stiglitz, Joseph. E., Amartya Sen, and Jean-Paul Fitoussi. "Report by the Commission on the Measurement of Economic Performance and Social Progress." Commission of the Government of France. September 2009. Accessed February 17, 2012. www.stiglitz-sen-fitoussi.fr/documents/rapport_anglais.pdf.

Tedeschi, Richard G. and Lawrence G. Calhoun. "A Clinical Approach to Posttraumatic." In *Positive Psychology in Practice*, edited by P. Alex Linley and Stephen Joseph. Hoboken, NJ: Wiley, 2004.

Urry, Heather, et al. "Making a Life Worth Living: Neural Correlates of Well-Being." *Psychological Science* 15, no. 6 (2004): 367–72.

Vaillant, George E. *Spiritual Evolution: A Scientific Defense of Faith*. New York: Broadway Books, 2008.

van Deurzen, Emmy. "Continental Contributions to Our Understanding of Happiness and Suffering." In *Oxford Handbook of Happiness*. Oxford: Oxford University Press, forthcoming.

Waters, Lea. "A Review of School-Based Positive Psychology Interventions." *The Australian Educational and Developmental Psychologist* 28, no. 2 (2011): 75–90.

Watson, David, Lee Clark, and Auke Tellegen. "Development and Validation of Brief Measures of Positive and Negative Affect: The PANAS Scales." *Journal of Personality and Social Psychology* 54, no. 6 (1988): 1063–70.

Wilson, John. "Introduction and Overview: A Positive Psychology of Trauma and PTSD." In *The Posttraumatic Self: Restoring Meaning and Wholeness to Personality*, edited by John Wilson, ed. New York: Routledge, 2006.

Wood, Allen W. "Kant vs. Eudaimonism." In *Kant's Legacy: Essays in Honor of Lewis White Beck*, edited by Predrag Cicovacki, 261–75. Rochester: University of Rochester Press, 2001.

World Health Organization. "Preamble to the Constitution of the World Health Organization." *Basic Documents*. Geneva, Switzerland: World Health Organization, 1964.

## NOTES

1. Aristotle, *Nicomachean Ethics* (Chicago: University of Chicago Press, 2011), I.iv.2.
2. Ibid., I.iv.2.
3. I am grateful to Dan Haybron for this point. See *The Pursuit of Unhappiness: The Elusive Psychology of Well-Being* (New York: Oxford University Press, 2008), 23–28, where he makes this point forcefully and at greater length.
4. Darrin M. McMahon, *Happiness: A History* (New York: Grove Press, 2006), 3. McMahon's history of happiness focuses on Western intellectual history. For a consideration of some of these same concepts in ancient Confucian and Daoist thought, see Philip J. Ivanhoe, "Happiness in Early Chinese Thought," in *The Oxford Handbook of Happiness* (Oxford: Oxford University Press, forthcoming).

5. Hesiod, "Works and Days," in *Hesiod: Theogony, Works and Days, Shield*, ed. Apostolos N. Athanassakis (Baltimore: Johns Hopkins University Press, 1983), lines 826–28.

6. We follow convention here and use happiness to translate eudaimonia, since it is less awkward than the alternatives. We are, however, very much aware of the problems involved in doing so.

7. McMahon points out that this connection goes beyond literature to etymology, as the word for *happiness* in virtually every Indo-European language is tied to words for luck, fortune, or fate. McMahon, *Happiness: A History*, 10–11.

8. Ibid., 25.

9. Ibid., 7.

10. In the ancient Greek world, a symposium was a hedonistic drinking party (the word itself meaning "to drink with"). A typical symposium was governed by an "archon" who determined what (large) quantities of wine each guest had to drink at what time and featured attractive wine-pourers, dancers, and flute girls. Depending on the wealth and taste of the guests, symposia might also feature *hetaera* (elegant, well-educated escorts) or cheaper call girls or male prostitutes. In Plato's hands, the symposium was transformed into a quest for a very different kind of happiness. The guests agreed that any drinking would be moderate and voluntary, and they decided to send the flute girl away. Instead of sensuous musical entertainment, the guests would provide their own intellectual entertainment by presenting a round of speeches in praise of love.

11. Julia Annas, *The Morality of Happiness* (New York: Oxford University Press, 1993), 46.

12. Aristotle, *Nicomachean Ethics*, I.vii.8.

13. Ibid., I.viii.15–16.

14. Cicero, *On Moral Ends* (Cambridge: Cambridge University Press, 2001), 78–79.

15. Mihaly Csikszentmihalyi, "Opening Remarks," Presentation at the First International Positive Psychology Summit, Washington, D.C., October 3–6, 2002.

16. Plato, *The Republic*, in *The Dialogues of Plato*, trans. B. Jowett (New York: Random House, 1892), VI, 509b.

17. Augustine, *Enchiridion on Faith, Hope, and Love*, trans. Thomas S. Hibbs (Washington, D.C.: Regnery Publishing, 1961), 11–12.

18. Gottfried Wilhelm Leibniz, *Theodicy: Essays on the Goodness of God, the Freedom of Man and the Origin of Evil*, trans. E. M. Huggard (New Haven: Yale University Press, 1952), 228.

19. A. J. Elliot and M. V. Covington, "Approach and Avoidance Motivation," *Educational Psychology Review* 13.2 (2001): 73–92.

20. Haybron, *The Pursuit of Unhappiness*, 29.

21. For a much more in-depth discussion of the nature of opposites and its implication for well-being, see James O. Pawelski, "Happiness and Its Opposites," in *Oxford Handbook of Happiness* (Oxford: Oxford University Press, forthcoming).

22. For an excellent discussion of this point in the field of psychology, see Shelly L. Gable and Jonathan Haidt, "What (and Why) Is Positive Psychology?" *Review of General Psychology* 9.2 (2005): 103–110.

23. The correlation is about r = -.2. David Watson, Lee Clark, and Auke Tellegen, "Development and Validation of Brief Measures of Positive and Negative Affect: The PANAS Scales," *Journal of Personality and Social Psychology* 54.6 (1988): 1063–70.

24. Corey L. M. Keyes, "Promoting and Protecting Mental Health as Flourishing: A Complementary Strategy for Improving National Mental Health," *American Psychologist* 62.2 (2007): 95–108.

25. Carol E. Ryff, et al., "Psychological Well-Being and Ill-Being: Do They Have a Distinct or Mirrored Biological Correlates?" in *Psychotherapy and Psychosomatics* 75.2 (2006): 85–95.

26. Friedrich Nietzsche, *Twilight of the Idols*, in *Twilight of the Idols and The Anti-Christ*, trans. R. J. Hollingdale (London: Penguin Books, 1990), 33.

27. Richard G. Tedeschi and Lawrence G. Calhoun, "A Clinical Approach to Posttraumatic Growth," in *Positive Psychology in Practice*, ed. P. Alex Linley and Stephen Joseph (Hoboken, NJ: Wiley, 2004).

28. Ann Marie Roepke, "Elevation as an Opportunity for Growth," part of a symposium presentation entitled "Elevating Experiences: Research on Moral Evaluation, Awe, and Transcendence." The Second World Congress on Positive Psychology, Philadelphia, PA, July 26, 2011.

29. Mihaly Csikszentmihalyi, *Flow: The Psychology of Optimal Experience* (New York: Harper Perennial, 1990), 52.

30. Roger Crisp. "Well-Being." *The Stanford Encyclopedia of Philosophy.* Edited by Edward N. Zalta. 2008. Accessed February 17, 2012. http://plato.stanford.edu/archives/win2008/entries/well -being/.

31. Immanuel Kant, *Foundations of the Metaphysics of Morals*, trans. Lewis White Beck (New York: Macmillan, 1985), 9–13; for an excellent analysis of Kant's views on happiness, see Julie Lund Hughes, "The Role of Happiness in Kant's Ethics," *Aporia* 14.1 (2004): 69.

32. Aristotle, *Nicomachean Ethics*, I.iv.1.

33. Ibid., I.vii.8.

34. Ibid., I.vii.9.

35. Ibid., I.iv.2.

36. Haybron, *The Pursuit of Unhappiness*, 36.

37. Annas, *The Morality of Happiness*, 46.

38. Aristotle, *Nicomachean Ethics*, I.vii.9.

39. For an overview of this critique by a number of continental philosophers, see Emmy van Deurzen, "Continental Contributions to our Understanding of Happiness and Suffering," in *Oxford Handbook of Happiness* (Oxford: Oxford University Press, forthcoming).

40. Friedrich Nietzsche, *Thus Spake Zarathustra*, trans. A. Tille (London: J. M. Dent & Sons, 1958), 9.

41. Sonia Lyubomirsky, Kennon M. Sheldon, and David Schkade, "Pursuing Happiness: The Architecture of Sustainable Change," *Review of General Psychology* 9.2 (2005): 116.

42. Jean-Jacques Rousseau, *The Social Contract*, trans. Willmoore Kendall (Chicago: Henry Regnery, 1954), 18.

43. Martin Seligman, "President's Address," The APA 1998 Annual Report, appearing in the August, 1999 *American Psychologist*. Accessed February 17, 2012. http://www.ppc.sas.upenn.

44. Martin Seligman and Mihaly Csikszentmihalyi, "Positive Psychology: An Introduction," *American Psychologist* 55.1 (2000): 5.

45. James O. Pawelski, "Beyond Healthy-Mindedness: William James and the Science of Well-Being," *William James Studies* (forthcoming).

46. Abraham Maslow, *Toward a Psychology of Being* (New York: John Wiley & Sons, 1968), 85; see also Carl Rogers, *A Therapist's View of Psychotherapy* (Boston: Houghton Mifflin, 1961), 350–51.

47. Marie Jahoda, *Current Concepts of Positive Mental Health* (New York: Basic Books, 1958), 23.

48. Carol E. Ryff, "Beyond Ponce de Leon and Life Satisfaction: New Directions in the Quest for Successful Aging," *International Journal of Behavioral Development* 12.1 (1989): 35–55.

49. Ed Diener, "Subjective Well-Being," *Psychological Bulletin* 95.3 (1984): 542–75.

50. Martin Seligman, *Flourish: A Visionary New Understanding of Happiness and Well-being* (New York: The Free Press, 2011).

51. American Psychiatric Association, *Diagnostic and Statistical Manual of Mental Disorders, Fourth Edition* (Washington, DC: American Psychiatric Association, 1994).

52. Corey L. M. Keyes, "Promoting and Protecting Mental Health as Flourishing: A Complementary Strategy for Improving National Mental Health," *American Psycholo-*

*gist* 62.2 (2007): 95–108. It is important to note that, while most of the models mentioned here focus on direct well-being, the models developed by Diener and Keyes are based on a notion of composite well-being.

53. World Health Organization, "Preamble to the Constitution of the World Health Organization," *Basic Documents* (Geneva, Switzerland: World Health Organization, 1964). This definition has remained unchanged in the Preamble since 1948.

54. Sheldon Cohen, et al., "Positive Emotional Style Predicts Resistance to Illness after Experimental Exposure to Rhinovirus or Influenza A Virus," *Psychosomatic Medicine* 68.6 (2006): 809–15.

55. Michael F. Scheier, et al., "Dispositional Optimism and Recovery from Coronary Artery Bypass Surgery: The Beneficial Effects on Positive Physical and Psychological Well-Being," *Journal of Personality and Social Psychology* 57.6 (1989): 1024–40.

56. Glenn V. Ostir, et al., "The Association between Emotional Well-Being and the Incidence of Stroke in Older Adults," *Psychosomatic Medicine* 63.2 (2001): 210–15.

57. Seligman, "Positive Health," *Applied Psychology* 57.1 (2008): 3-18.

58. For more information about the Center for Investigating Healthy Minds, visit www.investigatinghealthyminds.org.

59. Heather L. Urry, et al., "Making a Life Worth Living: Neural Correlates of Well-Being," *Psychological Science* 15.6 (2004): 367–72.

60. Ryff, et al., "Psychological Well-Being and Ill-Being: Do They Have a Distinct or Mirrored Biological Correlates?" *Psychotherapy and Psychosomatics* 75.2 (2006): 85–95.

61. For more information on this initiative, visit www.posneuroscience.org.

62. Robert Kennedy, "Remarks of Robert F. Kennedy," University of Kansas, March 18, 1968. Accessed February 17, 2012. www.jfklibrary.org/Research/Ready-Reference/RFK-Speeches/Remarks-of-Robert-F-Kennedy-at-the-University-of-Kansas-March-18-1968.aspx.

63. Joseph. E. Stiglitz, Amartya Sen, and Jean-Paul Fitoussi, "Report by the Commission on the Measurement of Economic Performance and Social Progress," Commission of the Government of France. September 2009. Accessed February 17, 2012. www.stiglitz-sen-fitoussi.fr/documents /rapport_anglais.pdf.

64. David Cameron, "Prime Minister Speech on Wellbeing: A Transcript of a Speech Given by the Prime Minister," Keynote Address. November 25, 2010. Accessed February 17, 2012. http://www.number10.gov.uk/ news/pm-speech-on-well-being/.

65. Kim S. Cameron, et al., "Foundations of Positive Organizational Scholarship," in *Positive Organizational Scholarship: Foundations of a New Discipline* (San Francisco: Berret-Koehler Publishers, 2003), 4.

66. Nel Noddings, *Happiness and Education* (Cambridge: Cambridge University Press, 2003), 1.

67. Lea Waters, "A Review of School-based Positive Psychology Interventions," *The Australian Educational and Developmental Psychologist* 28.2 (2011): 75–90. See also Martin Seligman, in *Flourish*, Chapter 5: Positive Education: Teaching Well-Being to Young People (New York: Free Press, 2011), 78–97.

68. Haybron, *The Pursuit of Unhappiness*, 33–36.

69. Martha Nussbaum, *Frontiers of Justice: Disability, Nationality, Species Membership* (Cambridge: Belknap Press, 2006).

70. Anna Alexandrova, "Doing Well in the Circumstances," *Journal of Moral Philosophy* (forthcoming).

71. Owen Flanagan, *The Really Hard Problem: Meaning in a Material World* (Cambridge, MA: MIT Press, 2007), 1.

72. Ibid., 4.

73. Sissela Bok, *Exploring Happiness: From Aristotle to Brain Science* (New Haven: Yale University Press, 2010), 105, 173–74.

74. Karen Armstrong, *Twelve Steps to a Compassionate Life* (New York: Alfred A. Knopf, 2011), 9.

75. Ellen Charry, *God and the Art of Happiness* (Grand Rapids, MI: William B. Eerdmans Publishing Company, 2010).

76. Paul Ricoeur, *Freud and Philosophy: An Essay on Interpretation* (New Haven, CT: Yale University Press, 1970).
77. Ibid., 40.
78. Eve Kosofsky Sedgwick, "Paranoid Reading and Reparative Reading; or, You're So Paranoid, You Probably Think This Introduction Is about You," in *Novel Gazing: Queer Readings in Fiction*, edited by Eve Kosofsky Sedgwick, 1–37 (Durham, NC: Duke University Press, 1997).
79. Ibid., 37.
80. Bruno Latour, "Why Has Critique Run Out of Steam? From Matters of Fact to Matters of Concern," *Critical Inquiry* 30.2 (2004): 225–48.
81. See "After Suspicion." *Profession* (2009): 28–35, and also "Suspicious Minds." *Poetics Today* 32.2 (2010): 215–34.
82. Felski, "After Suspicion," 30.
83. Felski, *Uses of Literature* (Oxford: Blackwell, 2008), 1.
84. Felski, "Suspicious Minds," *Poetics Today* 32:2 (2011): 217.
85. Ibid., 218.
86. Heather Love, "Close but not Deep: Literary Ethics and the Descriptive Turn," *New Literary History* 41.2 (2010): 388.
87. Stephen Best and Sharon Marcus, "The Way We Read Now," *Representations* 108 (2009): 3.
88. Ibid., 9–13.
89. Ibid., 18.
90. Vivasvan Soni, *Mourning Happiness* (Ithaca, NY: Cornell University Press, 2010), 13.
91. Charles Altieri, *The Particulars of Rapture: An Aesthetics of the Affects* (Ithaca, NY: Cornell University Press, 2003), 5.
92. Mark Knight and Emma Mason, *Nineteenth-Century R eligion and Literature* (Oxford: Oxford University Press, 2006).
93. Robert Barth, *Romanticism and Transcendence: Wordsworth, Coleridge and the Religious Imagination* (Columbia, MS: University of Missouri Press, 2003).
94. D. J. Moores, *Mystical Discourse in Wordsworth and Whitman: A Transatlantic Bridge* (Dudley, MA: Peeters, 2006).
95. Stephen Greenblatt, "Resonance and Wonder," In *Exhibiting Cultures: The Poetics and Politics of Museum Display*, edited by Ivan Karp and Stephen D. Levine, 42–56 (Washington: Smithsonian Institute, 1991).
96. Susan Sontag, *"Against Interpretation" and Other Essays* (New York: Farrar, 1966).
97. Charles Bernstein, *A Poetics* (Cambridge: Harvard University Press, 1992).
98. Elizabeth Long, "Textual Interpretation as Collective Action," In *The Ethnography of Reading*, edited by Jonathan Boyarin, 180–211 (Los Angeles: University of California Press, 1993).
99. Jonathan Bate, *Romantic Ecology: Wordsworth and the Environmental Tradition* (New York: Routledge, 1991).
100. Ibid., 5.
101. Don Bialostosky, *Wordsworth, Dialogics, and the Practice of Criticism* (New York: Cambridge University Press, 1992), 5.
102. Martha Nussbaum, *Poetic Justice* (Boston: Beacon Press, 1997).
103. Martha Nussbaum. *Love's Knowledge: Essays on Philosophy and Literature* (New York: Oxford University Press, 1992).
104. Marjorie Garber, *Academic Instincts* (Princeton: Princeton University Press, 2001).
105. Dorothy Hale, "Aesthetics and the New Ethics: Theorizing the Novel in the Twenty-First Century," *PMLA* 124.3 (2009): 898.
106. Love, "Close but not Deep: Literary Ethics and the Descriptive Turn," 372.
107. Felski, "Suspicious Minds," 217.
108. Potkay, *Wordsworth's Ethics* (Baltimore: Johns Hopkins University Press, 2012), 3.

109. For a more complete discussion, see Maria Magdalena Farland, "'That Tritest/ Brightest Truth': Emily Dickinson's Anti-Sentimentality," *Nineteenth-Century Literature* 53.3 (1998): 3674–89.

110. Moores, D. J., ed. *Wild Poets of Ecstasy: An Anthology of Ecstatic Verse*. (Nevada City, CA: Pelican Pond, 2011).

111. A forthcoming anthology edited by D.J. Moores, James Pawelski, Adam Potkay, Emma Mason, Susan Wolfson, and James Engell.

112. David P. Haney, "Recent Work in Romanticism and Religion: From Witness to Critique," *Christianity and Literature* 54 (2005): 265–82.

113. M. M. Bakhtin and P. N. Medvedev, *The Formal Method in Literary Scholarship*, trans. A. J. Wehrle (Baltimore, MD: Johns Hopkins University Press, 1978), 37.

114. Ibid., 38.

115. Ryan Cull, "Beyond the Cheated Eye: Dickinson's Lyric Sociality," *Nineteenth-Century Literature* 65 (2010): 38–64.

116. Nouri Gana, "War, Poetry, Mourning: Darwish, Adonis, Iraq," *Public Culture* 22 (2010): 33–65.

117. John Wilson, introduction to *The Posttraumatic Self: Restoring Meaning and Wholeness to Personality*, ed. John Wilson (New York: Routledge, 2006), 3.

118. Richard G. Tedeschi and Lawrence G. Calhoun, "A Clinical Approach to Posttraumatic Growth," in *Positive Psychology in Practice*, ed. P. Alex Linley and Stephen Joseph, (Hoboken, NJ: Wiley, 2004), 405.

119. Haidt, *The Happiness Hypothesis*, 146.

120. Ibid., 154.

121. Tedeschi and Calhoun, "A Clinical Approach to Posttraumatic Growth," 405.

122. Linley and Joseph, "Toward a Theoretical Foundation for Positive Psychology in Practice," 725.

123. Cited in Valliant, *Spiritual Evolution*, 150.

124. Letter to George and Georgiana Keats, 21 April (1819), In *Letters of John Keats: Volume 2, 1819-1821*, edited by H. E. Rollins (New York: Cambridge University Press, 2012).

125. Leon Festinger, "A Theory of Social Comparison Processes," *Human Relations* 7.2 (1954): 117–40.

126. Gerard Huther, *The Compassionate Brain* (Boston: Shambhala, 2006), 114.

127. Susan Wolfson, *Formal Charges: The Shaping of Poetry in British Romanticism* (Stanford, CA: Stanford University Press, 1999).

128. See Norman Holland, *Literature and the Brain* (Gainesville, FL: 2009).

129. Marghanita Laski, *Ecstasy in Secular and Religious Experiences* (Los Angeles: Tarcher, 1961), 26.

130. M. Csikzentmihalyi, *Flow: The Psychology of Optimal Experience* (New York: Harper & Row, 1990), 50.

131. See Christopher Peterson, Steven Maier, and Martin E.P. Seligman, *Learned Helplessness: A Theory for the Age of Personal Control* (New York: Oxford University Press, 1995).

# ONE

# Pound's Challenge to Rancière's Treatment of the "Aesthetic Regime"

## *Why Nietzsche Is Necessary for a Positive Account of Modernism in the Arts*

Charles Altieri

> "The existence of the world is justified only as an aesthetic phenomenon. . . . Nothing could be more opposed to the purely aesthetic interpretation and justification of the world which are taught in this book than the Christian teaching, which is, and wants to be, *only* moral and which relegates art, *every* art, to the realm of *lies* [italics added]."
> —Nietzsche, *The Birth of Tragedy*

I have always distrusted the word *flourish* in all of its grammatical forms. Prior to recent developments in various disciplines, the word seemed to me a tad pompous and more than a tad evasive. The seeming pomposity stemmed from the fact that this is not an expression much used in ordinary conversation, so that it seems a distinctively academic means of inflating the values negotiated in standard discourse. And it seemed evasive for closely related reasons. *Flourish* seemed intended to evoke idealizing potential powers within human nature. But which powers? What could be excluded as not some aspect of flourishing so long as there is an intensification of any of our powers?

However, I have also gradually come to think that any plausible attempt to preserve the significance of idealizing human powers may need precisely this pompous and evasive academic term. Philosophers, psychologists, and literary scholars need a space for insisting that there are plausible idealizations about human beings that can play significant roles in how we establish goals for ourselves that sometime make a positive difference in our behavior. Perhaps more important, having a term for such possibilities may help us to fight off the temptation to make our ideals subject to constant irony that allows us to claim lucidity while handling our immense disappointments about what we have to settle for as images of our powers. And the vagueness of the term proves useful because those idealizations that might make differences in our lives have a wide range of applications—from varieties of professional lives to the expanse of practical ideals that we imagine bring added significance and intensity to our lives. Given this range, it is probably more important to keep the space of idealization open rather than force conceptual specificity upon it. The concept of flourishing thus matters.

Still, my conversion is not so thorough that I can comfortably offer explicit arguments about flourishing. Instead, I am going to deal directly with the space of idealization itself by showing how important it is for two aspects of the study of modernist American poetry. Keeping open the space of idealization enables us at least to consider the imaginative visions that shaped the poet's own purposes. And that spirit of openness gives readers an opportunity to try out modes of response that recognize and grapple with these purposes, especially those purposes that develop as rationales for resisting the appeal of self-defensive ironic postures. More specifically, in this chapter I will propose a simple contrast in order to evaluate theoretical models we can use for appreciating what is distinctive and powerful about modernist American poetry. I will claim that Jacques Rancière offers a keen analytic perspective on the large shifts that occurred in nineteenth century aesthetics that were the ultimate foundations of modernism in all the arts. But his essentially structural model characterizing the contrasts between a regime of representation and one shaped by the primacy of relations among sensations seems to me not sufficient for orienting ourselves to the poetry because it does not address statements about intentions and so cannot make articulate the level of purposes and challenges to purposes that drive this work.

In fact, while Rancière is a superb critic of those who impose the moral and the political onto the aesthetic, his own refusal to talk about purposes replicates a void into which those discourses will always rush. So I go to the opposite pole: I want to show how Nietzsche provides the poets' ideals of values possible in an art that can accompany Rancière's basic theoretical observations and at the same time provide what was a focal point for the shaping of artists' intentions. By trying to spell out Rancière's basic picture of what becomes modernism we can develop by contrast what Nietzsche adds to the picture that helps us resist the appeal of political and moral accounts for the values involved in such work. Nietzsche's is an account of art that provides an image of human flourishing that is capable of challenging both those models and of defining one path for articulating why artists make a difference in what becomes possible for life.[1]

My test case for the limits of Rancière's analyses is the interpretation of what imagination does with and within the life of the senses posed by the central scene in Pound's second canto. Let me set the scene by offering two comments about the passage that opens the canto and sets its fundamental motif. (But I cannot quote because of permission issues, so I must ask the reader to consult the texts when I refer to poems.)

Notice that Pound refuses to treat his poetry as rhetorical energy, extending what a natural scene offers to an attentive eye and needy "I." Instead, the poem is insistently a making that is capable of shifting registers whenever the authorial will seems to find possibilities for going on. When identification with Browning proves problematic, the poem manages to go on by following sound echoes. Ultimately, it arrives at blind Homer, condemned to making poetry of those echoes. The poem arrives at a much richer epic than Browning's story.

Now I must move to the narrative central panel of the canto. The action begins with a ship in Scios picking up a young boy who turns out to be Dionysius. The boy gets assurances that this is a "straight ship" from the captain, Acoetes, who narrates the events. The crew mutinies and Acoetes is taken prisoner. Later the boy comes on deck, sees that the boat is taking a different course than the one promised to him, and releases Dionysian magic, to which the captain is extraordinarily attentive. Because the captain is so alert to the changes in atmosphere created by the power of Dionysius, and because the poem is so attentive to replicating these sensual movements, both captain and reader are aligned in realizing what such witnessing entails. "And worship / I have seen when I have seen," the captain asserts. There is nothing more to say; and nothing less than full commitment to assert. For Pound, poetry is validated by the staging of a conversion based primarily on the very experience in which the readers are asked to participate. The dramatic moment renders an incarnation; however, there is no transcendence. Devotion to seeing and refusal of the temptations of the slave trade suffice to put someone in a position to affirm something close to absolute commitment based simply on what becomes available to the life of the senses, without doctrine. Seeing suffices for this commitment but only if we recognize that this is a made seeing, or constructed sensorium, that activates a sense of value coming into existence because of poetry's capacity to reach beyond itself through itself. There is no interpreting of symbols; there is only an awareness of how fully the sensorium can affect the mind by affording a sense of meaningfulness that is beyond any moral register. Or, to make the same point another way, the emphasis on the aural in the beginning casts poetry as not describing sensations but extending them and transposing them into a register where the God dwelling in them becomes visible. This sense of power sanctions Acoetes's advice to Pentheus that he listen to Teiresias—not as moral wisdom but simply as respect for sheer power, without any qualifying evaluative concerns that derive from social intercourse.

Now recall my epigraph. Nietzsche is precise: Aesthetic phenomena are not justified by their truth or usefulness to the world; rather the existence of the world has to be justified by how aspects of that world come to stand within our artistic practices.[2] Such a reminder seems to me especially important now, because I think Jacques Rancière's otherwise very powerful account of "the aesthetic regime" cannot fully capture Nietzsche's sense of the possible power of art. As a result, he fails to make good on his efforts to sustain the claims of the aesthetic against the claims of the ethical and the political because his refusal of languages, like those of flourishing, fail to provide a sufficient alternative model of values. The political and the moral will always reemerge to provide idealizations of what the artists disclose. Rancière produces this dilemma because he insists on using aesthetic as a historical concept rather than a merely theoretical one concerning judgment. As a historical concept, aesthetics becomes a matter of "horizontal distributions" rather than depth models of "surface and substratum."[3] Rather than deal with all art, aesthetics becomes relevant only for the shifts in cultural thinking that our aesthetic objects have shaped in the past 150 years. So Rancière can offer fresh and compelling criticisms of figures like Badiou, Lacan, and Lyotard, because the urgencies of contemporary cultural life lead them to isolate "art from aesthetics, only to prostrate it before the indistinction of ethics."[4] But his fundamentally historico-structuralist way of establishing the domain of the aesthetic creates two fundamental problems.

First, because Rancière is content with an account of the aesthetic that "permits us to identify what pertains to art, i.e. its objects, modes of experience, and modes of thought,"[5] he feels no need to speculate on intentions or motives: the aesthetic is not a projection by the mind but an effect of how language is deployed. Yet I fear what we gain in objectivity we lose in the capacity to articulate a range of subjective intentional states that are rarely content with this vision of the aesthetic as fundamentally a matter of means rather than of ends. Without a sufficient effort to understand the artists' intentions, Rancière can only produce an aesthetics without sufficient projections about values.[6] And then, ironically, he reproduces a situation he complains about—that the arts seem to offer impoverished models of value that need the supplements provided by models of value borrowed from morality and politics.

My second criticism makes a further claim about this lack of concern for the values projected by statements of intention. An essentially formal and structural account of the aesthetic just eliminates ethics; it does not contest its specific claims to show how art works have power in the actual world. Yet works that rely on the means Rancière characterizes in his aesthetic regime often have the capacity to "realize" distinctive powers that emerge through their ways of deploying the imagination. For example, Pound's Acoetes statements of testimony reach far beyond the formal grounds on which they originate. His particular experience matters for how he projects values. Yet these values, this faith in a divine force that poetry seems capable of carrying, is not something that can be given an adequate hearing in ethical or political terms.[7]

It should not come as a surprise that I develop these critical comments by contrasting Rancière's version of the aesthetic with Nietzsche's. Nietzsche is an active participant in the aesthetic regime. But he also insists on exploring the values that the regime pursues, which might extend beyond the aesthetic domain by intervening in discourses that had previously been dominated by politics and ethics. Ultimately Nietzsche not only extends our sense of what powers can be attributed to the aesthetic regime, he also shows how they are capable of struggling against, and even dominating, what politics and ethics have to offer cultural life. Nietzsche affords a conceptual model in which the arts not only differ from ethics but also have the role of continually challenging the hegemony of ethics, because the arts seem to offer the richest understanding of what valuing can be. Indeed it is arguable that Nietzsche best articulates a change in thinking about art from how knowledge might be supplemented by feeling to how constructive powers can define values capable of challenging the culture's emphasis on epistemology.

The Romantic tradition in poetry tends to be characterized by its emphasis on enhancing what knowledge can involve when the agent can ally self-consciousness with the full energies of sensuous experience. The paradigm here would be Wordsworth's return to Tintern Abbey and his discovery of the expansive rhetorical resources that become available to him when he is moved by his expanded awareness of what a place can involve. Modernist poetry, on the other hand, is suspicious of knowledge and even more suspicious of any claims that an individual is "entitled" to offer the self as determining what might be representative values. Instead it concentrates on how the making of art brings direct modifications of our capacities to determine and to enjoy the values made present by the work. The artist's task is not to renew religion by fresh encounters with the objective world but to alter what counts as significant objects, and hence also as significance-bearing subjects. (As Rancière puts it, in the aesthetic regime, making and deploying the senses, or poesis and aesthesis, must occupy the same plane, without the mediation of any idea of human nature beyond the individual work of art.)

Nietzsche articulates this shift in two ways. His critiques of "truth" and the epistemic disciplines devoted to it make it much more difficult for the arts to build on any claim to epistemic authority or attempt to locate the powers of rhetoric within the recovery of what had been forceful modes of attention. Rather than finding the energies of *making* within sensitivity to appearances, *making* becomes responsible for all that appearance can carry as significance. And the primary question for art becomes not whether it is true in any sense but whether its ways of making can be exemplary and can specify domains in which imaginative energies become valuable for what they bring to the world. Second, Nietzsche develops the urgency for this making of values by his critique of nihilism—that is, a critique not of aspects of his culture but of the very pressure of what it means to live within this cultural dispensation. The challenge for the arts becomes something more than responding to an increasingly mechanistic and rhetorical culture. The task becomes engaging a total cultural climate in which all our instruments of knowledge present us with a world that refuses to reflect any distinctive human imaginative concerns. So making must take priority over interpreting, and the concern for what can be willed as engaged inspiration for states of making replaces the concern for how willing might be justified by knowing.[8]

Rancière defines his "aesthetic regime" as the last of three basic dispensations in Western culture. There was first an ethical regime for the arts shaped by Platonic thinking in which all art was political because it was seen as directly affecting the life of the community and immediately judged by its effects on that life.[9] With Aristotle there emerged the representative regime that offered an art devoted to holding together a threefold relation among "a productive nature, a sensible nature, and a legislative nature."[10] This art posits the correlation of a poesis, or way of doing, an aesthesis, or way of sensing, and a way of interpreting the interplay of these two as a demonstration of something exemplary about human nature.[11] Finally the aesthetic regime can be seen as working with these same three categories, but now there is a tension between its images of productive nature and of the sensible nature, because poesis and aesthesis have to occupy the same plane without the mediation of any legislative function beyond the individual work of art. Without this stable legislative function, poesis must seek not exemplary representativeness but rather a singularity that uproots stable orders of perception. It is as if poesis and aesthesis can achieve stable relations only by "the very gap of their ground" that emerges when one has to recognize that the concept of human nature "is either lost" or becomes present only in a "humanity to come."[12]

We can test the value of these claims by offering particular contrasts between four aspects of what Rancière attributes to this aesthetic regime and corresponding motifs that Nietzsche's work made available. First, the primary concern for Rancière is describing the historical situation for artists after the demise of the regime of representation. The new art still seeks an impact on society. But it is constrained because it offers content different from what had been typical historical functions of art, so its audience becomes not ritualized addressees but "a new undifferentiated public"[13] without the resources of usable genre assumptions.[14] The "modern aesthetic revolution . . . is the abolition of the parallelism that aligned artistic hierarchies with social hierarchies." "Everything is a subject for art," so there is no longer a point to distinguishing what is noble and what is base.[15] That refusal, in figures like Flaubert, generates a democratic politics of indifference that avoids "all forms of political intervention."[16] Art offers a "sheer presence that is no longer exchanged for anything."[17] So an autonomous art based on indifference proves inseparable from a radical heteronomy because it abolishes "the boundaries that allowed a regime of representation to distinguish art objects from other objects in the world."[18]

Second, Rancière understands the aesthetic regime's relation between active and passive modes of experience as setting the life of the senses at a tangent to efforts to impose continuity by thought.[19] Making takes the form of an uneasy relation between the willed and the unwilled, with sensation cast as sometimes actively sought and sometimes unbid violation of intentions. The result is the "immediate union of pure voluntary activity and pure passivity" in a dizzying explosion of multiplying sensations that refuse the satisfactions of older modes of coherence: "Inventive activity and sensible emotion encounter one another 'freely' as two aspects of a nature which no longer attests to any hierarchy of active intelligence over sensible passivity."[20] So aesthetics has to work out changes in forms of intelligibility that honor "ways of sensible being" rather than ways of doing (poesis).[21]

Third, Aesthetics must orient itself toward thinking of the "paradoxical sensorium" as released from human nature and representational demands. That thinking has to take place under the sign of a "lost human nature," which is to say of a lost norm of adequation between an active faculty and receptive faculty."[22] This loss of mutual relations between active and receptive faculties explains why the thinking of art proves confusing and why critics want to replace (or supplement) that thinking by invoking politics and ethics. But to give in to that temptation is to ignore the strange and thrilling sites that the new art can construct. At one pole the newly liberated senses can be said to produce an effect of sublimity that "places art under the sign of an immemorial debt toward the absolute—either in the form of radical singularity defeating every concept or in the form of a radical politics opposing in art's name every trace of commodification.[23] At the other pole, the democratic tendencies that accompany the loss of hierarchy promise to construct spaces that make visible the territory of the "common"—think Andy Warhol's subject matter and also his commitment on every level to lack of boundaries between art and life. Conversely, producing a thinking for this art by turning to the political and the ethical imposes a continuity of practical possibility that denies the art's basic challenge to come to terms with discontinuity and proliferation.

Fourth, the emergence of the aesthetic must take the place of any coherent sense of human nature. For Rancière the greatest challenge posed by the aesthetic regime is its utter dismissal of all the concepts that sociology depends on for its analyses and for its normative projections.[24] The aesthetic invites fresh concepts for what might hold society together. But, again, all the concepts philosophers work with cannot avoid replacing the art by politics or by ethics. The only alternative Rancière imagines is the possibility of resisting concepts by taking from art only its power to produce the heterogeneous without forcing interpretations upon the resulting dispositives of the sensible. Then might we have an art-driven politics that does not explain art but tries to learn from how it treats the new freedom to recompose the senses.[25]

Rancière is obviously not wrong. He captures an instability, a restlessness, a mixture of joy with anxiety and a mysterious openness to the inhuman that has pervaded the arts since the mid-nineteenth century, and he locates the rationale for that in often brilliant readings of Kant and of Schiller. Yet his account also seems somewhat myopic, in part because he accepts a dichotomy between the passive and the active that seems better read as an always incomplete but always dynamic dialectic in which an active force labors to give shapes to its own awareness of an irreducible passivity driving affective life. For example, there is the role of witness to what Dionysius can do. In not according intentionality its due, Rancière's four categories of analysis seem predictably negative, as if modernism were best defined by its refusals and losses rather than by what values become available for its new constructive practices. (Adorno is actually positive by comparison because he gives clear constructive uses of his version of the relevant negativities).

I suspect that the only way we can correct the situation is to provide a general account of the positive shapes that the artists' intentions gave to their thinking about the permissions afforded by this new regime. But I can only offer a substitute for that project. I will argue that the most typical intentions for how the arts might produce a new culture can be found in Nietzsche's work because he was the most articulate thinker at characterizing expressivist alternatives to the limitations inherent in the regime of representation. The importance of that work should be clear if we draw contrasts between Nietzsche and Rancière on each of the four points I have been developing.[26]

First, Nietzsche would agree with Rancière's picture of the historical situation facing the artists who explored this new aesthetic regime:

> The artists could not know their audiences; in the place of a consensual "human nature" there had emerged a void that invites constant refiguration; and sensations were breaking free from any inherent hierarchy of faculties or meanings so that the artists' images of what thinking in their medium involves had to undergo major changes.[27]

For Nietzsche, however, one has to realize that the undoing of representation was not simply a historical shift but also an opportunity to provide alternatives to problematic notions of truth" produced by scientists' versions of Christian asceticism:

> They [philosophers] all pose as if they had discovered and reached their real opinions through the self-development of a cold, pure, divinely unconcerned dialectic . . . ; while at bottom it is an assumption, a hunch, indeed a kind of 'inspiration'—most often a desire of the heart than has been filtered and made abstract that they defend with reasons they have sought after the fact.[28]

The old regime of representation had left Europe on the brink of total nihilism because it had given authority to empiricism's strength—its capacity to secure objective and unequivocal descriptive terms. So the new art could not just propose democratic leveling, it also had to create the experience of possible new hierarchies that could treat democratic objectivity as a deformed mode of valuing built on Christian ressentiment. Models of value based on truth had to be replaced by those attentive to "physiological demands for a certain type of life."[29] "The noble type of man experiences *itself* as determining values; it does not need approval; it judges. . . . It knows itself to be that which first accords honor to things; it is *value-creating* [italics added]. Everything it knows, as part of itself, it honors."[30] Analogously, realization had to replace representation. Once the arts were released from the obligations of the regime of representation, they might be able to cultivate their manifest differences from the disciplines established for the pursuit of truth. And they might then interpret their own sense of formal freedom as the permission to explore how they might directly manifest powers to establish values that the culture had repudiated. The emphasis on individual *making* might become a theater for displaying the possible capacities of the individual will.

Perhaps then a philosophical aesthetic could locate what is conceptually significant about the sense of particular values cultivated by the arts. For example, what if the powers Kant had to attribute only to artistic composition (where he could speculate beyond what was required to secure understanding) might provide powerful images of what the psyche might become in any process of creating values? Nobility might depend simply on the self's coming to treat "everything it knows as part of itself"[31] that it is in the process of honoring (so that one could "become who one is") "The individual appears, obliged to give himself laws and to develop his own arts and wiles for self-preservation, self-enhancement, self-redemption"[32] And the actions of such individuals may even be capable of rebuilding an aristocratic culture that philosophy had been trying to destroy for two thousand years:

> Every artist knows how far from any feeling of letting himself go his most 'natural' state is—the free ordering, placing, disposing, giving form in the moment of 'inspiration'—and how strictly and subtly he

> obeys thousandfold laws precisely then, laws that precisely on account of their hardness and determination defy all formulation through concepts (even the firmest concept is, compared with them, not free of fluctuation, multiplicity, ambiguity).[33]

Second, this last quotation offers a striking example of how Nietzsche does not accept a general contrast between active and passive because that contrast does not recognize how thoroughly the two modes can be wrapped each in the other. Passivity can be activity in its receptive mode: The multiplication of sensations without sponsorship by concepts is not a weakness or vulnerability of the art but a sign of revolutionary power to revel in excess that is not bound by "truth." Passivity becomes something the will can attune to and address and utilize as a felt condition, allowing the agent to develop new identifications. Indeed this is why the artists can imagine radical formal experiments that provide conditions of intense readerly activity: intense submission is the precondition for the transfer of power. The path from impressionism to suprematism and noniconic abstraction is above all a series of celebrations of what can be created as value when the domain of the concept can no longer determine categories for processing sensations or distinguishing active from passive.

This need to align oneself with complex conditions for identification is one reason

Nietzsche was fascinated by the processes of writing (and by analogy any form of imaginative creation). Writing is different from thinking epistemically because it is irreducibly from a point of view that is not impersonal and also not quite recognizably personal, in the sense that the writing self is not predictable from other manifestations of one's empirical nature. Forces become present in the imaginative constructive activity that often one cannot control by reason or habit. Yet the writing itself becomes a taking of responsibility by adapting these forces to the world and letting the product stand as something other than a lie. Writing takes up the possibility of overcoming any division between what is released as a life of sensations and what is projected by one's expressive metaphors giving a unique twist to those sensations.[34]

The best example of Nietzsche's understanding of writing as a distinctive mode of valuing is his treatment of metaphor—in ways that substantially illuminate the force of the commitment to correspondences fundamental to Symbolist art and how it shapes principles like collage. For Nietzsche there is no need for metaphor to be constrained by empiricist divisions between tenor and vehicle, or content and expressive activity. Science-driven distinctions need no longer establish general conditions for literal description. Rather metaphor extends how writing offers irreducible syntheses of what seems passive and what seems active, each supplementing and each denying the other's authority. Notice for example how the following passage puts psychological features on the same level as sensuous existence: "Perhaps there is nothing about so called educated people and believers in 'modern ideas' that is as nauseous as their lack of modesty and the comfortable insolence of their eyes and hands with which they touch, lick, and finger everything."[35] And notice too how collage extends that power to establish a new literalness by creating a space in which different registers of sensual objects combine on a single mysterious plane, as in the series of transformations in Picasso's *Guitar, Sheet Music, and Glass*.[36]

Third, how can thinking bring concepts back into play while acknowledging that they have no ground in human nature or control over the play of sensations that bring liveliness to experience? And why come to terms with "discontinuity and proliferation?" Rancière is mostly interested in the failures of contemporary thinking to preserve this aesthetic register in the face of the urgencies it produces for these new concepts that in fact subject it to the political and the ethical. I want to develop how Nietzsche offers a representative modernist responsiveness to this problem that denies the terms of Rancière's characterization. Nietzsche often suggests that separating human life into domains like ethics and aesthetics is an aspect of nihilism that can have no promising outcome. Instead we have to recognize why moral thinking is doomed, so that we can treat value as a relation to life that has no disciplinary custodian. Art is privileged only in the sense that it often recognizes the problems with moral practices and so offers itself as a direct expression of life values intensified by their resistance to the moral. On the basis of these Nietzschean arguments I want to suggest that the best critical path now would not follow Rancière's effort to hold on to art as a separate mode of thinking from ethics and politics. Instead, it is probably more productive to identify with the art of the aesthetic regime's capacity to challenge these overall distinctions and focus on how the sheer vitality of the work establishes different attitudes toward values. The work is not simply the construction of a singular state resistant to concepts; rather it calls attention to its ability to affect how we regard what ethics or politics might bring to the scene. Art puts the process of forging singular states of being to work in the actual world—as content and as states of desirable intensity. Art does not so much evade the moral as enter into mortal combat with it to determine what the ultimate models of valuation will become.

For Nietzsche the "ethical" is wrong from the start, at least in so far as it is based on any general model of evaluation to which particular wills to power are told they must conform. Because value resides in an individual's expressive acts, the domain of the moral can only haunt the expressive as its negation, as a mark that the individual has conformed to some version of the pressure of the general and subsumed action into making a copy of something:

> The whole of morality is a long undismayed forgery which alone makes it at all possible to enjoy the sight of the soul. From this point of view much more may belong in the concept of 'art' than is generally believed.[37]

Morality is forgery because it claims authenticity as the realization or construction of the agent's character. But the idealizations of morality intervene between agent and act, so there is no possibility of authenticity, there is only attuning the self to the idea rather than to the situation.[38] So morality is inherently antithetical to self-expression, unless one constructs the self as finding some kind of latent truth within the effort to be moral. And this way lies metaphysical madness.

The entire domain of expression, then, must for Nietzsche be conceived as the antithesis to what morality could provide. This is why "much more may belong in the concept of 'art' than is generally believed." And connecting this "more" to the concept of expression is probably Nietzsche's most intimate, and most illuminating, relationship to the aesthetic register. The new art does not simply register conditions characterized by a multiplicity of sensual registers cut free from conceptual controls. Rather the art uses that fluidity and multiplicity to allow the possibility that selves or situations can be realized or find expression in ways that were not possible when representations had to be correlated to concepts. One can fold a moral value into expressivist schemes because responsibility is still necessary—but this is located in the simple accepting of responsibility for what can be realized in the particular, without any dependency on concepts. One simply finds the product satisfying because the self would rather be part of it than excluded from it.

Manner becomes matter in an endless struggle to absorb value into particular modes of activity intensified by the artist. And trusting in manner is how one becomes free from entering the forgeries inherent in those concepts that claim to explain freedom in terms of adapting moral identities. This expressive value will be a feature of any state whose unfolding absorbs subjectivity and makes it manifest in a new integration with the orders of the senses—whether the state be intensely subjective or an impersonal effort to render energies that seem anchored in the objectivity of the work's stance toward the world. There is no production of significant value without a sense of obeying law. But there is also no production of significant value if the law issues from a domain that is not an actual force in the shaping of experience.[39]

Fourth, the denial of any authority for concepts of human nature within the aesthetic regime is only half of the story. Rancière does not take up the fact that this lack affords a corresponding domain of possibility, or what Wallace Stevens called the search of "a possible for its possibleness" (*Collected Poetry and Prose,* 411). Again Rancière has to stress the negative to retain sufficient distance from those who would absorb even that sense of possibility within the political and the ethical. But he then misses an opportunity to value the kind of freedom art gives distinctively as art, so that art can be poised in active struggle with what would appropriate it (without art being merely utopian). If there is no human nature, then we have to compose what might suffice as plausible senses of human possibility. There is a continually open future because there is no determinate present. And art has a distinctive role within this process of construction because its versions of possibility offer examples of concrete ways for not only distributing sensations but also for composing attitudes capable of transforming acts of description into living modes of evaluation responsive to the nihilism rampant in the West.

The commitment to the future born in the aesthetic regime is difficult to talk about because there is no objective formal device we can isolate that responds to this desire. And the topic is inherently vague because there can be no adequate description of possibility: The sense of possibility is under constant testing and revision. Yet opening a future is a constant fantasy for the new art. And, again, Nietzsche is a most discursively articulate spokesperson for artists because he was so deeply disappointed by every gesture to give authority to society's version of the present tense. In part, Nietzsche dramatizes the pathos of having to believe in the future because in the present few readers understand or appreciate his critical and reconstructive efforts. But he also shows the value of embracing that pathos and letting it at the least provide a direction for redirecting alienation from society into possibility, and hence irony into trust in figurality.

We probably have no choice but to risk the incomprehension that opens ways into new possible dispositions of attention and negotiations for social life.[40] Even Pound's Acoetes mixes into his testimony to the god the need to warn Pentheus to become a careful reader of what this power bodes for the future. Rancière offers a powerful mode of that caution, especially in relation to the claims of the political and the moral. But it may be time for criticism to honor Nietzsche's faith that art's leveling of the old order has sufficient energy and self-possession to inaugurate a positive new dispensation capable of honoring the philosophical import of individual acts of refusing to settle for description.

## BIBLIOGRAPHY

Nietzsche, Friedrich Wilhelm. *Beyond Good and Evil: Prelude to a Philosophy of the Future.* Translated by Walter Kaufmann. New York: Vintage, 1989.

———. *Ecce Homo.* New York: Dover, 2004.

Pound, Ezra. *The Cantos of Ezra Pound.* New York: New Direction Publishing Corporation, 1996.

Rancière, Jacques. *Aesthetics and Its Discontents.* Malden, MA: Polity Press, 2009.

———. *The Politics of Aesthetics.* Translated by Gabriel Rockhill. New York: Continuum International Publishing Group, 2007.

Stevens, Wallace. *Collected Poetry and Prose*. New York: Library of America, 1997.

## NOTES

1. This project forces me into well-worn critical territory. I rely on Aaron Ridley's terrific "*Nietzsche on Art* (Routledge, 2007) for an account of Nietzsche's ideas of art, and I am familiar with most of the many studies that articulate how specific Nietzschean ideas shape possible values for specific writers, most noteworthy Erich Heller, *The Importance of Nietzsche* (University of Chicago Press, 1988). But my concern is less with spelling out Nietzsche's specific ideas than with speculating on how the popular understanding of his work might have helped a wide range of writers to determine distinct paths for pursuing these values that cannot be contained within the moral or political domains. I am less interested in Nietzsche's ideas about art than about how Nietzsche's thinking might affect artists' understandings of what was possible in their work. Even those writers we cannot claim to be Nietzschean probably took some inspiration from his style and his renderings of what a will to power might involve for expressions emphasizing the resources of a particular medium.

2. For specific possible references to what Pound sees in Dionysius, consider the description of him in section 295 of *Beyond Good and Evil*: "The genius of the heart, who makes everything loud and self-satisfied fall silent and teaches it to listen, who smoothes rough souls and gives them a new desire to savor—the desire to lie still as a mirror, that the deep sky may mirror itself in them—; the genius of the heart who teaches the stupid and hasty hand to hesitate and grasp more delicately; who divines the hidden and forgotten treasure, the drop of goodness and sweet spirituality under thick and opaque ice, and is a divining-rod for every grain of gold which has lain long in the prison of much mud and sand; the genius of the heart from whose touch everyone goes away richer, not favored and surprised, not as if blessed and oppressed with the goods of others, but richer in himself, newer to himself than before, broken open, blown upon and sounded out by a thawing wind, more uncertain perhaps, more delicate, more fragile, more broken, but full of hopes that as yet have no names. . . ."

3. Rancière defines aesthetics as that discourse that "permits us to identify what pertains to art, i.e. its objects, modes of experience, and forms of thought" (Rancière, *Aesthetics and Its Discontents*, 4). So from the start he refuses the supplementary question of formulating how art pertains to our interests in the various domains that comprise our sense of actual life. That way, he thinks, lies confusion with ethics. Then in *Aesthetics and its* Discontents (but not in other books) he further narrows aesthetics (Rancière, *Aesthetics and Its Discontents*, 8) to pertain only to one of the three basic dispensations he attributes to the arts in the West (all of which he determines by something very close to the aesthetics that this definition delimits).

4. Rancière, *Aesthetics and Its Discontents*, 87.

5. Ibid., 4.

6. Even works that rely on roughly the same shifts in how the senses and authorship are imagined can differ substantially in purposes and in the affective experiences engendered by these purposes. One of Rancière's great achievements is showing deep affinities between Balzac and Mallarmé. But these affinities do not make for common purposes or visions of what different genres can accomplish. I suspect that Balzac, like most novelists and many poets, did not consider his works primarily as aesthetic objects but something closer to rhetorical objects shaped by specific interpretive values applied to the actual world. And even when writers and painters do embrace the aesthetic, it is often as means rather than as end. How ambitious work functions from the mid-nineteenth century in Europe to the beginnings of postmodernism was probably determined largely by what Rancière identifies as the predicates distributed by the aesthetic regime. Why the elements are deployed as they are, however, might be a very different matter. Cézanne and Mondrian have similar rejections of representational values but to very different purposes that shape how they envision the aesthetic

object forming an interface with the actual world and doing practical work within that world. And then the ultimate test of value is whether aesthetic means suffice to accomplish ends that are not limited to the aesthetic domain.

7. I am not unaware that resistance to the political and the moral can sanction problematic claims about the power of art. But even those problems indicate how we might need a language of human powers and desires focused on how individuals might shape their significant ends.

8. This Nietzschean context also helps explain why the concept of autonomy never took hold among the American poets (by contrast to what occurred in France)—probably because they could not align their own labors with disinterested judgment. Autonomy at most meant the capacity not to be bound by the past: the poets did not seek disinterest but tried to enhance and realize their own interests in finer tones and more fluent evocations. I think Stevens's "Idea of Order at Key West" is an exemplary statement of the powers of art that refuse or redirect claims about autonomy for art.

9. Rancière, *The Politics of Aesthetics*, 12–18.

10. Rancière, *Aesthetics and Its Discourse*, 7.

11. Ibid., 7.

12. Ibid., 8.

13. Ibid., 9.

14. Ibid., 9: Painting has to become "an archive of its own processes."

15. Jacques Rancière, *The Future of the Image*, trans. Gregory Elliott (New York: Verso, 2009), 106.

16. Rancière, *Aesthetics and Its Discontents*, 40.

17. Rancière, *The Future of the Image*, 17.

18. Rancière, *Aesthetics and Its Discontents*, 101.

19. Ibid., 10.

20. Ibid., 13.

21. Ibid., 11.

22. Ibid., 11–12.

23. Ibid., 22.

24. Ibid., 12–14.

25. Ibid., 32–39.

26. The bad news is that this comparison will be unfailingly abstract in spelling out what was at stake for artists in hollowing out of the representative surface to make another topic appear under the appropriate subject. The good news is that this abstraction will allow us to see what is held in common by those artists and writers in the aestheticist regime who chose to stress the subjectivity of the making and those who develop more objective or impersonal versions for transforming how thought and the senses might be arranged.

27. Nietzsche, *Ecce Homo*, 12.

28. Ibid., 12.

29. Ibid., 11.

30. Ibid., 205.

31. Ibid., 205.

32. Ibid., 211.

33. Ibid., 100–101.

34. Ridley is surprisingly uninterested in this dimension of Nietzsche's internalized sense of how art enters philosophy, despite, or perhaps because, it played such a central role in poststructuralism.

35. The point is sufficiently important for modernist art to warrant two more examples:

> "We have been spun into a severe yarn and shirt of duties and *cannot* get out of that—and in this we are "men of duty," we too. Occasionally . . . we dance in our "chains" and between our "swords"; more often, . . . we gnash our teeth and feel impatient with all the secret hardness of our destiny." (Nietzsche, *Beyond Good and Evil*, 213).

> "Their fundamental faith simply has to be that society must *not* exist for society's sake but only as the foundation and scaffolding on which a choice type of being is able to raise itself to its higher task and to a higher state of being—comparable to those sun-seeking vines of Java . . . that so long and so often enclasp an oak tree with their tendrils until eventually, high above it but supported by it, they can unfold their crowns in the open light and display their happiness." (Nietzsche, *Beyond Good and Evil*, 213)

36. I labor to introduce collage because Rancière is often quite good on collage, especially on its transformations in contemporary art ( Rancière, *Aesthetics and Its Discontents*, 46–47; 55). But he refuses to acknowledge how collage especially creates the space where we have to be concerned with intentions and purposiveness and individual acts of valuation. Collage in fact is probably the best example of how in modernism the central quality is not sensuousness but a literalness that fuses the senses with imaginative states insistent on their own capacity to confer meaning within the sensuous.

37. Nietzsche, *Beyond Good and Evil*, 230.

38. Sartre developed a version of this logic when he argued that one cannot be sincere and direct because the effort to be sincere requires fidelity to an idea that is not an aspect of the concrete situation.

39. The very next section after the passage I quote on moral forgery defines a philosopher as one who "is struck by his own thoughts as if they came from the outside," followed by the inevitable play on what is metaphor and what is literal: "who is perhaps himself a storm pregnant with new lightnings" (Nietzsche, *Beyond Good and Evil*, 230).

40. Had I the space I would elaborate the consequences of Nietzsche's commitment to the future. The first is his sense that the originality of unmasking Christian Morality "breaks the history of mankind into two parts. One lives before him, one lives after him" (Nietzsche, *Ecce Homo*, 133). This originality entails that the time before him will be alien, and those at home in it will be incapable of understanding the prophet. The prophet depends on the future for vindication. This dependency is first of a straightforward need for readers that will allay the prophet's utter loneliness. But there is also a richer dependency because only those readers will in fact show "how one becomes what one is" because only they will be able to match the prophet's words with reality and recognize that in fact the writer was prophetic. Only in the future will the evil man be allowed to become the affirmative character he always was (Nietzsche, *Ecce Homo*, 134).

# TWO

# Thoreau and Health

## *Physician, Naturalist, Metaphysician*

James Engell

> I feel that I draw nearest to understanding the great secret of my life in my closest intercourse with nature. There is a reality and health in (present) nature; which is not to be found in any religion—and cannot be contemplated in antiquity—I suppose that what in other men is religion is in me love of nature.
>
> —Thoreau, *Journal* entry for October 30, 1842 (*Journal* 2, 55)

In his "Conclusions" to *The Varieties of Religious Experience*, William James states that nature "interpreted religiously" must not be merely "the materialistic world over again, with an altered expression," but must reveal, "over and above the altered expression, *a natural constitution* different at some point from that which a materialistic world would have. It must be such that different events can be expected in it, different conduct must be required. . . . It is only transcendentalist metaphysicians who think that, without adding any concrete details to Nature, or subtracting any, but by simply calling it the expression of absolute spirit, you make it more divine just as it stands."[1]

In his phrase "interpreted religiously," James takes *religiously* in the way that spiritual life is experienced daily, practically, by one individual, how it's felt on the pulse and in the heart, not how it's memorized or merely repeated from others or from institutions.

Thoreau experienced and then expressed a natural constitution of the world, a constitution of Nature, different from that which a baldly materialistic world would present. He experienced the natural world as a form of health, of human health, and even as a kind of heaven. Thoreau is a transcendentalist physician who calls those who would hear him to a pragmatic insight and healing, one that interprets nature and diagnoses our own ills. He does so in a way that reorients how we conceive of the "natural constitution" of the environment and our own natural constitutions together. This reorientation, he believes, brings us to better health mentally and physically.

Throughout his *Journal* and in work published both during his lifetime and posthumously, Thoreau wrote about health. It is a constant subject. Yet, he never collected his many reflections on health in one concentrated essay or chapter. Instead, health in all its interrelated aspects—physical, mental, spiritual, the senses, nutrition, and ethical well-being—informs just about all that he wrote, much in the way that a heartbeat sustains us all day but may not be noticed or studied consciously. A few years after Thoreau died at age forty-four, James Russell Lowell, apparently still piqued by Thoreau's attitude to Lowell's actions as periodical editor of Thoreau's narrative on the Maine woods, remarked, "Mr. Thoreau had not a healthy mind, or he would not have been so fond of prescribing. His whole life was a search for the doctor." Lowell addresses Thoreau's vision of nature and continues the medical image: "We look upon a great deal of the modern sentimentalism about Nature as a mark of disease." It is a disease that Lowell claims has taken as its victims "sentimentalists, unreal men, misanthropes on the spindle side." Despite this animus, Lowell closes on notes of praise. "His whole life," says Lowell, repeating that phrase he had just used in a negative context, "was a rebuke of the waste and aimlessness of our American luxury, which is an enslavement to tawdry upholstery." There is something of the diagnostician that Lowell sees in Thoreau, too: "he had watched Nature like a detective who is to go upon the stand; as we read him, it seems as if all-out-of-doors had kept a diary and become its own Montaigne." The printed "leaves" of Thoreau's writing, concludes Lowell in a lovely image, especially appropriate given Thoreau's enchantment with the leaf as emblematic of many natural processes and systems, "shed their invisible thought-seed like ferns."[2] If someone's vision causes such strong reactions—denial and affirmation—it seems worth attending to with care.

Yet, despite the prevalence of Thoreau's concern for health as a form of human flourishing, only one treatment touching it has appeared in literary journals, and that in a fairly specialized form more than sixty years ago.[3] Preparing this essay, originally given at the Thoreau Society Annual Gathering in Concord, Massachusetts, in July 2010, I located only two other pertinent studies, one in the journal *Literature and Medicine*, the second in the journal *Environmental Values*.[4] Both these interdisciplinary essays recognize that Thoreau's writing on health connects profoundly with environmental concerns and offers much to modern medical understanding and behavior. So, too, in a more scattered but perceptive way does Robert D. Richardson, Jr.'s *Henry Thoreau: A Life of the Mind.*[5] In short, Thoreau's ideas about health have not been nullified by scientific and medical advances. Because they focus on human relationships to the environment and *its* health, his ideas have grown more urgent and valuable.

## HEALTH AND NATURE, IDEAL AND REAL

Two brief statements from Thoreau's *Journal* during 1853 and 1854 sum up his insistence on human health as fully realized only in relation to the sustainable health of the larger environment and the ecosystems that surround and sustain us: "For all nature is doing her best each moment to make us well—she exists for no other end, Do not resist her. . . Why nature is but another name for health" and "Health is a sound relation to nature."[6] These rather cryptic statements Thoreau had earlier foreshadowed in his "Natural History of Massachusetts" (1842), where he claims, "In society you will not find health but in nature. Unless our feet at least stood in the midst of nature, all our faces would be pale and livid." Regarding society—human beings acting in isolation from nature—he says, "There is no scent in it so wholesome as that of the pines, nor any fragrance so penetrating and restorative as the life-everlasting in high pastures." It is not only the direct contact of the senses, it is also the mental knowledge of natural processes that together provide a tonic. A combination of the directly empirical and the conceptual or even ideal is key. "I would keep some book of natural history always by me as a sort of elixir, the reading of which should restore tone to the system. To the sick, indeed, nature is sick, but to the well, a fountain of health."[7]

That last sentence suggests that our own state of being governs how we view our relation to nature; it is when we are healthy that nature provides an almost unconscious source of strength, "a fountain of health." This helps explain Thoreau's remark in his *Journal* that "Only the convalescent are conscious of the health of nature."[8] Only as we become aware of an improvement in the changing state of our own health (and therefore are most concerned about its progress) do we grasp that nature untouched by "society" holds a reservoir of well-being. In "Walking," Thoreau confessed his own experience of a mode of constant convalescence, or rather, of ongoing preventive care: "I think that I cannot preserve my health and spirits unless I spend four hours a day at least—and it is commonly more than that—sauntering through the woods and over the hills and fields absolutely free from all worldly engagements" (*Excursions*, 187). And here we see it is not only physical health but "spirits" too (and not "animal spirits") that Thoreau links to contact with the natural world untrammeled by the pressures and stress of human obligation.

Behind these remarks rests the larger idea that our bodies and minds have evolved with nature and are inextricably connected to it, that what we are and even what we think enjoy an intrinsic, connatural relation to the ecology of other modes of life. In more metaphysical terms, what we are and how we regard nature—our cognition and powers of conceptualization—are constitutive with, rather than merely regulative of, natural phenomena and natural laws. This may be identified as a "romantic" attitude, and it does echo themes and statements in writers such as Wordsworth and Coleridge, both of whom Thoreau read. Yet, this attitude attracted William James, too, and marks certain strains of modern environmental thought.

Two passages, again from Thoreau's *Journal,* exemplify this value of the constitutive bond between human "health and spirits" and nature. One passage slants to the mental or even ideal:

> By some fortunate coincidence of thought or circumstance I am attuned to the universe—I am fitted to hear—my being moves in a sphere of melody—my fancy and imagination are excited to an inconceivable degree—This is no longer the dull earth on which I stood—It is possible to live a grander life here—already the steed is stamping—the knights are prancing.

Here lurks deep awareness of a correspondence with the external world, of belonging, of a harmony of being so strong that it elevates thoughts, prompts creative power, and gives vision beyond mere eyesight, "melody" and music beyond mundane sound. "Already our thoughts bid a proud farewell to the so called actual life and its humble glories," Thoreau continues. "Now this," he concludes, "is the verdict of a soul in health. But the soul diseased says that its own vision and life a-lone is true & sane."[9]

Yet, the ecstasy Thoreau describes has roots, or inspiration, directly in the things and productive systems of Earth. You cannot have senses to be out of unless you have senses to begin with. The two—ideal ecstasy and flesh-and-blood rhythms—are connected. They join as elements of one larger existence, as Thoreau outlines in this second passage, just a little earlier in his *Journal*:

> What is called genius is the abundance of life or health so that whatever addresses the senses—as the flavor of these berries—or the lowing of that cow [a favorite sound for Thoreau]—which sounds as if it echoed along a cool *mt* side just before night—where odiferous dews perfume the air and there is everlasting vigor serenity—& expectation of perpetual untarnished morning—each sight & sound & scent & flavor—intoxicates with a healthy intoxication.

Taste, sound, smell, sight: all the senses but touch he directly invokes, yet touch virtually, too, for the passage has a palpable feel to it, what William Hazlitt calls "gusto." Then, a few lines later, Thoreau reminds us that this is not a circle of the senses only, but linked to something other than sense, a deeper perception, a more complex power, and rejuvenation, too:

> If we have not dissipated the vital the divine fluids—then is there a circulation of vitality beyond our bodies. The cow is nothing—Heaven is not there—but in the condition of the hearer—I am thrilled to think that I owe a perception to the commonly gross sense of taste—that I have been inspired through the palate—that these berries have fed my brain. After I had been eating these simple—wholesome—ambrosial fruits—on this high hill side—I found my senses whetted—I was young again.

Thoreau then claims of the berries, "They fed my brain—my fancy & imagination—and whether I stood or sat I was not the same creature" (*Journal 5*, 215–16).

If we cast back over the two *Journal* passages just quoted, we realize how they run the scale from lowest sense to "a grander life," and that they share one phrase *in common*: "my fancy and imagination" ("my fancy & imagination") occurs crucially in both. These faculties—rather, this *one* faculty of imaginative power, for Thoreau does not seem here to distinguish them—provides the nexus for sense and spirit, for "bodies" and "brain." This is, as Thoreau affirms, part of "what is called genius" and involves "the abundance of life or health"; it is "the verdict of a soul in health."

This is a heady, encompassing reach, from small berries that metamorphose into "ambrosial fruits," from "the lowing of that cow" that becomes heaven "in the condition of the hearer." It is a self-affirming joy, positive and healthy. We realize it most, Thoreau contends, when we are in the direct presence of the natural world. In *Wild Fruits* he exclaims, "What a healthy out-of-door appetite it takes to relish the apple of life, the apple of the world, then!"[10] One way to view this may be as an "uneasy tension between empiricism and idealism" or transcendentalism,[11] yet it is just such tensions that prove vital and sustaining for both material and mental wellness. And this requires a balancing act, too, for Thoreau regards health, physical and mental, as in many respects avoiding both excess and deprivation, where the secret of medicine is a habit of simplicity and deliberation, very hard to obtain and maintain—society all the time tempts us away from such a habit and seduces us with others—but all-important in its moderation.

## BALANCE AND "MENTAL HEALTH"

So, Thoreau pronounces that "All places, all positions—all things in short are a medium happy or unhappy. Every Realm has its centre and the nearer to that the better while you are in it." This immediately sparks another observation: "Even health is only the happiest of all mediums . . .

there may be excess or there may be deficiency—in either case there is disease. A man must only be *virtuous* enough." Thoreau even suggests that one may survive well enough physically without virtue ("Nature is very kind and liberal to all persons of vicious habits—and does not exhaust them with many excesses"), but then, of course, it is spiritual and mental health that suffer (*Journal 2*, 207, 42). In other words, as he points out in the chapter "Higher Laws" in *Walden*, there is a side of nature that is purely physical, "an animal in us, which awakens in proportion as our higher nature slumbers." The key is to balance the two and not permit the lower nature to prevail. It is in that sense that he says, a few pages later in the same chapter, "If you would avoid uncleanness, and all the sins, work earnestly, though it be at cleaning a stable. Nature is hard to be overcome, but she must be overcome." This appears to contradict many other statements about health and nature until we realize that in this context "Nature" stands for that "animal in us," which "is reptile and sensual, and perhaps cannot be wholly expelled." This distinction, he says, was prompted by seeing the "lower jaw of a hog, with white and sound teeth," apparently unlike the diseased teeth and gums of some virtuous people, and that jaw "suggested that there was an animal health and vigor distinct from the spiritual" (*Walden*, 219, 221, 219).

The larger point, again, is balance, the avoidance of excess. "Any excess," says Thoreau, even "to have drunk too much water even the day before is fatal to the morning's clarity" (*Journal 5*, 194). This is not only moderation in the physical or animal; it is likewise moderation and lack of fanaticism in the spiritual. It is, moreover, a finely practiced sense that the physical and spiritual depend on and inform one another, what today we might call a holistic sense of health.

What today we call mental health is part of Thoreau's picture, too. He uses the phrase "mental health" in the chapter "Solitude" (*Walden*, 136). Near the beginning of that book, in "Economy," he peers into our constant sense of stress and worry, worry over work, "all the day long on the alert," and our worry over change we cannot control. There is one illness that seems to admit little help and no final remedy: "The incessant anxiety and strain of some is a well nigh incurable form of disease" (*Walden*, 11). One way to counter this is newly familiar to us as a byword found in various forms of therapy: live in the present, live in the moment. We are incapable of controlling everything that affects us, and thus so often we redouble our efforts to do so. For such an endless cycle of stress Thoreau has no easy cure, but he does state at least once what is needed for us to develop internally: "Health requires this relaxation this aimless life. This life in the present" (*Journal 5*, 392).

Moreover, if we merely sit and ruminate, if we remain forever indoors, our health will likewise suffer. Of shopkeepers and mechanics—and today we might think of office workers, employees who stare at screens for endless hours, and academics—who stay in their shops or cubicles and cross their legs rather than walking on them, Thoreau muses, in "Walking," that "I think that they deserve some credit for not having all committed suicide long ago" (*Excursions*, 187). In other words, a cramped imagination or a cramped body will each engender the other, and together they will eventuate in unhealthy desperation, a sense that life is stuck, meaningless.

Solitude and contact with nature may counteract this, but not carried to the point of isolation (again, balance enters in). In that chapter "Solitude," Thoreau paints the picture of a lost, starving man whose weakness produces a "diseased imagination." In contrast to him, "owing to bodily and mental health and strength, we may be continually cheered by a like but more normal and natural society"—more normal and natural than the ill man's "grotesque visions"—and so "come to know that we are never alone" (*Walden*, 136).

A symbol of this combined physical and mental health, and of living in the present, comes in *Walden* at the end of the previous chapter, "Sounds." That symbol is one of Thoreau's favorites, the "brave Chanticleer. He is more indigenous even than the natives," the native songbirds. "His health is ever good, his lungs are sound, his spirits never flag" (*Walden*, 127). The sound lungs are poignant, given the consumption that worked its way through Thoreau's family and ended his own life. Yet, as he says in one *Journal* entry, "I would brag like the chanticlere in the morning—with all the lustiness that the new day imparts—without thinking of the evening when I & all of us shall go to roost."[12] No matter how much the uncertainties of life and our lack of control over them plague and worry us, we are better off plunging in, storming the main gate, and fretting less over a future whose pitfalls we are imagining are, almost by definition, not the ones into which, often through no fault of our own, we fall.[13] In short, as he remarks in "Solitude," there "can be no very black melancholy to him who lives in the midst of Nature and has his senses still," that is, open and receptive (*Walden*, 131).

Sherman Paul has written eloquently about sound and particular sounds as fundamental to Thoreau's sense of health, and it would make little sense to repeat at length his fine argument here (see note 3, above). It is enough perhaps to say that there are countless instances in Thoreau's writing of sound as an index or messenger of health, sometimes with the implied pun of "sound" as healthy (Chanticleer's lungs that make such a lusty call are "sound"). It is a leitmotif in Thoreau that natural sounds often convey a sense of health or harmony, what Paul refers to as "the agency of correspondence," the means or harmony by which the bodily and animal integrate with the mental, spiritual, and moral. In "A Winter Walk," to cite just one example, Thoreau speaks of "feeling our pulse by listening to the low of cattle in the street, or the sound of the flail in distant barns." This heard, ever-present connection with nature, even when we live inside, provides a kind of aural thermometer. "No doubt," he continues, "a skilful physician could determine our health by observing how these simple and natural sounds affected us" (*Excursions*, 75).

## ENCOUNTERING AND CONFRONTING, CHEER AND JOY

Left entirely to ourselves and to the habits of our own society—to our strictly town concerns without the aid and ministrations of direct contact with the natural world—we harbor a large, latent capacity for making ourselves sick, physically and mentally. The farther and longer the remove from direct contact with nature, the more difficult it becomes to treat those illnesses, which can become habitual. No amount of philosophizing, and least of all no long list of prescription medicines, can alter that; rather, walking and observing, and touching and seeing and smelling natural, vital life and its habitats counteract it. Without this natural diagnosis, without its healing, and without openness to this physician-like presence of the *natural constitution* of the world we will, as Anaximander feared, damage our own constitution and end by suffocating in our own waste. This, at least, becomes Thoreau's conviction, one that his own experience confirms to him.

Since we each experience this awareness of the natural constitution of the world individually, you will have your recounting, but here is one of mine:

On April 24, 2010, I was walking a powerline trail on the side of Penobscot Mountain in Pennsylvania, near Lake Nuangola, where, on its shore, my uncle and grandfather had built a cottage in the woods seventy years ago, and to which every year of my life I have repaired several times, at longer or shorter stretches, to restore myself. On that trail, over forty years, I'd seen fox and deer, tadpoles in two-month pools, bluebirds, turkey vultures, larks, hawks innumerable, and countless species of wildflowers and butterfly. That day I spotted only deer tracks and a solitary, large hawk, too high up for me to identify. It seemed that, at 1:00 p.m, actually nature's noon, the fauna, at least, were quiet or elsewhere. On retracing my steps, I began distractedly to think of this essay, and to imagine if I could acquire a decent edition of Thoreau on my electronic book reader in order to search his texts for several passages I recalled imperfectly (an acquisition that never happened). Along the trail I heard a rapid clicking to the left. I thought it first a dragonfly, for I'd already seen one, though it seemed early in the season. But the clicking increased suddenly in rhythm and loudness. It was, I then plainly saw, a rattlesnake, with rattles on its slightly elevated tail now in full vibration. My footsteps stopped about fifteen feet from its head. It was two or three feet off the trail before me. I hadn't halted more than a second or two before instinctively, yet slowly, taking a half step backward. In another few seconds the rattles ceased, and the snake—I could now fully see, about three or four feet long—reversed its direction and moved with surprising speed into the underbrush, almost as fast as anyone could jog. Well, here I had been thinking of Thoreau and health and nature and his texts, and an encounter that could have been harmful, or even worse, seemed avoided only by the merest chance of timing. What kind of health was that?

Yet, the snake had stopped before I had. When I halted it was already still. Our paths were about to intersect, but it wanted no more of that direct meeting than I did. This snake warned me, and to its warning signal I was and remain deeply grateful. I finished the walk a healthier man than when I began it two hours earlier. For all that the snake knew, I carried a gun. (I have carried a rifle up there before, to target shoot with my son, and hunters are up there all the time in the fall.) The snake kept life and I kept limb. The warning of the rattles seemed to me only minutes after the encounter not unlike the early warnings we receive, often, of possible or impending ill health: stay this course, keep this up, do as you've been doing, and damage likely will occur, possibly serious damage. So, this warning, I concluded, was a *good* thing, not a signal of purposive harm—if the snake had moved to hunt me, surely it could have done so with real success—but an early-warning sign that, if heeded, would ensure the health of both of us. Now, that is a natural constitution pointing not to some Absolute but to a working out of living things. This became the passage to remember from that walk, one not easily forgotten.

That encounter, to revert to William James's criteria mentioned at the start of this essay, doesn't seem to me simply materialistic. It was living, vital. And in it, both the human and reptilian had choices to make, choices determined, in part, by evolution, but actual choices nevertheless. The agencies of a living world, therefore, seem not only different in degree but actually in kind from whatever agency inhabits a material world only; and from such a living world so naturally constituted we can expect different events, and those events require a choice of conduct. Reading those events and making those choices is a way to diagnose not only the material body but also the spirit that elects to live deliberately. It's at once a natural and transcendental way to health, something real that reflects on an ideal in mind.

You may already be recalling the last paragraphs of "Spring" in *Walden,* which begin, "Our village life would stagnate if it were not for the unexplored forests and meadows which surround it. We need the tonic of wildness,—to wade sometimes in marshes where the bittern and the meadow-hen lurk, and hear the booming of the snipe. . . . We can never have enough of Nature" (*Walden,* 317–318). We know what Thoreau means by *tonic* here, and it isn't the New England name for a carbonated beverage—he means medicine, health, healing, and something that gives vigor.

To drive home this natural medicine and the health it promotes, he thinks of the inevitable death that all living things face, but in a light unexpected: "We are cheered when we observe the vulture feeding in the carrion which disgusts and disheartens us and deriving health and strength from the repast." He says it brings *cheer* (animates, brings joy, makes us clear headed). He goes on to a fact even harder to swallow: "There was a dead horse in the hollow by the path to my house, which compelled me sometimes to go out of my way, especially in the night when the air was heavy, but the assurance it gave me of the strong appetite and inviolable health of Nature was my compensation for this." The consciousness is not of nature red in tooth and claw but of a "Nature . . . so rife with life that myriads can be afforded to be sacrificed and suffered to prey on one another." He gives examples, even so much "that sometimes it has rained flesh and blood!" Then he offers a penetrating judgment: "With the liability to accident, we must see how little account is to be made of it. The impression made on a wise man is that of universal innocence. Poison is not poisonous after all, nor are any wounds fatal. Compassion is a very untenable ground. It must be expeditious. Its pleadings will not bear to be stereotyped" (*Walden*, 318).

There's another pertinent section of *Walden*, in the earlier chapter "Solitude," in the last paragraphs that begin similarly: "The indescribable innocence and beneficence of Nature,—of sun and wind and rain, of summer and winter,—such health, such cheer, they afford forever!" (*Walden*, 138). Again, *cheer,* used in a way that Wordsworth uses it in *The Prelude* ("chear," "cheared," and "chearful") to describe human interaction with nature, for example, "Thus long I lay / Cheared by the genial pillow of the earth / Beneath my head" (1805, I, ll. 87–89). Thoreau notes in his essay "Thomas Carlyle and His Works," setting up a contrast, "The poet is blithe and cheery ever, and as well as nature. Carlyle has not the simple Homeric health of Wordsworth" (*Early Essays*, 248). The sympathy that the presence of the natural world can afford us as human beings is so powerful that if we were to grieve for a just cause, then "the winds would sigh humanely," says Thoreau, "and the clouds rain tears, and the woods shed their leaves." He asks, "Shall I not have intelligence with the earth? Am I not partly leaves and vegetable mould myself?" (*Walden*, 138). Here is a materialistic world more than materialistic—it's also intelligential, moral, and at times sympathetic.

This attitude John Muir echoes beautifully. I'm thinking especially of *My First Summer in the Sierra,* where many passages harmonize with Thoreau's: "What pains are taken to keep this wilderness in health,—showers of snow, showers of rain . . . floods of light . . . interaction of plant on plant, animal on animal, etc., beyond thought! How fine Nature's methods!" Muir asks why his enjoyment of Nature in the Sierra should appear extravagant. "It is only common sense, a sign of health, genuine, natural, all-awake health." The life Muir witnesses brings "cheer" and "joy." He claims, "We soon cease to lament waste and death, and rather rejoice and exult in the imperishable, unspendable wealth of the universe." Shortly after this observation Muir ventures: "More and more, in a place like this, we feel ourselves part of wild Nature, kind to everything," meaning akin to everything, though he seems also to pun.[14] Muir himself sought personal health, mental and physical, in contact with nature.

The point here is not so much that Wordsworth's or Thoreau's *thought* is passed down, but rather that their quality of experience is in fact re-experienced in a completely different place and time, so that for a later soul similarly awakened, the natural world is not merely materialistic either, but vital. Speaking of fragile butterflies Muir remarks: "How are their little bodies, with muscles, nerves, organs, kept warm and jolly in such admirable exuberant health? Regarded only as mechanical inventions, how wonderful they are! Compared with these, Godlike man's greatest machines are as nothing."[15]

## BODY AND SOUL, PHYSIC AND METAPHYSIC—AND HEAVEN

That was a digression. Returning to "Solitude" in *Walden,* Thoreau pushes the metaphor of health and medicine until it's no longer a metaphor but a symbol in the Coleridgean sense, it *is* itself even as it *also* represents a greater whole of which it is a part. "What is the pill which will keep us well, serene, contented? Not my or thy great-grandfather's, but our great-grandmother Nature's universal, vegetable, botanic medicines, by which she has kept herself young always." Thoreau rejects the medicine bottle sold out of the traveling salesman's wagon and instead pleads, "let me have a draught of undiluted morning air. Morning air!" Then, to bring together this natural world, health, and a religious sense all in one he proclaims, "I am no worshipper of Hygeia, who was the daughter of that old herb-doctor Æsculapius," and commonly represented as the goddess of health; "but rather of Hebe, cupbearer to Jupiter, who was the daughter of Juno and wild lettuce, and who had the power of restoring gods and men to the vigor of youth" (*Walden,* 138–39). Here, as when he recorded in his *Journal,* "I was young again" (see above), is rejuvenation.

There's not time to explore the connection fully, but all this links up with Thoreau's interest in yoga, yogis, and his experiment in what we'd call transcendental meditation, an interest explored by Stefanie Syman in her book *The Subtle Body: The Story of Yoga in America* (2010). Thoreau's work also has clear affinities with certain modern mental health treatments, for example, Stephen S. Ilardi's *The Depression Cure: The 6-Step Program to Beat Depression Without Drugs* (2010), which emphasizes exercise, a healthy diet with more omega-3 fats, engagement rather than morbid rumination, sleep, and sunlight exposure—getting outside.

When the Environmental Protection Agency was founded and associated federal legislation passed in the early 1970s, that agency was foremost and largely linked to concerns of human health, the clean water, the clean air act, and similar statutes—though one might just as well have said that clean air and clean water would contribute, too, to the health of fish, birds, mammals, even of certain microbes. There's not enough space here to give it more than suggestive treatment, but Thoreau today alerts us to so-called environmentally linked or environmentally caused diseases, that is, diseases caused by our remove from nature, or our pollution of it (cancer, mental health, ADD?). President Obama received in May 2010 a report from the President's Cancer Panel, appointed by President Bush in the previous administration, stating that the extent of environmentally caused and aggravated cancers in the United States has been "grossly underestimated." On another medical front, as this essay was being prepared for the press in late summer 2011, a major, large-scale study of 192 pairs of identical and fraternal twins concluded that the causes of autism—a condition diagnosed with alarmingly increasing frequency—are more predominantly environmental than genetic. Exposure to certain medications and toxins may play a role.[16]

How, more exactly then, is Thoreau's interest as a physician *transcendental*? Let me approach that through Schelling's remark as Coleridge rephrases it in his *Biographia Literaria,* a remark, therefore, that Thoreau almost certainly read, the statement that any worthwhile transcendental idealism "is only so far idealism, as it is at the same time, and on that very account, the truest and most binding realism." If genuine, the two, in any ultimate analysis, cannot be viewed separately. Some transcendental philosophers, such as Fichte, could, in Coleridge's opinion, show "a boastful and hyperstoic hostility to Nature."[17] However, for Schelling, for Coleridge, and for Thoreau, transcendental thought is legitimated only when rescued from an abstract play of concepts, words, and forms by the tangible, empirical world of living nature, of berries, slime moulds, and sunsets. And living nature is only known and experienced by us fully as human beings when we learn through self-conscious, inner examination, through a transcendental as well as an empirical reckoning.

In "'Another name for health': Thoreau and Modern Medicine," Michael P. Branch and Jessica Pierce contend that Thoreau has much to offer current medical practice. They acutely remark, "Thoreau argued that true health would result only from the integration of physic and metaphysics: 'Good for the body is the work of the body, and good for the soul is the work of the soul, and good for either the work of the other—let them not call hard names, nor know a divided interest.' . . . To Thoreau, the 'perfect body' was the expression of the combined physical and spiritual well-being that he identified with the natural world."[18] The only true idealism and the only true realism must exist together: a transcendental physician, a swamp and meadow metaphysician.

Just as discussion continues about the degree of allegiance Thoreau gave to empirical science balanced against transcendental philosophy and religious experience, and whether the former, the empirical, came to dominate late in his life, so there is larger debate about the balance of these two elements in American Transcendentalism generally. I am here suggesting that over many years Thoreau recognized the interplay of the two, the *necessity* of their mutual existence as constituting both the only true realism and the only true idealism. They are not mutually exclusive. They are symbiotic. We feel on our pulse, we *experience* both. In his last years, Thoreau seems to have felt that scientific observation and discovery simply had more work left to do, and more open fields in nature to explore, than philosophy had in continuing to develop idealism or metaphysics. So, he set about to do the work most in need of doing.[19]

Finally, where might Thoreau experience in the natural world a kind of heaven, the image or actuality of a place of rest and restoration for the spirit? This he sees multiple times, and we might see it ourselves multiple times, too, but here is just one instance from his journal about Cape Cod. Fully aware of violence and death in nature, Thoreau nevertheless describes a heaven on Earth:

> There is scarcely a white-pine on the forearm of the Cape. Yet in the northwest part of Eastham, near the Camp Ground, we saw, the next summer, some quite rural, and even sylvan retreats, for the Cape, where small rustling groves of oaks and locusts and whispering pines, on perfectly level ground, made a little paradise. The locusts, both transplanted and growing naturally about the houses there, appeared to flourish better than any other tree. There were thin belts of wood in Wellfleet and Truro, a mile or more from the Atlantic, but, for the most part, we could see the horizon through them, or, if extensive, the trees were not large. Both oaks and pines had often the same flat look with the apple-trees. Commonly, the oak woods twenty-five years old were a mere scraggy shrubbery nine or ten feet high, and we could frequently reach to their topmost leaf. Much that is called "woods" was about half as high as this—only patches of shrub-oak, bayberry, beach-plum, and wild roses, overrun with woodbine. When the roses were in bloom, these patches in the midst of the sand displayed such a profusion of blossoms, mingled with the aroma of the bayberry, that no Italian or other artificial rose-garden could equal them. They were perfectly Elysian, and realized my idea of an oasis in the desert. Huckleberry-bushes were very abundant, and the next summer they bore a remarkable quantity of that kind of gall called Huckleberry-apple, forming quite handsome though monstrous blossoms. But it must be added, that this shrubbery swarmed with wood-ticks, sometimes very troublesome parasites, and which it takes very horny fingers to crack. ("Across the Cape," chapter VII, *Cape Cod*, 101–102)

There is a heaven, and it is on Earth, an Elysium, a paradise with wood ticks and rattlesnakes. It's Eden, so we may learn to be better gardeners, for heaven is under our daily care and cultivation, as is our health, from Penobscot Mountain even to the summit of Ktaadn.

In 1851, Thoreau wrote in his *Journal*, "Disease is not the accident of the individual nor even of the generation but of life itself. In some form & to some degree or other it is one of the permanent conditions of life."[20] He seemed to realize that the body always harbors some pathogen, it is only a question whether our defenses, what today we call the immune system, can gain control: "Life is a warfare a struggle" (*Journal 4*, 35). From December 1860 until he died May 6, 1862, tuberculosis sapped his strength. He traveled to Minnesota, a journey that took about two months, in part to seek relief. The climate there was then recommended for its dry, restorative power. Back in Concord in mid summer 1861, he spent time ordering his papers and writings, but lost weight, became weak, eventually had to stay indoors, and finally could barely sit up or speak. His sister Sophia, his friend Ellery Channing, and others such as Theo Brown remarked on his great equanimity, his buoyancy, his lack of complaint, his insistence that there was as much comfort in perfect disease as in perfect health, that it was as good to be sick as to be well.[21] In the course of his unrelenting illness he was maintaining as much health as anyone could, for as long as he could, even until neither health nor disease remained.

## BIBLIOGRAPHY

Branch, Michael P. and Jessica Pierce. "'Another name for health': Thoreau and Modern Medicine." *Literature and Medicine* 15, no.1 (1996): 129–45.

Coleridge, Samuel Taylor. *Biographia Literaria*. Edited by James Engell and W. Jackson Bate. Princeton: Princeton University Press, 1983.

Da Rocha, Antonio Casado. "The Value of Health in the Writings of Henry David Thoreau." *Environmental Values* 18 (2009): 201–15.

Dean, Bradley P., ed. *Wild Fruits: Thoreau's Rediscovered Last Manuscript*. New York: Norton, 2000.

Hallmayer, Joachim, M.D., et al. "Genetic Heritability and Shared Environmental Factors Among Twin Pairs with Autism." *Archives of General Psychiatry* (2011). Accessed September 12, 2011. doi: 10.1001/archgenpsychiatry.2011.76.

Hodder, Alan D. *Thoreau's Ecstatic Witness*. New Haven: Yale University Press, 2001.

James, William. *The Varieties of Religious Experience: A Study in Human Nature*. London: Longmans, 1911.

Johnson, Rochelle L. *Passions for Nature: Nineteenth-Century America's Aesthetics of Alienation*. Athens: University of Georgia Press, 2009.

Lowell, James Russell. "Thoreau's Letters." *The North American Review* 101 (October 1865): 597–608.

Muir, John. *My First Summer in the Sierra*. Boston: Houghton Mifflin, 1911.

Paul, Sherman. "The Wise Silence: Sound as the Agency of Correspondence in Thoreau." *The New England Quarterly* 22, no. 4 (1949): 511–27.

Richardson, Jr., Robert D. *Henry Thoreau: A Life of the Mind*. Berkeley: University of California Press, 1986.

Thoreau, Henry David. *Cape Cod*. Edited by Joseph J. Moldenhauer. Princeton: Princeton University Press, 1988.

———. *Early Essays and Miscellanies*. Edited by Joseph J. Moldenhauer and Edwin Moser, with Alexander Kern. Princeton: Princeton University Press, 1975.

———. *Excursions*. Edited by Joseph J. Moldenhauer. Princeton: Princeton University Press, 2007.

———. *Journal, Volume 2: 1842–1848*. Edited by Robert Sattelmeyer. Princeton: Princeton University Press, 1984.

———. *Journal, Volume 4: 1851–1852*. Edited by Leonard N. Neufeldt and Nancy Craig Simmons. Princeton: Princeton University Press, 1992.

———. *Journal, Volume 5: 1852–1853*. Edited by Patrick F. O'Connell. Princeton: Princeton University Press, 1997.

———. *Journal, Volume 6: 1853*. Edited by William Rossi and Heather K. Thomas. Princeton: Princeton University Press, 2000.

———. *Journal, Volume 7: 1853–1854*. Edited by Nancy Craig Simmons and Ron Thomas. Princeton: Princeton University Press, 2009.

———. *Journal, Volume 8: 1854*. Edited by Sandra Harbert Petrulionis. Princeton: Princeton University Press, 2002.

———. *The Maine Woods*. Edited by Joseph J. Moldenhauer. Princeton: Princeton University Press, 1972.

———. *Walden*. Edited by J. Lyndon Shanley. Princeton: Princeton University Press, 1971.

Walls, Laura Dassow. *Seeing New Worlds: Henry David Thoreau and Nineteenth-Century Natural Science*. Madison: University of Wisconsin Press, 1995.

Wordsworth, William. *The Prelude 1799, 1805, 1850*. Edited by Jonathan Wordsworth, M. H. Abrams, and Stephen Gill. New York: W. W. Norton, 1979.

## NOTES

1. William James, *The Varieties of Religious Experience: A Study in Human Nature* (London: Longmans, 1911), 518.

2. James Russell Lowell, "Thoreau's Letters," *The North American Review* 101 (October 1865): 597-608; 604, 605, 607, 608. For the disagreement between Lowell and Thoreau, see Thoreau, *The Maine Woods*, ed. Joseph J. Moldenhauer (Princeton: Princeton University Press, 1972), 360-63.

3. Sherman Paul, "The Wise Silence: Sound as the Agency of Correspondence in Thoreau," *The New England Quarterly* 22.4 (1949): 511–27.

4. Michael P. Branch and Jessica Pierce, "'Another name for health': Thoreau and Modern Medicine," *Literature and Medicine* 15.1 (1996): 129–45; Antonio Casado Da Rocha, "The Value of Health in the Writings of Henry David Thoreau," *Environmental Values* 18 (2009): 201–15. I am thankful to Joshua G. Wilson for assistance in research and to Kevin Van Anglen and Jacob Risinger for helpful comments and suggestions.

5. Robert D. Richardson, Jr., *Henry Thoreau: A Life of the Mind* (Berkeley: University of California Press, 1986), 119, 123, 157–59.

6. *Journal, Volume 7: 1853-1854*, ed. Nancy Craig Simmons and Ron Thomas (Princeton: Princeton University Press, 2009), 16; *Journal, Volume 8: 1854*, ed. Sandra Harbert Petrulionis (Princeton: Princeton University Press, 2002), 229.

7. *Excursions*, ed. Joseph J. Moldenhauer (Princeton: Princeton University Press, 2007): 4–5. Hereafter cited as *Excursions*.

8. *Journal, Volume 2: 1842-1848*, ed. Robert Sattelmeyer (Princeton: Princeton University Press, 1984), 209. Hereafter cited as *Journal 2*.

9. *Journal, Volume 5: 1852-1853*, ed. Patrick F. O'Connell (Princeton: Princeton University Press, 1997), 272. Hereafter cited as *Journal 5*.

10. Bradley P. Dean, ed., *Wild Fruits: Thoreau's Rediscovered Last Manuscript* (New York: W. W. Norton, 2000), 87.

11. Da Rocha, Antonio Casado. "The Value of Health in the Writings of Henry David Thoreau," *Environmental Values* 18 (2009): 202.

12. *Journal, Volume 6: 1853*, ed. William Rossi and Heather K. Thomas (Princeton: Princeton University Press, 2000), 172.

13. For Chanticleer, contact with nature, and "living in the present," see also Da Rocha, 207–08.

14. John Muir, *My First Summer in the Sierra* (Boston: Houghton Mifflin, 1911), 170, 287, 14, 168, 325, 326.

15. Ibid., 215.

16. Joachim Hallmayer, M.D. et al, "Genetic Heritability and Shared Environmental Factors Among Twin Pairs with Autism," *Archives of General Psychiatry* (2011): accessed September 12, 2011, doi: 10.1001/archgenpsychiatry.2011.76.

17. Samuel Taylor Coleridge, *Biographia Literaria*, ed. James Engell and W. Jackson Bate (Princeton: Princeton University Press, 1983), 1.261: 158–59.

18. Michael P. Branch and Jessica Pierce, "'Another name for health': Thoreau and Modern Medicine," *Literature and Medicine* 15.1 (1996): 131.

19. For three of many possible examples, see Laura Dassow Walls, *Seeing New Worlds: Henry David Thoreau and Nineteenth-Century Natural Science* (Madison: University of Wisconsin Press, 1995); Rochelle L. Johnson, *Passions for Nature: Nineteenth-Century America's Aesthetics of Alienation* (Athens: University of Georgia Press, 2009), 208–17, 266n46, 267n58; Alan D. Hodder, *Thoreau's Ecstatic Witness* (New Haven: Yale University Press, 2001), 169–73.

20. *Journal, Volume 4: 1851-1852*, ed. Leonard N. Neufeldt and Nancy Craig Simmons (Princeton: Princeton University Press, 1992), 35.

21. See Richardson, *Henry Thoreau*, 385–89; Hodder, *Thoreau's Ecstatic Witness*, 301–05.

# THREE

# Falling from Trees

## *Arborescent Prosody in John Clare's Tree Elegies*

Erin Lafford and Emma Mason

This chapter brings together the experiences of reading and listening to think about the relationship between rhythm and well-being in John Clare's elegies on trees. We propose that the tree-like structure and rhythms of Clare's tree elegies forward a model of health and well-being that the poet uses to overcome feelings of grief and sickness provoked by the mass destruction of the environment and land caused by enclosure in the early nineteenth century. To foreground what we mean by tree-like or "arborescent" rhythms, we turn to Peter Broderick's thirty-minute sequence for piano and strings, *Music for Falling from Trees* (2009). Broderick, we argue, creates a rhythm of falling down as a prelude to being pulled back up into tonal, metrical, and emotional stability, a process that is apparent from the performed sound of the sequence as well as the visual elements of the score. We discuss Broderick's score to show how its arborescent content provides a map into health for the grieving or fallen listener and use this as a model for reading Clare's own poetic transcriptions of what he hears when he listens to and with trees. Both Broderick and Clare work from moments of sadness and despair: Broderick's sequence aurally produces the experience of a hospitalized mental patient undergoing a nightmarish drug therapy and electric shock treatment before finding a way to recovery through human compassion and attention; Clare painfully mourns the devastation of his rural neighborhood by declaiming the "cant" behind enclosure while engaged in an ultimately futile struggle to avoid his own hospitalization for mental illness. Yet we hear a redemptive, *eudaimonic*, and distinctly arborescent rhythm in Broderick's sequence and Clare's elegies, especially "The Mores" and "To a Fallen Elm," one that guides the listener through troubling emotion to enable and foster well-being. Locating listeners inside a rhythmic motion of falling through sadness, Broderick and Clare hold us safely within steadfast and regular forms and teach us how to bear negative emotion in the positive meters of their texts.

In addition to offering a critical reading of Clare's elegies through Broderick's music, we also wish to contribute to current debates on the *eudaimonic* potential of prosody. Prosody is still regarded by many readers as a set of fixed and circumscribed rules that must be fully adhered to in the process of calculating how a text should sound. Like Gilles Deleuze and Félix Guattari's famous indictment of vertical, "arborescent" thinking, to which we return in Part I of this chapter, the critical vilification of prosody is based on its assumed role as a dictatorial and dogmatic system of code cracking that unnecessarily distances readers from their own idiosyncratic hearing of a poem. A recent debate about Keats's pronunciation of the word *Lamia* on the North American Society for the Study of Romanticism's online mailing list, for example, surged into a furious discussion about the relative value of prosody. When one contributor suggested stressing the middle syllable of *Lamia* (like *Maria*), a respondent replied that it is "impossible metrically to stress the *i*"; when another contributor raised the possibility that *Lamia* might be a dactyl, the same respondent declared that "*Lamia* is not a dactyl and the meter consistently shows that. If you want to believe it's a dactyl, which has no meaning in English versification, please feel free. Provide a scansion to support your claim. We are not Humpty Dumpties in metrics, deciding on a whim to make this is a 'dactyl' and that an 'iamb.' There are rules."[1] The discussion, contributed to by some of the most prominent prosodists working in the field of Romanticism, became so heated that the proponent of "rules-based" prosody eventually resigned his membership from the list. Following this impassioned debate, Susan Wolfson reminded colleagues of Keats's posthumously published sonnet, "If by dull rhymes our English must be chain'd," a poem that exhorts readers to "inspect the lyre, and weigh the stress / Of every chord, and see what may be gain'd / By ear industrious, and attention meet" (ll.7–9). We concur with Wolfson's recommendation that prosody is a process of close listening and "industrious" attention, a law that must be read through spirit in order to instigate an interpretive rigor driven by creativity and imagination. As Meredith Martin and Yisrael Levin argue in their recent special issue of the journal *Victorian Poetry* on "Victorian prosody": "Though still attentive, always, to the ways that poems are made and received" scholars newly working in this field "no longer view prosody as an aesthetic category that is distinct from the political or cultural sphere; indeed, not only does the study of Victorian culture help us understand Victorian prosody, but the study of Victorian prosody . . . helps us to understand Victorian culture."[2]

Our close readings of Clare's elegies contribute to this renewal of interest in prosody by showing how Clare's use of rhythm and meter produce feelings of well-being even when the poem's content is mournful and sad. Both Broderick and Clare allow their readers to recover from their painful narratives by guiding us through tree-like texts that are vertical but branching, apical but budding. The listener is invited to begin at the top of these tree-like forms and fall down through them, a downward motion that metaphorically registers their sorrowful content. For us, Broderick and Clare understand the tree as a structure that guides and holds the arching and dividing shoots of accidentals and syllables adept at cradling and sustaining listeners as they fall down the rooted bough of the text. Part I of this essay outlines our understanding of the relationship between such tree-like form and well-being. We define "arborescent" rhythm in relation to Deleuze and Guattari's critique of arborescence in their work on rhizomes, and suggest that, contrary to their reading, a "vertical" and stable experience of sound can be more healing than a mutating horizontal one. In Part II we turn to how this rhythm works aurally and visually in Broderick's composition and in Clare's "The Mores" and "To a Fallen Elm," arguing that all three texts engender an aural falling experience as a way of imagining the emotional content of suffering. We argue, however, that the listener is repeatedly held and gentled within this falling experience by branching rhythms, sounds, rests, and stresses as a way of allowing for well-being amidst periods of pain and sadness.

## I

While the "eudaimonic turn" in literary studies has beneficially insisted on the worth and intellectual rigor of texts that discuss or embody positive emotions and experiences, we are interested in investigating how an emotionally sorrowful text might work eudaimonically. We read the term *eudaimonic* as a process, an active element within the text that can work affectively upon the reader. This active element, we propose, is poetic rhythm, already critically established as a textual component able to affectively impact on readers and listeners. Iambic pentameter is notoriously considered to be a subjective representation of the human heartbeat and thus the most engaging and "natural" of all rhythms; and trochaic prosody is frequently discussed as an audile instrument for lulling and soothing those who read it because of its acoustic affinity with children's songs and nursery rhymes. We wish to move beyond merely representative readings of prosody to embrace a methodological approach that uncovers an active and benign element in rhythm. It is the task of our project to explore one route into what Tennyson calls "a use in measured language" (*In Memoriam*, V, l.6), one that we argue lies in arborescent rhythm as a steady beat that promotes feelings of well-being even in texts that do not initially seek to represent positive experience. As a form of human flourishing, well-being signifies movement, development, thriving, and growth, analogous to a tree or plant that progresses from germination to bloom, or the patient that "flourishes" under treatment and care. This development might be a fluctuating one in which the patient moves between pain and relief, suffering and physical health, recovery and death. But in the midst of suffering and pain, the measure of arborescent rhythm creates a sense of security and rootedness in which emotional health can always flourish within the controlled form of the poem. By engaging with a poem that is shaped like a tree, readers are steadily drawn down the page by the trunk-like form of the words, but they are granted moments of relief from this falling by the occasional branching out offered by extra syllables and accents. The reader is also held by the arborescent structure of the poem, especially apparent in Clare's "The Mores," wherein its eighty lines of varying lengths with no stanzaic breaks give it the "concrete" visual effect of a tree. The absence of punctuation in Clare's poetry compounds its arborescence, the eye invited to tumble vertically down a page of words that are free of end-stopped lines and typographical marks but then encouraged to return to the start of the poem by the omission of a final period point.

Clare's formal technique subverts the notion that the tree offers only a continuous, circumscribed model of experience. Our specific use of the term *arborescent,* for example, signals our engagement with Deleuze and Guattari's famous critique of aborescent form to endorse "rhizomatic" form and thinking in *A Thousand Plateaus: Capitalism and Schizophrenia* (1980). A companion piece to their previous book, *Anti-Oedipus* (1972), both studies sketch Deleuze and Guattari's deconstructive attack on unified, hierarchical "tree-like" thought in favor of an arbitrary, unregulated, wandering, nomadic thought conducive to experience as breakdown. Rhizomatic thought disbands the fixed, pointed, and directed movement of vertical, ordered thought in order to allow for involuntary ideas ("lines of flight") to explode out horizontally but connect "back to one another" to prevent the genesis of "a dualism or a dichotomy."[3] The rhizome is celebrated as an unrestrained, heterogeneous, rupturing, fleeing, flowing assemblage capable of displacing the tree's phallocentric, stratified, limited, and taxomonic structure, one that has "dominated Western reality and all of Western thought, from botany to biology and anatomy, but also gnosiology, theology, ontology, all of philosophy."[4] "Arborescent systems are hierarchal systems," Deleuze and Guattari argue, because they enclose individuals, nations and societies behind a frontier of state-enforced "preestablished, arborified and rooted" social edifices.[5] By contrast, there "are no points or positions in a rhizome, such as those found in a structure, tree, or root. There are only lines. . . . We do not have units of measure, only multiplicities or varieties of measurement."[6] Rhizomatic thought, unlike arborescent thought, multiplies outward, grafting itself endlessly into and onto new territories and experienced as a kind of "drunkenness" in which we stumble here and there, caught in a state of "in-betweeness":

> A rhizome has no beginning or end; it is always in the middle between things, interbeing, *intermezzo*. The tree is filiation, but the rhizome is alliance, uniquely alliance. The tree imposes the verb 'to be,' but the fabric of the rhizome is conjunction, 'and . . . and . . . and . . .' This conjunction carries enough force to shake and uproot the verb 'to be.' Where are you going? Where are you coming from? What are you heading for? These are totally useless questions.[7]

Rhizomatic experience is disorienting, dizzying and without (unified) meaning, a "nonsignifying system" that leaves us "without an organizing memory or central automaton, defined solely by a circulation of states."[8] It is, then, profoundly uncomfortable and anti-well-being, forcing the individual into a process of constant "becomings" and schizophrenic multiplicity, a syndrome similar to that which modern psychiatry calls dissociative identity disorder and one that we are less willing to idealize than Deleuze and Guattari.

Deleuze and Guattari are, of course, deliberately provocative in their elevation of a "hallucinatory" and mutating way of being that serves as a counter to the war machines of capitalism, accounting, bureaucracy, and power. Trees, they demand, have "made us suffer too much. . . . Nothing is beautiful or loving or political aside from underground stems and aerial roots, adventitious growths and rhizomes."[9] While we agree politically with Deleuze and Guattari's radical promotion of a "beautiful" and "loving" way of being that rejects suffering, we suggest that the arborescent is a route into, rather than an obstruction of, such experience. We take issue with Deleuze and Guattari's assumption, for example, that the act of asking questions such as "Where are you going? Where are you coming from? What are you heading for?" is inherently reactionary because it presupposes an inclination for a fixed identity of stability and composure. For the sick patient desperately in need of equilibrium and a decelerated pace of life, Deleuze and Guattari's rhizomatic obsession with "picking up speed," "coming and going" and doing "away with foundations . . . endings and beginnings" is unhelpful.[10] Specifically, we wish to suggest that the "units of measure" Deleuze and Guattari denounce the tree-root for representing in fact offer a steady and dependable rhythm of well-being to those struggling with illness and grief: we locate this rhythm in both music and poetry. Deleuze and Guattari argue that "musical form, right down to its ruptures and proliferations, is comparable to a weed, a rhizome" and preface their introduction to *A Thousand Plateaus* with an extract from a score by Sylvano Bussotti[11]:

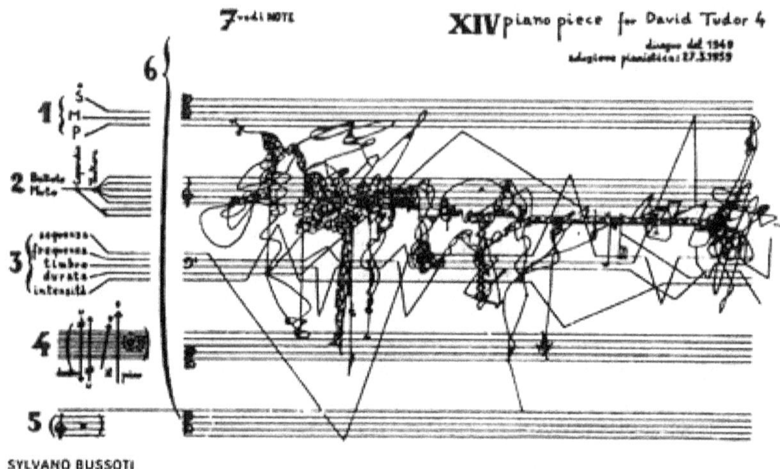


**Figure 3.1. Bussotti score. (Reproduced by kind permission of MGB Hal Leonard.)**

The score is intentionally bewildering, refusing interpretation and exemplifying rhizomatic sound. We suggest that arborescent sound, while not disconcerting and obscure, is still open to interpretation, creating a healing listening experience through its capacity to ground and root the auditor, holding the listener still in an experience of calm and equanimity. We do not mean to imply that arborescent sound and rhythm are in any way simple or straightforward, or that they lull the individual into a removed and detached state of being safe from the world's intrusions, political or otherwise. Rather, we assert that habitual and unbroken rhythms can autonomously coil and bloom up and down the vertical axis of a tree structure while being gently anchored in its frame. Most species of tree, for example, are flowering plants comprised of roots, trunks, branches, twigs, and leaves that grow in spirals, creating growth rings as new wood emerges concentrically over older wood. Unlike the drunken, hallucinating rhizome, tree roots at once move through the ground and also moor the tree, spreading to absorb water and soil nutrients, while stabilizing the trunk and its proliferating offshoots. Communal, empathetic, and loving, the tree roots directly relate to the branches and leaves above, even to the extent that when roots on one side of a tree are damaged, the foliage on that same side will also wilt or die. Arborescent rhythm embodies such communal care by drawing the reader down toward the security of the ground, always guiding him or her within the embrace of its many boughs and twigs.

## II

We hear this process made audible in Broderick's *Music for Falling from Trees* (2009), a sequence that aurally re-creates the experience of falling and recuperation. The piece maps this process through seven narrative tableaux that musically sound out the story of a man's struggle to preserve his personal identity while inside a psychiatric hospital. Broderick wrote the sequence on violin, viola, and piano for Adrienne Hart's modern dance piece, *Falling from Trees* (2008), and he completed it in just three weeks, writing alone in an empty barn and improvising around short themes and rhythms. A composition of postminimal classical drone, the music builds and flourishes, twists and collapses, and resonates with an unpunctuated and incessant moving rhythm. While each section begins mildly, usually with a series of soft-pedalled piano notes that rise into a surge of indistinct sounds, the music shifts into moments of folk-like tunefulness that are then held in abeyance before sliding and repeating into silence. "An Introduction to the Patient" begins the composition, a single minute of jarring and relapsing sound that immediately evinces the patient's isolation, solitude, and emotional instability. This discordant opening is followed by the heightened and paranoid piece, "Patient Observation," commencing with the sound of a ticking clock that Broderick creates by tapping his fingers on his violin. Running underneath the whole three-minute piece, this proprioceptive tapping steadies the chilling sound of a violin bow scraped across the strings and the monotone toll of a single low piano note, holding the listener steadily in its regular, directed rhythm. Just as Bussotti's score embodies the rhizomatic, so Broderick's score is arborescent, its four-part harmony working together in a structured and neat symbiosis. While Broderick has not yet transcribed his improvised score in published form, our own transcription of the first fifteen bars is illustrative of these formal elements:

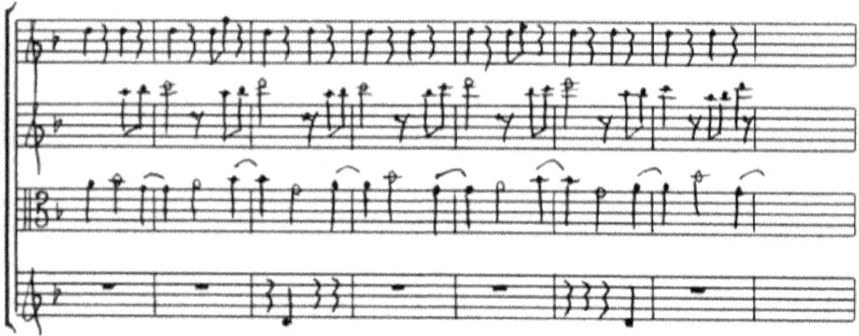

**Figure 3.2. Transcription of Broderick score. (This extract from Peter Broderick's score *Music for Falling from Trees* (2009) is reprinted with the kind permission of the composer.)**

The tentatively played first violin note (the top line of the score) speaks antiphonally to the single-noted piano here (the lowest line of the score), moving the listener down through the harmony within a communal and reciprocal trajectory of sound speaking to sound. The falling experience is tempered by the repeated deployment of rests, which visually bud out of the piece as tiny waving crotchet sprigs, slowing and regulating the listener's descent. Broderick's recollection that he composed the sequence by sending each day's work to Hart for comment is indicative of the music's at once extemporized and controlled affect, spontaneously written within the safe confines of an attentive and sympathetic dialogue. Just as the back-and-forth creative process between Broderick and Hart permits the composition to flourish, so, like the patient, the listener is urged to observe and hear in order to engage with the affective benefits of the piece. The written score and music work as an exercise in attention, memory, and (ultimately) trust. The listener must hear each new rhythm as it is introduced and repeated, and then assimilate that new rhythm into what has previously been heard, waiting patiently for the piece to unfold, and allowing him or herself to plummet through the piece while trusting in the route its structure offers.

The listener is recurrently thrown around and held by the sequence, then, caught between the branching rests wherein moments of repose are found and secured by the tonal centres of the music that provide resolution amidst musical chaos. Each part is intended to be materialized within the movements of dancers, and the soundscape of the piece is one into which the listener enters through his or her body: while the music is marked by a confusing and distressing pitch, its rhythm always holds the listener alert and in check. Only in "Pill Induced Slumber" is there a suggestion that the listener might be tranquillized by Broderick's measures, functioning, as Tennyson writes, as a "sad mechanic exercise, / Like dull narcotics, numbing pain' (*In Memoriam*, V, ll.7–8). Unlike Tennyson, however, Broderick pushes the drowsy security of his most balmy refrains into an energized if threatening cacophony of converging sounds at the end of this piece and uses this as a way to introduce the fourth and mellifluously lighter "The Dream." While the frightening slicing strings that fill "Awaken / Panic / Restraint" and "Electroconvulsive Shock" throw the patient and listener alike into a harsh and alienating period of aesthetic debilitation, relief is always provided. It is as if we fall through the music attached to a safety belt of rhythm and melodic colloquy until all tension is resolved in the final "The Path to Recovery." While the end of the sequence recalls the antiphonal back and forth of "Patient Observation" and dissolves the tension of the sequence in a tender and steadying triple meter, it does not simply dissolve into resolution. The listener falls through the sequence, not to reach the security of the ground or to be distracted from its moments of dissonant noise, but to bodily enter into sound and remain there, attentive and quiet. The event of hearing oneself sustained in the motion of falling from a tree gives us a template for reading Clare's elegies because it refuses both complacent and despairing emotions. Broderick's music does not map out a course at the end of which the listener is left physically and emotionally fallen. Rather, the score suspends the listener in an experience of auscultation in which that attention to the body's falling allows for an engagement with one's environment based on hearing: the tree becomes, in Jean-Luc Nancy's terms, "rhythmed space" and its arborescent direction a line to be scanned.[12]

If *Music for Falling from Trees* trains the listener how to scan the movement of falling from a tree, Clare's tree elegies teach us how to hear the falling of trees. Both Broderick and Clare evoke an aural falling experience as a way to imagine separation, the former from the self, the latter from the landscape. Just as the listener of Broderick's sequence is dropped down through the music as a way of accessing the patient's anxieties, so the reader of Clare's elegies is plunged prosodically through the poem to encourage an empathy with those stricken by enclosure. Clare creates an arborescent poetics to find a way through the distress of enclosure, one that connected him back to the landscape while also granting him well-being. The arborescent rhythm that heals and stabilizes Broderick's sick and hospitalized patient offers elegiac relief to Clare's narrator, easing feelings of uprootedness through a tree-like stability of form. Such stability was paramount for Clare, his sense of well-being dependent on feelings of home and familiarity rooted in a landscape devastated by enclosure. The historical impact of enclosure on Clare has been widely commented on, most notably by Jonathan Bate and John Barrell.[13] Our project, however, explores how Clare works through the suffering caused by enclosure by sustaining a listening experience as a practice of care equivalent to Heidegger's *sorgen*, one that substitutes the negligent violence imposed by mass tree felling.[14] Clare felt the brutality of tree clearing not just through the economic and social changes forced on his fellow smallholders and now landless labourers: he also mourned the loss of specific trees as intimate friends. Writing in his *Journal* in 1824, Clare describes his reaction to the removal of "an old woodstile taken away from a favourite spot which it had occupied all my life . . . it hurt me to see it was gone for my affections claim a friendship with such things but nothing is lasting in this world last year Langly bush was destroyd an old white thorn that had stood for more than a century full of fame."[15] Clare's corresponding tree elegy, "Langley Bush," appears as a stump of growth on the page, its twenty unpunctuated lines a degraded representation of its now damaged form. But while the remains of the trunk "mullder[s]" and rots (l.16), the poem's softly balladic *abab* rhyme transforms the verse from being a simple memorial to a once admired whitethorn and into a paean praising the "sacred shade" (l.1) of its leaves and "boughs" (l.7), the reverence it inspired in even "lawless gipseys" (ll.9–10), and the "love" (l.13) it provoked in the "withering age" (l.12) of enclosure.

We hear solace rather than find it in "Langley Bush," as Clare's stress on the tree's affective capacities is communicated through the cheerful and assured rhymes—shade/made, me/see, knew/true, alows [sic]/boughs—that ring through the poem. Clare similarly points to rhyme's redemptive faculty in a short essay called "The Woodman or the Beauties of a Winter Forest" (c.1820), in which he tracks the journey of a woodman over a "frosty plain," past "His favourite tree" and "shuffling" through snow and ice, but always with a "heart-felt glee."[16] The woodman institutes this positive affect, Clare writes, by cheering his way with a song that makes "the rhymy-feather'd thickets resond [sic] in rural melody."[17] Embraced by the natural world, the woodman hears, rather than sees, the detail of its beauty:

> [H]e pursues his journey over many new made hills and valleys of new fallen snow with 'heart-felt glee' cheering the rugged way with the oft-repeated scrap of an harmless old song making the rhymy-feather'd

> thickets resond in rural melody . . . O'er his head the hugh rugged oaks stretch forth their spreading grains crouching closely together in romantic arches—On every side the feather'd rhyme lodges on the smallest twig and shines in all the variety of forms which Imagination can suggest or the fairy visions of playful fancy picture to his view—the green moss spreads on every [*del* stone] stovin nay it flourishes to adorn the bank and decorate the ground[18]

The passage vividly reveals Clare's emotional affinity with local wildlife and places of natural beauty, documenting as it does his investment in habitual encounters with beloved geographical spots. Clare finds in the Woodsman's view of forest trees a level of aesthetic detail that resonates as both a poetic technique and an affective listening experience. Twice he describes the trees as possessing "rhymy feathers" or "feather'd rhymes," an observation that is both sensitive and anatomically accurate in its representation of tree-like shapes and sounds. "Feather'd rhymes" directly marries the visual and aural to make a space for a poetics that mimics organic shapes: the base trunk of a tree "feathers" off into branches and shoots that are at once different from one another yet share a similarity, each branch "rhyming" with the next as it provides a variation on the initial taproot and foundational trunk of the tree. A poem similarly uses the frame of a structured meter and rhyme scheme to branch out into new rhymes: it "feathers" and turns on a prosodic foundation that roots its embellishments and cadences. The trees in this excerpt provide, not just a poetic method for Clare but also a positive experience of "imagination" and "fancy," states of poetic inclination that permit the woodsman to imbue the very landscape with well-being: even the moss "flourishes" under this enchanting affect while the landscape "resond[s] in rural melody."

We hear this "rural melody" as a form of elegy in two further poems by Clare: "The Mores" and "To a Fallen Elm" both decry enclosure as an experience of suffering and imprisonment, but one that Clare is able to control and transform through poetic form. His choice of formal devices reveals a poet who uses prosody to navigate his own personal distress while at once working to produce the poem as a communal, empathetic space of well-being for his readers. The tree-like qualities of each poem guide readers but do not "enclose" them: rhymes and emotions alike go budding and branching down in a movement that generates an experience of *eudaimonic* falling for those who hear and read them.

"The Mores" is one of Clare's most powerful critiques of enclosure, articulating as it does a broad attack on its effect upon the landscape and those who seek an emotional connection with it. It is a poem that speaks of personal hurt while also opening out to communal feeling, a simultaneously private and open mode of writing that enables an arborescent way of being. Thematically and formally tight, its rigid visual trunk rooted into the page, "The Mores" is also flexible, its branching lines allowing for reader interpretation and empathetic engagement. Clare's narrator engages a politically radical and emotionally sensitive tone to mourn the loss of the natural world he found so freeing as a child:

> Now this sweet vision of my boyish hours
> Free as spring clouds and wild as summer flowers
> Is faded all—a hope that blossomed free
> And hath been once no more shall ever be
> Inclosure came and trampled on the grave
> Of labours rights and left the poor a slave (ll.15–20)

This comparison between freedom and imprisonment is constant throughout the poem, and it is through the interplay of these two opposing states that Clare creates a poetic form that is measured, but flexible; solid, but pliable. These repeating images of liberation are matched by a relentless, rolling syntax devoid of end-stopped lines or pauses: the brook "dribble(s) on" (l.31), the Moors are "loosing" (l.37), the landscape "lengthens" (l.36), and groups of sheep "unfold" (l.27) in a symbiosis of physical lengthening and deliverance from confinement. Clare seems determined to recapture the uninhibited experience of the natural world that he cherished as a boy: "Unbounded freedom ruled the wandering scene / Nor fence of ownership crept in between" (ll.7–8). In recalling this lost memory, however, he is forced to create his own "fence of ownership" in poetic form. To rekindle emotional well-being and a whole sense of self, Clare must mark out a poetic boundary of his own, one that permits an emotional free-fall guided and tended to by its rhythms.

These rhythms are positioned against what Clare calls the "lawless law" of enclosure, a phrase that captures his sense of the moral as well as environmental failure inherent to tree felling. Yet his arborescent prosody works as a counter to this emotional hurt, an aesthetic "lawless law" that is constantly blooming and flourishing with rhythms that pull the reader into the poem and invite him or her into affective experience. This experience is one of aural and visual "falling": the lack of punctuation causes the lines to "fall" on top of one another and cascade downward, piling into a long column of unchecked sentences. This somewhat rhapsodic style reads, at a glance, very quickly, the reader tumbled down constant images of free movement: the dribbling brook, the sweeping plover, the singing lark, wandering sheep. Yet the form is also a visually solid structure, as each line of the poem acts as a ring or layer of a tree trunk, all composite parts of a pillar of stability. There is comfort in this strong, hardy presence on the page. Clare's investment in vertical, arborescent images is an antidote to enclosure's horizontal partitioning of the land. "The Mores" is full of recurring references to blocked pathways and hindered progression, fence meeting "fence in owners little bounds" (l.47), garden grounds shrunk into "little parcels" (l.49), and "stopt" paths (l.65) appearing everywhere "cowslaps" and "daisys" and "corn fields" (ll.59–61) once grew:

> Each little tyrant with his little sign
> Shows where man claims earth glows no more divine
> On paths to freedom and to childhood dear
> A board sticks up to notice 'no road here' (ll.67–70)

Clare retaliates against this restricting maze of horizontal pathways with the vertical, arborescent form of his verse. Viewed in this way, each sentence reads like a pathway, a rhizome even, that is assimilated into a new thriving structure that moves downward, rooted into the page and allowing each line to consequently sway and flourish. This flourishing is permitted rhythmically, as the iambic pentameter inherent to the prosodic workings of the poem keeps the reader in check. The meter, with its level stresses, stops readers from "falling" completely through this poetic landscape, allowing them to rest for a moment on each branch-like line until the meter gently pushes them down onto the next. This movement is itself underpinned by the unbroken stability of the moors, that which Clare calls a "level scene . . . that never felt the rage of blundering plough" (ll.1–3). This rhythmic stability manifests itself aesthetically throughout "The Mores," arborescence being continually revealed in its poetic structure and prosody. However, where "The Mores" enables a prosodic comfort, "To a Fallen Elm" manifests arborescence as friendship, the elm embracing the narrator, and the listener, amidst its branching frame.

Clare's "To a Fallen Elm" is a direct address to the elm as a companion, an approach that allows the narrator to engage aurally with the tree's form, structure, and sound. Clare constructs and imagines a *eudaimonic* way of being as one of sound and rhythm modeled on "thy music making Elm" (l.65) that continues to sing in the space of the poem even after it is felled. "To a Fallen Elm" is a more personal elegy than the directly political "The Mores": the narrator, for example, calls out to the tree as a familiar and domesticated member of his family and home and suffers the subsequent grief when the tree is felled by the enforcement of enclosure boundaries. The elm is more than just a homely landmark, however. It is a source of buoyant companionship for Clare, a "friend not inanimate" that plays an active role in his emotional well-being:

> Friend not inanimate—tho stocks and stones
> There are and many clothed in flesh and bones
> Thou ownd a language by which hearts are stirred
> Deeper than by the attribute of words
> Thine spoke a feeling known in every tongue
> Language of pity and the force of wrong (ll.29–34)

In these lines Clare lays bare how he and the tree exist in an affective relationship. This relational mode is aural, a special kind of "language" that ties Clare and the tree into a qualitative "feeling" that "stirs" and comforts those who experience it. It is how Clare depicts this "language"—"deeper than by the attribute of words"—that frames it as a bodily sensation, a way of communicating with the world and those emotions that can be felt and measured. We suggest that this "language" is rhythm, one that resonates out from the sounds emitted from the tree and into a pattern of being that secures feelings of stability and joy.

Just as the arborescent prosody of "The Mores" guides the reader through the poem, so do the rhythms of the tree guide Clare into moments of calm and respite from emotional suffering. Indeed, from the opening lines, the "Old Elm" is bestowed with an aural affective quality: Clare celebrates the sounds of the tree blowing around the chimney top as "the sweetest anthem autumn ever made" (ll.1–2), his use of the word "anthem" signifying the sound's rousing and emotionally stirring element. He develops this "anthem" into a specifically arborescent rhythmic sound that is at once stabilizing and restorative:

Old Elm that murmured in our chimney top
The sweetest anthem autumn ever made
And into mellow whispering calms would drop
When showers fell on thy many colored shade
And when dark tempests mimic thunder made
While darkness came as it would strangle light
With the black tempest of a winter night
That rocked thee like a cradle to thy root
How did I love to hear the winds upbraid
Thy strength without while all within was mute
It seasoned comfort to our hearts desire
We felt thy kind protection like a friend
And pitched our chairs up closer to the fire
Enjoying comforts that was never penned (ll.1–14)

In this passage, the elm is a reassuring presence, a constant to rely and focus upon as a compass to navigate fear and trauma. Although the elm is constant here, it is not static: Clare stresses that the tree is "not inanimate" but rhythmic and communicative. Even when subjected to the harsh elements of wind and rain, the elm is still able to "whisper" to those sheltering at home, sending soothing instants of sound to those who patiently listen inside. Yet it is the physical movements of the tree that tie it so deeply to the model of arborescent prosody we have established in our reading of both Broderick's sequence and "The Mores." As it "rock[s]" those who listen to it "like a cradle to thy root" (l.8), the elm moves back and forth in a motion that is stabilized by its tree form, firmly rooted into the ground like the prosody of "The Mores" and the tonal centres of *Music for Falling from Trees*. The elm sways in a gesture of security, producing comforting sounds while simultaneously remaining fixed and steadfast. Clare is now able to engage with the sounds of trees in a manner analogous to the listener of "The Mores" and Broderick's score: the reader of "To a Fallen Elm" must thus listen to Clare listening. We hear Clare guided through the tree's comforting creaks and waves, "dropped" through its "whispering calms" in a controlled and measured way.

The tree becomes a poem for Clare, then, pulling him rhythmically into its structure in order to soothe him back to a state of well-being: "It seasoned comfort to our hearts desire" (l.11). While the poem is written from hindsight to a tree that is "fallen," we as readers receive the tree in a continual process of falling: we are guided through and protected from the sporadic and painful "ruin" (l.65) to which the elm is subjected in a rhythmic state of control and measurement. This is apparent in the running pace of the poem's rapid prosody, one that builds through repeated and constant references to images and sounds, but that is tempered by natural pauses. The opening description of the storm, for example, with its dark tempests, strangled light, and upbraiding winds is gentled by the line "rocked thee like a cradle to thy root," one that is lulling in both connotation and also prosody. As the line eases this frenetic scene it also draws the listener into a state of reflection in the ensuing rhythmic lines: "How did I love to hear the winds upbraid / Thy strength without while all within was mute" (ll.9–10). The quiet fortitude of the elm's boughs and branches, underneath which children play (l.23) and birds sing (l.25), produces a "happiness" (l.27) in Clare, one that might be materially undermined by the elm's falling but is emotionally secured in the listener's experience of such movement. The poem's insistence on enclosure's ravaging cruelty is sharply clear—laborers cheated, cottages devastated, rabbits dislodged from their dens, and cows driven away from their habitats: "No matter—wrong was right and right was wrong / And freedoms brawl was sanction to the song" (ll.63–64). Yet this "song" is immediately countered by the following invocation of the tree as Clare's "music making Elm" (l.65): that music is what we as listeners are left with even amid the glutting tyranny (ll.70–71) of felling. While the final lines of the poem are preoccupied with this tyranny, it is the pentameter and linked rhymes ("laws," "powers," "maws," "devours") that the listener is left with, a *eudaimonic* metrics that deafens us to the barking axe (ll.49–50) Clare finds so hateful. Like Broderick, Clare finds well-being in sound, and by describing those experiences he finds most painful in a form that offers aesthetic pleasure, he is able to formulate and bestow an arborescent prosody that is repeatedly and rhythmically curative.

## BIBLIOGRAPHY

Barrell, John. *The Idea of Landscape and the Sense of Place 1730-1840: An Approach to the Poetry of John Clare*. New York and London: Cambridge University Press, 1972.

Bate, Jonathan. *John Clare: A Biography*. London: Picador, 2003.

Broderick, Peter. *Music For Falling from Trees*. Erased Tapes, 2009.

Clare, John. "John Clare's Journal." *John Clare By Himself*. Edited by Eric Robinson and David Powell. Manchester: Carcanet, 1996.

———. *John Clare: A Critical Edition of the Major Works*. Edited by Eric Robinson and David Powell. Oxford: Oxford University Press, 1984.

———. "The Woodman or the Beauties of a Winter Forest." *The Natural History Prose Writings 1793-1864*, edited by Margaret Grainger, 1–9. Oxford: Clarendon Press, 1984.

Deleuze, Gilles and Felix Guattari. *A Thousand Plateaus: Capitalism and Schizophrenia*. London: Athlone Press, 1980.

Heidegger, Martin. *A History of the Concept of Time*. Translated by Theodore Kisiel. Indiana: Indiana University Press, 1992.

Martin, Meredith and Yisrael Levin. "Victorian Prosody: Measuring the Field." *Victorian Poetry* 49, no. 2 (2011): 149–60.

Nancy, Jean-Luc. *Listening*. Translated by Charlotte Mandell. New York: Fordham University Press, 2007.

North American Association for the Study of Romanticism (NASSR) listserv, 'Lamia' thread, March 16, 2011–March 23, 2011. http://listserv.wvu.edu/cgi- bin/wa?A0=NASSR-L Web.

## NOTES

1. North American Society for the Study of Romanticism (NASSR) listserv, 'Lamia' thread, March 16, 2011–March 23, 2011. Web accessed June15, 2011. http://listserv.wvu.edu/cgi-bin/wa?A0=NASSR-L.

2. Meredith Martin and Yisrael Levin, "Victorian Prosody: Measuring the Field," *Victorian Poetry*, 49.2 (2011): 149–60 (150).

3. Gilles Deleuze and Felix Guattari, *A Thousand Plateaus: Capitalism and Schizophrenia* (London: Athlone Press, 1980), 9.

4. Deleuze and Guattari, *Thousand Plateaus*, 18.

5. Deleuze and Guattari, *Thousand Plateaus*, 17, 19.

6. Deleuze and Guattari, *Thousand Plateaus*, 8.

7. Deleuze and Guattari, *Thousand Plateaus*, 25.

8. Deleuze and Guattari, *Thousand Plateaus*, 25.

9. Deleuze and Guattari, *Thousand Plateaus*, 15.

10. Deleuze and Guattari, *Thousand Plateaus*, 25; we accept that certain forms of psychological health, most notably Jungian multiplicity, can be fast moving by comparison with the fragmentation and multiplicity associated with conditions such as PTSD.

11. Deleuze and Guattari, *Thousand Plateaus*, 11–12.

12. Jean-Luc Nancy, *Listening*, trans. Charlotte Mandell (New York: Fordham University Press, 2007), 39; by *auscultation* we refer to the diagnostic process of listening to the sound of internal organs through a stethoscope.

13. See John Barrell, *The Idea of Landscape and the Sense of Place 1730-1840: An Approach to the Poetry of John Clare* (New York and London: Cambridge University Press, 1972); and Jonathan Bate, *John Clare: A Biography* (London: Picador, 2003).

14. See Martin Heidegger, *A History of the Concept of Time*, trans. Theodore Kisiel (Indiana: Indiana University Press, 1992).

15. John Clare, "John Clare's Journal." In *John Clare By Himself*, edited by Eric Robinson and David Powell, 179 (Manchester: Carcanet, 1996).
16. Clare, "John Clare's Journal," 4.
17. Clare, "John Clare's Journal," 5.
18. Clare, "John Clare's Journal," 5.

# FOUR

# Happiness, Catharsis, and the Literary Cure

John Channing Briggs

Studies of the origins, functions, and significance of human flourishing are eventually confronted with the question of whether some kind of catharsis—involving pain, pleasure, or both—is necessary for that flourishing to take place. Without attempting to resolve the questions of whether happiness is a legitimate goal of human existence or whether we must all eventually endure Job-like lives or some mixture of both conditions, ancient questions persist: Must we undergo some form of catharsis for the sake of achieving what happiness is available to us? If so, what does literary catharsis offer us in that process? How deeply can certain literary experiences of suffering, release, and enlightenment be involved in the pursuit of happiness and the full exercise of the best of human qualities commonly associated with human flourishing? In what way do they fulfill that function, particularly when we turn our attention to the cathartic powers of great literature—the kind of literature we keep, perhaps for these reasons? How might the moving tensions and resolutions of literary catharsis influence human flourishing? Interest in the curative effects of literary catharsis—especially their importance for the flourishing of the *polis* and its inhabitants—is at least as old as Aristotle's employment of the word *catharsis* in the *Poetics* and the *Politics*.[1] The son of a physician, he characterized the effects (or some would say, the literary dynamics) of the phenomenon as a repeated, individual, and collective participation in what is more or less analogous to a medical cure of purgation (or as some would say purification) of fear and pity. The means of that release, the nature of what is released, and indeed the meaning of catharsis itself—including its end, value, site of action, and its relation to psychological, emotional, moral, physical, intellectual, and religious well-being—have been the stuff of recurrent controversy and reactive neglect for two thousand years. Is it possible to understand literary catharsis more clearly now in the light of a renewal of interest among students of literature in the basis of human flourishing?

The new academic fascination with happiness and human flourishing emerges from an era in which literary catharsis was relatively neglected. Even though audience response and various hypotheses about catharsis were a subject of importance among the New Critics and others writing just after World War II, catharsis has attracted comparatively little attention where we would expect it most: in English departments. In the theory-driven or activist interpretation that has dominated the academy for the last generation, attention has been turned elsewhere. Meanwhile, in other academic fields the topic, if not always the term, continues to attract interest. Beyond the academy we have seen rising interest in cathartic therapy, and at least fifty years of massive participation in various activities that are undeniably if vaguely or diffusely cathartic: long-march demonstrations, arduous and ecstatic musical festivals, therapeutic boot camps, secular and religious pilgrimages, extreme athletic ordeals, unending presidential campaigns, and daring political-religious vigils that might best be understood as contests of endurance for distinguishing sincerity from hypocrisy. This is not to mention the prevalence of theatrical experiences on film and stage that habitually or self-consciously cultivate (or manipulate) responses of pity and fear, indulgence and shock, sometimes expertly and other times creating indifference or exhaustion, both moral and somatic.[2] What can a new look at an old question about catharsis—asking whether there are demanding, curative, and enlightening forms of literary catharsis—offer us under these conditions?

## I

The idea that catharsis, including literary catharsis, is a type of cure that promotes human flourishing is not useful unless we get down to cases. But the cases, especially those outside of literary environs, are not all that clear. The traditional religious idea of the cure of souls, for the sake of which many Christian priests of judgment and mercy have been called curates, is fraught with controversy. Does the change come from within or without? If from both, what preparations and motions, if any, are appropriate or justified? Is it a process of pain or pleasure, or are these categories beside the point? How does one know a religious cure has taken place? Psychological cures, likewise, take a host of forms, devote themselves to different aspects of the mind and body, and despite apparent successes are frequently deemed ephemeral or false. So too, is the longstanding ubiquity of the placebo and the drama accompanying and perhaps bringing about its cures in medical practice. Successful placebo treatment does not guarantee legitimacy in the medicine chest. While placebos' minimal side effects and cost have helped make them an intriguing subject of medical research (see below), the notion that placebos can be incorporated into standard medical practice raises fundamental questions for investigators about whether they and those who skillfully administer them adhere to science or perform licensed quackery. Forms of catharsis also attract large audiences to violent and erotic films, promoted by the assumption that the vicarious pleasure of witnessing the release of passions is merely entertaining or perhaps curative of repressed emotions. Meanwhile, parents' groups and some scholars energetically condemn all such cathartic displays as incitements to excess. How might a renewed inquiry into literary catharsis and its connection to human flourishing reopen these almost automatically divisive issues without pretentious elevation to a study of the mysteries of religious conversion, or without being reduced to a study of recreational therapy, psychological manipulation, or what Hollywood calls "sensational releases"?

The modern medical discussion of placebos is paradoxically full of suggestive observations about the nature of drama and literary catharsis, their characteristic attributes and their potentially deleterious or curative effects. First, placebos are known to cure, in some circumstances, for reasons more related to drama than connected to ordinary biological processes, sophisticated technologies of medical intervention, or even our notion that alleviating distress is good for health. The successful administration of placebos has been, of necessity, to some degree deceptive. From the traditional medical perspective, the physician puts on a show, providing a treatment that conceals from the patient that the treatment is a pleasing vacuity. Other researchers see a deeper level of curative action. Writing in a recent issue of *Philosophical Transactions of the Royal Society*, an issue dedicated to placebo research, Irving Kirsch describes a new and successful treatment designed to overcome this paradox, one that retains the qualities of traditional placebo treatments while rendering them more artfully, in a more convincing way. The new experimental treatment takes advantage of physicians' and patients' remarkably persistent confidence in certain placebo effects with a set of quasi-theatrical strategies such as indirection, distance, identification, and anticipation. The narrative detail of the passage is worth quoting at length:

> The biggest barrier to the use of placebos in clinical practice is the almost universal perception that for a placebo to be effective it must be administered deceptively. Since expectancies appear to play a major role in placebo responding, informing people accurately that they are being given a placebo should prevent it from being effective. There is a way around this, however. If a convincing rationale can be presented,

> perhaps placebos can be prescribed openly without deception. Recently, my colleagues and I developed and tested such a rationale. We told patients suffering from irritable bowel syndrome (IBS) that placebos have been shown to be effective for their condition, that their effects are induced at least in part by a well-known mechanism (that of classical conditioning), and that for that reason, the act of taking a placebo pill could work as a new mind–body treatment that could reduce IBS symptoms. We found that the patients in our study accepted this rationale, took their placebo pills as prescribed (two pills twice a day), and got better in comparison with patients in a control group that were not given the placebo pills. The effect was as large as that produced by commonly prescribed medication for IBS. Furthermore, it could not be completely accounted for by the therapeutic relationship, because time and attention were held constant across the two groups.[3]

Administered in the right manner under the right circumstances, certain placebos, like literary effects in tragic drama, for example, seem to work in ways that rival or surpass conventional alternatives. Sheer deception—secret administration of the placebo without patients' knowledge they are receiving any sort of treatment—is worthless. Treatment without requiring a relatively challenging regime of placebo medicine is also relatively ineffective. So is administration without attending to patients' expectations of meaningful treatment from a truthful and sympathetic physician. Here the patients are "let in on" the inner workings of the placebo cure: they are told it is a "well-known mechanism." The more complete explanation, in parentheses, is presumably not fully known to the patient, and is circular: that the mechanism is the "social conditioning" of placebo administrations, which generally have positive effects. Yet the explanation is convincing to the degree that the patients embrace the indirect yet veracious first part of the explanation and to the extent that they see it conveyed under fruitful circumstances: by a professionally distanced yet caring physician in a manner that responds credibly to their anticipation of meaningful treatment. The analogies one might draw between this phenomenon and a theatrical performance—one the audience looks forward to as a release or abreactive diversion—are many.

A relatively arduous placebo treatment is apparently more effective than one that makes no demands. When patients are told they are being treated with a neutral substance or a procedure with unproven effects, the most marked results occur when they undergo "physical placebo interventions" such as "sham acupuncture" that imitate surgery or inoculation.[4] The expectation of suffering and risk taking under the close care of a physician can have detectable benefits that seem greater than those of other placebo treatments.[5] Successful placebo treatments pay attention to patients' anticipations—their desire for healthful release and their often-inarticulate fears and understandings of their condition. Significant placebo responses occur, according to Colloca and Miller, when "'the meaning of the illness experience for the patient is altered in a positive direction,' and the factors that contribute to that positive change in the mind-body unit are essentially the patient's awareness of being listened to and attended by the caregiver." Care and understanding are needed together when health and life are in question. Their combined support is supposed to provide a sense of "mastery and control over the illness," so much so that the placebo response might be understood more accurately as a "'meaning response.'"[6] The cure is somatic as well as psychological: the skillful physician, Colloca and Miller argue, engages a bodily expectancy—a responsive predisposition for health. There is at least a partial identification with the "presence of the clinician—the way he or she relates to the patient through sight, speech, body language, and touch" as the bearer of the cure that is also working within.[7] What they call the paradigmatic "good doctor" accesses the patient's inner resources, encouraging hope to the extent that she sympathizes "with" rather than "next to" the patient. When that communication has to do with "shared meanings," the affordances of healing that flow from fulfillment of those expectancies results in a "meaning response" that can produce "a huge difference for patients in the objective and subjective dimensions of their illness."[8] To read these prominently published arguments for the credibility of placebo cures is to note a shift in some researchers' understanding of the field. Another investigator, Oron Frenkel, argues that a wide range of curative effects might be brought about by a bodily expectancy or physiological avidity for health. He hypothesizes that that capacity responds to other health-conducive actions by the body and the physician that operate below consciousness and above the level of reflexes. Such expectancies embody and express, Frenkel contends, what Merleau-Ponty has called "motor intentionality."[9] They are mind-body complexes whose actions tell us about what it means to be embodied beings, activated here during the ordeal of illness. They operate in a manner beyond mere somatic response because they are an "absorbed coping" (67).[10] Meissner joins Frenkel, Colloca, and Miller by calling these strange yet common ameliorations of disease "affordances." When they activate, they bring about changes in blood pressure and other somatic functions below the level of "conscious representations." At the same time, they go beyond conventional understandings of how the body works because they somehow move within "'lived experience'" as the body-mind anticipates and responds to the effects of curative treatments.[11] Disrupted by illness, such expectations are in the process of losing, yet working to restore, their ability to "aim at" recovery.[12] It is difficult to conceive of such activity without positing some sort of activity appropriate to an audience caught up in a curative, moving drama: a body-mind reaching toward health, an incipient recognition of what once was and what might be brought back into existence.

We know that under certain conditions the brain chemistry of Parkinson's patients changes as a result of an administration of a placebo drug when the patients are admitted into a clinical trial.[13] Being invited into that ordeal of experimentation indicates that they are *worthy of undergoing* a medical trial, and that they are candidates for some form of alleviation of their all-too-mortal condition. They are invited to envision their at least partial recovery by means of an ordeal. It is as though the idea of health (not of disease) that Aristotle understood to be the guide of the true physician were to return as the body's ability to maintain—or, in the absence health, to at least remember—the power and true nature of health. The new placebo literature suggests that successful treatment for conditions beyond the reach of surgery and conventional drugs must involve an ordeal, and that the mind-body desire for health and the necessity of the ordeal require dramas and rituals of curing that ultimately include both patient and physician. It appears that in order for medicinal gestures to effectively engage, over time, patients' capacity to enlarge themselves—free themselves—from what often seems to be the overriding power of illness, the physician must somehow credibly participate in and influence the ordeals of hope brought on by illness. There are certainly circumstances in which the patient and good physician have the opportunity to participate in mutual dramas of hope and understanding in the face of death. Some would say the effects of that relationship might hold whether the prognosis was for recovery or impending death. In both cases the power of the illness would be broken.

## II

We see the pertinence of these observations about curative medical dramas in a much more charged setting: the use of classical literature in the treatment of veterans suffering from posttraumatic stress disorder (PTSD). Of course, the general idea of providing cathartic therapy to soldiers is not new. In the modern era, psychological therapy using catharsis was attempted as early as the Second World War, perhaps earlier. A remarkably large number of motion pictures from the nineteen forties and fifties, including the best of the fifties westerns on screen (e.g., those featuring Jimmy Stewart) and on television (e.g., the first two years of *Rawhide*), include ingenious and sometimes moving demonstrations of attention to the returning veteran's need for some form of curative ordeal and release in a peacetime world. So too in the ancient world of warring Greek city states, Sophocles and other playwrights often created dramas that engage those soldiers' internal conflicts and aspirations in the context of the political, ethical, and religious values of the polis.

As the deleterious effects of PTSD on human flourishing have become a renewed cause of concern, Homer and the ancient Greek dramatists have been rediscovered as sites of cathartic action for men and women embattled in internal conflicts long after they have returned home. Each work offers an occasion for an imaginative reengagement of episodes and patterns of experience that have built up corrosive reservoirs—particularly of somatic and moral shock and grief—that are resistant to normal personal adjustments and conventional therapy. Although it is not possible to delineate with scientific assurance the mechanisms by which these works achieve catharsis, or to ascribe certain success to specific experiences of the drama, it is worth hypothesizing the action of at least five literary devices which, in their interaction, are among the most effective contributors to the cathartic effect. These five, and no doubt others, work together in an expert poet's hands to displace and yet somehow open and work upon the sources of deep trauma. They seem (1) to provide a means to elicit the audience's *wonder* at strange stories that (2) despite and because of those stories' *distance*, awaken a desire for (3) *identification*, and (4) a consequent *release or overcoming* of resistance when an analogous trauma is (5) *endured, undergone, and seen in a new light.* The claim here worth making is that once stirred to take on the experience by these means, a resistant yet searching audience is more likely to undergo—and see more in—the curative ordeal.[14] The Philoctetes Project, a theater organization named after Sophocles's play about the agony of stigma suffered by a guiltless soldier-archer disabled by a snakebite and abandoned as unclean by the Greek army on its way to Troy, performs the play in settings that stimulate recuperative, therapeutic discussion.[15] The theater group also performs Sophocles's *Ajax*, about a guileless, faithful warrior who goes berserk when he sees himself dishonored in the awarding of Achilles's armor to his wily rival, Odysseus. A number of factors partly displace and yet strangely identify these actions with the modern agony of many returning soldiers' lives. Not only do time, historical/mythological context, and mode of warfare obviously separate Philoctetes and Ajax from their modern counterparts; so does the surprising public, ritualized license the playwrights give to the frankness and vehemence of the wronged soldier, who in each case takes center stage. And yet these devices, in the way they are rendered in these intriguing plots, are conducive to forms of wonder. They also apparently open the way to meaningful identification with the suffering Greek heroes. A brief summary of the plot alone seems to evoke some of the effect of the drama. In it we witness the agony and triumph of Philoctetes ten years after his abandonment, when his fellow Greeks determine that they need his bow to win the war, return to his island of exile to request it, and through a series of dramatic turns and speeches, determine that their deception of Philoctetes must give way, with the help of a god, to their acknowledgement of the army's need for the warrior they shunned. He must return with his bow to Troy. The story of Ajax is less appealing to the audience looking for a happy ending but is perhaps more probing in its treatment of a supremely courageous, honor-driven soldier whose vengeful loss of control upon a point of honor endangers his fellow soldiers. Again, there is a concentration of attention upon the aggrieved warrior's outrage, including, from the beginning of the play, a concentration on Ajax's horrified shame over the results of his anger after he threatens and curses his commanders and Athena maddens him. He has wildly and disgracefully avenged himself upon a herd of sheep. Recognizing what he has done in his imperfection, the hero comes to his senses and, as we gradually realize from the unfolding of his thoughts, dedicates himself with lucid, self-reflective resolution to an honorable death by his own hand. One need not accept this final resolve as a model for imitation. In fact what we witness far more prominently is Ajax's flawed, insightful articulation of his doubly dishonored condition and his desire to act justly. This doubly articulate gesture presents to his sympathetic witnesses with a moving inoculation against self-undoing rage. Jonathan Shay's widely noticed account of his experience reading and discussing Homer with groups of veterans, based on decades of experience, follows a similar pattern. His therapeutic practice and his books (*Achilles in Vietnam* and *Odysseus in America*) have been endorsed by high members of some of the armed services. In that practice, the *Iliad*'s central story of Achilles is an epic drama not only with regard to the many causes and disastrous consequences of a great soldier's misdirected grief and moral outrage but also as an impressive enactment of the Homeric poetry's ancient care for opening channels of grief. In the process, as readers of Homer remember, the epic engages the consequences of irresponsible command: Agamemnon's disrespectful mishandling of his subordinates' attachment to honor. Conversely, the story of Odysseus is an opportunity to reexperience, in curative form, the ordeal of a heroic veteran's return to a world that does not easily welcome him, and for which he cannot easily prepare himself. In both cases, Shay rediscovers with his audience an ancient function of the Homeric poems as cathartic engagements of the losses and darkly freighted glories of war.

By these means and others, Shay's modern audiences are challenged and invited to enter or reenter a particular experience of ancient battle trauma remote to their circumstances and understanding, yet strangely close to deep sources of what Shay in *Achilles in Vietnam* has argued are the roots of PTSD. Protectively and yet insistently, the plays and the epic poetry seem to speak to—and draw out—blocked or inhibited sensibilities and imaginations. Deepened by the "brother witnessing" of fellow veterans, the workings of these dramas also create a space for noncombatants to feelingly witness, as did ancient audiences, the veterans' return.[16]

## III

In his interpretation of the drama of Oedipus set out in *The Interpretation of Dreams*, Freud argues that Sophocles's treatment of that legend of the ill-fated king is valuable precisely because it is a "moving" imitation of psychoanalysis. In order to free Thebes from its mysterious curse, Oedipus struggles to remember and comprehend the cause, which increasingly centers upon his memory and his power to recognize what is perhaps unbearable in his own history. The fictional drama enacts and draws us in to reenact the process of a kind of psychoanalytic cure by undergoing—in an artfully heightened and mitigated form—a heroic, trauma-doubling event. Given the resistance of the psyche to face the knotted conflicts that block the way to a cure, psychoanalytic inquiry resembles the playwright's. In the case of *Oedipus Rex*, Freud praises the "cunning" twists and turns of the king's inquiry and the dramatist's handling of it. The unfolding story half reveals—and yet leads to deeper layers of—the vexed history of the hero's life.[17] In this movement, Sophoclean drama and psychoanalysis not only share a clinical history[18] they also reflect upon and illuminate one another. We witness Oedipus gradually recognizing—and *resisting* recognition of—key events in his past as he dares, admirably and dangerously, to thread his way to the truth that will break the curse of Thebes's disease. With the chorus, we draw near to that struggle, and in responding with awe and pathos to the agon of the king we witness how it shadows—displaces and yet draws into view—something awful and deeply impressive about the heroic, self-undoing qualities of a great man in extremis. For Freud, healthy psyches need such psychoanalytic dramas precisely because they are falsely convinced of their healthiness in an environment of enforced repression. In the psychoanalytic frame, they risk illness if they do not themselves repeatedly undergo a type of Sophoclean or analytic cure. To do so, they need somehow to identify with what they resist seeing: the sick psyche's experience of descent and reemergence. Oedipus's admirable stature and strange imperfection is a catalyst for the audience's imagining itself in that far worse state, not as tourists but as witnesses and travelers working their way toward a painfully familiar light.

Freud's analysis of the human prospect is famously dour: human beings are bound to deceive themselves. A cure that would make their neuroses at least manageable is often unlikely unless they enter the psychoanalytic agon. But how? To be psychologically healthy under the conditions he describes as typical in the life of the psyche, there must be ways for relatively healthy audiences to strengthen their constitution against their tendency to avoid seeing the causes of their illnesses. The best means for this change, Freud at one point argues, is to witness a sympathetic and admirable protagonist *become* neurotic. Great literature permits and indeed invites this experience without professional deceit.

The psychoanalyst's favorite example of such a sympathetic figure is Hamlet. As in the drama of Oedipus, in the Shakespearean play the distance between audience and the royal protagonist is great, though bridgeable by displacement and identification. The plots of both plays are threaded paths in a minotaur's labyrinth—a trap leading back to a source of distress and, for the hero who threads it, a pathway to freedom. The obscure goal of the adventure is something repressed for which the audience half-consciously yearns. Freud explains the phenomenon somewhat more mechanistically in his essay "Psychopathic Characters on the Stage":

> It appears to be one of the prerequisites of this art form that the struggle of the prepressed impulse to become conscious, recognizable though it is, is so little given a definite name that the process of reaching consciousness goes on in turn within the spectator while his attention is distracted and he is in the grip of his emotions, rather than capable of rational judgments. In this way resistance is definitely reduced, in the manner seen in psychoanalytic treatment, when the derivatives of the repressed ideas and emotions come to consciousness as a result of a lessening of resistance in a manner denied to the repressed material itself.[19]

It is unfortunate, given the suggestiveness of this description, that Freud did not support the idea that catharsis was a viable psychoanalytic treatment. Its effects were transient, and it relied upon irrational responses to a degree that was not compatible with what was for him the indispensably rational work of analysis. His analysis of aesthetic catharsis went unelaborated, overshadowed by another, more mechanical and pessimistic catharsis: the "death-instinct" and the compulsion to repeat. What mattered most was the game, yet ultimately vain, tendency of the psyche to repeat traumatic stimuli in order to imitate and incorporate an entropic tendency toward death. Despite these reservations, however, Freud grants the power of Sophoclean and Shakespearean drama to yield pleasure by means of their revealingly displaced enactments of deep psychological conflicts. What is a grim resistance to death is also in these great works of literature a repetition that activates life-giving resources. The compulsion to repeat in that sense is capable of a measure of success in *getting it right,* not just acceding to grim reality but also returning to the conflicts with renewed if imperfect powers so as to live one's life as well as possible as a mortal human being.[20] The compulsion to repeat might be an expression of that desire for health and a higher, more virtuous level of being.

## IV

Two prominent Elizabethan revenge tragedies—*The Spanish Tragedy* and its surpassing cousin, *Hamlet*—can be read as instructive examples of immersive literary catharsis that result from broadly similar psychological and philosophical currents. Without being reenactments of specific traumas, each one returns circuitously to a set of corrosive personal and political/philosophical conflicts. Their plots displace yet somehow reenact those conflicts for cathartic ends, each complicating and redirecting the protagonist's (and by analogy the audience's) desire for revenge by displacing, releasing, crossing, and tempering it in ordeals of wonder and woe that induce reflection.[21] Despite and because of its peculiar brand of violence and the notorious excesses of its protagonist's vengeful madness, *The Spanish Tragedy* (attributed to Thomas Kyd with possible collaborators in the period 1582–92) is a good example of such a complex cathartic action. Arising out of a long historical period of rivalry, conflict, and diplomatic maneuvering between England and Spain, the play's opening moment mixes the vengeful aftermath of war with hopeful (fictional) negotiations of a marital alliance. In the world of the play the kingdoms in conflict and possibly at peace are Portugal and Spain, a displacement that releases and focuses English attention upon the causes of their enmity and their prospect of reconciliation. The result engages the age's chivalrous tensions *within* war and love and in the conflicts *between* war and love that characterize each kingdom as well as its courtly supporters.

*The Spanish Tragedy* is no sublimely cathartic classical tragedy. It is a messy, intriguing sequence of scenes that compete with one another for cathartic effects, some perverse and others pointing toward higher—more truly courtly—modes of being. Tortuous digression and progress draws audiences into a labyrinth of admirable courtly aspirations that turn into pathologies, then (sometimes) turn back again to higher things. In this pleasingly displaced, tortuous world one moves from hope to shock and sometimes to the recognition that courtly ideals contain the means to elevate as well as destroy themselves. In dramatic fashion, love and honor turn cruelly to lust and vengeance, which become more terrible and fascinating as love and honor reassert themselves. These are actions within the play and, in a mediated sense, within the audience. The cathartic effects of this swing and layering of opposing impressions indulges yet *stimulates and tests* an attentive audience's capacity to flourish. It offers opportunities to glimpse and identify with a more complete kind of virtue amid examples of its own moral disintegration. The play provides the means for audiences to act repeatedly—by their risky openness as well as their preference and power of choice—in accordance with that higher virtue as it rises in the dark or goes into eclipse. Audiences' success in these experienced choices makes for a happiness in themselves, a happiness characteristically induced by lasting literature of this kind. It is a way of human flourishing that is a suffering, aspiring activity. The situation is intriguingly simple, suggestive, fluid, and complex. In Act I, we see that the conclusion of the war has immediately engendered kingly gestures of diplomatic brotherhood even as the ghost of a fallen Spanish soldier plots revenge on his Portuguese nemesis. We see courtly love promising happiness despite the losses of war, then provoking rivalrous hatred. Orderly social ranking enforces the peace and stirs poisonous resentment. After the appearance of the famous soon-to-be-avenger, Hieronimo (it is likely that audiences saw the play repeatedly or at least with knowledge of its notorious outcome), we still encounter good reasons to hope for the allayment of vengeful war through the arts of peace. Horatio, grieving for his friend Andrea, falls in love with Bel-Imperia, who is distraught over the loss of Andrea; for a moment their love promises grief's repair (before she uses that love to take revenge on Andrea's killer, Balthazar). Early on, Hieronimo provides sound counsel about humility to the victorious King of Spain, whom he reminds of English victories over his realm and the need to recognize his own limits. Later, Hieronimo is the appointed judge to determine with careful deliberation the guilt of Lorenzo's murderous agent. He carries out his charge in due process of the law. Even in his grief after Horatio's death Hieronimo approaches the King in an attempt to make vengeance the work of his ruler, not himself. Turned away before he has a chance to speak and after his madness overtakes him, his vengeful plotting is activated by a terrible opportunity to foster reconciliation: he is put in charge of the courtly entertainment supposed to celebrate the two kingdoms' treaty of peace.

The cathartic development of the play consists of an agony of transgressions repeated, and repeatedly averted or momentarily overcome, by courteous gesture. The circumstances of war are repaired amid eruptions of dark desires for personal justice.

A series of malevolent and unlucky subversions break the standoff, leading to the murder of the innocent Horatio and the unleashing of his grief-maddened father as a licensed avenger. When Hieronimo finally clears the stage with secret plots and appalling thoroughness, the slaughter of guilty conspirators, lured to play the part of their own victimhood, yields a type of vengeful satisfaction. Justice, such as it is, has been served. But the scale of the carnage, which includes more deaths of innocents, provokes horror. The urge to see more blood for blood—whether in personal or monarchical blood feuds, rivalry for a woman's favor, or as a result of grieving madness—is exercised, countered, and subdued by this dramatic realization of its ultimate costs. The ghost of Don Andrea, the specter of the aggrieved Spanish soldier we see at the play's beginning, watches over the action in silent anticipation of retribution for his unchivalrous death and his separation from his love Bel-Imperia at the hands of the scheming Portuguese, Balthazar. But before he receives that satisfaction, he must gaze upon the Spanish plotter Lorenzo joining with Andrea's enemy to entrap and kill Don Andrea's friend Horatio over a new rivalry for grieving Bel-Imperia's favor. A faithful servant must die as well, caught up in a web of vengeful purposes. That is not enough. Andrea must see Hieronimo's wife kill herself in grief at the death of her son Horatio, then he must observe how Horatio's father loses his courtly mind, killing Lorenzo in a fiendishly elaborate play that ends with Bel-Imperia taking her own life in a spectacle of woe. The innocent Duke of Castile, father of Lorenzo and Bel-Imperia, must fall as well. Wild justice blights and destroys lives that should not have been caught in revenge. In all these moments we see sentiments of civility raised higher than seems possible, then made monstrous or dashed to ever greater effect, until the final entertainment becomes the victims' imperfectly justified, pitiable, and then shocking encounter with death. The evildoers and an innocent bystander are brought into the drama as actors close to the play's offer of cathartic insight until they are disbelievingly killed. The hanged, still unburied body of Hieronimo's son, cruelly displayed in death by the parent who calls on his ancient right to avenge his son, becomes a stage prop for the father's grim delight in a new tragedy of revenge, in which Horatio's body serves as the play's most convincing and outrageous lure. Hieronimo slays his power to speak of these events when he bites off his tongue.

Whatever our expectation of punishment for the murderers of Horatio, Hieronimo's shocking catastrophe forces attention away from old, conventionally articulable understandings of retributive justice. Notions about the injustices brought on by differences of class—those distinctions that provocatively separate the ambitions of the yeoman-like Andrea and Horatio from the aristocratic station of Bel-Imperia and her resentful brother Lorenzo—seem almost inconsequential when Hieronimo's madness does its work. We might say the same about violations of courtly conduct in war: Are they really the cause of what has happened? Even the secret murder of innocents must take its place in the context of the final spectacle of revenge played to its outer limits. Presiding over the play but never interfering in his action is the ghost Andrea's companion, the figure of Revenge, whom the Queen of the Underworld Proserpine has provided as a companion to the ghost of Andrea. From the beginning, the audience is invited to recognize Andrea's motive for revenge as double, possibly much larger and more diffusely uncontrollable than a particular grievance. Doubled in this way, it is potentially the motiveless motive of Revenge itself, whose merciless power is beyond any man's will to restrain it. The influence of this unlimited Revenge throughout the play, complementary to Andrea's grievance yet forebodingly separate, threatens to flood the drama with a pitiless and baleful—sometimes and to some extent, perhaps, justifiable—energy of retribution that we finally see embodied in Hieronimo. One sympathizes to a degree with the course of the drama, then recoils. The play moves toward a catastrophe that is a form of justice, but one that is beyond human limits and the moral capacity to imitate it. The sympathies and judgments aroused and allayed in the course of that action, some in favor of revenge, are tempered if not rebuked, and when they combine with the sense of shock that accompanies the last act they make that resistance a source of curative power. It is right, it feels right, that we cannot accept the final disembodied judgment of Andrea's ghost and of Revenge that all is well. For all its excesses, *The Spanish Tragedy* remains cathartic in its strangely familiar distance from geopolitical and chivalrous facts, and in the haunting thoroughness with which it provokes reflection and moral choice regarding the attractive, apparently ineradicable, baleful, malleable, partly redeemable, woeful, wonder-provoking motives of revenge.

## V

Shakespeare's *Hamlet* is a revenge tragedy *tour de force*. Its cathartic action relies, as does *The Spanish Tragedy*, on devices of distancing and identification that draw audiences (and characters) into conflicts otherwise inaccessible or unendurable, and then offer ways to bring them out. In *Hamlet* this happens in various cathartic enactments of Hamlet's grieving powerlessness, which wars intermittently with his inchoate conviction that his father has met an unnatural death. Struggling within this turmoil, often pulled from it by events, the protagonist encounters his original dilemma in the form of displaced, cathartic situations and events. The process energizes and tests him, or finds him wanting, as he attempts to recover his princely self. In his flourishing toward tragedy one sees something of his cause in one's own: the awakened aspiration—flawed though it might be—toward human flourishing or happiness that is an activity of one's inner and outer being seeking harmony with a higher end.[22] In this agony of indecision and aspiration, we have ample evidence of Hamlet's energy and decisiveness as he misdirects them in quibbles and distractions. The most dramatic instances are patterns of ordeal and release that open lines of action and reveal truths while compromising his cause and provoking misunderstandings of motive and fact. We witness or hear about his dangerously daring encounter with the revelatory, perhaps misleading ghost; his self-dramatization as he breaks his passion for Ophelia; his recklessly frank yet subtle play-within-the-play to capture Claudius's guilt; his ruthless thrusting through the arras that unfortunately kills the wrong (or is it the right?) man; his tormented and unsleeping discovery of his own death warrant, which he turns against unknowing messengers; his swashbuckling kidnap by the pirates; his perverse and strangely triumphant descent into Ophelia's grave with grieving Laertes; and his acceptance of the fatal duel with Laertes arranged by his now certain enemy, the king. All lead him away from, and toward, a resolution of his quandary that could not have been waited for, or chosen directly, or brought to issue by means of heroic resolve.

The ghost confides in Hamlet and his prophetic ambition without giving him adequate proof that the message is true. Ophelia inspires his disclosure of torments of love and grief that she cannot comprehend or bear to learn, and which he cannot make into a lover's pledge. His presentation of his modified version of the Players' drama, *The Murder of Gonzago*, seems to expose Claudius's guilt while obscuring it in a nephew's murder of his uncle king. Claudius's startled response is not in itself distinguishable (as Horatio's lack of response confirms) from the behavior of a king who has just seen a nephew-sponsored play about a nephew murdering his uncle. Hamlet strikes through the curtain and finds Polonius, Claudius's double, proving his capacity to do the deed in the moment he sees he has been grievously reckless and ineffective. On his way to exile after baiting the king with his play and killing the king's agent, Hamlet opens the seals of Claudius's message to reveal his uncle's deadly intentions—without discovering whether those intentions are connected to King Hamlet's death. When a pirate ship attacks his vessel (as we hear in retrospect in Hamlet's letter to Horatio), the melancholy prince reexperiences the test he faced with the ghost on the parapet. As in the first encounter with the armed figure of King Hamlet, he must grapple with the warlike threat, be taken alone as a prisoner (as he was alone with the ghost, next to the abyss), and find a way to ransom himself (as he was given the charge to revenge his father) for his freedom.

> A pirate of very warlike appointment gave us chase. Finding ourselves too slow of sail, we put on a compelled valour, and in the grapple I boarded them. On the instant they got clear of our ship, so I alone became their prisoner. They have dealt with me like thieves of mercy; but they knew what they did. I am to do a good turn for them.[23]

These arduous and distanced reenactments of prior conflicts mix entrapment with noble bravado, and further confusion with the possibility of insight, even revelation.

Returning to Denmark and aware of the king's intention to take his life, Hamlet permits himself to undergo that threat indirectly in at least three complementary ways: first in the very act of returning to the kingdom that has condemned him to die; second, in the leap he takes—in the mourning presence of the king—into Ophelia's grave with Laertes (who of course is himself contemplating revenge against the killer of his father and sister); and again, in his acceptance of the challenge to fight Laertes in a dangerously appointed duel. Variously in all three, Hamlet enacts his meditation upon Yorick's skull, placing himself— testing himself and his fitness for life on the edge of death—in what might be his own grave. The display of Hamlet's facility in these foreboding scenes marks another characteristic of the play's most cathartic forms of literary catharsis: the protagonist's experiencing (and the audience at a distance experiencing with him) an immensely responsive and heightened sensitivity to the double existence of being a princely, versatile determiner of his fortunes and yet a pawn of events. From moment to moment, Hamlet walks the tightrope assuredly when he is not pausing to find, or lose, his balance over the abyss. The engaged audience develops a sense of exhilaration and care stimulated by these alternations, but there must also be a pressing sense of incompleteness in that participation. Hamlet keeps secrets, and the emotional and intellectual resolution of the play is not in its conclusion, which is markedly unfinished. Hamlet never learns that Claudius killed his father even though he has the mortal satisfaction of seeing the work of his poison in his mother. The price of what he learns is doubled by the death of Laertes, whom he had once sought to make a brother, and the destruction of Denmark's royal house with the accession of the heir of King Hamlet's enemy Norway (by necessity through election, if not by conquest). Even the philosophical Horatio resolves to join the carnage, restrained only by his friend's request that he tell the prince's story, as though the retelling of what is notably incomplete would make all clear. A striking sense of incompleteness persists to the end, whatever satisfaction one draws from Horatio's faithful pledge to tell Hamlet's story. In his forecast of that tale, Hamlet's friend begins the story with a startling lie that is known to the audience and to himself: that Hamlet did not have anything to do with the deaths of Rosencrantz and Guildenstern (V.ii.318). We know as witnesses of all five acts that the rest of the story, once Horatio fulfills his promise to Fortinbras to bring closure to the play's moving yet truncated conclusion, is bound to suffer from further discontinuities, more incompleteness. In a sense, it will be the play we have, the *Hamlet* we are compelled to see again. Why this desire to repeat and reflect and repeat such a perplexing, moving action when the result is incomplete? Is it possible we are drawn back by a yearning to reexperience and transcend our last impressions by dwelling on the possibility of resolution amid such fatally fascinating distractions? Of finding clarifying truths as much as, or more than, cathartic closure? Is the latter process of reflective repetition another, perhaps higher form of catharsis? The mind and sensibility of an engaged audience, one that has witnessed *Hamlet* and returned to it again and again, might best be understood as yearning for something beyond catharsis. Higher virtue? Wisdom? Can we characterize that audience's strange desire to experience suffering and light as the pursuit of a more lasting happiness? Yes, if we return to the play and other great works of literature again and again, in ways that better dispose us to answer and act upon such questions—however imperfectly—in our flawed, persistent capacity to become better versions of ourselves.

## BIBLIOGRAPHY

Aristotle. *Art of Rhetoric*. Loeb Classical Library, 1926.
———. *Nicomachean Ethics*. Loeb Classical Library, 1926.
———. *Poetics*. Loeb Classical Library, 1995.
———. *Politics*. Loeb Classical Library, 1932.
Bowers, Fredson. *Elizabethan Revenge Tragedy*. Princeton: Princeton University Press, 1940.
Brunius, Teddy. "Catharsis." *The Dictionary of the History of Ideas*. Edited by Philip P. Wiener. New York: Charles Scribner and Sons, 1968, 1973.
Dreyfus, H. L. "The Primacy of Phenomenology over Logical Analysis." *Philosophical Topics* 27, no. 2 (2000): 3–24.
Erikson, Erik. *Childhood and Society*. New York: Norton, 1963.
Frenkel, Oron. "A Phenomenology of the 'Placebo Effect': Taking Meaning from the Mind to the Body." *Journal of Medicine and Philosophy* 33 (2008): 58–79.
Freud, Sigmund. The Standard Edition of the Complete Works of Sigmund Freud. Translated by James Strachey. 24 vols. London: Hogarth, 1953–74.
Hiltunen, Ari. *Aristotle in Hollywood: The Anatomy of Successful Storytelling*. Bristol, UK: Intellect Books, 2002.
Kisch, Irving. "Preface." *Philosophical Transactions of the Royal Society* B 366 (2011): 1781–82.
Kyd, Thomas. *The Spanish Tragedy*. Prepared by W. W. Greg and D. Nichol Smith. London: Oxford University Press, 1949.
Luana Colloca and Franklin G. Miller. "Harnessing the Placebo Effect: The Need for Translational Research." *Philosophical Transactions of the Royal Society* 366 (2011): 1922–30.
Meisner, Kim. "The Placebo Effect and the Autonomic Nervous System: Evidence for an Intimate Relationship." *Philosophical Transactions of the Royal Society* B 366 (2010): 1808–17.
Merleau Ponty, M. *Phenomenology of Perception*. Translated by C. Smith. London: Routledge, 1962.
Philoctetes Project. www.philoctetesproject.org.
Portman, John. "Physician Patient Relationship: Like a Marriage Without Romance." *Western Journal of Medicine* 173 (2000). 279–82.
Scheff, T. J. *Catharsis in Healing, Ritual, and Drama*. Berkeley: University of California Press, 1979.
Shakespeare, William. *Hamlet*. In *The Norton Shakespeare*, edited by Stephen Greenblatt, Walter Cohen, Jean Howard, and Katharine Eisaman Maus. New York: W. W. Norton, 1997.
Shay, Jonathan. *Odysseus in America: Combat Trauma and the Trials of Homecoming*. New York: Charles Scribner and Sons, 2002.
———. *Achilles in Vietnam: Combat Trauma and the Undoing of Character*. New York: Charles Scribner and Sons, 1994.
Smith, David H. "Communication as a Reflection of, and a Source for, Values in Health." *Journal of Applied Communication Research* 16 (1988): 29–38.

## NOTES

1. *Poetics* VI.2–3; *Politics* VIII.7. For related passages, see *The Art of Rhetoric* II.5 and 8; *Nicomachean Ethics* II.6.

2. For a unique book-length attempt by a Hollywood insider to connect Aristotle's Poetics to Hollywood plots, see Ari Hiltunen, *Aristotle in Hollywood: The Anatomy of Successful Storytelling* (Bristol, UK: Intellect Books, 2002).

3. Irving Kirsch, "Preface," *Philosophical Transactions of the Royal Society* B 366 (2011): 1781b.

4. Luana Colloca, and Franklin G. Miller, "Harnessing the Placebo Effect: The Need for Translational Research," *Philosophical Transactions of the Royal Society* 366 (2011): 1922–30, 1924b.

5. Ibid., 1928b.

6. Ibid., 1923b.

7. Ibid., 1923b.

8. Ibid., 1923b.

9. See M. Merleau-Ponty, *Phenomenology of Perception*, trans.C. Smith (London: Routledge, 1962); and Oron Frenkel, "A Phenomenology of the 'Placebo Effect': Taking Meaning from the Mind to the Body." *Journal of Medicine and Philosophy* 33 (2008), *passim*.

10. The phrase is from H. L. Dreyfus, "The Primacy of Phenomenology over Logical Analysis," *Philosophical Topics* 27.3.

11. Kim Meisner, "The Placebo Effect and the Autonomic Nervous System: Evidence for an Intimate Relationship," *Philosophical Transactions of the Royal Society* B 366 (2010): 1809, 1814. For a taste of recent discussions of Aristotle's *Rhetoric*, arts of persuasion, and placebo effects, see John Portmann, "Physician-Patient Relationship: Like a Marriage without Romance," *Western Journal of Medicine* 173 (2000): 279–82; and David H. Smith, "Communication as a Reflection of, and a Source for, Values in Health," *Journal of Applied Communication Research* 16 (1988): 29–38.

12. Cited in Frenkel, 67.

13. Ibid., 60 and *passim*.

14. For a psychologist's helpful account of the mechanisms of literary and therapeutic catharsis, see T. J. Scheff, *Catharsis in Healing, Ritual, and Drama* (Berkeley: University of California Press, 1979).

15. Philoctetes Project. www.philoctetesproject.org.

16. Jonathan Shay, *Odysseus in America: Combat Trauma and the Trials of Homecoming* (New York: Scribner, 2002), *passim*. See also Shay's *Achilles in Vietnam: Combat Trauma and the Undoing of Character* (New York: Scribner, 1994).

17. Sigmund Freud, *The Standard Edition of the Complete Psychological Works of Sigmund Freud*, 24 vols. trans. James Strachey (London: Hogarth, 1953–74). 4.261–63.

18. Sophocles's background as a physician of souls is obscure, but according to Teddy Brunius, he was "the first Asclepian priest in Athens," who dedicated an altar to Asclepius and wrote an Asclepian Hymn. In the therapeutic methods and case studies of the Asclepian center in Epidaurus we find the use of drama and music, and there was a practice of psychiatric as well as chirurgical character. Shock treatment and athletics were important in the therapy. Catharsis was a key word in this medicine and religion." Teddy Brunius, "Catharsis," In *The Dictionary of the History of Ideas*, edited by Philip P. Wiener 269a (New York: Charles Scribner and Sons, 1968, 1973).

19. Freud, 7.309.

20. According to Freud's student Erik Erikson, Freud had in mind a seemingly more modest goal. In answer to a question about what a normal person should be able to do well, he gave his informal, much-quoted answer: to work and to love. Erickson explains that Freud understood love as genital fulfillment and work as productive work that did not interfere with that love: "He meant a general work-productiveness which would not preoccupy the individual to the extent that he loses his right or capacity to be a genital and a loving being." See Erik Erikson, *Childhood and Society* (New York: Norton, 1963), 264–65.

21. The analysis that follows draws from the foundational study of revenge tragedy by Fredson Bowers, while arguing that the play is more unified in its design and effect than Bowers is willing to grant. See Fredson Bowers, *Elizabethan Revenge Tragedy*, (Princeton: Princeton University Press, 1940).

22. Here I am alluding, of course, to the locus classicus of studies of human flourishing: Aristotle's definition of eudaimonia in the Ethics, I.vii.

23. *Hamlet* in *The Norton Shakespeare,* eds. Stephen Greenblatt, Walter Cohen, Jean Howard, and Katharine Eisaman Maus (New York: W. W. Norton, 1997), IV.vi.13–19.

# FIVE

# Ramblers, Hikers, Vagabonds, and Flâneurs

## *America's Peripatetic Romantics and the Rituals of Healthy Walking*

Michael West

Supposedly exemplified by Poe, popularized by Baudelaire, and Marxized by Walter Benjamin, the concept of the flâneur as a gentlemanly detached stroller in the city is often invoked to describe the ambivalent response of nineteenth-century writers to increasing urbanization. How useful is it in explaining the various rituals of walking cultivated by writers in the American Renaissance? Less than one might imagine, for American Romanticism bred few boulevardiers. Upon closer inspection, parallels with Baudelaire tend to evaporate. Benjamin's concept is grounded in a dour and deterministic economic analysis of culture that most eminent American Romantics did not share. Nature's nation left individuals free to pursue happiness and thrive, in their view. Even in urban environments, even facing such poignant challenges as disease and death, one might enjoy the sense of well-being earned by responding positively and energetically to adversity. Whether rambling down country lanes or ambling down city pavements, what drove them was not so much a flâneur's fascination with the spectacle of available wealth as the possibility of cultivating personal health holistically through various modes in which human flourishing manifests itself, ranging from satisfying work, sportive athleticism, and physical therapy through friendly sociability, appreciation of beauty, and nature-based spirituality.

The main outlines of Benjamin's concept of the flâneur are sketched in *Charles Baudelaire: A Lyric Poet in the Era of High Capitalism*. While England pioneered industrial production, midcentury Paris introduced modern marketing with such innovations as the photograph, its commercial daily press, and its glass-roofed shopping arcades, precursors of the department store. Through the anonymous window-shopping crowds in pursuit of commodified fashion strolled the flâneur, described and to some extent exemplified by Baudelaire, a self-styled expert at observing urban life. Perhaps a poet and dandy, such a flâneur might make his living selling prose sketches of urban character types to newspapers aimed at nervous readers craving orientation within this novel, bewildering maze, for the unprecedented size and anonymity of the modern metropolis could frighten city dwellers, exposing them to a phantasmagoria of constant shocks.

Yet, simultaneously, the monotony of city life bred boredom, especially in intellectuals with revolutionary sympathies who were barred any political role by conservative reaction in the wake of 1848. The flâneur combated boredom by immersing himself in the crowd, pursuing novel fashions, half surrendering himself to "the intoxication of the commodity around which surges the stream of customers." Sauntering, he "demanded elbow room and was unwilling to forego the life of a gentleman of leisure."[1] Idling ostentatiously and rarely buying, he dramatized his aloofness from commerce, labor, and any purposive destination as well as from the crowd, for he was "unable to rid himself of a sense of their essentially inhuman make-up." Nevertheless, he became "their accomplice even as he dissociates himself from them."[2] His was a complex ambivalence toward the spectacle of consumerism, for while he pretended to aristocratic detachment from the economic considerations, within the thronged arcades his role combined seller's and consumer's roles; he came there as to a market, seeking material for writing that he hoped to sell to the press. Even if he promenaded a turtle *pour épater les bourgeois*, he also promenaded the idea of bourgeois consumption itself. His pretension to sophisticated knowledge of the city was a sham, for the shop windows in which he peered or preened himself offer only a superficial image that conceals the actual means of production demanding Marxist class analysis. A sense of his superficiality haunted him, however, so Baudelaire "battled the crowd—with the impotent rage of someone fighting the rain or the wind."[3] For Benjamin "the defining characteristic of metropolitan life is the desire for the commodity and the concomitant commodification of desire," according to Graeme Gilloch. "The erotic impulse finds satisfaction only in the voyeuristic and the inorganic," so ultimately "the crowd is the haunt of the melancholic" like Baudelaire.[4]

Benjamin's view of modernity is indeed a profoundly melancholy one, lacking the brash confidence of orthodox Marxist utopianism. But it is site-specific. Navigating Moscow's narrow sidewalks made him wonder whether the flâneur could have ever flourished there; likewise, he suggested that the dandy could become a true flâneur only when transplanted from London to Haussmann's ample boulevards. London and Paris were both bigger and more densely populated than New York City in the 1840s and 1850s. The antebellum American city could seem less an anonymous metropolis than a polis, an urban town with a history, environment, and communal ethos; its vibrant politics were shaped by energies that did not need to be sublimated in shopping. Moreover, the belief that city and country were reconcilable was manifest in much nineteenth-century American city planning, and writers like Emerson, Hawthorne, and Whitman often suggest a possible synthesis incorporating pastoral and small-town values in an urban environment of "organic cities."[5]

From Addison and Steel's *Spectator* essays observing early eighteenth-century London, New Yorkers derived a conception of the city walker more appropriate to a nascent metropolis that one might compass on foot in a day. Continued in the nineteenth century by writers like Lamb, Leigh Hunt, De Quincey, and Dickens, the British tradition of city sauntering was readier to see crowds as benign. Perambulating both rural and (less frequently) urban milieux, Geoffrey Crayon, the urbane strolling narrator of Washington Irving's sketches, begat the Knickerbocker manner of roving Manhattan editors like Lewis Gaylord Clark and the dandiacal Nathaniel Parker Willis. These city wits were unsure at first that Manhattan could accommodate would-be boulevardiers, and they were eager to celebrate the prosperous consumerism at which the flâneur cocks a wary eye. Such literary men about town displayed no conflicted angst over encroaching capitalism's making midcentury Gotham a phantasmagoria, and the influential moral-reform press would hardly have tolerated pleasure-seeking American writers trying to set up as Broadway Baudelaires. "Though 'spectator' and 'flâneur' seem to mean the same thing, they come from different literary traditions and urban structures," argues Wyn Kelley, who finds the latter term unsuited to antebellum literature, since "the American sensibility resisted flâneurial tendencies until later in the century."[6]

Thus, despite Baudelaire's claiming Poe as his spiritual brother, James V. Werner's *American Flâneur: The Cosmic Physiognomy of Edgar Allan Poe* fails to develop the parallel convincingly. For one thing, Poe "very seldom depicts the city as such (if ever)."[7] When he does, his cities often seem "unnaturally void of inhabitants" like "The City in the Sea."[8] Whereas Benjamin's Parisian flâneur delights in the arcades that turned the street into an exterior dwelling place and subverted the bourgeois domestic interior's pretension to an individual life, Poe's stories focus relentlessly on claustrophobic buildings or rooms, suggesting his preoccupation was not social but individual psychological pathology. Descriptions of detached metropolitan observers like Poe's archetypal detective C. Auguste Dupin and the narrator of "The Man of the Crowd" are not plentiful—and Poe goes out of his way to set these figures in the foreign metropolises of Paris and London. The latter tale is almost unique in Poe's fiction in offering a detailed description of an ambulatory observer scrutinizing an urban crowd. While the story helped inspire Baudelaire's ideas about the flâneur, Benjamin misreads Baudelaire as viewing the mysterious man of the crowd himself as a flâneur, a role the French poet instead linked to the narrator. Benjamin "remains trapped within his own error," as John Rignall points out, unable to apply his own concept persuasively to Poe's tale.[9]

Rather than relishing fashionable London most, when pursuing the man of the crowd Poe's narrator shows more interest as the chase leads them at night into disreputable lowlife haunts—a preference that scarcely corresponds to the Baudelairean flâneur's. Since Poe's work offers almost no examples of pedestrian observers pleasurably preoccupied with crowds and fashionable life, Werner's study treats Poe as a flâneur largely because Poe shows interest in physiognomies, the commodification of literature, and scientific exploration of the cosmos if not the metropolis.

But if the flâneur is not a walker in the city, what is he? Surely to treat Benjamin's concept so metaphorically is to risk emptying it of content and verging upon the kind of "allegorical" interpretation that Benjamin himself professed to scorn: "the allegorist plucks an item from his chaotic fund of knowledge and holds it up next to another to see whether they match: that meaning to this image, or this image to that meaning."[10] Neither Poe's writings nor his life (most of it spent as a devoted family man unlike the Parisian flâneur) suggests that urban pedestrian window-shopping was a pastime he found important. In his city sketches he regretted that omnibuses had "changed exercise into inertia" and rejected the idea that Bulwer-Lytton was "a mere dandy" by stressing that he once toured England and Scotland on foot (*Doings of Gotham*, 80, 43). Poe's claim to have walked ten miles within an hour himself may not exaggerate too grossly, for the most significant walk he ever described was no casual urban stroll but rather a thirty-mile hike from Baltimore to Washington and then back, energetically undertaken in 1829 to convince his dubious foster father of his determination to save money and secure a West Point appointment.

In Hawthorne, however, we do encounter a writer whose narrators in the sketches often portray themselves as saunterers. Thus in "Footprints on the Seashore" the narrator exclaims, "I eschew the presence of any meditative stroller like myself, known by his pilgrim staff, his sauntering step, his shy demeanor, his observant yet abstracted eye" (*Works*, 9:458). But despite resemblances, such timid gentlemen hardly seem Baudelairean boulevardiers. They ramble in nature, not cities, or they are village vagabonds like the narrators of "The Village Uncle" and "Little Annie's Ramble." If they can claim a French ancestor, he would not be Baudelaire but the nature-loving narrator in Rousseau's *Reveries of the Solitary Walker*, filtered through the English Romantic poets and Hawthorne's beau ideal, Washington Irving. Hawthorne's *American Notebooks* record how it was his "invariable custom" to lose his way on woodland rambles. "Nothing is more annoying than a walk of this kind—to be tormented to death by . . . innumerable . . . petty impediments; it incenses and depresses me at the same time," he complained. "Always when I flounder into the midst of a tract of bushes, which cross and intertwine themselves about my legs, and brush my face, and seize hold of my clothes with multitudinous gripe; always . . . I feel as if it were almost as well to lie down and die in a rage and despair, as to go one step further. It is laughable, after I have got out of the scrape, to think how miserably it affected me for the moment . . ." (*Works*, 8:340–341). As Dana Brand remarks, Hawthorne's writings often explore "the dilemma of an American who tries to be a flâneur in an environment that is almost comically inhospitable to his efforts."[11]

In *Our Old Home* (1863) Hawthorne described wandering from Britain's busier city districts into the slums as offering "a sort of somber phantasmagoric spectacle" that is "unknown on our side of the Atlantic" (*Works*, 5:277). Thus, "My Kinsman, Major Molineux" mocks the country boy Robin's naive conviction that on entering the little provincial capital of colonial Boston after hiking more than thirty miles he has stepped into a foreign metropolis dominated by bewigged "gay and gallant figures" where "traveled youths, imitators of the European fine gentlemen of the period, trod jauntily along, half dancing to the fashionable tunes which they hummed, and making poor Robin ashamed of his quiet and natural gait" (*Works*, 11:215). He has yet to learn that the city is neither so alien nor so brutal as he and Benjamin imagine it. What first struck him as a baffling nocturnal phantasmagoria succumbs to rational explanation in a few hours. Unlike the fashionably Europeanized gentry Robin encountered earlier (most presumably members of the waning court party like the Major), the rioters are not blasé urban sophisticates sublimating political energies stifled by a failed revolution—they are American citizens preparing for a successful one.

*The Blithedale Romance*'s bachelor narrator Miles Coverdale relishes "my morning lounge at the reading room or picture gallery; my noontide walk along the cheery pavement, with the suggestive succession of human faces, and the brisk throb of human life, in which I shared" (Hawthorne, *Works*, 3:40). But the novel ruthlessly exposes the inadequacies of the spectatorial mode that he and the other urban pastoralists transplant to Blithedale in a futile effort to gain privileged insight into people. His detached gaze yields no solution to the mysteries posed by other characters, only deeper detachment. "Unraveling the social postures and interpretive presumptions of the urban spectators," as Brand observes, Hawthorne "unravels the flâneur."[12]

Melville likewise viewed flâneurial pretensions with suspicion. Indeed, his first publication, "Fragments from a Writing Desk, No. 1," appeared in 1839 over the initials L. A. V. as a letter to the editor of the *Lansingburgh, (N.Y.) Democratic Press* spoofing the Knickerbocker city wits. "Pollux! What a comfortable thing is a good opinion of one's self!" L. A. V. proclaims. "Why, I walk the Broadway of our village with a certain air . . . as a *distingue* of the purest water," unlike "the little sneaking vermin who dodge along the street" and so "set off to advantage my own slow and magisterial gait, which I can at pleasure vary to an easy, abandoned sort of carriage." Allegedly "beautiful as Apollo, dressed in a style which would extort admiration from Brummel," L. A. V.'s preposterous small-town conceit about "my own metropolis" suggests that his nineteen-year-old creator regarded Gotham's strolling dandies as only slightly less absurd (*Writings*, 9:192–93). A similar technique of comic dislocation characterizes observer-figures in the early novels. "One cannot imagine the Addisonian spectator or the Parisian *flâneur* wandering the Pacific," as Kelley says, so by deploying such figures in an exotic landscape "Melville challenges the genteel urban culture" that spawned them, using "various subtle and some violent methods of discrediting the spectator."[13]

Though very much a part of New York's urban culture, Melville often described city life harshly, as in the case of the descriptions of New York and Liverpool in *Redburn*. When he found himself in London in 1849 as a prospering young author of thirty, he indefatigably walked its streets. Occasionally he visited conventional tourist attractions or fashionable haunts like the Burlington arcade, where he bought a cigar case while waiting to call on his publisher. But usually for his walks he sought out areas far off the beaten tourist track, "commonly the most desperate, the vilest and most degraded of the greatest commercial metropolis of the western world."[14] A prominent motive seems to have been to observe with heartfelt concern (as Hawthorne would do tracking his steps a few years later) what Melville described as "the poverty and misery of so large a portion of the London population" (*Journal*, 51).

Another leading motive was healthy exercise. When Melville bought his Berskshire property next year, he "thought nothing of going with his sisters and the Morewoods on a casual hike of more than ten miles."[15] Such bucolic excursions were "the great joy of his Berkshire days," and those for whom he organized these sportive jaunts found him "almost extravagantly fond" of them.[16] On one outing, companions noted how Melville clambered energetically up a tree "with the agility of a well-trained sailor," hallooed lustily, then made the woods ring with his axe—feats seldom seen in the Bois de Boulogne.[17] He endowed *Pierre*'s country-bred hero with similar athleticism, unable to sleep without "walking his twelve miles a day, or felling a fair-sized hemlock . . . or performing some other gymnastical feat" (*Writings*, 7:17). Later, when Pierre is reduced to living in New York, he at first takes a regular walk "through the greatest thoroughfare of the city" so that "the utter isolation of his soul, might feel itself more intensely from the incessant jogglings of his body against the bodies of the hurrying thousands." But he soon abandons such outings, preferring night walks when storms thin the crowds, then dark side streets frequented by "social castaways," until finally "nothing but the utter night-desolation of the obscurest warehousing lanes would . . . be at all sufferable to him" (*Writings*, 7:340-41). As a boy growing up in Manhattan, Melville had relished country rambles in the then Elysian Fields of Hoboken, and in old age the preference remained. His daily constitutional often saw him "tramping through the Fort George district or Central Park, his roving inclination leading him to obtain as much outdoor life as possible," the *Tribune* obituary noted.[18] Sometimes he would walk the still-wild Riverside Bluffs seven miles from City Hall, impressing observers with his "health and vigor" as he "walked with rapid stride and an almost sprightly gait." If the weather was too cold, he "worked off excess energy by walking back and forth on the back porch."[19] Unlike the flâneur, he did not saunter casually down commercial avenues but purposefully pursued physical exercise, not crowds, which he avoided as much as possible.

Like Melville, other American writers positively relished the rural hiking challenges that daunted Hawthorne. Thus in his journal Francis Parkman boasted of walking sixteen hours daily for days in a row to see rural sights; his pugnacious forays into Nature prepared him as a historian to record the conquest of a continent. The 250-mile walk that Audubon took up the Ohio to Louisville with his young son in 1823 taxed the boy at first, as his father recorded in "A Tough Walk for a Youth." But the concern yielded to paternal pride when by the end he and his now-hardened stripling left other men in their party limping in their wake. Quadrupling that mileage, just after the Civil War, John Muir set out solo from Louisville on the adventurous expedition described in his *A Thousand-Mile Walk to the Gulf* (1916), observing many plants but precious few city folk en route while surviving storms, would-be robbers, malaria, and alligators.

Scribbling American women had more difficulty emulating such heroic nature hikers, of course. Reminiscent of the timid Hawthornean narrators, Amherst's wannabe flâneurs—"Sauntering Gentlemen with Canes"—still seemed nonchalant to Emily Dickinson beside the sun-shy "Ladies—with Parasols . . . /And little Girls—with Dolls" perambulating the village main street in summer (*Poems*, 1:273 [#342]). Liability to misconstruction as a streetwalker discouraged upper-class American women from going out on foot in cities except to shop. Either in pursuit of commodities or regarded as a commodity herself, a strolling urban woman aspiring to become a flâneuse would inevitably have found it harder to dissociate herself from commerce than the flâneur. In her essay "Fashionable Invalidism" (1867) Fanny Fern vigorously attacked genteel men and women who felt obliged to ride around the corner. "How I rejoice in a man or woman with a chest; who can look the sun in the eye and step off as if they had not wooden legs," she roundly declared. "I walk, not ride. I own stout boots—pretty ones, too . . . I dash out in the rain because it feels good on my face" (*Writings*, 341). With her husband's amused support she experimented with men's garb as more suitable than skirts for walking the city at night. She was convinced that women inmates would continue to outnumber men in insane asylums until "physical education becomes a religion with the mothers of this country" (*Writings*, 246).

With some American fathers physical education had already become a religion, among them Timothy Fuller, who redeemed himself from sickliness with a vigorous exercise program and encouraged his gifted daughter Margaret in the same direction. As a ten-year old in Cambridge she leapt at the chance to trek three miles to a better school in Boston: "It will be rather fatiguing walking in and out again every day," she conceded, "but then again I shall have a pleasant walk to pay for it."[20] Not content with a daily constitutional to stave off migraines, she may also have walked in her sleep. Throughout her life vigorous walking served this neurotic and emotionally deprived woman as therapy for what she saw as the debility induced by an overly intellectualized upbringing that separated her from other schoolgirls except when she joined them in "active games," for "I liked violent bodily exercise" (*Portable Margaret Fuller*, 20). On the Midwestern tour that she recorded in *Summer on the Lakes* (1844), she walked aggressively in cities like Chicago and Milwaukee. After hilly New England, her first experience of the Illinois prairies was off-putting: ". . . to walk, and walk, and run, but never climb, oh! It was too dreary for any but a Hollander to bear . . ." But she soon found grandeur in the thought that, if endowed with seven-league boots, "I might continue that walk for hundreds of miles without an obstacle and without a change" (*Portable Margaret Fuller*, 91). Effete Eastern women needed exercise before they would be ready to settle on the prairies among Midwestern girls, she decided, and she was impressed by the immigrants landing in Milwaukee who would then "walk off into the country, the mothers carrying their infants, the fathers leading their little children by the hand." In Cooper's *The Prairie* Natty Bumppo had preferred walking to riding, and Fuller lamented that her own party's prairie excursion in a carriage disappointingly offered no chance to explore on foot "some strange woodland path in search of whatever might befall. It was . . . almost as tame as New England" (*Portable Margaret Fuller*, 138). Working on her manuscript in Cambridge the next spring, she walked from five till darkness every day and celebrated its completion with a meditative stroll among the graves in Mt. Auburn Cemetery.

As a journalist in New York City, she chose to live with her editor Horace Greeley at some remove from lower Manhattan, leaving herself a substantial walk after the omnibus to return to her lodging, and she "often traipsed around the city (with an escort) well past midnight," occasionally showing what her biographer terms with mild exaggeration "a *flâneur*'s studied fascination with the city's grotesque spectacles."[21] Visiting a mesmerist French doctor for chronic backaches, she may have enjoyed as much relief from her twice-weekly four-mile walks to his office as from his treatments. She delighted at the thought of "climbing the hills" with friends like Anna Barker Ward. By the time she found herself in Italy, she was capable of romantic mountaineering on her own as she described in a letter to Caroline Sturgis Tappan: "I had another good day, too, crossing the Apennines. The young crescent moon rose in orange twilight, just as I reached the highest peak. I was alone on foot; I heard no sound; I prayed" (*Portable Margaret Fuller*, 525, 520). Dispatches from Rome during the Revolution describe her as abroad without an escort during street demonstrations and returning from long walks at night alone. As a journalist in New York, her aggressive reformist agenda had left her discontented with spectatorial detachment, and she hardly admired European flâneurs or flâneuses when she saw them. English mill girls "strolling bareheaded, with coarse, rude and reckless air, through the streets," prompted curiosity and pity, to be sure, but also mild disdain, while on the Champs Elysées she had recoiled from "the files of men sauntering," finding the Parisian boulevardier's superior air, "half-military, half-dandy, of self-esteem and savoir-faire . . . not particularly interesting" (*At Home and Abroad*, 124, 217–18). Now in Rome she found that political involvement rendered the flâneur's role impossible. Deemphasizing the architectural cityscape, she portrayed crowds as politically self-conscious, self-determining citizenry, on whose struggles "I cannot look merely with a pictorial eye."[22]

On his first visit to Rome in 1833 Emerson's pictorial eye had been mightily taken by its art and architecture but not by its pedestrians. "It is a majestic city, & satisfies this craving imagination," he averred. "And yet I would give all Rome for one man such as were fit to walk here" (*Letters*, 1:372). Rome was an exception to his general distaste for cities, where "I always . . . suffer from loss of faith" (*Correspondence*, 260). Upon reaching Paris he found it "a loud modern New York of a place" (*Journals and Miscellaneous Notebooks*, 4:197). Although as a tourist he did "stare & stare at the thousand thousand shop windows" (*Letters*, 1:387), he "despised the flâneur as much as he disliked the city's easy, fat, amused life."[23] Emerson's misgivings about the urban environment were by no means absolute, nor did he think nature an automatic panacea for what ailed the city sophisticate: "the fop of fields is no better than his brother of Broadway" (*Complete Works*, 3:177). But Emerson's cosmopolitan idealism did little to foster the emergence of American boulevardiers.

If there were an impressively talented American urban flâneur, however, the Transcendentalist Whitman might seem the likeliest candidate in his predilection for promenading Broadway. Indeed, for the *N.Y. Aurora* he wrote sketches imitating Willis's, while many poems describe him sauntering through his Mannahatta. But as "one of the roughs" Whitman's pose involved neither foppish gentlemanly aloofness from the masses nor skeptical critical detachment from the metropolis (*Leaves of Grass*, 1:31n). Rather he seems passionately attached to all the urban phenomena he encounters while his myth of the open road takes him out of the city entirely into romantic nature worship. To be sure, after a lengthy expression of powerful longing to escape from the city to country solitude, the second section of "Give Me the Splendid Silent Sun" reverses course:

> Give me faces and streets—give me these phantoms incessant and
> endless along the trottoirs!
> Give me interminable eyes—give me women—give me comrades
> and lovers by the thousand!
> Let me see new ones every day—let me hold new ones by the hand
> every day!
> Give me such shows—give me the streets of Manhattan!
> (*Leaves of Grass*, 2:499)

But while this second section ends by celebrating "Manhattan crowds, with their turbulent musical chorus," parallelism suggests that the two sections mirror each other, "that nature and the city are complementary realms of similar experience," so that the longing for urban social contact actually harmonizes with the desire for peaceful pastoral isolation.[24]

The craving for superficial contact with crowds compensated this solitary singer for the intimacy they could not really provide. While he may have gazed longingly on potential new comrades and lovers every day, holding hands with many of them smacks of wish fulfillment on the part of a poet who "saw many I loved in the street or ferryboat . . . yet never told them a word" (*Leaves of Grass*, 1:222). His oft-proclaimed desire to be positively absorbed by crowds contrasts strikingly with Baudelaire's aloof stance, and he shows relatively little fascination with the spectacle of consumerism per se. He thought elegantly dressed women in Central Park had "much style, (yet perhaps little or nothing, even in that direction, that fully justified itself)," so that "there is nothing in them which we who are poor and plain need at all envy," alienated from nature as they were by "limitless wealth, leisure, and . . . gentility." Perambulating Philadelphia's Chestnut Street, he was most intrigued by a window display featuring two fine sheep reposing on hay and straw in a little corral, "altogether a queer sight amidst that crowded promenade of dandies, dollars, and dry goods" (*Prose Works 1892*, 1:199, 190). Though he did plenty of idle sauntering, what most appealed to him about crowds was the sense of dynamic bustle and movement, so that "one begins to feel that it was not the city that captivated him, but motion, change, and energy themselves or as instruments for ushering in the anticipated ideal democracy."[25] Such a vision may keep the actual city at a distance, like the panorama he famously observed in "Crossing Brooklyn Ferry," where the passengers are faceless avatars of the speaker and his reader, embodying "not a world in motion and alive but only the assertion of motion and life," with the poet's vision of an eternal present firmly anchored not in the cityscape but in permanent aspects of nature like sunlight, water, breezes, and seagulls.[26]

Seeking to apply the concept of the flâneur to Whitman, Jonathan Arac has perceptively compared his "To a Stranger" with Baudelaire's sonnet "A une Passante," which Benjamin treats as paradigmatic of "the stigmata which life in a metropolis inflicts on love."[27] Baudelaire describes seeing a beautiful woman passerby wearing deep mourning and the fleeting exchange of glances that convinced not only him but her too (in his view) that they were potential lovers, soul mates fated never to meet again in the anonymity of the city. Despite superficial resemblances, Whitman's poem differs strikingly:

Passing stranger, you do not know how longingly I look upon you,
You must be he I was seeking, or she I was seeking (it comes to me as of a dream)
I have somewhere surely lived a life of joy with you,
All is recalled as we flit by each other, fluid, affectionate, chaste, matured,
You grew up with me, were a boy with me or a girl with me,
I ate with you and slept with you, your body has become not yours only nor left
    my body mine only,
You give me the pleasure of your eyes, face, flesh, as we pass, you
    take of my beard, breast, hands, in return,
I am not to speak to you, I am to think of you when I sit alone or
    wake at night alone,
I am to wait, I do not doubt I am to meet you again,
I am to see to it that I do not lose you. (*Leaves of Grass*, 2:392)

For Baudelaire and Benjamin the city sunders two individuals whom it has transiently united, and the painful sexual shock of the encounter is its simultaneously anguishing evanescence. For Whitman the city reunites children previously separated who seem not so much individuals as androgynes for whom sexual differentiation is irrelevant. Baudelaire's city condemns him to frustrated love; Whitman's guarantees the joyful continuation into the future of a chastely matured affection that may have begun in the country.

"Benjamin's Baudelaire wrote against his age," Arac concedes, whereas "Whitman wrote with his age" in sympathy with capitalism.[28] But when one takes into account their other dissimilarities, one may wonder whether applying the concept of the flâneur to Whitman obscures more than it illuminates. Whereas Baudelaire makes no imaginative connection between metropolitan Paris and the Île de France, "Whitman's urban scenes are always in harmony with nature; are really merely projections of it, the bustle and abundance being extensions of the creative energy and fecundity of nature."[29] For all the unease about urban culture that he often projected in portraying prostitutes, one cannot imagine the French poet exclaiming with Whitman, "Sweet, sane, still Nakedness in Nature!--ah, if poor, sick, prurient humanity in cities might really know you once more!" (*Prose Works 1892*, 1:152). Haunted by the illnesses plaguing most of his family, the poet who thus described his therapeutic program for naked sunbathing and exercise in old age had always been a valetudinarian. His greatest poem opens by celebrating his "delight alone or in the rush of the streets, or along the fields and hillsides, / The feeling of health" (*Leaves of Grass*, 1:2n). An important part of what drove the American poet to ramble through city and country alike was less a morbid fascination with crowds than sheer delight in healthy bodily exercise. Rather like the convalescent narrator of Poe's "Man of the Crowd," Whitman soaks up vital energy from crowds rather than simply basking in an observer's presumptive social and intellectual superiority.

Indeed Whitman's sauntering tendencies simply extend into an urban setting the devotion to walking of the era's supreme literary saunterer, Thoreau, whose marked disdain for cities and crowds squares awkwardly with Benjamin's notion of the flâneur. Thoreau's magnificent essay "Walking" takes fanciful flight from a bogus etymology deriving *saunter* from the phrase *á la Sainte Terre* allegedly used by medieval vagabonds to explain that they were going to the Holy Land. Though the forays into Concord described in *Walden*'s chapter "The Village" sometimes link his pose to other village flâneurs, he hated the grit of gravel beneath his feet and was primarily a bucolic rambler, visiting Boston occasionally but always with a destination in mind rather than just to promenade there. Whereas Benjamin's flâneur botanizes for human physiognomies on Parisian boulevards, Thoreau's botanizing focuses on learning the names and faces of all the flora and fauna of Walden woods. The flowers of evil that Baudelaire plucked in Parisian bordellos Thoreau found growing wild in deserted swamps. Poison dogwood seemed "beautiful as satan" (*Journal*, 4:214). But though the fungus Devil's Phallus might provoke the Baudelairean frisson of evil, the aesthete's ultimate sensation, Thoreau recoiled in disgust from its stench.

But this woodland aesthete in whom Emerson rightly saw resemblances to the dandy Beau Brummel also harbored a potential invalid's desire to toughen himself through walking to master Nature's challenges, the greatest of which in his case was incipient tuberculosis. Whereas other Romantic nature writers often subordinate the activity of walking to the sights it reveals, locomotion per se remained central for Thoreau. Though his ideal sauntering was not "akin to taking exercise . . . as the sick take medicine at stated hours," he walked four hours or more almost every day (*Excursions*, 89). According to Emerson, "walking has the best value as gymnastics for the mind" (*Complete Works*, 12:141), and Thoreau likewise preferred to "go a-huckleberrying in the fields of thought" (*Writings*, 12:400). Walking provides the structure of many of his literary "Excursions." Indeed, like Rousseau, whose *Reveries du promeneur solitaire* found regular pedestrian rhythm uniquely conducive to trance-like creative meditation, Thoreau claimed to be unable to write without walking. "The writing which consists with habitual sitting is mechanical wooden dull to read," he felt, and he developed an elaborate theory of biofeedback to explain how by stimulating the circulation walking forestalled intellectual constipation by establishing proper drainage for bodily wastes: "Methinks that the moment my legs begin to move, my thoughts begin to flow—as if I had given vent to the stream at the lower end & consequently new fountains flowed into it at the upper."[30]

"When we walk, we naturally go to the fields and woods," claims Thoreau, observing that even "some sects of philosophers have felt the necessity of importing the woods to themselves" by planting groves and walks where they strolled like the Stoics in open-air porticos. "What would become of us if we walked only in a garden or a mall?" he concludes (*Excursions*, 190). No such reservations troubled Parisian flâneurs, of course. "An arcade was never more than a mall," as Rebecca Solint observes, and for all the philosophical pretensions with which Benjamin strives to invest them, his flâneurs sometimes seem simply progenitors of today's more déclassé mall rats.[31] America's pastoral imagination inhibited the emergence of literary conventions for ritualized urban spectatorship like Europe's, and Benjamin's concept is of limited usefulness in explaining the pedestrian styles celebrated by midcentury American writers. With the exceptions of Poe and the later Melville, our canonical Romantic authors tended to be ebullient optimists whose evolutionary meliorism and belief in social progress were colored by faith in participatory democracy and the individual's potential for self-determination independent of society. After their country declared liberty to pursue happiness, many chose to pursue it on foot. Often humorous stylists, theirs was basically a comic rather than a tragic view of life. They did not naively ignore its darker aspects, but felt that even illness and mortality did not leave the individual absolutely helpless. "I am trying . . . the effect of air and exercise," wrote Henry Wadsworth Longfellow. "Today I have walked ten miles [with Dickens in Boston]. I am disappointed in not getting well" (*Letters*, 2:381). The valetudinarian vigor with which so many actively cultivated health by city and country walking makes them poor examples of a concept grounded like Benjamin's model of the window-shopping flâneur in lugubrious social and economic determinism.

Our Romantic authors came of age when newspapers like New Haven's *Connecticut Herald* celebrated ambulatory heroics gleaned from the system of complimentary exchanges that bound the nation's journals together.

*Extraordinary Pedestrian*

John Wilson, better known as "Walking Wilson," commenced trading to New-Orleans in the spring of 1800; completed his forty-eighth voyage during the last summer, averaging nearly two and a half trips per season; and during that period, has travelled by land and water one hundred and twenty-eight thousand miles, in the prosecution of that trade, which will appear from the following exhibit.

| | |
|---|---|
| 46 trips to New-Orleans. 1600 miles. | 76,800 |
| Walked twenty trips through the wilderness, returning. 800 each, | 16,000 |
| 12 do. on horseback, do. | 9,600 |
| 16 do. in steam-boats, 1600 do. | 25,600 |
| | 127,400 |

Wilson has more than once beaten the United States mail, whilst walking; man never could keep side and side with him; has never been overtaken by man on foot or horseback; is about forty years of age; possesses a constitution apparently unimpaired; has amassed a portion of "earthly goods," and is now in the "full time of successful experiment," making his forty-ninth trip. Wilson is native of Mason county, Ken.

*Maysville, Eagle.*[32]

What chiefly drove the dauntless Wilson on his expeditions was a motive shared with many other Americans who like Hawthorne's Robin Molineux stepped off briskly to seek their fortunes? No sauntering backwoods boulevardier, Wilson walked purposefully across very rough country to build up a flourishing trade. When Poe tramped from Baltimore to Washington or Margaret Fuller and Fanny Fern trudged about New York and Rome as reporters or Thoreau toted compass and chain around farms to proclaim himself monarch of all he *surveyed,* they were all likewise pursuing "earthly goods."

But Wilson's motives were not limited to profit, for while ballyhooing his "successful experiment" in business the *Maysville Eagle* proudly noted an element of challenge propelling this native son to outdistance all competitors on foot. One doubts that he emulated the technique of today's Olympic race walkers, but if he could actually keep pace with Tennessee Walking Horses he was perhaps one of the country's earliest recorded joggers; anyone never overtaken by trotting horses (if we may believe that claim) sustained the gait of modern ultramarathoners daylong. Wilson apparently approached walking as the pedestrian peer of Mike Fink the Riverboatman, ready to vanquish all comers, and may well have earned a jogger's high. Poe, Melville, Parkman, and Audubon all on occasion describe walking almost as a form of competitive sport where success might warrant feelings of triumphant exhilaration. Worth noting is the fact that this motive can be distinguished from exercising for health.

The noun *constitutional* denoting a walk undertaken for healthy exercise postdates Wilson's feats. Rather than suggest that walking has improved his constitution, the *Maysville Eagle* seems more concerned to assure readers that his heroic trips have not actually impaired it. Thus Thoreau distinguishes his ideal sauntering from medicinal exercise by arguing that "the chivalric and heroic spirit which once belonged to the Rider seems now to reside in . . . not the Knight, but Walker Errant," for "every walk is a sort of crusade, preached by some Peter the Hermit in us, to go forth and reconquer this holy land from the hands of the Infidels" (*Excursions*, 185–86).

But whether or not Wilson walked for exercise, Thoreau surely numbered that among his motives. As the phrase *daily constitutional* became common parlance, American Romantics by the score indulged in frankly salubrious strolling. Virtually every author here discussed mentions walking for health. Emily Dickinson's modest forays outdoors were encouraged by her schools, but they pale beside the intrepid pedestrian regimens of Fanny Fern and Margaret Fuller. Moreover, for these women walking also served as a mode of sociability. Dickinson and Fuller often mention their desire to walk with friends, and one such typical female social ritual is glimpsed in Whitman's "Song of Myself" when "on the piazza walk five friendly matrons with twined arms" (*Leaves of Grass*, 1:19n). Their male counterparts too combined camaraderie with exercise, Longfellow logging his ten miles through Boston with Dickens in the hope of shaking off sickness, Hawthorne and Melville forsaking sedentary deskwork to renew their friendship in England with "a pretty long walk together" (Hawthorne, *Works*, 22:163). And before the phrase *walking out together* came in the later Victorian era to connote courtship, propriety sanctioned the sexes walking together in contexts where innocent friendship could be exalted into the heatedly romantic. "Couldn't Carlo, and you and I walk in the meadow an hour—and nobody come out but the Bobolink," Dickinson queried the shadowy man who dominated her early erotic imagination. "I waited a long time—Master—but I can wait more—wait till my hazel hair is dappled—and you carry the cane . . ." (*Letters*, 2:314–15).

If health, friendship, and romance do not propel Wilson's solo hikes, neither do they figure significantly in Benjamin's model of the flâneur. Moreover America's Romantics went beyond both in other important ways. When Wilson commenced trading on foot with New Orleans in 1800, there was probably no copy of Wordsworth's and Coleridge's *Lyrical Ballads* (1797) in Maysville. Nothing suggests that this indefatigable entrepreneur paused en route to indulge in raptures over the scenery like a Southern avatar of Natty Bumppo the Pathfinder. But by the 1820s Romanticism was beginning to permeate Nature's Nation, and Cooper was in the van of those happily endorsing it. Even if they sometimes sauntered in cities, virtually all the major authors who followed in his wake both described and enjoyed rambling cross-country to commune with nature. Hawthorne, one of the more urbane and eighteenth-century spirits among them, was capable of strikingly sentimental religio-aesthetic effusions on "a solitary walk to Walden," where he concluded that "if I were to be baptized, it should be in this pond" (*Works*, 8:394–95). Though hardly a nature worshiper, even Poe in his "Sonnet—To Science" expresses conventional Romantic regret that we are murdering the beauty of the natural world in dissecting it. In her *Summer on the Lakes* or his summers in the Berkshires, Fuller and Melville could both wax Wordsworthian about country walks, while a village stroll sufficed for Emerson. "Crossing a bare common, in snow puddles, at twilight, under a clouded sky . . . I have enjoyed a perfect exhilaration," he famously wrote at the beginning of *Nature*, explaining how a "wild delight" seized one outdoors, an ecstatic experience in which "I become a transparent eye-ball. I am nothing. I see all. The currents of the Universal Being circulate through me; I am part or particle of God" (*Collected Works*, 1:9–10). Later Transcendentalists like Thoreau, Whitman, and Muir all followed his lead in making nature walks a gateway to aesthetic and pantheistic experience. "How glad I am that spring has come," wrote Dickinson while resisting revivalist indoctrination at Mount Holyoke Female Seminary, "and how it calms my mind . . . to walk out in the green fields and beside the pleasant streams in which South Hadley is so rich" (*Letters*, 1:66). Massachusetts offered green pastures where beside still waters she preferred to restore her soul hunting distant wildflowers amid muffled echoes of the Twenty-third Psalm.

America's Romantics walked for various reasons—health and wealth, sport and sociability—but mingled with these motives were ecstatic peak experiences linking walking with aesthetic and spiritual fulfillment. Even on the economic level their motives tend to differ from those of Benjamin's urban flâneur, obsessed with the spectacle of consumption but denied true Marxist understanding of industrial production. If the flourishing trade that "Walking Wilson" trekked laboriously cross-country to build up depended partly on slave labor, he was presumably aware of that fact. And successful personal labor of most sorts is an important form of human flourishing. Like our other authors the work on which Thoreau most prided himself was of course artistic: his writing. But for all his criticism of the American work ethic, he could regard our widespread prosperity as the basis for future cultural improvements that we could readily afford like schools and libraries, for insofar as our democracy's "circumstances are more flourishing, our means are greater than the nobleman's" (*Walden*, 110). Whitman went even further in viewing economic dynamism like Wilson's as the basis for the emergence of a new and more fully human people, convinced that both democracy and individuality, "with unimpeded branchings, flourish best under imperial republican forms" (*Prose Works*, 2:392). Among the branches in which democratic individualism flowered he would surely have included the forms of human flourishing especially cultivated by America's Romantic walkers: sportive athleticism, physical therapy, amative friendship, aesthetic sensitivity, and spirituality in the guise of nature-worship. All of these conduce to people's total health, but few are marked concerns of Benjamin's Parisian flâneurs.

## BIBLIOGRAPHY

Anon. "Extraordinary Pedestrian." In *Connecticut Herald* (New Haven), XX, no. 2 (Feb. 26 1823): 2.

Arac, Jonathan. "Whitman and Problems of the Vernacular." In *Breaking Bounds: Whitman and American Cultural Studies*, edited by Betsy Erkila and Jay Grossman, 44–61. New York: Oxford University Press, 1996.

Benjamin, Walter. *Charles Baudelaire: A Lyric Poet in the Era of High Capitalism*. Translated by Harry Zohn. London: Verso, 1983.

Brand, Dana. *The Spectator and the City in Nineteenth-Century American Literature*. New York: Cambridge University Press, 1991.

Capper, Charles. *Margaret Fuller: An American Romantic Life*. New York: Oxford University Press, 1992–2007.

Dickinson, Emily. *Letters*. Edited by Thomas H. Johnson. Cambridge, MA: Harvard University Press, 1958.

———. *Poems*. Edited by Thomas H. Johnson. Cambridge, MA: Harvard University Press, 1958–1965.

Emerson, Ralph Waldo. *Collected Works*. Edited by Alfred Riggs Ferguson et al. Cambridge, MA: Harvard University Press, 1971.

———. *Complete Works*. Boston: Houghton Mifflin, 1883–1893.

———. *Correspondence of Emerson and Carlyle*. Edited by Joseph Slater. New York: Columbia University Press, 1964.

———. *Journals and Miscellaneous Notebooks*. Edited by William H. Gilman et al. Cambridge, MA: Harvard University Press, 1960–1982.

———. *Letters*. Edited by Ralph L. Rusk. New York: Columbia University Press, 1939.

Fern, Fanny [Sarah Payson Willis]. *Ruth Hall and Other Writings*. Edited by Joyce W. Warren. New Brunswick: Rutgers University Press, 1980.

Fuller, Margaret. *At home and abroad; or, Things and thoughts in America and Europe*. Edited by Arthur B. Fuller. 1856; rpt. Port Washington, New York: Kennikat Press, 1971.

———. *The Portable Margaret Fuller*. Edited by Mary Kelly. New York: Penguin, 1994.

Gilloch, Graeme. *Myth and Metaphor: Walter Benjamin and the City*. Cambridge, UK: Polity, 1996.

Hawthorne, Nathaniel. *Centenary Edition of the Works*. Edited by William Charvat et al. Columbus, OH: Ohio State University Press, 1962.

Horsford, Howard C. "Melville and the London Street Scene." *Essays in Arts and Sciences* 16 (May 1987): 23–25.

Kelley, Wyn. *Melville's City: Literary and Urban Form in Nineteenth-Century New York*. New York: Cambridge University Press, 1996.

Leyda, Jay. *The Melville Log: A Documentary Life of Herman Melville*. New York: Harcourt, 1951.

Longfellow, Henry Wadsworth. *Letters*. Edited by Andrew Hilen. Cambridge: Harvard University Press, 1966–1982.

Machor, James L. "Pastoralism and the American Urban Ideal: Hawthorne, Whitman and the Literary Pattern." *American Literature* 54 (1982): 329–53.

Melville, Herman. *Journal of a Visit to London and the Continent, 1849–1850*. Edited by Eleanor Melville Metcalf. Cambridge, MA: Harvard University Press, 1948.

———. *Writings*. Edited by Harrison Hayford et al. Evanston, IL: Northwestern University Press, 1968–1991.

Parker, Hershel. *Herman Melville: A Biography: Volume II, 1851–1891*. Baltimore: Johns Hopkins University Press, 2002.

———. "Melville and the Berkshires: Emotion-Laden Terrain, 'Reckless Sky-Assaulting Mood,' and Encroaching Wordsworthianism." In *American Literature: The New England Heritage*, edited by James Nagel and Richard Astro, 65–81. New York: Garland, 1981.

Poe, Edgar Allan. *Doings of Gotham . . . with . . . Comments by Thomas Ollive Mabbott*. Pottsville, PA: Spannuth, 1929.

Raynaud, Jean. "Rural and Urban Visions in Poe's Tales." In *Mythes ruraux et urbains dans la culture américaine*, 121–34. Aix-en-Provence: Université de Provence, 1990.

Rignall, John. *Realist Fiction and the Strolling Narrator*. London: Routledge, 1992.

Schöpp, Joseph C. "'We come out to Europe to learn what man can': Emerson's Grand Tour of 1833." In *Walking on a Trail of Words: Essays in Honor of Professor Agnieszka Salska*, edited by Jadwiga Maszewska and Zbigniew Maszweski, 11–25. Lodz: Wydawniatwo Universytetu Lodzhiego, 2007.

Smith, J. E. A. "Herman Melville" (1891–1892). In *The Early Lives of Melville: Nineteenth-Century Biographical Sketches and their Authors*, edited by Merton M. Sealts, Jr., 119–49. Madison: University of Wisconsin Press, 1974.

Solint, Rebecca. *Wanderlust: A History of Walking*. New York: Viking, 2000.

Steele, Jeffrey. "Margaret Fuller." In *American Travel Writers, 1776–1864*, edited by James Schramer and Donald Ross, 126–38. Detroit: Gale, 1997.

Stout, James P. *Sodoms in Edens: The City in American Fiction before 1860*. Westport, CT: Greenwood, 1976.

Tanner, Stephen L. "Whitman as Urban Transcendentalist." *South Dakota Review* 14, no. 2 (1976): 6–18.

Thoreau, Henry. *Excursions*. Edited by Joseph J. Moldenhauer. Princeton, NJ: Princeton University Press, 2007.

———. *Journal*. Edited by John C. Broderick et al. Princeton, NJ: Princeton University Press, 1981–.

———. *Walden*. Edited by J. Lyndon Shanley. Princeton, NJ: Princeton University Press, 1971.

———. *Writings*. Edited by Bradford Torrey. Boston: Houghton Mifflin, 1906.

Warren, Joyce W. *Fanny Fern: An Independent Woman*. New Brunswick: Rutgers University Press, 1992.

Werner, James V. *American Flaneur: The Cosmic Physiognomy of Edgar Allan Poe*. New York: Routledge, 2004.

West, Michael. *Transcendental Wordplay: America's Romantic Punsters and the Search for the Language of Nature*. Athens, OH: Ohio University Press, 2000.

Whitman, Walt. *Leaves of Grass: A Textual Variorum*. Edited by Sculley Bradley et al. New York: New York University Press, 1980.

———. *Prose Works 1892*. Edited by Floyd Stovall. New York: New York University Press, 1963–1964.

## NOTES

1. Walter Benjamin, *Charles Baudelaire: A Lyric Poet in the Era of High Capitalism*, trans. Harry Zohn (London: Verso, 1983), 54–55.
2. Walter Benjamin, *Charles Baudelaire*, 128.
3. Walter Benjamin, *Charles Baudelaire*, 154.
4. Graeme Gilloch, *Myth and Metropolis: Walter Benjamin and the City* (Cambridge, UK: Polity, 1996), 172, 146.

5. James L. Machor, "Pastoralism and the American Urban Ideal: Hawthorne, Whitman, and the Literary Pattern," *American Literature* 54 (1982): 330

6. Wyn Kelley, *Melville's City: Literary and Urban Form in Nineteenth-Century New York* (New York: Cambridge University Press, 1996), 69–70.

7. Jean Raynaud, "Rural and Urban Visions in Poe's Tales." In *Myths ruraux et urbains dans la culture américaine* (Aix-en-Provence: Université de Provence, 1990), 126

8. James P. Stout, *Sodoms in Edens: The City in American Fiction before 1860* (Westport, CT: Greenwood, 1976), 60.

9. John Rignall, *Realist Fiction and the Strolling Narrator* (London: Routledge, 1992), 13.

10. Walter Benjamin, qtd. and trans. John Rignall, *Realist Fiction*, 16.

11. Dana Brand, *The Spectator and the City in Nineteenth-Century American Literature* (New York: Cambridge University Press, 1991), 107.

12. Dana Brand, *Spectator and the City*, 154.

13. Wyn Kelley, *Melville's City*, 62.

14. Howard C. Horsford, "Melville and the London Street Scene," *Essays in Arts and Sciences* 16 (May 1987): 24.

15. Hershel Parker, "Melville and the Berkshires: Emotion-Laden Terrain, 'Reckless Sky-Assaulting Mood,' and Encroaching Wordsworthianism," in *American Literature: The New England Heritage*, ed. James Nagel and Richard Astro (New York: Garland, 1981), 69–70.

16. J. E. A. Smith, "Herman Melville" (1891–1892). In *The Early Lives of Melville: Nineteenth-Century Biographical Sketches and Their Authors*, edited by Merton M. Sealts, Jr., 131 (Madison: University of Wisconsin Press, 1974),.

17. Jay Leyda, *The Melville Log: A Documentary Life of Herman Melville* (New York: Harcourt, 1951), 1:424.

18. Qtd. in Smith, "Herman Melville," 121.

19. Hershel Parker, *Herman Melville: A Biography: II, 1851–1891* (Baltimore: Johns Hopkins University Press, 2002), 914–19.

20. Margaret Fuller, qtd. in Charles Capper, *Margaret Fuller: An American Life* (New York: Oxford University Press, 1992-2007), 1:58.

21. Charles Capper, *Margaret Fuller*, 2:212.

22. Margaret Fuller, qtd. in Jeffrey Steele, "Margaret Fuller." In *American Travel Writers, 1776–1864*, edited by James Schramer and Donald Ross, 134 (Detroit: Gale, 1997).

23. Joseph C. Schöpp, "'We come out to Europe to learn what man can': Emerson's Grand Tour of 1833." In *Walking on a Trail of Words: Essays in Honor of Professor Agnieszka Salska*, edited by Jadwiga Maszewska and Zbigniew Maszewski, 20 (Lodz: Wydawniatwo Universytetu Lodzhiego, 2007).

24. James L. Machor, "Pastoralism and the American Urban Ideal," 333.

25. Stephen L. Tanner, "Whitman as Urban Transcendentalist," *South Dakota Review* 14.2 (1976): 11.

26. James L. Machor, "Pastoralism and the American Urban Ideal," 338.

27. Walter Benjamin, *Charles Baudelaire*, 125.

28. Jonathan Arac, "Whitman and Problems of the Vernacular." In *Breaking Bounds: Whitman and American Cultural Studies*, edited by Betsy Erkila and Jay Grossman, 58 (New York: Oxford University Press, 1996).

29. Stephen L. Tanner, "Whitman as Urban Transcendentalist," 13–14.

30. *Journal*, 3:378–9; see further Michael West, *Transcendental Wordplay: America's Romantic Punsters and the Search for the Language of Nature* (Athens: Ohio University Press, 2000), 196–200.

31. Rebecca Solint, *Wanderlust: A History of Walking* (New York: Viking, 2000), 289.

32. *Connecticut Herald* (New Haven), XX, No. 2. (Feb. 25, 1823): 2.

# SIX

# Spenser's "vertuous . . . discipline" and Human Flourishing

Paola Baseotto

The aim of the present article is to propose Spenser's allegorical epic poem, *The Faerie Queene,* as a focal text for studies of the nature and practice of human flourishing in the perspective indicated by recent research in psychology. Baltes and Freund argue that "psychological work on ideas such as flourishing and a good life benefit from consideration of philosophical and humanist work."[1] I think that *The Faerie Queene* performs this function particularly well: Spenser's poetic mastery stimulates aesthetic peak experiences in readers who are offered philosophical and ethical lessons about the meaning of human flourishing.

Since my very first contact with *The Faerie Queene* as a young student of English literature, I have experienced the intensity of the reader-response it stimulates. The poem possesses a remarkable power to excite "*feeling-into and identification,* the psychophysiological processes whereby we come temporarily to resonate to external objects and events as if their dynamics, motives, and experiences occurred in us."[2] As I hope to show, *The Faerie Queene* is characterized by a profound "orientative impact," to use the terminology of art psychology, which expands "the observer's awareness of meanings, implications, and even potentialities for action."[3] The end of the "action" promoted by the poem is the unfolding of a well-functioning, virtuous personality. Keyes's enunciation of the central goal of positive psychology as the understanding of "what builds positive character, and what makes life worth living" is a perfect description of the subject matter of *The Faerie Queene.*[4]

In the letter to Sir Walter Raleigh appended to the 1590 edition of the poem, Spenser declares that the "generall end" of *The Faerie Queene* is "to fashion a gentleman or noble person in vertuous and gentle discipline" (714):[5] "virtue" and "discipline" are cornerstones of the Spenserian discourse of flourishing. A crucial element of Spenser's view of virtue is a moral and spiritual understanding of the significance of living a full and productive life; the authorial letter characterizes the poem as instrumental to the acquisition of this understanding and of the abilities to actualize it. While the term *discipline* in Spenser's work is certainly also understood as "mental and moral training," it is above all an "instruction imparted to disciples" in order to form them to "proper conduct and action" in the perspective of the spiritual, ethical, and social responsibilities of earthly life.[6] The gentleman (and, by implication, the reader) Spenser's work aims at fashioning, in fact, is clearly no contemplative or hermit unconcerned with worldly affairs. Spenser's narratives consistently suggest a notion of heroism based on exposure to trials that test the endurance of characters and boost their moral and spiritual energy. In *The Faerie Queene* only characters who fully embrace the "painfull toile" (II.iii.40.9) of their quest figure as well-functioning individuals progressively unfolding their potential. The poem offers several dramatizations of the process of human flourishing, depicting a range of intermediate steps between the "excellency" ("Letter" 715) of Prince Arthur and the dehumanization of Fradubio (I.ii.28–44).

The centrality of reflections on the nature of and requirements for human flourishing within the Spenserian discourse of fashioning virtuous and active members of society has a clear Aristotelian cast, as Spenser himself declares in the "Letter" by repeatedly naming Aristotle as the philosophical father of *The Faerie Queene*.[7] Spenser's idea of flourishing, in fact, reflects the teachings of "the schools of Hellenistic ethics that scholars denote, collectively, as eudaimonistic."[8] As McMahon points out, Socrates, Plato, Aristotle, the Epicureans, and the Stoics indicated *eudaimonia*—rendered in English as "happiness," "well-being," or "flourishing,"—as the "final aim of philosophical reflection and virtuous activity."[9] Often differing as to the ultimate goal of the good life, Hellenic *eudaimonists* agreed that individuals flourish when they fulfill their natures or functions as human beings.[10]

This is not the place to deal with Spenser's reception of various eudaimonistic theories throughout his canon. The present study privileges an analysis of what I consider the crucial influence on *The Faerie Queene* as a handbook of human flourishing: the Aristotelian emphasis on full exercise of individual capacities as a precondition for full humanity and the "process of learning or training" necessary to become eudaimonic individuals.[11] Aristotle states that eudaimonia is "the activity of a complete life in accordance with complete excellence" and specifies that virtuous activity is the most desirable end of life and the essential component of eudaimonia.[12] The Aristotelian identification of flourishing with the virtuous life offers the standard against which the degree of participation in full humanity of the Spenserian characters is measured.

"For Aristotle, *eudaimonia* consisted of the possession of a virtuous character predisposed to practice, and actively practicing, virtuous behavior."[13] The two fundamental concepts at the base of the Aristotelian view of flourishing, perfectionism and *praxis* (action), inform the Spenserian dramatization of the nature and practice of human flourishing in *The Faerie Queene*.[14] "Neither by nature, then, nor contrary to nature do excellences arise in us; rather we are adapted by nature to receive them, and are made perfect by habit:" this passage exemplifies the rationale behind the narrative framework of Spenser's poem.[15] Each completed book of *The Faerie Queene* illustrates a specific virtue and the "fashioning" of a character who is endowed with the potential to become its champion.[16]

In the perspective of the virtue ethics that informs their work, both Aristotle as the philosophical father of the perfectionist theory of flourishing and Spenser as its skillful teacher identify the capacities central to human nature as virtues.[17] Hence Aristotle provides a detailed description of the life of "complete excellence" in *Nicomachean Ethics* and Spenser enlarges on the moral virtues "as Aristotle hath deuised" ("Letter" 715), each championed by a hero-to-be who is invariably characterized by a virtuous potential that needs developing and actualization.[18] This process of development and actualization is what the poem is all about: its rhetorical strategy is based on a complex network of dramatizations of successful or aborted efforts towards this goal, with parts of the main plot and subplots illustrating a very large range of impulses and attitudes that hinder or facilitate this process. The protagonists of *The Faerie Queene* possess a constitutional inclination to the virtue they champion, but the text makes it clear that when they start off they are inexperienced and often unaware of the very basics of the virtue they represent. That is why they need guidance from other characters who display a much deeper understanding and command of specific aspects of that virtue. All would-be patrons of virtues, moreover, benefit from confrontation with the opposites of their virtuous teachers and receive special enlightenment through visions or during their stay in houses of instruction and in places of testing. An illustrative example of this narrative strategy is the story of Red Cross, the Knight of Holiness, whose virtuous nature unfolds thanks to the help of, among others, Una, Arthur, Fidelia, and Contemplation, as well as through confrontation with Duessa, Error, Archimago, Orgoglio, Sansfoy, and Despair.[19] Red Cross is tested in Lucifera's house, Orgoglio's castle, and Despair's cave. Perfected in Coelia's House of Holiness, he is granted a vision of the New Jerusalem and of his own destiny as Saint George.

Spenser's insistence on his knights' imperfection and lack of full possession of their virtue, apart from being clearly suggestive of the limits of their fallen nature, by dilating narrative space allows full illustration of the whole process of unfolding of potentialities. This strategy perfectly serves the Spenserian discourse of full humanity not as a given but as a conquest. The virtuous disposition of the Spenserian would-be heroes and the long preparation needed for its full actualization illustrate very well the Aristotelian claim that eudaimonia "comes as a result of excellence and some process of learning or training," given that "all who are not maimed as regards excellence may win it [eudaimonia] by a certain kind of study and care."[20] "Study and care," "learning or training:" this beyond doubt is the focus of *The Faerie Queene* as shown by its narrative framework. Most of the twelve cantos composing each completed book, in fact, are devoted to the training and testing of the protagonist, to his or her long apprenticeship as patron of a specific virtue through a series of achievements and setbacks. Unproblematic and unambiguous accounts of the protagonist's acquisition of his or her virtue and completion of the assigned quest—in the few cases when quests are completed at all—are given only a few stanzas. Spenser's artistic and ethical energy is only occasionally spent on commenting on his heroes' accomplishments. He seems less keen on counting the arrows that hit the target than he is on describing the training and diligence of the archer, his or her willingness to try again and again, overcoming frustration and exhaustion. Spenser's heroes are those resilient individuals whose unfolding as human beings does not come to a standstill on the occasion of trials but gains new impetus. In this regard, *The Faerie Queene* answers the call of positive psychologists for illustrations of "what it means to thrive under challenge" and "how human strengths . . . are sometimes forged in trial and tribulation."[21]

*The Faerie Queene* functions particularly well as a great instructional work on human flourishing when it teaches lessons regarding the centrality of endurance and resilience in personal growth and the deadly potential of its main enemy: the impulse to withdraw from life's battles. Both the *Nicomachean Ethics* and Spenser's poem represent flourishing as an activity, not as a feeling or a fixed state of being. We have seen that Aristotle lays great stress on *praxis*, insisting that moral virtues are produced by habits of conduct and are realized in action: "excellences we get by first exercising them. . . . We become just by doing just acts, temperate by doing temperate acts, brave by doing brave acts." [22]

In *The Faerie Queene* only characters who navigate life's "seas of troubles and of toylesome paine" (VI.ix.31.6) eventually achieve the stature of heroes despite the incompleteness of their quest, because by not giving up, and by exercising their capacities to the utmost, they have flourished. Conversely, those who immure themselves in isolation and inaction stop flourishing and become, as I shall demonstrate, debased figures of human beings leading sterile and futile lives. In this regard the poem is a masterful and persuasive literary illustration of the central tenet of Aristotelian ethics: the importance of goal striving for human flourishing. Aristotle declares:

> [W]e must enjoin every one that has the power to live according to his own choice to set up for himself some object for the good life to aim at . . ., with reference to which he will then do all his acts, since not to have one's life organized in view of some end is a mark of much folly.[23]

Modern science has endorsed Aristotle's linking of goal striving and flourishing. Research indicates that goal striving "is vital to 'the good life:'" "when asked what makes for a happy, fulfilling, and meaningful life, people spontaneously discuss their life goals."[24] *The Faerie Queene* conveys the idea that having a quest and engaging in it make flourishing possible. Spenser's knights are required to quest not just for God, church, monarch, and England, but first and foremost for their own self-growth because only full humanity produces virtuous and heroic actions. Moreover, as the narrative of the Knight of the Red Cross indicates, only by first flourishing in the here and now can one hope to enjoy eternal life as a saint. While by reason of its Christian framework *The Faerie Queene* represents eternal bliss as the ultimate goal of individuals, it nonetheless lays great stress on the earthly nature of the efforts required to unfold as good Christians. The poem's more open (and more often commented upon) reminder of the necessity to embrace secular duties is addressed to the Knight of the Red Cross by Contemplation. Red Cross, following an experience that positive psychologists would describe as a perfect state of flow and enlightenment regarding his future as Saint George, misjudges his own progress toward complete unfolding. Contemplation has to remind a would-be saint anxious to "streight way on that last long voiage fare" (I.x.63.4) that he has earthly duties to fulfill. This is one of the many endorsements in the poem of a "*theologia vitae* that is to be lived to the full in the secular world . . . in allegiance to the 'Powers that be' that are 'ordained of God' (Romans 13.1)."[25] Approving references to secular endeavours contribute significantly to the pragmatic and instructional quality of *The Faerie Queene*.[26]

Besides its expediency for the actualization of human capacities, hence for flourishing, engaging in earthly duties is also crucial as proof of individuals' awareness of their own state as fallen humans in a fallen world, a precondition for salvation in Protestant theology. The open formulation of this crucial concept that elsewhere in the poem is often highlighted in the narrator's remarks or in stories such as that of Ruddymane in the first canto of Book II, is uttered by Belphoebe, a paragon of virtue, who in her reminder that "God did Sweate ordaine" (II.iii.41.5) echoes Genesis 3.19, "In the sweat of thy face shalt thou eat bread, til thou returne to the earth." Evans points out that

> The Quest, itself made necessary by the Fall, must be achieved by means of fallen human nature. . . . The degree to which the characters sweat in the pursuit of virtue is a measure of their heroism.[27]

Unsurprisingly, appreciative remarks regarding "the sweating" of characters in pursuit of virtuous quests recur throughout the poem: thus for instance Britomart is portrayed as she "forward rode, and kept her ready way" (III.iv.18.2) and Sir Guyon as he "Him selfe addresst to that aduenture hard," rising "early before the Morne" (II.xi.3).

More numerous than eulogistic descriptions of the forward impetus of would-be heroes are references to their painful apprehension of the daunting amount of "toil and paine" (VI.x.2.2) required by their quests. The poem represents the temptation to withdraw from life's struggles as a very understandable human instinct, but at the same time it accentuates its destructive potential with regard to human wholeness. This discourse is developed across the six completed books by means of theme-related narratives of various reactions to escapist impulses and their effects on flourishing: some stories focus on successful attempts at overcoming exhaustion (Sir Calidore's, for example; see my discussion below), others describe the outcome of withdrawal from the stream of life (see for instance the narrative of the knights who prefer the ease and inaction of the Bower of Bliss to the pursuit of their tasks, II.v and xii).[28]

*The Faerie Queene* depicts no sin, no slackening of moral or spiritual energy as equally detrimental to human wholeness as sloth.[29] In view of the poem's instructional message about flourishing as a lifelong process entailing energetic engagement, sloth is appropriately a pervasive theme. Spenser calls upon all his resources as a poet and moral teacher to anatomize this temptation, offering lessons about the attitudes that facilitate the dissemination of its paralysing poison into people's minds and souls. Three of them receive greater emphasis: (1) the impulse to prefer ease to toil, (2) fatalistic views of human action as futile, and (3) inappropriate responses to trauma.

Regarding the first attitude, Spenser offers an impressive demonstration of his ability to infuse music into words and vibrancy into images in the hypnotic allurements to rest spoken within Edenic settings by tempters endowed with rare rhetoric gifts that clearly signify the endangering potential of this very human inclination to prefer ease to toil.[30] By conjuring the utter tranquillity of Phaedria's island and Acrasia's garden, the smells, colors and lulling sounds of a welcoming natural setting, the smiles and quiet sleep of its guests, Spenser skillfully excites in his readers an ecstatic experience. Phaedria's urging not to waste "ioyous howres in needlesse paine" and her invitation to reject "fruitlesse toile, and present pleasures chuse" (II.vi.17.4, 9) sound persuasive and innocent. The condition of the knights who dwell in Acrasia's garden, "the most daintie Paradise on ground" (II.xii.58.1), their "warlike Armes, the ydle instruments / Of sleeping praise, . . . hong vpon a tree" (80.1), seems enviable. However reluctant to emerge from such pleasing enchantment, Spenser's reader is progressively made aware of multiple signs of the sinful quality of this kind of ease and reflects that because invitations are by wicked speakers, they cannot be conducive to spiritual, moral, and physical flourishing.[31] When enticements to rest are uttered by the likes of Acrasia, whom Spenser's "Letter" identifies as an "Enchaunteresse" (717) or the Sirens who evoke the Homeric temptresses, the reader easily understands that the ease they promote is improper. The reader-response that the text dramatizes as appropriate, however, comes as a result of a more complex process of interpretation when speakers are honest characters like the shepherds in Book VI. Their offer of refreshments and hospitality to Sir Calidore, "yet sweating" (VI.ix.5.7) in his pursuit of the Blatant Beast, seem devoid of moral danger. And yet the recurrent textual emphasis on the absence of toil and strife characterizing the pastoral community alerts the reader to Calidore's false expectation of an earthly paradise. Within the poem's Christian framework, a life untouched by change, death, and loss is not a possibility for fallen humans in the fallen world.[32] Innocence and happiness in a Christian perspective are regained through spiritual regeneration and active engagement, not through retreat. Calidore's "sweating" is necessary: the narrative dramatizes the knight's attitude in the pastoral haven—unwilling to "sew / His former quest, so full of toile and paine," he is "vnmyndfull of his vow and high beheast" (VI.x.2.1-2; x.1.3)—as understandable, but nonetheless censurable.

Dramatized as more devious and hence opposing more effectively the forward impulse that enables human flourishing, is fatalism, which entails an apprehension of human striving as futile. This is a sensitive issue for a poet writing within the framework of Protestantism; as McCabe observes, "Calvin's doctrine of the relationship between grace and free will was one of the most contentious tenets of reformed theology."[33] Indeed, the tension between two competing discourses, the ideal of virtuous action and the Protestant emphasis on human incapacity to perform it unless divinely predetermined to it, a view that may stimulate fatalistic attitudes, often characterizes Spenser's narratives of the nature and practice of flourishing. His texts represent excessive emphasis on this aspect of Protestant theology and its implications—devolvement of responsibility and demotivation—as hindrances to the energetic performance of the worldly duties that are vital for individual and collective flourishing. Orthodox in their formulations, references to human powerlessness by both wicked and virtuous speakers are interpreted as powerful incitements to disengage by characters who are already weary of their quest or doubtful about their own suitability as questers. One spokesperson of fatalistic views is Night, "the evil demiurge of Spenser's cosmology,"[34] who declares that nobody "can turne the streame of destinee, / Or breake the chayne of strong necessitee, / Which fast is tyde to *Ioues* eternall seat" (I.v.25.4–6). The Red Cross Knight's condition marked by lack of spiritual energy and psychological helplessness in the face of obsessing doubts about his own ability to "striue with strong necessitie" (I.ix.42.6) is another evocative depiction of the persuasive and disheartening power of arguments regarding the corruption of human will.[35]

In an illuminating discussion of treatments of the theme of fatalism in *The Faerie Queene*, Jessica Wolfe rightly identifies the central point of Spenserian concern with the excuse of determinism: "Her [Night's] belief in a 'fatal chain' that binds the will in turn fuels a hopelessness that discourages both the active pursuit of virtue and the avowal of personal responsibility for sin."[36] Several stories and comments by the narrator throughout *The Faerie Queene* underline individual responsibility for errors and the crucial role of energetic virtuous action assisted by Grace: humans are called to participate in God's design, not just contemplate it.[37] This is clearly stated for example by Merlin who, having disclosed Britomart's future as bride of the Knight of Justice and mother of a king, refutes her nurse's fatalistic observation, "what needes her to toyle, sith fates can make / Way for themselues, their purpose to pertake?" by remarking: "Indeede the fates are firme, . . . Yet ought mens good endeuours them confirme, / And guyde the heauenly causes to their constant terme" (III.iii.25). In this perspective, views of the futility of virtuous striving are exposed as false: all through the poem it is lives that have lost meaning and purpose that are depicted as futile. This pervasive discourse is developed to the full in the Spenserian narratives of various reactions to trauma.

The motif of trauma is at the core of *The Faerie Queene*: the degree of the characters' acceptance of traumatic experiences as necessary and the transformation of their personality in terms of growth or regression are litmus tests of their spiritual state and virtuous energy, hence, within the view of flourishing dramatized in the poem, of the degree of their participation in full humanity.[38] The poem's pragmatic and instructional strength is probably best expressed in its representations of various types of trauma and minute descriptions of the range of possible outcomes. A corresponding Spenserian character for each personality described in Wilson's seminal taxonomy of posttraumatic conditions may easily be found. Una, for instance, could well function as a representative figure of the "Accelerated Self" who is characterized by resilience and whose post-traumatic "self-metamorphosis" is a "protean transformation of . . . inner resources."[39] While her loved one, Red Cross, languishes in Orgoglio's dungeon, Una despairs and manifests loss of will to live. Prince Arthur functions as a facilitator of flourishing pressing her with a series of warnings and words of encouragement (I.vii.38–42) aimed at rousing her from the mood of self-pity and indulgence in despair signalled by her description of herself as "the laughing stocke of fortunes mockeries" (43.2) and her comment that there is nothing left for her to do than her "woes to weepe and waile" (39.9). Arthur points out to Una that immurement in despair is overcome through holding on to the perspectives of faith and to the rule of reason. These words revive "her chearelesse spright" (52.8); significantly, the canto ends on the image of a resilient Una energetically engaging in her quest to save her knight with Arthur's (that is, Grace's) help, "so forth they went" (52.9): following her trial, Una's forward impetus intensifies.[40]

Not surprisingly, the impression on the reader's imagination of scientific descriptions of the main characteristics of posttraumatic personalities is not in the least comparable to Spenser's literary renderings. Suffice it to consider, as an example, the bare facts of the condition of the "Inert Self," the "most severely damaged person," "diminished in humanness," deprived of "motivational striving," showing an "unexpressive" face,[41] compared with the unforgettable, haunting portrait of the Knight of the Red Cross emerging from one in a series of spiritual and psychological trials: he is a "ruefull spectacle of death and ghastly drere," "His sad dull eies deepe sunck in hollow pits," "his visage pale and wan," "his vitall powres / Decayd, and al his flesh shronk vp like withered flowres" (I.viii.40–42).

*The Faerie Queene* offers many instructive accounts of a state, languishing, that is the object of great attention and deep concern in modern psychology. Described as a condition marked by "the absence of meaning, the absence of purpose, and the absence of anything positive in life," languishing is "an overlooked malady that is the counterpart to mental health."[42] American scientists have raised the alarm regarding this "silent and debilitating epidemic . . . associated with poor emotional health, with high limitations of daily living, and with a high likelihood of a severe number (i.e., six or more) of lost days of work."[43] Narratives of languishing characterized by the recurrent motif of waste and futility linked to inaction and disengagement are crucial to the Spenserian endeavour to fashion flourishing individuals. A typical story dealing with what modern science describes as the "emotional distress and psychosocial impairment" characteristic of individuals diagnosed with this condition is that of Timias, Prince Arthur's squire.[44] A very active "fresh budd of vertue" (I.viii.27.1) in the first three books of *The Faerie Queene*, by the seventh canto of Book IV Timias is depicted as a "wofull wight" (38.6) who lives in a cabin in the depths of the forest entertaining suicidal thoughts. Unjustly accused of unfaithfulness by his beloved Belphoebe, he turns into the living image of "sad melancholy" (38.9). To discourage identifications with the cliché of the melancholy lover of Elizabethan sonnet sequences, the narrator points out that it is the "fowle dishonor" (IV.vii.37.9) deriving from Belphoebe's accusation that takes away from him his joie de vivre; "since Timias's name signifies honour, dishonour makes him 'like a pined ghost' (41.4)."[45] His voluntary seclusion and his abandoning of duty and social role (he breaks his "wonted warlike weapons" and throws them away "with vow to vse no more," (39.1–2) make him like a living dead: he is significantly described as a "ghost late risen from his graue" (IV.viii.12.7). The text emphasizes the importance of goal striving for the development and maintenance of a fully human identity: as soon as Timias abdicates his duty and divests his role, he becomes ghostlike; he loses his humanity. His physical transformation is so radical, Arthur and Belphoebe hardly recognize him when they meet, thus signifying that he is not himself anymore. Expressing his self-hate through nearly starving himself to death, "The more his weakened body so to wast" (IV.vii.41.8), he tells Belphoebe that his torments have made him "loath this life, still longing for to die" (IV.viii.16.9). Having vowed "in that wildernesse, of men forlore, / . . . / His hard mishap in dolor to deplore, / And wast his wretched daies in wofull plight" (vii.39), he spends his life "in dolour and despaire" (43.2), weeping and wailing "night and day" (viii.2.8). A reiterated use of expressions such as "*wast* his wretched daies," "*wearing out* his youthly yeares," "*wore* away" (vii.39.8; 41.2; viii.2.6; italics mine), emphasizes the motive of waste and of the futility of a life that has lost its purpose. Timias's willful immurement in a useless life that is a living death is condemned by Belphoebe:

> He whose daies in wilfull woe are worne,
> The grace of his Creator doth despise,
> That will not vse his gifts for thanklesse nigardise
> [niggardliness]. (IV.viii.15.7–9)

While the Red Cross Knight's and Timias's painful recovery from a state of total paralysis of their will to "forward fare" (I.ix.2.5) functions as a lesson regarding the crucial role of patience, endurance, and resilience in the formation and maintenance of a fully human, flourishing identity, allegorical representations of a state that modern science would describe as an irreversible posttraumatic immurement in dehumanizing stasis teach this same lesson by negative example. Malbecco is a paradigmatical example: his allegory traces the degeneration of a mortal human to an undying abstraction. When his young wife runs away with his wealth Malbecco loses the objects of his jealous and sterile attachment and is driven to utter despair. Incapable of involvement in virtuous action, he assumes the ghostlike appearance of one "from Limbo lake . . . late escaped" (III.x.54.9). His repeated attempts at committing suicide are unsuccessful because

> Through long anguish, and selfe-murdring thought
> He was so wasted and forpined quight,
> That all his substance was consum'd to nought,
> And nothing left . . . (III.x.57.1–4)

Malbecco loses his human features and turns into an "aery Spright;" he "is woxen so deform'd, that he has quight/ Forgot he was a man, and *Gealosie* is hight" (III.x.60.8–9). He has become so identified with vice that he has lost the humanity that alone promises deliverance from mortal life. Forever trapped in a state of frightful immutability, he can "neuer dye, but dying liues" (III.x.60.1).

*The Faerie Queene* is a powerful poetic transcription of mythology's universal theme of "trauma and the transformation of identity."[46] Following the pattern of archetypal tales depicting the protagonist Hero as he or she "journeys into the abyss of dark forces, endures trials of spirit, soul, and body," Spenser's poem evokes the challenges of life and the consequences of moral choices. It provides readers with a "fayre mirrhour" to "behold [their] face[s]" (II.Proem.4.7) and stimulates their desire to see the image of a Red Cross Knight, not a Malbecco in it, the image of someone who has been bruised but not overwhelmed by life's struggles, someone who has had to learn to be a man before even dreaming of becoming a saint.

## BIBLIOGRAPHY


Aristotle, *The Complete Works of Aristotle.* Edited by Jonathan Barnes. 2 vols. Bollinger Series LXXI. Princeton, NJ: Princeton University Press, 1984.

———. *Eudemian Ethics.* Translated by J. Solomon. In *The Complete Works of Aristotle,* Volume 2, edited by Jonathan Barnes. 2 vols. Bollinger Series LXXI. Princeton, NJ: Princeton University Press, 1984.

———. *Nicomachean Ethics.* Translated by W. D. Ross. In *The Complete Works of Aristotle,* Volume 2, edited by Jonathan Barnes. 2 vols. Bollinger Series LXXI. Princeton, NJ: Princeton University Press, 1984.

Baltes, Paul B. and Alexandra M. Freund. "The Intermarriage of Wisdom and Selective Optimization with Compensation: Two Meta-Heuristics Guiding the Conduct of Life." In *Flourishing: Positive Psychology and the Life Well-Lived,* edited by Corey L. M. Keyes and Jonathan Haidt, 249–73. Washington, DC: American Psychological Association, 2003.

Baseotto, Paola. *"Disdeining life, desiring leaue to die:" Spenser and the Psychology of Despair,* Studies in English Literatures 10. Stuttgart: *ibidem,* 2008.

———. "Godly Sorrow, Damnable Despair and *Faerie Queene* I.ix." *Cahiers Elisabéthains* 69. 1 (2006): 1–11.

———. "Theology and Interiority: Emotions as Evidence of the Working of Grace in Elizabethan and Stuart Conversion Narratives." In *A History of Emotions, 1200–1800,* ed. Jonas Liliequist. London: Pickering and Chatto, 2012.

Berger, Harry Jr. *Revisionary Play: Studies in the Spenserian Dynamics.* Berkeley and Los Angeles: University of California Press, 1988.

Berry, Lloyd E., ed. *The Geneva Bible: A Facsimile of the 1560 Edition.* Madison, WI: University of Wisconsin Press, 1969.

Darwall, Stephen. "Valuing Activity." In *Human Flourishing,* edited by Ellen Frankel Paul, Fred D. Miller Jr. and Jeffrey Paul, 176–96. Cambridge: Cambridge University Press, 1999.

Eagleton, Terry. *After Theory.* New York: Basic Books, 2003.

Eid, Michael and Randy J. Larsen, eds. *The Science of Subjective Well-Being.* New York: Guilford Press, 2008.

Emmons, Robert A. "Personal Goals, Life Meaning, and Virtue: Wellsprings of a Positive Life." In *Flourishing: Positive Psychology and the Life Well-Lived,* edited by Corey L. M. Keyes and Jonathan Haidt, 105–28. Washington, DC: American Psychological Association, 2003.

Escobedo, Andrew. "Spenser and Classical Philosophy." In *The Oxford Handbook of Edmund Spenser,* edited by Richard A. McCabe, 520–37. Oxford: Oxford University Press, 2010.

Evans, Maurice. *Spenser's Anatomy of Heroism: A Commentary on 'The Faerie Queene.'* Cambridge: Cambridge University Press, 1970.

Frankel Paul, Ellen, Fred D. Miller Jr. and Jeffrey Paul, eds. *Human Flourishing.* Cambridge: Cambridge University Press, 1999.

Gregerson, Linda. "*The Faerie Queene (1590).*" In *The Oxford Handbook of Edmund Spenser,* edited by Richard A. McCabe, 198–217. Oxford: Oxford University Press, 2010.

Hamilton, A. C., Donald Cheney, David A. Richardson, and William W. Barker, eds. *The Spenser Encyclopedia.* Toronto, Buffalo and London: University of Toronto Press, 1990.

Haybron, Daniel M. "Philosophy and the Science of Subjective Well-Being." In *The Science of Subjective Well-Being,* edited by Michael Eid and Randy J. Larsen, 17–43. New York: Guilford Press, 2008.

Hiller, Geoffrey G. "Night." In *The Spenser Encyclopedia,* edited by A. C. Hamilton, Donald Cheney, David A. Richardson, and William W. Barker. Toronto, Buffalo and London: University of Toronto Press, 1990.

Horton, Ronald A. "Virtues." In *The Spenser Encyclopedia,* edited by A. C. Hamilton, Donald Cheney, David A. Richardson, and William W. Barker. Toronto, Buffalo and London: University of Toronto Press, 1990.

Hurka, Thomas. *Perfectionism.* Oxford: Oxford University Press, 1993.

———. "The Three Faces of Flourishing." In *Human Flourishing,* edited by Ellen Frankel Paul, Fred D. Miller Jr. and Jeffrey Paul, 44–71. Cambridge: Cambridge University Press, 1999.

Keyes, Corey L. M. and Jonathan Haidt, eds. *Flourishing: Positive Psychology and the Life Well-Lived.* Washington, DC: American Psychological Association, 2003.

Kraut, Richard. *Aristotle: Political Philosophy.* Oxford: Oxford University Press, 2002.

Kreitler, Hans and Shulamith Kreitler. *Psychology of the Arts.* Durham, NC: Duke University Press, 1972.

Lyons, Bridget Gellert. *Voices of Melancholy: Studies in Literary Treatments of Melancholy in Renaissance England.* London: Routledge, 1971.

MacLachlan, Hugh and Philip B. Rollinson. "Magnanimity, Magnificence." In *The Spenser Encyclopedia,* edited by A. C. Hamilton, Donald Cheney, David A. Richardson, and William W. Barker. Toronto, Buffalo and London: University of Toronto Press, 1990.

McCabe, Richard A., ed. *The Oxford Handbook of Edmund Spenser.* Oxford: Oxford University Press, 2010.

———. *The Pillars of Eternity: Time and Providence in 'The Faerie Queene.'* Dublin: Irish Academic Press, 1989.

———. "Providence". In *The Spenser Encyclopedia,* edited by A. C. Hamilton, Donald Cheney, David A. Richardson, and William W. Barker. Toronto, Buffalo and London: University of Toronto Press, 1990.

McMahon, Darrin M. "The Pursuit of Happiness in Life." In *The Science of Subjective Well-Being,* edited by Michael Eid and Randy J. Larsen, 80–93. New York: Guilford Press, 2008.

Miller, David L. "Abandoning the Quest." *ELH* 46.2 (1979): 173–92.

Nohrnberg, James. *The Analogy of 'The Faerie Queene.'* Princeton, NJ: Princeton University Press, 1980.

Patrides, C. A. and J. Wittreich, eds. *The Apocalypse in English Renaissance Thought and Literature.* Manchester: Manchester University Press, 1984.

Rasmussen, Douglas B. "Human Flourishing and the Appeal to Human Nature." In *Human Flourishing*, edited by Ellen Frankel Paul, Fred D. Miller Jr. and Jeffrey Paul, 1–43. Cambridge: Cambridge University Press, 1999.

Ryan, Richard M. and Edward L. Deci. "Hedonia, Eudaimonia, and Well-Being: An Introduction." *Journal of Happiness Studies* 9.1 (2008): 1–11.

———. "On Happiness and Human Potential: A Review of Research on Hedonic and Eudaimonic Well-Being." *Annual Review of Psychology* 52 (2001): 141–66.

Ryff, Carol D. and Burton Singer. "Flourishing Under Fire: Resilience as a Prototype of Challenged Thriving." In *Flourishing: Positive Psychology and the Life Well-Lived*, edited by Corey L. M. Keyes and Jonathan Haidt, 15–36. Washington, DC: American Psychological Association, 2003.

Sandler, Florence. "*The Faerie Queene*: An Elizabethan Apocalypse." In *The Apocalypse in English Renaissance*, edited by C. A. Patrides and J. Wittreich, 148–74. Manchester: Manchester University Press, 1984.

Spenser, Edmund. *The Faerie Queene*. Edited by A. C. Hamilton. London: Longman, 2001.

Wilson, John P. *The Posttraumatic Self: Restoring Meaning and Wholeness to Personality.* New York: Routledge, 2006.

Wilson, Rawdon R. "Character." In *The Spenser Encyclopedia*, edited by A. C. Hamilton, Donald Cheney, David A. Richardson, and William W. Barker. Toronto, Buffalo and London: University of Toronto Press, 1990.

Wolfe, Jessica. "Spenser, Homer, and the Mythography of Strife." *Renaissance Quarterly* 58. 4 (2005): 1220–88.

## NOTES

*Note on texts:* Quotations from *The Faerie Queene* are from the annotated 2001 edition by A. C. Hamilton (London: Longman, 2001). References to Spenser's "Letter" and to the text of the poem are cited parenthetically in the text by page number and book, canto, stanza, line numbers respectively (roman numerals are used for books and cantos).

1. Paul B. Baltes and Alexandra M. Freund, "The Intermarriage of Wisdom and Selective Optimization with Compensation: Two Meta-Heuristics Guiding the Conduct of Life." In *Flourishing: Positive Psychology and the Life Well-Lived*, eds. Corey L. M. Keyes and Jonathan Haidt, 249–73 (Washington, DC: American Psychological Association, 2003), 249.

2. Hans Kreitler and Shulamith Kreitler, *Psychology of the Arts* (Durham, NC.: Duke University Press, 1972), 28.

3. Ibid., 324.

4. Keyes, introduction to *Flourishing*, xiii.

5. "A Letter of the Authors expounding his *whole intention in the course of this worke: which* for that it giueth great light to the Reader, for the better vnderstanding is hereunto annexed": hereafter, "Letter." As Nohrnberg points out, "In the Renaissance the purposes of literature in general and the epic poem in particular are understood to be continuous with this notable genre of intellectual prose, that is, the educational treatise, or 'institution', which gets out to fashion an ideal vocational or social pattern and invites emulation by the elite to whom it is addressed." *The Analogy of 'The Faerie Queene'* (Princeton, NJ: Princeton University Press, 1980), 26.

6. My three quotations are from *The Shorter Oxford English Dictionary,* 3rd ed., s.v. "discipline." Regarding the term *discipline,* see Aristotle's reference to the centrality of "some sort of discipline" for acquisition of the virtuous habits that produce the "good life." *Eudemian Ethics*, trans. J. Solomon, in *The Complete Works of Aristotle*, Volume 2, edited by Jonathan Barnes, 2 vols. Bollinger Series LXXI (Princeton, NJ: Princeton University Press, 1984), 1922, I.1.1214a.

7. Scholasticism, which harmonized Christian theology with classical philosophy, was the mainstay of Spenser's education at Pembroke College, Cambridge; Aristotle and his medieval commentators (Thomas Aquinas above all) was prescribed reading.

8. Daniel M. Haybron, "Philosophy and the Science of Subjective Well-Being." In *The Science of Subjective Well-Being*, edited by Michael Eid and Randy J. Larsen, 24 (New York and London: Guilford, 2008). Haybron points out that "Aristotle's writings are so influential that commentators often use 'eudaimonistic' or 'eudaimonic' simply to denote Aristotelian theories of well-being or views that emphasize perfection or virtue," 24.

9. Darrin M. McMahon, "The Pursuit of Happiness in History." In *Science of Subjective Well-Being*, Eid, 82.

10. A review of ancient and modern eudaimonic concepts is found in Richard M. Ryan and Edward L. Deci, "On Happiness and Human Potential: A Review of Research on Hedonic and Eudaimonic Well-Being," *Annual Review of Psychology* 52 (2001): 141–66 and "Hedonia, Eudaimonia, and Well-Being: An Introduction," *Journal of Happiness Studies* 9, no. 1 (2008): 1–11.

11. Aristotle, *Nicomachean Ethics*, trans. W. D. Ross. In *The Complete Works of Aristotle*, 2:1737, I.8.1099b.

12. Aristotle, *Eudemian Ethics*, 1930, II.1.1219a. In this light, as Terry Eagleton notes, Aristotle clearly identifies happiness with virtuous behavior: "It is not as though the reward for virtue is happiness; being virtuous *is* to be happy. It is to enjoy the deep sort of happiness which comes from fulfilling your nature." *After Theory* (New York: Basic Books, 2003), 117. Andrew Escobedo observes that "the automatic association between happiness and virtue has a distinctly odd ring to modern ears. Our philosophers, starting most notably with Kant, have taught us that virtue is a duty, one that may require us to sacrifice our happiness for the sake of the good." "Spenser and Classical Philosophy." In *The Oxford Handbook of Edmund Spenser*, edited by Richard A. McCabe, 522 (Oxford: Oxford University Press, 2010).

13. Escobedo, "Spenser and Classical Philosophy," 521. For an excellent review of Aristotle's conceptions of virtue, human good, and well-being, see Richard Kraut, *Aristotle: Political Philosophy* (Oxford: Oxford University Press, 2002), 20–97.

14. Regarding Aristotle's perfectionist theory, Douglas B. Rasmussen remarks that "To 'perfect,' to 'realize,' or to 'actualize oneself is not to become God-like, immune to degeneration, or incapable of harm, but it is to fulfil those potentialities and capacities that make one human. This is to achieve one's natural end or perform one's natural function." "Human Flourishing and the Appeal to Human Nature," in Ellen Frankel Paul, Fred D. Miller Jr. and Jeffrey Paul, eds., *Human Flourishing* (Cambridge: Cambridge University Press, 1999), 37. See Thomas Hurka's important study *Perfectionism* (Oxford: Oxford University Press, 1993). Stephen Darwall suggests that in the light of a perfectionist reading of Aristotle's ethics, "a proper understanding of what we are includes an understanding of what we are *to become*. By approximating this standard, we better realize our nature, and hence, ourselves." "Valuing Activity," in *Human Flourishing*, Frankel Paul, 180.

15. Aristotle, *Nicomachean Ethics*, 1743, II.1.1103a.

16. As Thomas Hurka observes, philosophical views based on the Aristotelian perfectionist idea of flourishing stress the etymological relation of the term *flourishing* to "flowering." In this light, "we are to understand human flourishing by analogy with similar states of other organisms such as animals and even plants. A plant or animal flourishes when the properties that constitute its nature are developed to a high degree. By analogy, it is said, there are properties central to human nature, and their development is what makes for human flourishing and a good human life." "The Three Faces of Flourishing," in *Human Flourishing*, Frankel Paul, 44.

17. Emmons points out that "The study of virtue as an aspect of personality is enjoying something of a renaissance in contemporary research . . . these constructs [of virtue ethics] are powerful tools for research in positive psychology." "Personal Goals, Life Meaning, and Virtue: Wellsprings of a Positive Life," in *Flourishing*, Keyes, 122.

18. Aristotle, *Nicomachean Ethics*, 1741, I.13.1102a. Numerous scholars have pointed to the lack of exact correspondence between Aristotle's and Spenser's moral virtues; Ronald A. Horton, "Virtues," in *The Spenser Encyclopedia*, ed. A. C. Hamilton et al. (Toronto, Buffalo and London: University of Toronto Press, 1990), provides a useful review of the critical debate. I think the expression "as Aristotle hath deuised" points less to a formal correspondence of single elements of Aristotle's virtue ethics, than to the broader influence of his philosophy and ethics on *The Faerie Queene*.

19. These characters are all externalizations of the Knight's own virtuous or sinful impulses and, as suggested by Elizabeth Heale in a personal communication, aspects of divine or satanic forces at work in the world. On Spenser's narrative strategies and especially his use of "virtue's antitypes or mirror inversions," see Linda Gregerson, "*The Faerie Queene (1590)*," in *The Oxford Handbook of Edmund Spenser*, McCabe, 209.

20. Aristotle, *Nicomachean Ethics*, 1737, I.8.1099b.

21. Carol D. Ryff and Burton Singer, "Flourishing Under Fire: Resilience as a Prototype of Challenged Thriving." In *Flourishing*, Keyes, 16.

22. Aristotle, *Nicomachean Ethics*, 1743, II.1.1103b. Escobedo remarks that "Tudor English writers used Aristotelian ideas about ethics with the full knowledge that some of their Protestant colleagues condemned Aristotle's notion of habituated virtue for failing to coincide with the doctrine of human depravity" and rightly argues that "Spenser saw both overlap and difference between classical philosophy and Christian theology." "Spenser and Classical Philosophy," 521.

23. Aristotle, *Eudemian Ethics*, 1923, I.2.1214b.

24. Emmons, "Personal Goals, Life Meaning, and Virtue," 106. Emmons suggests that "The goals construct has given form and substance to the amorphous concept of 'meaning in life' that humanistic psychology has long understood as a key element of human functioning. . . . The scientific and clinical relevance of the personal meaning construct has been demonstrated in the adjustment literature, in which indicators of meaningfulness (e.g., purpose in life, a sense of coherence) predict positive functioning . . . , whereas indicators of meaninglessness (e.g., anomie, alienation) are regularly associated with psychological distress and pathology," 107.

25. Florence Sandler, "*The Faerie Queene*: An Elizabethan Apocalypse." In *The Apocalypse in English Renaissance Thought and Literature*, edited by C. A. Patrides and J. Wittreich, 155 (Manchester: Manchester University Press, 1984). See Sandler's interesting discussion at pp. 154–56 of the episode of the Red Cross Knight's instruction by Contemplation in the light of the Erasmian view of secular duties as preliminary, not contrary to achieving "the contemplative vision," 155.

26. The Protestant theology that informs the *Faerie Queene* views good works as the fruits of faith, "a means not of gaining salvation but of verifying the existence of the necessary true and lively faith," Hugh MacLachlan and Philip B. Rollinson, "Magnanimity, Magnificence," in *The Spenser Encyclopedia*, Hamilton, 448.

27. Maurice Evans, *Spenser's Anatomy of Heroism: A Commentary on 'The Faerie Queene'* (Cambridge: Cambridge University Press, 1970), 31.

28. In my study of despair, *"Disdeining life, desiring leaue to die:" Spenser and the Psychology of Despair*, Studies in English Literatures 10 (Stuttgart: *ibidem*, 2008), I examine numerous narratives of trauma in the entire Spenserian canon.

29. In her not recent, but amply documented discussion of literary treatments of melancholy, Bridget Gellert Lyons notices that from the Middle Ages forward criticism of sloth or acedia has focused especially on its inclination to generate impulses at "letting one's talents and virtues rot, and failing to accomplish one's task in a more worldly sense also." *Voices of Melancholy: Studies in Literary Treatments of Melancholy in Renaissance England* (London: Routledge, 1971), 88. On sixteenth-century concepts of sloth and Spenser's idea of moral purpose, see David L. Miller, "Abandoning the Quest," *ELH* 46, no. 2 (1979): 173–92.

30. R. Rawdon Wilson notes that "Spenser adapts a standard method of characterization which derives from medieval romances, especially those by Chrétien, in which the hero typically finds himself caught between the claims of duty and pleasure.

Ultimately this method is classical and derives from the narrative practice of Homer and Virgil and in particular Ovid." "Character," in *The Spenser Encyclopedia*, Hamilton, 142.

31. Evans rightly argues that Spenser's descriptions "make a deep appeal to the senses but at the same time, by drawing on the great patterns of image or myth throughout the poem, they have built-in moral signposts which force the reader to recognize and evaluate truly the experiences." *Spenser's Anatomy of Heroism*, 74.

32. The Edenic peace of the pastoral community is appropriately disrupted by the irruption of a tiger and a group of Brigands. A thoughtful treatment of Spenser's criticism of the arcadian state of mind is Berger's "Re-verting to the Green Cabinet," in Harry Berger Jr., *Revisionary Play: Studies in the Spenserian Dynamics* (Berkeley and Los Angeles: University of California Press, 1988).

33. Richard A. McCabe, *The Pillars of Eternity: Time and Providence in 'The Faerie Queene'* (Dublin: Irish Academic Press, 1989), 171.

34. Geoffrey G. Hiller, "Night," in *The Spenser Encyclopedia*, Hamilton, 511.

35. These lines are spoken by Despair. However, as I have argued in "Godly Sorrow, Damnable Despair and *Faerie Queene* I.ix," *Cahiers Elisabéthains* 69, no. 1 (2006), 6, the seeming dialogue with Despair is an internal debate, a spiritual fight. Despair is an objectification of the Red Cross Knight's psychic and spiritual state, as well as a figure of the devil and the abstraction of despair.

36. Jessica Wolfe, "Spenser, Homer, and the Mythography of Strife," *Renaissance Quarterly* 58, no. 4 (2005), 1239.

37. I agree with McCabe's view that Spenser "greatly values human endeavour and the concept of spiritual trial which seems to inform most of the quests bespeaks a keen interest in the workings of the will," *Pillars of Eternity*, 177. On the complex and controversial issue of Spenser's idea of providence and predestination, see McCabe's important discussion in *Pillars of Eternity*, 160–87, and his article "Providence" in *The Spenser Encyclopedia*, Hamilton.

38. The Protestant view of suffering as a necessary step in the *ordo salutis* provides the context of Spenser's narratives of trauma. On the paradigm of salvation and the difference between productive and sterile suffering leading respectively to spiritual flourishing and damnable despair, see Paola Baseotto, "Theology and Interiority: Emotions as Evidence of the Working of Grace in Elizabethan and Stuart Conversion Narratives." In *A History of Emotions, 1200–1800*, ed. Jonas Liliequist (London: Pickering and Chatto, 2012) and "Godly Sorrow, Damnable Despair and *Faerie Queene* I.ix."

39. John P. Wilson, "The Posttraumatic Self." In *The Posttraumatic Self: Restoring Meaning and Wholeness to Personality*, edited by John P. Wilson, 44–45. (New York: Routledge, 2006).

40. The Arthur of *The Faerie Queene* is a human instrument of divine grace.

41. Wilson, "The Posttraumatic Self," 41.

42. Corey L. M. Keyes, "Complete Mental Health: An Agenda for the 21st Century," in *Flourishing*, Keyes, 298.

43. Ibid., 294, 307.

44. Ibid., 294.

45. Edmund Spenser, *The Faerie Queene*, 463.

46. John P. Wilson, "Trauma and the Epigenesis of Identity," in *Posttraumatic Self*, Wilson, 69.

# SEVEN

# The Choices of *Can You Forgive Her?*

## *Literary Realism, Freedom, and Contentment*

Amanpal Garcha

Though Anthony Trollope's fiction has a reputation for aesthetic and ideological conservatism, it might also be distinguished by its frequent representations of a particular kind of psychological openness, a kind of openness that has close associations, in modern Western culture, with personal freedom. One of Trollope's signal novelistic innovations is his unprecedented attention to characters' acts of internal, mental deliberation: while novelists since the eighteenth century have represented characters' personal thoughts and feelings, more than any other writer before him, Trollope devoted considerable amounts of space in his works to characters' processes of decision making and, frequently, indecision. *Can You Forgive Her?* (1864–1865), which inaugurated Trollope's Palliser series, might constitute his most sustained examination of the relationship between contentment and decision making. The novel focuses on Alice Vavasor's tortured deliberations as she decides whether it is best—for her, for others, and for society's rules of propriety—to marry John Grey or her cousin George Vavasor. The novel's other characters routinely experience the same kind of fraught self-questioning and weighing of options. When Burgo Fitzgerald dances with Glencora Palliser, she possesses an "unsettled mind—quite unsettled whether it would be best for her to go or stay!"[1], and Trollope goes to some length to represent Glencora's internal struggle as she decides whether or not to leave Palliser for Fitzgerald; the substantial subplot centered around Mrs. Greenow charts how she keeps alive the possibilities of marrying Cheesacre and Bellfield, and Trollope shows how she comes to find an answer to the questions she asks herself: "should she marry for love; and if so, should Captain Bellfield be the man?" (499). And of course, through the novel's title, Trollope calls upon the reader to engage in a lengthy process of deliberation as to whether or not Alice should be forgiven.

In his fiction, examples of Trollope's interest in decision making are not hard to find, and they do not all relate to women and their marriage plots. *The Warden* focuses on Septimus Harding's long process of deciding to abandon his post at Hiram's Hospital. It represents what Elaine Hadley calls Harding's "mental substantiation of devil's advocacy," as Trollope shows Harding "rehearsing opposing positions" and evaluating the moral, ethical, and legal reasons why he might go or stay.[2] Much of the pathos in *Phineas Redux* comes from Finn's uncertainties as to whether or not he desires the political life he lives in London. Finn often wonders about his decision to reenter Parliament, as at the beginning of the novel when he finds himself remembering how parties, power, and Countesses' "drawing rooms" had (as shown in the novel's prequel, *Phineas Finn*) been open to him, before he abandoned them for a relatively secluded domestic existence with his Irish wife. "He had left all those things [of Parliamentary privilege] of his own free will, as though telling himself that there was a better life than they offered to him. But was he sure that he found it to be better? He had certainly sighed for the gauds which he had left."[3]

Trollope's interest in such self-questionings—as to how characters' choices might accord with those characters' own sense of rightness and might result, or not result, in happiness—registers the increase of a certain kind of freedom in mid-Victorian society. This kind of freedom is that of self-determination, and it is important in several different contexts: the history of political liberalism, which seeks to preserve subjects' capacity for choosing their own "pursuit of happiness" with minimal interference from the state; the basic operations of capitalism, which depend on buyers' and sellers' acts of choice as they pursue self-interest in the marketplace; and recent psychological research, which suggests that individuals' happiness depends on their abilities to choose among different courses of actions.

Trollope's representations of decision making and freedom are to some extent representative not just of the individual-centered, liberatory ideals that inform the discourses of liberalism, capitalism, and (some strains of) psychology, but also of the problems—of regret, procrastination, anxiety, confusion, and helplessness—that such freedom routinely creates among subjects in modern Western cultures. In conducting this analysis, I will try to further two of this volumes' critical aims: (1) I will explicitly address the topic of human happiness, in particular by tying Trollope's representations of choice making to psychologist Barry Schwartz's revisionary account of the relationship between autonomy, freedom of choice, and feelings of happiness; and (2) question the assumptions about self-determination and happiness that seem to underlie literary critics' conclusions that characters in nineteenth-century realist fiction exist as "repressed" or "disciplined" subjects primarily because the very kinds of self-determinative acts of decision making that Trollope represents are too moderate and conservative, or in other words, not sufficiently open-ended or unstructured. Yet Schwartz's and others' psychological conclusions suggest that critics' equation of openness, freedom, and individual happiness (an equation that is often implicit and that will need to be unpacked) is simplistic: as Trollope shows and Schwartz suggests, an individual's sense of the openness of his or her options, even if those options are not radical and are not many, does not necessarily produce a sense of contentment or meaningful self-determination.[4] The process of decision making itself can be torturous and deeply unsatisfying, and having a variety of possible avenues open can make one experience a state that Schwartz provocatively calls "the tyranny of freedom."[5]

In their deliberations as to how to pursue a correct, contentment-making course of action, Trollope's characters enact what psychologist Daniel Gilbert identifies as the fundamental cognitive move associated with human happiness and its (often incomplete) realization: they "preview in their imagination chains of events that [have] not come to pass" with the aim of securing "the welfare of [their] future selves."[6] Even Finn, who tries to discern whether or not he *was* happy when he was married, looks inward not to find out the truth of the past but rather to assess the potential for obtaining happiness in his future political career. Gilbert asserts that this future-orientation is both uniquely human and is evolutionarily advantageous. By locating the human capacity for prospection firmly in biological essence, though, he misses the historical circumstances that have made these capacities particularly important to modern, especially capitalistic, life. However much prospection helped prehistoric *homo sapiens* outmaneuver less intelligent animals around them, the intense emphasis that modern Western societies place on this capacity is in fact what leads Gilbert to associate it closely with "happiness."

In his work on philanthropy and the rise of capitalism between 1750 and 1850, the historian Thomas Haskell argues that because the marketplace relies so heavily on people who can plan ahead and, especially, meet contractual obligations, Western economies from the eighteenth century onward have rewarded and ultimately created individuals possessing a "cognitive style" allowing them to "live partly in the future." Like most of the deals that drive economic exchange, a contract forces one to think ahead; it makes each party "[commit] himself to bring to pass some designated future event" in order for that contract to be fulfilled.[7] The nineteenth-century realist novel, whose rise coincided with modern capitalism's, takes this future-orientation as perhaps the central principle of its main characters and its plots. As Peter Brooks suggests, one of the nineteenth-century novel's defining characteristics is that it views ambition, "aspiration, [and] getting ahead seriously rather than simply as the object of satire." "Ambition provides not only a typical novelistic theme but also a dominant dynamic of plot: a force that drives the protagonist forward."[8] Again, these accounts of prospection, which emphasize the cultural, ideological factors that have placed such stress on looking to the future since the advent of modernity, help contextualize Gilbert's theory of human happiness. For one thing, these accounts suggest that Gilbert's model, which asserts happiness's dependence on future satisfaction, might not be the only one that *can* account for happiness: for instance, this model has very little to do with *present* satisfaction or the kinds of intense, momentary feelings of ecstasy that, for instance, many lyric poems seek to record. For another, the fact that Gilbert's model for understanding happiness resonates with twenty-first century individuals means that those same individuals might look to nineteenth-century novels for insights about happiness, since those novels, especially Trollope's, gave careful consideration to how characters went about striving, scheming, planning, and deciding for future happiness.[9]

Yet literary critics have, by and large, been suspicious of these novels' capacity to depict anything like the freedom of action that progressive, or contemporary, kinds of happiness would seem to require. As the next few paragraphs will suggest, even though critics writing in the past few decades rarely explicitly invoke such a broad idea as "human happiness," they have argued that realistic novels present both characters and characters' options for agency as too constrained, too disciplined. With this line of argument, these critics all but suggest that something like "happiness" is dependent upon an individual's possession of a number and range of choices, in terms of whom they have sex with, what work they perform, what they can say or not say, where they travel, and importantly, how many different possibilities of actions they can mentally entertain. According to this line of thought, human flourishing can best be secured by individuals' release from the relatively meager choices and options that, for instance, face characters in many realist novels.

In his 1994 book *Narrative and Freedom: The Shadows of Time*, Gary Saul Morson presents a good example of this line of argument—an example that, because it explicitly addresses ideas of freedom, agency, and temporality, resonates especially well with this essay's main concerns. According to Morson, a scholar of Russian literature, the most liberating, and thus seemingly the most valuable, realist novels are those that imagine time as "open" and the future as containing "various paths"; such novels, for Morson, suggest that individuals' lives are not determined by external laws but are rather available to be changed because humans are free to make "a choice among a range of possibilities."[10] Thus, according to Morson's argument, novels that refuse deterministic, "closed" time are best at depicting and resonating with individuals' sense of freedom. Those novels—including Trollope's *Can You Forgive Her?*, which Morson mentions in passing—that embrace alternatives, or "real possibilities that could have happened even if they did not," most satisfyingly work against the structured nineteenth century narratives that often seem "predisposed to convey a sense of fatalism, determinism, or otherwise closed time."[11]

The equations Morson makes here, between individual freedom and the presence of a number of possibilities that an individual might choose, between a restriction of possibilities and human oppression, and between open, nonlinear narrative structures and an embrace of human agency and creativity, might seem unremarkable. Similar equations are at least implicit in many critical accounts of realist fiction. In part remarking on how in realist novels, "chronological time" becomes an "ordering principle" that contributes to the novels' "commanding structure of significance" and "extraordinary tightness of meaning," Leo Bersani in his 1971 essay "Realism and the Fear of Desire" takes such novels to task for using their emphasis on narrative coherence to put forth a normative vision of character and selfhood in which "psychological complexity is tolerated as long as it doesn't threaten an ideology of the self as a fundamentally intelligible structure unaffected by a history of fragmented, discontinuous desire."[12] In contrast with realism's narrative, psychological, and philosophical "tightness" is postmodernist fiction's relative openness, which Bersani associates with unclear chronology, a "diffusion of meaning," and a lack of "predictable direction"—all of which resist realism's "containment of desire" and nineteenth century fiction's overall reinforcement of the most repressive, normalizing features of Western ideology.[13]

More recent critics, working with a paradigm of individuality and desire that casts suspicion on previous assumptions that individual desires are subject to social repression, have nonetheless popularized a concept—that of Foucauldian "discipline"—which has done little to displace our fundamental imagination of how characters and readers might happily experience freedom. Like many of the most sophisticated thinkers that adopted his ideas about social power, Foucault himself does not put forth an ideal of a kind of wholesale freedom, in which an individual might find him or herself liberated to choose among an enormous number of possible avenues to future contentment. *A History of Sexuality* is mostly devoted to the opposite of such freedom. In it, Foucault elaborates one of the diabolical ways power asserts itself: modern disciplinary systems put forth individuals' sexuality as the ultimate truth of their selves, and this assertion of sexuality's "truth" then forces individuals into a web of bureaucratic, scientific, and political modes of normalization as subjects endlessly describe and confess their sexual desires to authorities. When Foucault in this work imagines a different, perhaps more liberating society, he does not imagine one with *no* constraints. In this society, Foucault writes, with its "different economy of bodies and pleasures, people will no longer quite understand how the ruses of sexuality, and the power that sustains its organization, were able to subject us to that austere monarchy of sex, so that we became dedicated to the endless task of forcing its secret, or exacting the truest confessions from its shadow" while "believ[ing] that our 'liberation' is in the balance."[14] With this oft-quoted passage, Foucault imagines a society that still enforces an "economy of bodies and pleasures"—in other words, even at this moment of quasi-utopian thinking, he maintains that this "better" world still structures individuals' experiences of pleasure and regulates their relationships to their bodies. This better world will place individuals in a *different* "economy of bodies of pleasures" but will not allow individuals to experience a radical, wholly open, unstructured set of possible pleasures that Bersani puts forth as an alternative to realism's ethos and that, in a different register, Morson seems to embrace when he writes of certain realist writers' imagination of an indeterminism "in which possibilities exceed actualities."[15]

Despite the implication of Foucault's statement—that some type of structure or containment of possibilities is inevitable, even in a reformed, more enlightened sociopolitical system—critics' use of his idea of "discipline" has made it seem as if realism's complicity in "coercion" and its reinforcement of Victorian society's push for "restriction" and "control" mean that true liberation can occur only in the absence of *any of* the structures that realism relies on to create order: predictability, linearity, and stability.[16] Said another way, even though poststructuralist theory's critiques of the idea of the "free individual" have motivated much recent work on the nineteenth-century novel, these critiques' focus on the diabolical ways in which modern, Western systems of power exploit individuals to maintain the status quo has (1) prompted few serious investigations of what contented freedom might look or feel like and thus (2) somewhat paradoxically done little to challenge the fantasy that freedom is the experience of being able to choose from a large, maybe infinite, variety of actions, life paths, and futures.

In spelling out these critical accounts' assumptions about freedom and contentment, this essay is not exactly attempting to make a surprising set of points. It is, though, attempting clearly to articulate how these accounts, at least in part, put forth specific and thus perhaps testable notions of how individuals how might achieve a sense of liberation (that is, they would achieve this sense by perceiving that their choices are not unduly limited by social coercion or norms) and how society might encourage individuals' happiness (that is, it would expand, rather than constrain, the individuals' opportunities to choose their own short- and long-term future paths). Some psychological research has indeed supported the idea that feelings of contentment, freedom, and agency go hand-in-hand with a subject's sense of his or her ability to choose from an open set of options on the basis of his or her individual desires. According to Richard Ryan and Edward Deci, psychologists who have written extensively on the subject of "self-determination," for instance, positive feelings of "self-esteem" and "general well-being" follow in part from an individual's exemption from "external regulation"—when an individual feels "intrinsic motivation" rather than the promise of "extrinsic rewards," he or she is able to "seek out novelty and challenges . . . to explore" and thereby develop "the positive potential of human nature"; thus, "choice . . . and opportunities for self-direction" can "enhance intrinsic motivation," allowing "people a greater feeling of autonomy" and thereby promoting contentment and well-being.[17]

Following this line of argument, the *less* constrained a subject feels by social regulation and the more open the subject feels are his or her options for action, the happier that subject will be. In Trollope's *Can You Forgive Her?*, the reader is presented with a character, Alice Vavasor, whose options are expansive in comparison with heroines of previous nineteenth-century English novels. More so than Austen's Emma, a character notable for the influence she yields on those around her, Alice is very cognizant that she is in a position to *choose* her husband, or more precisely, to choose *between* her two suitors, each of whom she in fact twice agrees to marry. Trollope's transformation of the marriage plot in regards to showing Alice's decision-making process is remarkable and unprecedented. Despite the fact that its most basic structure—two rivals competing for one woman's hand—is perhaps the most commonplace plot element in English fiction (and a very common one in English literature more generally), few if any novelists before Trollope represent the beloved woman as possessing an opportunity to consider both rivals at the same time and being able to exercise the power to choose which one she would like to marry. That is, by representing his heroine as able not just to choose between saying "yes" or "no" to a potential marriage partner (as for instance, Emma is able to choose to deny Elton her hand and to imagine herself refusing Frank Churchill's offer if he made it), but also actively to consider which of two men would make her happier, to weigh the two men's personalities against each other, and to entertain both options at the same time, Trollope foregrounds the act of decision making in a way that no other novelist had done. For all the psychological richness that their authors endow them with, Emma, Elizabeth Bennett, Jane Eyre, Catherine Earnshaw, or for that matter, David Copperfield and Arthur Pendennis, prior to their commitment to their eventual spouses, never rationally and explicitly compare the relative merits of marrying Knightley or Frank Churchill, Darcy or Wickham, Edgar or Heathcliff, Dora or Agnes, Blanche Amory or Laura in the way Alice is able to consider her two marital options:

> As the mental photographs of the two men forced themselves upon her, she could not force herself to forget those words—'Look here, upon this picture—and upon this.' How was it that she now knew how great was the difference between the two men, how immense the pre-eminence of [John Grey] whom she had rejected—and that she had not before been able to see this on any of those many previous occasions on which she had compared the two together? . . . [S]he thought of her cousin George's face when he left her room a few days since, and remembered Mr. Grey's countenance when last he held her hand at Cheltenham. (386)

In previous novels, the option of marrying one rival rather than another is never a matter of conscious deliberation for the main characters: for Emma, Frank Churchill has already been ruled out as a possible spouse before she is surprised to find herself in love with Knightley; for Catherine, the idea of marrying Heathcliff has never been a real possibility to her, as she explains to Nelly, "It would degrade me to marry Heathcliff now";[18] and for David, Dora is dead before he acknowledges Agnes's superior suitability for him. Alice, though, is represented primarily by what one early reviewer called her "vacillations" between her cousin and Grey, and this vacillation, as she "compare[s] the two together" and considers her suitors' relative values, takes up a significant portion of the text. Moreover, in *Can You Forgive Her?*, this active comparison of two simultaneously present suitors is not exclusive to Alice: Mrs. Greenow's parallel plot concerns her construction of a situation in which Captain Bellfield and Mr. Cheesacre constantly assert their individual superiority as potential husbands, very often in the presence of each other. For Trollope, marriage is not only a matter of falling in love or deciding whom to marry but also a matter of carefully and almost constantly comparing two potential suitors on the way to determining which is the better match.

Trollope's modification of the marriage plot, providing his women increased agency in the processes of mentally considering future husbands and making an actual choice, reflects liberal individualism's transformative effects on English culture by the mid-Victorian era. In part, liberal individualism enters Trollope's fiction in a very particular, historically grounded way—as what Elaine Hadley has termed mid-Victorian liberalism's "practices of moralized cognition" that emphasized "specific techniques of thought production and judgment, such as 'free thought,' reflection, abstraction, logical reasoning, and internal deliberation."[19] According to theories of liberalism put forth by John Stuart Mill and others, this model of deliberative "logical reasoning" would ideally guide the decision-making processes of both individual subjects—as, in Trollope's novel, Alice weighs her suitors' qualities against one another—and of Great Britain's political system—again, as in the novel, Plantagenet Palliser hopes to persuade Parliament of liberal policies' validity by using the facts and figures he continually accumulates. Recent critics' attention to political liberalism's impact on Victorian fiction has often centered around Trollope's novels as, in them, Trollope represents the characteristic liberal habits of careful judgment, rational argument, and devil's advocacy as inhering in many different kinds of conversations, including those between different political parties, between characters holding different values, and as in Alice, between different parts or aspects of a single character.[20]

Both in his personal political convictions and in his novels, Trollope did not fully embrace liberal models of self- and national governance. His partial skepticism of these models' notion that deliberation will yield wisdom and contentment explains critics' interest in his novels, as those novels reveal not just liberalism's reach but also its limits in terms of affecting popular opinion; and this skepticism also explains why his narratives sometimes achieve closure through an assertion of a kind of old-fashioned, patriarchal power.[21] In the present discussion of realism's depictions of freedom and happiness, though, it is important to look at Trollope's skepticism of another kind of liberalism: the more nebulous, but historically more long-lasting, idea that individuals possess a freedom of choice that social structures should infringe upon as little as possible. It is this more vague liberal value that influences not just Trollope's modes of characterization but also democratic ideas that have defined Western culture since at least the eighteenth century—and that have produced present-day convictions that an expansive sense of personal freedom yields happiness.

Like many other Victorians, Trollope saw this more individual-centered, less rationally oriented liberalism as a set of values that subjects should embrace partially, as it could lead to violent, anarchic revolution. Certainly, he was not sympathetic to the burgeoning feminist movement in England that called for society to extend respect for individual rights to women. This movement explicitly asserted that women should not just enjoy political and social privileges—the right to vote, the opportunity to pursue educational and professional opportunities, and so on—but also that they should be able to exercise self-determination in choosing among a large variety of future paths. As Harriet Taylor asserted in her 1851 work *The Enfranchisement of Women*, women must be allowed a large scope of freedom of action and thought: "The proper sphere for all human beings is the largest and highest they are able to attain to. What this is cannot be ascertained without complete liberty of choice."[22]

Trollope opposed such arguments in favor of women exercising self-determination in wider, less socially conventional ways while at the same time, as Sharon Marcus has shown, he maintained surprisingly close ties to figures in England's burgeoning feminist movement.[23] This somewhat conflicted relationship to feminist assertions that women need "liberty of choice" goes some way in explaining Trollope's depiction of Alice's vacillations. While Alice exercises her choice in a manner that registers women's increased scope of agency since, say, Ann Radcliffe's Emily fairly passively falls in love with Valancourt in *Mysteries of Udolfo*, she feels neither the sense of power nor the sensations of happiness or contentment that this increased choice might produce. Instead, Trollope consistently portrays Alice as deeply unhappy, even tortured, by her exercise of choice: as she affiances George, then Grey, and then George before finally marrying Grey, her vacillations cause her pain. Alice sees her state of self-determination as profoundly depressing: "upon the whole it was a grievous task to her in these days—this having to do something with her life. Was it not all vain and futile?" (342). What she calls "her fling at having her own will" results not in feelings of achievement or agency but rather in helplessness: "She had assumed command of the ship, and had thrown it upon the rocks, and she felt that she never ought to take the captain's place again" (774).

In sum, if a reader believes that, for actual individuals, freedom of choice is psychologically beneficial, then Trollope's negative depiction of Alice's choice making may wholly be explained by his fearful or dismissive attitude toward women's social empowerment. That is, Trollope endows Alice with the "liberty of choice" for which feminists were appealing, but then as a way of undermining this liberatory appeal, he falsely and misogynistically shows Alice as unhappy with choice and wishing to abdicate her decision-making position. The remainder of this essay, though, will put forth an alternate explanation for Trollope's depiction of Alice's unhappiness. Trollope's consistent focus on indecisive figures, both male *and* female, arises only partially from changes in gender roles in the nineteenth century and more so from a particular set of psychological or cognitive difficulties that liberalism's emphasis on "free choice" creates for modern individuals: these difficulties might be understood as a function of liberal society's tendency to proliferate choice-making opportunities and in so doing, create a situation in which, in the words of psychologists Sheena Iyengar and Mark Lepper, "choice is demotivating."[24]

Schwartz has accurately pointed out that this expansion of choice, and the unhappiness resulting from it, is not an ahistorical, existential truth but rather a distinctively modern phenomenon. For Schwartz, modernity brought with it an ideal of a "fully self-determined self . . . that is unconstrained—by habit, by social convention, or by biology" and a capitalistic economic system that offers a bewildering array of products in the marketplace while emphasizing that the individual's ability to choose among those products constitutes an important exercise of his or her liberty. Individuals face an increasing number of options—however incomplete "freedom of choice" might be for many subjects in twenty-first century America, more people have more options as to what educational paths to pursue, what kind of career to try to follow, whom to marry, where to live, and at any given moment, what to buy, what kind of entertainment to consume, and what to do than at any other historical moment.[25]

Despite these options and this sense of a relatively "unconstrained" self, modern Americans are not becoming increasingly happy. Schwartz attributes the stunning increase in rates of depression among Westerners directly to the expansion of choices, and he makes this attribution on the basis of several lines of argument: first, that liberalism's emphasis on self-determination increases subjects' "*expectations* about control," so that individuals are bound to become unhappy when they inevitably realize that many key aspects of their lives and futures are not, in fact, determined by their desires or actions; second, the same emphasis makes subjects blame themselves—their own lack of talent, effort, or persistence—for various kinds of failures as opposed to attributing those failures to external factors; third, individualism weakens social bonds and group activities that offer "a crucial vaccine against depression" but require the kind of "submerging [of] one's self" that liberalism devalues; and fourth, it paralyzes effective action, as individuals refuse to make choices because they come to believe that, with so many options, it is likely they "will make a nonoptimal choice" and feel that they can never gather adequate information to feel sure they will make the right choice.[26]

Like Iyengar and Lepper, Schwartz associates the unhappiness proceeding from choice with an individual facing an enormous array of options—an array that is much larger than the set of two men that Alice must choose between in *Can You Forgive Her?* Still, Trollope's representation of an *un*happiness that comes with choice, of a sense of paralysis and hopelessness that follows from possessing a somewhat open set of future paths, suggests that in his novels, he is recording the same kind of response to "openness"—a response of "demotivation," of regret, and paralysis—that Schwartz diagnoses as widespread in democratic, modern societies. To contextualize Trollope's work in this way is not to cover over, or defend against, the obvious misogyny he shows toward Alice but rather to emphasize that Alice's unhappiness in the face of open choices is in important ways identical to other individuals' unhappiness—indeed, in Trollope's work, it is identical to many indecisive *male* characters' unhappiness. Trollope expresses his misogyny less in his depiction of Alice's depression than in the dismissive attitude his narrator has toward Alice's desire for self-determination. In *Barcester Towers,* for instance, Trollope produces a male character, Arabin, who also perceives a sense of open possibility and with it, a paralyzing inability to make decisions: "It is the bane of my life that on important subjects I acquire no fixed opinion. I think, and think, and go on thinking, and yet my thoughts are running ever in different directions."[27] What defines Alice's "feminine" powerlessness is not her tendency toward vacillation—Arabin is only one of Trollope's many characters who share this tendency—nor this vacillation's depressive effects on her mood and sense of agency but rather ultimately her decision to give up on the struggle to decide and to put her future in the hands of a man, a deferral of responsibility that Trollope never feels the need to make his male characters enact.

To move this argument back to the wider topic of realist aesthetics' relationship to happiness and freedom, it is necessary to analyze a little more closely how Trollope's representation of the unhappiness of choosing is tied to the capitalist marketplace—a site of choice making that is very important to Schwartz's and Iyengar's critiques of psychological theories emphasizing "self-determination" and that might be as important to Trollope's aesthetics as liberal politics, which forms so much of the Palliser series' content. In fact, perhaps the most instructive representation of choice making (instructive in the sense that it might tell us the most about Trollope's depictions of modern decisions) in *Can You Forgive Her?* is one that shows a consumer choosing among a variety of goods. In the novel's opening pages, the reader meets Alice's father, Mr. Vavasor, whose most consistent, distinctive trait is his desire to eat at his club each night rather than at home with Alice. "After his wife's death he dined at his club every day," the narrator writes, and he "was rarely happy except when so dining." Mr. Vavasor's most powerful delight in his nightly dinners, though, proceeds from his experience of choosing among the various dishes on the menu and not from the food itself.

> They who have seen him scanning the steward's list of dishes, and giving the necessary orders for his own and his friend's dinner, at about half past four in the afternoon, have seen John Vavasor at the only moment of the day at which he is ever much in earnest. All other things are light and easy to him—to be taken easily and to be dismissed easily. Even the eating of dinner calls forth from him no special sign of energy. (41)

In this passage, Trollope sums up the way "freedom of choice" can exert a seductive power over individuals and the possible negative effects of succumbing to that power. Anyone who has enjoyed window shopping or web- or channel-surfing can understand Mr. Vavasor's attraction to the moments when he feels many options open to him and in quick succession evaluates those options according to how much he thinks he will enjoy consuming each.

Yet (as those of us who *most* enjoy living in this phantasmatic state of thinking that almost anything might be available to us also know), the enjoyment Mr. Vavasor feels at such moments of open choice—when multiple future paths are open to him—results in a *diminution* of satisfaction in his exercise of agency, as the consequences of choosing only one meal of the many is significantly less delightful and less intense than his pleasure in openness. As the novel continues, the reader finds out that Mr. Vavasor is constitutionally irresponsible and ineffective: he can provide no helpful or serious direction to Alice when she is troubled by her own indecision. This ineffectiveness stems directly from his strong attachment to the power he feels when he is contemplating many options—and thus his relative dislike of actually exercising his power of choice, of choosing *only* one path and thus eliminating other possibilities. Mr. Vavasor's desire for open choices also explains why he is drawn repeatedly to his club. Whereas life outside the club inevitably presents him with restrictions—such as the small scope of opportunities that his modest income allows him—and with commitments and responsibilities—such as caring for Alice—the action of perusing the menu provides him with a feeling of relatively unconstrained power to determine his future. This feeling has significant parallels with that of Alice as she tries to exercise her "will" by prolonging the state of *choosing*—as a process of potentially endless comparison and vacillation—instead of by entering the state of *having made a choice.*

There are important differences between Alice and her father as well, as Alice comes to find her state of indeterminacy oppressive, while Mr. Vavasor is repeatedly drawn to it. However, this difference works mostly to establish Alice as ultimately the more responsible and happier character, as she possesses not only the drive to experience a sense of "open freedom" but also one to close down her options, to find satisfaction in what Trollope might maintain as the real world of restrictions. Another important difference is the fact that while Alice's indecision applies to her marital fate, Mr. Vavasor's applies to a much less consequential "future path," that of what he will eat. But in Vavasor's case, the site of his powerful enjoyment of choice making is, importantly, that of economic as well as alimentary consumption. As many commentators on liberalism's emphasis on freedom of choice have remarked, the capitalistic economic market provides perhaps the most important practical and theoretical paradigm for the exercise of freedom through individual preference. In fact, Alice's own comparisons between her cousin and Grey are, in part, a function of her capacity to view the two of them as in some ways products in the market, with qualities that she might abstract from them and evaluate. Providing insight into the historical circumstances that pushed Trollope to alter the marriage plot by depicting a woman actively deciding between two suitors, Ayse Çelikkol says the following of modern ways of comparing and judging:

> As economic theories of circulation reveal, the act of comparison lies at the heart of the marketplace. A commodity acquires a specific amount of exchange value only when it is to be exchanged with another commodity with which its worth can be compared. Because marketplace relations are firmly embedded in social and domestic registers, the comparative gesture might be more ubiquitous than it first appears.[28]

Çelikkol's point—that the "act of comparison" is at once rooted in capitalist modes of exchange and "ubiquitous" because those modes determine so many of modernity's social interactions—suggests that Alice's exercise of her freedom to compare her two suitors has as much to do with the kinds of consumer calculations that occupy her father as with the political ideals of liberal freedom that to some extent inform *Can You Forgive Her?*'s political plots. Even Trollope's representation of Alice's act of comparison—in which she sees the "mental photographs of the two men" and evaluates the men based on those "photographs"—evokes the marketplace. As Daniel Novak has argued, though photographs would come to be associated with the faithful representation of subjects' particularities and personal idiosyncrasies, in the mid-Victorian era, they "became both a visual and literary art to the extent [they were] able to transform *all* . . . bodies . . . into interchangeable and abstract forms" that, as Novak points out, were thus structurally identical to commodities.[29]

This recognition of the connections between Trollope's representations of open choices and the economics of market exchange, consumer choice, and capitalist desires leads us to a few concluding ideas about realism, freedom, and happiness. The first is a different, critical way of understanding the assertions of such theorists as Morson, Bersani, and others, whose works imply that the most satisfying existence is one that is most "open," most full of possibilities, and that realist fiction often militates against this vision of unbounded possibilities. As the previous pages have argued, there is good reason to believe that (1) the experience of having a large number of options and future paths is likely to create depression, confusion, and inaction; and (2) this experience itself is one that has its origins in the capitalist marketplace and works both to attach ourselves to consumption (as Mr. Vavasor compulsively returns to his club to enjoy the menu's choices) and to lessen the enjoyment and significance of our lives outside the marketplace.

The second is a reassessment of what psychologists and literary critics alike mean by happiness. One might expect that the "lesson" of the previous pages to be the following: that to achieve contentment, individuals should try to break their addiction to "free choice" and reject the market's assertion that there are optimal, or perfect, options that will closely match our desires. In an echo of Georg Lukacs' articulation of what the hero of a realist novel must learn—that the expansiveness of his "soul" can never find fulfillment or even adequate accommodation in a social world of limitations, structures, and barriers—Schwartz suggests that modern individuals need to move away from choosing with a desire for "optimization" and instead become "satisficers" who "settle for something that is good enough and not worry about the possibility that there might be something better."[30] We should cease our endless deliberations by choosing adequacy—by preemptively expecting that choices will yield results that are somewhat imperfect, disappointing, and compromised.

Yet another lesson might be the following: that our various conceptions of happiness are, *in one way or another*, overly invested in the future.

As all of these arguments—the one implicit in Trollope's narrative of Alice's unhappy attempts to become "the captain of her own ship"; Gilbert's assertions of the link between prospection and contentment; Schwartz's ethic of moderate contentment; and even the more idealist moves of Morson, Ryan, and Deci—suggest, modern happiness might only be able to be conceived in terms of *future* happiness, of either making good, realistic decisions about what Gilbert calls our "future selves," of avoiding the depressing effects of endlessly deciding, or of being able to envision and enact possibilities different from those that external social structures try to impose. By analyzing the relationship between happiness and choice and by showing the surprising ways in which choice and happiness by no means go hand-in-hand, the present analysis might lead us to consider critically how modernity has led us to think of happiness and freedom in terms of temporal deferral—as having to do with making good decisions *for the future.* Trollope may in fact have had an alternate model of contentment in mind: when he was developing the plot of *Can You Forgive Her?*, he was to some extent considering the period of the American and French Revolutions and of British Romanticism—he based the novel on his early, failed play, *The Noble Jilt*, that takes place in France in the 1790s. As many of the present-tense lyric poems written by Wordsworth suggest, Romantic authors routinely portrayed liberty and freedom as much as *immediate feelings* as the prospect of future possibilities. After the last few decades, in which criticism has seemed to equate happiness with individuals' abilities to dictate the course of their futures, it might be worth considering how tricky such acts of self-determination can be and the cost of our emphasis on choice as an expression of freedom—and instead, consider the extent to which freedom and happiness are affective states that can be achieved in the present, however much this "presentness" is anathema to the future orientation of psychologists, realist authors, and modern society alike.

## BIBLIOGRAPHY


Bersani, Leo. *A Future for Astyanax: Character and Desire in Literature.* New York: Columbia University Press, 1976.

Brontë, Emily. *Wuthering Heights*. New York: Penguin, 2004.

Brooks, Peter. *Reading for the Plot: Design and Intention in Narrative.* Cambridge: Harvard University Press, 1985.

Çelikkol, Ayse. "*The Morgesons*, Aesthetic Predicaments, and the Competitive Logic of the Market Economy." *American Literature* 78 (2006): 29–52.

Dames, Nicholas. "Trollope and the Career: Vocational Trajectories and the Management of Ambition" *Victorian Studies* 45 (2003): 247–78.

Earle, Bo. "Policing and Performing Liberal Individuality in Anthony Trollope's *The Warden.*" *Nineteenth Century Literature* 61 (2006): 1–31.

Foucault, Michel. *The History of Sexuality, Part I: An Introduction.* Translated by Robert Hurley. New York: Vintage, 1990.

Goodlad, Lauren. *Victorian Literature and the Victorian State: Character and Governance in a Liberal Society*. Baltimore: Johns Hopkins Univ. Press, 2003.
Hadley, Elaine. *Living Liberalism: Practical Citizenship In Mid-Victorian Britain*. Chicago: University of Chicago Press, 2010.
Haskell, Thomas L. "Capitalism and the Origins of the Humanitarian Sensibility." *American Historical Review* 90 (1985): 339–61, 547–66.
Iyengar, Sheena and Mark Lepper. "When Choice Is Demotivating: Can One Desire Too Much of a Good Thing?" *Journal of Personality and Social Psychology* 79 (2000): 995–1006.
Levine, George. "Can You Forgive Him? Trollope's 'Can You Forgive Her?' and the Myth of Realism." *Victorian Studies* 18 (1974): 1–30.
Marcus, Sharon. "Contracting Female Marriage in Anthony Trollope's *Can You Forgive Her?*" *Nineteenth-Century Literature* 60 (2005): 291–325.
Morson, Gary Saul. *Narrative and Freedom: The Shadows of Time*. New Haven: Yale Univ. Press, 1994.
Novak, Daniel. *Realism, Photography and Nineteenth-Century Fiction*. Cambridge: Cambridge Univ. Press, 2008.
Roberts, Lewis. "Disciplining and Disinfecting Working-Class Readers in the Victorian Public Library." *Victorian Literature and Culture* 26 (1998): 105–32.
Rogers, Helen. "Women and Liberty." In *Liberty and Authority in Victorian Britain*, edited by Peter Mandler. Oxford: Oxford Univ. Press, 2006. 124–50.
Trollope, Anthony. *Barcester Towers*. New York: Penguin, 1984.
Ryan, Richard M., and Edward L. Deci. "Self-Determination Theory and the Facilitation of Intrinsic Motivation, Social Development, and Well-Being." *American Psychologist* 55 (2000): 69–70.
Schwartz, Barry. *The Paradox of Choice: Why More Is Less*. New York: HarperCollins, 2004.
———. "Self-Determination: The Tyranny of Freedom" *American Psychologist* 55 (2000): 76–86.
Trollope, Anthony. *Barcester Towers*. New York: Penguin, 1984.
———. *Can You Forgive Her?* New York: Penguin, 2004.
———. *Phineas Redux*. Oxford: Oxford University Press, 2000.

## NOTES

1. Anthony Trollope, *Can You Forgive Her?* (New York: Penguin, 2004), 534. Hereafter, this edition will be cited parenthetically in the text.
2. Elaine Hadley, *Living Liberalism: Practical Citizenship In Mid-Victorian Britain* (Chicago: Univ. of Chicago Press, 2010), 79.
3. Anthony Trollope, *Phineas Redux* (Oxford: Oxford Univ. Press, 2000), 54.
4. See Barry Schwartz, *The Paradox of Choice: Why More Is Less* (New York: HarperCollins, 2004).
5. Schwartz, "Self-Determination: The Tyranny of Freedom" *American Psychologist* 55 (2000): 79.
6. Daniel Gilbert, *Stumbling on Happiness* (New York: Vintage, 2006), 10, xiv.
7. Thomas L. Haskell, "Capitalism and the Origins of the Humanitarian Sensibility," *American Historical Review* 90 (1985): 553.
8. Peter Brooks, *Reading for the Plot: Design and Intention in Narrative* (Cambridge: Harvard Univ. Press, 1985), 39.
9. Perhaps the best critical treatment of Trollope's aesthetic reliance on the ambitious plans that constitute a "career," for both today's reader and for so many of Trollope's characters, see Nicholas Dames, "Trollope and the Career: Vocational Trajectories and the Management of Ambition" *Victorian Studies* 45 (2003): 247–78.
10. Gary Saul Morson, *Narrative and Freedom: The Shadows of Time* (New Haven: Yale Univ. Press, 1994), 5

11. Morson, 8.

12. Leo Bersani, "Realism and the Fear of Desire." In *A Future for Astyanax: Character and Desire in Literature,* 52–56 (New York: Columbia Univ. Press, 1976).

13. Bersani, 51–52.

14. Michel Foucault, *The History of Sexuality, Part I: An Introduction,* trans. Robert Hurley (New York: Vintage, 1990), 159.

15. Morson, 10.

16. For an example of the way current cultural criticism uses "discipline" to describe a purely negative state of coercion—and thus leaves the idea of "freedom" critically unexamined—see, Lewis Roberts, "Disciplining and Disinfecting Working-Class Readers in the Victorian Public Library" *Victorian Literature and Culture* 26 (1998): 105–32.

17. Richard M. Ryan and Edward L. Deci, "Self-Determination Theory and the Facilitation of Intrinsic Motivation, Social Development, and Well-Being," *American Psychologist* 55 (2000): 69–70.

18. Emily Brontë, *Wuthering Heights* (New York: Penguin, 2004), 152.

19. Hadley, 9.

20. For critical accounts of the relationship between liberalism and Trollope's fiction, see Hadley; Lauren Goodlad, *Victorian Literature and the Victorian State: Character and Governance in a Liberal Society* (Baltimore: Johns Hopkins Univ. Press, 2003); and Bo Earle, "Policing and Performing Liberal Individuality in Anthony Trollope's *The Warden*" *Nineteenth Century Literature* 61 (2006): 1–31.

21. For an influential account of how Trollope closes off such free deliberation through an imposition of older forms of morality and conventionality, see George Levine, "Can You Forgive Him? Trollope's 'Can You Forgive Her?' and the Myth of Realism" *Victorian Studies* 18 (1974): 1–30. See also, Sharon Marcus, "Contracting Female Marriage in Anthony Trollope's *Can You Forgive Her?*" *Nineteenth-Century Literature* 60 (2005): 291–325.

22. Quoted in Helen Rogers, "Women and Liberty." In *Liberty and Authority in Victorian Britain,* edited by Peter Mandler, 128 (Oxford: Oxford Univ. Press, 2006).

23. See Marcus, 293.

24. Sheena Iyengar and Mark Lepper, "When Choice is Demotivating: Can One Desire Too Much of a Good Thing?" *Journal of Personality and Social Psychology* 79 (2000): 995–1006.

25. Schwartz, "Self-Determination," 80.

26. Schwartz, "Self-Determination," 85–86.

27. Anthony Trollope, *Barcester Towers* (New York: Penguin, 1984), 475.

28. Ayse Çelikkol, "*The Morgesons,* Aesthetic Predicaments, and the Competitive Logic of the Market Economy," *American Literature* 78 (2006): 29.

29. Daniel Novak, *Realism, Photography and Nineteenth-Century Fiction* (Cambridge: Cambridge Univ. Press, 2008), 37.

30. Schwartz, *Paradox,* 91.

# EIGHT

# The Crosses We Bear

## *Religion, Readers, and Woman's Intellect in Augusta Jane Evans's* St. Elmo

David Bordelon

> "The perfection of womanhood . . . is the wife and mother, the center of the family, the magnet that draws man to the domestic altar, that makes him a civilized being, a social Christian. The wife is truly the light of the home."
> —Godey's Lady's Book, 1860

> "Never complain of your birth, your employment, your hardships; never fancy that you could be something if you only had a different lot and sphere assigned you. God understands his own plan, and he knows what you [need . . .] better than you do."
> —The Ladies' Repository, 1865

> "Pure and undefiled religion is, to do good; and it follows, very plainly, that, if God be the Author and Friend of society, then, the recognition of him must enforce all social duty, and enlightened piety must give its whole strength to public order."
> —McGuffey's New Fifth Eclectic Reader, 1866

> "The family state is the aptest earthly illustration of the heavenly kingdom, and in it woman is its chief minister."
> —American Woman's Home, 1869[1]

These, and thousands of similar quotes, provide the evidence for modern views of religion as a conservative, controlling force in nineteenth-century America—and rightfully so. Too often religion was used to silence women, confine them to the home, and relegate them to a mere helpmeet status. A literary manifestation of this religious fervor appeared in the domestic fiction that emerged in the antebellum period and remained popular throughout the century.[2] With narratives typically tracing a young woman's bumpy course towards marriage, these works offered fictional homiletics in praise of the subject's circumspect, pious life. And it is this piety that gives many critics pause. As Elizabeth Fox-Genovese observes, "Feminist literary critics have generally embraced the prevailing hostility of contemporary critics to religion, dismissing formal religion as inherently repressive, especially of women."[3] Given this dismissive attitude, how would scholars approach one of the most popular works of domestic fiction, Augusta Jane Evans's *St. Elmo or Saved at Last* (1866), which opens with the protagonist singing a bible verse and concludes with a marriage to a preacher who ends her writing career with the command "There shall be no more books written!"(365)?

They could be excused for reading this text, with its sacralization of female submission and male dominance, as part of the Victorian library extolling the "Angel of the Hearth" and as a primer on religious self-control. But the novel's historical reception tells a different tale: where many modern readers see religion as repression, most of Evans's contemporaries saw religion as renewal.[4] The critical commentary on the novel reveals this tension. In her introduction to a modern reprint of the text, Diane Roberts struggles to reconcile the novel's endorsement of "militant Christianity" and relegation of women to the "domestic domain" with Evans's public persona as a "successful conservative woman."[5] In contrast, an 1867 review of *St. Elmo* saw no conflict or repression, and instead links religion with empowerment: it argues that one of the "*morale*[s]" of the book is to "show [. . .] the achievements of an educated, self-reliant Christian woman."[6]

The wide and enduring popularity of the novel demonstrates the broad appeal of this "morale." Four months after its initial printing, the publisher, G. W. Carleton, reported that a million volumes had been sold, amounting to a copy for every thirty-seven Americans.[7] These remarkably high initial sales were followed by decades of continuing readership. In 1894, *The Boston Sunday Globe* conducted interviews with twenty-five female "wage earners" on their reading habits and found that *St. Elmo* was a favorite. From 1891 to 1902 it remained one of the most borrowed adult titles of the Muncie (Indiana) Public Library. And in 1898, thirty-two years after it was first published, the Siegel Cooper department store in Manhattan offered *St. Elmo* for half price as a loss leader, a bait to lure shoppers into the store.[8] This long demand points to *St. Elmo's* position as a steady seller, a class of books, like Dickens's *A Christmas Carol* and Robert Browning's poetry (also featured in the Siegel Cooper advertisement), which remained popular long after they were first published. To put this in context, in the nineteenth century *St. Elmo* was the third most popular novel in America, behind Harriet Beecher Stowe's *Uncle Tom's Cabin* and Lew Wallace's *Ben Hur*.[9]

While *St. Elmo* fulfills the conventions of domestic fiction (the attractive orphan heroine, the perseverance through tribulations, the reward of marriage) many readers found a more empowering message: a rationale for intellectual work by women. The novel suggests that if women's minds are strong enough for religious devotion, then they are strong enough for rigorous scholarship. This stands in contrast to other popular works of domestic fiction, such as Susan Warner's *Wide, Wide World* and Maria Cummins's *The Lamplighter*, in which the heroines, while possessing the native intelligence and requisite piety deemed a true woman's vocation, are no scholars. The heroine of *St. Elmo*, Edna Earle, possesses the requisite piety but has also mastered Latin, Greek, Hebrew, and Chaldean, on an ambitious quest to write a book proving that all the world's mythologies and "every system of religion . . . could be traced to Moses and Jesus" (86).[10] For Edna and Evans, piety functions as a cover; it secures the veil of a culturally approved attribute—religion—to mask the influence of a culturally suspect practice—women pursuing scholarship.

This deification of education lies at the core of the novel's concept of well-being. For most nineteenth-century American women, a faith in God denoted not only the spiritual realm but also contentedness on earth—what Evans labels in an 1859 letter as "the ways of pleasantness and the paths of peace."[11] In particular, the emphasis on the immediate, emotional rewards of religion instead of the eventual, heavenly end marks an acknowledgement that there is more to spiritual life than demurely suffering the whips and scorns of time. In a later letter explaining the life of "literary women," Evans more fully explicates this marriage of religion, education, and fulfillment. She writes that such women, "experience a deep peace and satisfaction, and are crowned with a glory such as marriage never gave."[12] The duality of the word choices—*peace, satisfaction, glory*—conflate the secular with the spiritual, linking their emotionally positive denotations to the coded lexicon of nineteenth-century religious discourse. Together these attributes form a nexus uniting religion, intellect, and well-being under the "crown" of a woman writer like Edna—and the letter writer herself.

While this marriage of intellect and devotion was second nature for Evans and her contemporaries, it poses a challenge for modern interpretations of domestic fiction.[13] Some critics, best exemplified by Ann Douglas, suggest the genre encouraged writers to confuse "theology with religiosity, religiosity with literature, and literature with self-justification,"[14] to which Evans can only reply "guilty as charged." Yet *St. Elmo* departs from Douglas's schema that domestic fiction "idealized [an] arrested femininity which forestalled the disappointments of maturation in a world uninterested at best in their intellectual and emotional adulthood."[15] The novel's emphasis on scholarship and attacks on materialism point to an embrace of an independent intellectual life. It suggests that the feminine ideal is rooted not only in the piety, submission, and duty of the stereotypical domestic heroine but also in a deep and abiding love of knowledge, a love exemplified in Edna's appeal to intellectual emancipation: after her desire to learn Greek is questioned by her guardian Mrs. Murray, Edna responds "I do not quite understand why ladies have not as good a right to be learned and wise as gentlemen" (55). Thus instead of supporting an aggressively anti-intellectual agenda, per Douglas, *St. Elmo* shows that one of the most popular postwar domestic novels espoused an aggressively intellectual agenda. And this view was not lost on contemporary women. In 1867, a female columnist in *Scott's Magazine* chastised male writers who criticized Evans's use of "big words" in "female books," noting with scorn that she deserved the "generous support to which her genius entitles her."[16]

The nineteenth-century dismissals of *St. Elmo* the writer alludes to were followed by similar comments in later critical works such as Fred Pattee's *The Feminine Fifties* and Herbert Brown's *The Sentimental Novel in America*. While feminist criticism opened the novel to more nuanced and subversive readings in works such as Nina Baym's *Woman's Fiction* and Sharon Harris's *19th-Century American Women's Novels: Interpretative Strategies*, debates about the conservative impulse of the novel remain. In *Private Woman Public Stage* Mary Kelley argues that *St. Elmo* "unwittingly reaches the ultimate in contradiction and absurdity" through its mixed message of woman's intellect and woman's submission.[17] More recently, Anne Boyd, in *Writings for Immortality: Women and the Emergence of High Literary Culture in America*, argues that the novel presents a conservative message of acquiesce and control.[18] I sympathize with this vision of the novel and agree with critics that religion lies at the root of this "problem." But Evans's readers did not necessarily follow the dictates of the author—or the literary critics of the future. What many modern critics see as a bar to growth—religious belief—many historical readers saw as an open door.[19] An 1897 review characterized Evans as "God-gifted," and just in case readers missed the implication, added that "she is a heaven commissioned story teller."[20] But this "commission" does not limit her to pastoral sentiments: the writer noted that "for a writer of learned treatises upon many deep and important subjects, she posses capabilities equaled by few and surpassed by no female on this continent."[21] These comments and other reviews, essays, diaries, and letters from the period document that for many nineteenth-century readers, *St. Elmo*'s religious imagery did not amount to an opiate for the reading masses. Tracing the novel's historical reception reveals how religion provided cultural "cover" for a decidedly progressive agenda: education for women. More broadly, this focus reveals how a novel could speak in two voices: conservative, for readers set on maintaining the status quo, and subversive, for those set on broadening women's roles.[22]

Eve Kosofsky Sedgwick's idea of "reparative criticism" can be usefully applied here. Moving from a "hermeneutics of suspicion" to a focus on the "transformative power" of books, Sedgwick argues, opens up a text to a more optimistic, constructive interpretation, and in the case of *St. Elmo*, a more accurate historical reading.[23] For modern readers, the exaggerated religiosity of the novel can seem faintly camp; instead of reading *St. Elmo* as a bildungsroman charting a course of empowerment, growth, and self fulfillment, critics are too often led astray by the novel's ostentatious religiosity and Edna's inevitable path toward the wedding altar. Sedgwick's emphasis on contextualization moves interpretation away from ideology to a more historical reading. Such a reading charts how the novel rigorously challenged the prevailing view that women lacked the mental acuity and stamina for serious academic study. Placing *St. Elmo* in its nineteenth-century context reveals its palliation of a society bent on contradictory impulses: self-improvement through education and commitment to the Christian ideal of subservient women.

This approach lies at the heart of the shift from interpretation as cultural pathology (how does a work reveal its ideological bias to critics) to interpretation as illumination (how does a work enlighten or benefit readers). *St. Elmo* presents a case study in the efficacy of reader-response or reception theory in making this transition to an alternate, and perhaps more positive readings of a text. In his classic work on reception theory, *Toward an Aesthetic of Reception*, Hans Robert Jauss posits that examining historical readers (the "addressees" of a text) enables a movement "from recognized aesthetic norms to a new production that surpasses them."[24] This mechanism allows a movement from the traditionalist "aesthetic norm" of religion as a force of control to a "new production" of religion, at least in *St. Elmo*, as an emancipatory agent. By relying "not on an organization of 'literary facts' that is established *post festum*, but rather on the preceding experience of the literary work by its readers,"[25] a reception or reader-response approach avoids the observer bias of literary criticism that castigates works that do not support a specific critical agenda. In its focus on the Other—in this case, historical readers—reception theory creates the intellectual breathing room necessary to separate from the subject, providing a framework to deal with a subjective topic, religion, objectively; in short, it helps modern critics shoulder the cross of a nineteenth-century audience.

From the "Second Great Awakening" of the antebellum period to the Chautauqua movement of the late Victorian Age, nineteenth-century America was steeped in religion. While both men and women professed their piety, the culture celebrated a perceived bond between women and home and religion. Josiah Holland's popular *Titcomb's Letters to Young People Single and Married*, first published in 1858 and then republished throughout the century, makes this union clear by first establishing women as the queen of the household and then elevating them to domestic priestesses. Directly addressing female readers, he wrote:

> [C]rowning every grace of person and mind, every accomplishment, every noble sentiment, every womanly faculty, every delicate instinct, every true impulse, I would see religion upon your brow—the coronet by token of which God makes you a princess in his family.[26]

This gendering of religion, with women transformed into holy vessels of sanctity, framed the discourse on woman's duties and rights. In effect, women had to genuflect before the cultural altar of religion, positioning their endeavors to ensure compliance within the strictures of what became, as suggested by the book's popularity, a holy mandate.

And these strictures also applied to books. Noah Porter, whose *Books and Reading: or, What Books Shall I Read and How Shall I Read Them?* went through several editions starting in 1870, argued that people should choose "Christian literature" for all their reading.[27] Such books demonstrated a "faith in the moral order of the universe as supreme and beneficent" and fostered "the belief in the ultimate triumph of the good and the right, the conviction that love to God and love to man comprehend all goodness."[28] For Porter, books were a metonymic force, a print manifestation of the Christian values he believed should animate and guide all human activity.[29] He would find a kindred spirit in *St. Elmo*'s Edna. Explaining the careful and deliberate progress on her second novel, she tells a friend that "books seem such holy things to me, destined to plead either for or against their creators in the final tribunal" (356). For Edna, all books are sacred. Invested with such Christian symbolism, they represented, much as Porter argued, the religious values of their creator. In *St. Elmo*, books—the material result of knowledge, intellect, and scholarship—are transformed into vehicles of piety.

Similar professions of devotion are found in Evans's correspondence. In an 1860 letter to a friend contemplating writing fiction, Evans warned, "be sure to *select* the *very highest types* of character for the standard has sadly deteriorated of late in works of fiction. . . . . The world needs *elevating* and it is the peculiar province of the Novelist to present the very highest *noblest types* of human nature."[30] *Elevation,* in nineteenth-century parlance, denotes improvement, with the added connotation of religion: such a rise necessarily looked heavenward. Evans makes her aims more explicit in a letter to her friend and political surrogate, the Confederate statesman Jabez Lamar Monroe Curry: "I am *inexpressibly gratified* that you esteem '*St. Elmo*' so highly; and I trust that with the blessing of God, my 'labor will not be in vain'—that I may be the humble instrument of doing *some good,* of leading some soul safely to Christ."[31] Here the cultural expectations of literature as an adjunct to religion are made clear. Instead of acknowledging her own ability or even gratification, the reference to a Corinthians verse ("labor will not be in vain" I 15:58) emphasizes Evans's role as a producer of what Porter would label "Christian literature." Both the quote and self-deprecating comment on her status as a mere conduit of grace ("humble instrument") illustrate the degree to which Evans had internalized the proscribed roles of woman writers in nineteenth-century America.

Evans's deference to religion is explained, in part, by the attacks against women developing their intellect. An 1852 review of *Woman and Her Needs* by the popular novelist and feminist Elizabeth Oakes Smith follows a familiar rhetorical trope of nineteenth-century discussions on women and intellect: acknowledge a religious basis for female education and then warn against it. First comes the olive branch—"There is nothing unwomanish in the fullest exercise by woman of the thought and mind, which, if God has given, he has given for use"; then the ax falls—such work "is *not her highest destiny.* It is *not her noblest life.*"[32] For this writer, and many in the culture at large, to be a true woman meant rigorous thinking was off limits. And the inclusion of "highest destiny," like the "elevating" of Evans's letter, establishes the religious rationale behind the warning. This concern about women and intellect was not relegated to the spiritual health of women. More ominously, given the expected role of women as child-bearers, Dr. Edward Clarke infamously warned in 1873 that women who attended college ran the risk of "undeveloped ovaries," which would make them "sterile."[33] It is under this pall of tepid support and strong antagonism that Evans labored to create characters, like Edna, who freely exhibited their learning.

Yet while educational opportunities for women gradually improved throughout the century, the established beliefs on women and intellect were hard to erase.[34] An 1882 diary entry from Adeline Graham, a young, middle-class woman in small-town Michigan, captures both the internalization of the religious values shown in Evans's work and the shift to more enlightened views. Adeline, who desires to become a "physician" and has aspirations to attend Wellesley, had been taking Latin lessons to prepare for college. After an illness she wrote "Ma lays it to my studying but I think differently."[35] The difference in opinion, in addition to the usual child/parent dynamic, illustrates the tension between those, like Adeline's mother, who follow the popular notion that study can lead to sickness in women and those, like Adeline, who enjoy the stimulation of intellectual challenges.[36] Even her verb choice here, *think,* with its emphasis on the cognitive, establishes the primacy of woman's thought and its separation from the body. Yet elevation of the intellect does not mean a decline of the sacred. Mirroring Edna, who combines a prodigious intellect with saintly piety, Adeline's desire for knowledge does not interfere with her faith. While at college, she kept up with her religious devotion, noting in one entry that "our Sunday evening bible classes are so pleasant."[37]

Adeline's interest in bible study emphasizes the intellect: a reader confronting a text and discussing it with others. This interest in texts is a hallmark of Evans's fiction. Indeed, the same *De Bow's* review that praises *St. Elmo*'s moralizing Christian influences criticizes its "grave mistake of studying books instead of human nature."[38] But in keeping with nineteenth-century reading practices, the main book Evans/Edna studies is the Bible. Evans lays out her religious credentials in the very first words of the novel: "He stood and measured the earth: and the everlasting mountains were scattered, the perpetual hills did bow" (1). The reference to Chapter 3:6 of Habakkuk establishes God's power over the earth; he literally moves mountains, establishing dominion through brute force. This opening sets the religious tone for the novel, with the heroine becoming a literal signifier of the Bible, singing the praises of the Christian God.[39]

This connection between books and religion is continually reinforced in the narrative; early in the novel, as Edna recovers from an injury, Mrs. Murray tells her "I shall send you a Bible, and you must make yourself as contented as possible" (30). Murray's present of a Bible reinforces the idea that it serves as the starting point for her intellectual ambitions, a spiritual locus for Edna's rigorous and exhaustive course of study. In this *St. Elmo* can be read as a precursor to social gospel novels such as Charles Sheldon's *In His Steps* (1897), which, as Erin Smith argues, make "clear that founding the kingdom of God here on earth depends on making appropriate use of books and literacy" (194).[40] While Evans's conservatism is at odds with the social gospel's struggle for social justice, its joining of God with intellect and literacy demonstrates a more general acceptance of such a practice.[41] The novel's union of education and Christianity was not lost on contemporary critics. One writer noted that Evans is both "Learned, pious" and in nineteenth-century America, the former would not be readily accepted in women without the latter.[42]

Yet some contemporary critics rejected the novel's displays of erudition. The *New York Times* sarcastically requested "a key to her volume" to help readers "know what the fine talk which people use in this book is about. Everybody cannot be expected to converse in Chaldaic and Hebrew."[43] Charles Henry Webb's parody of the novel, *St. Twel'mo*, gains much of its comic energy by satirizing its target's high-flown dialogue and obscure references. And a review in *Godey's Lady's Book* demonstrates that even the periodical most recognized for having its finger on the pulse of American feminine thought could misjudge its readers: "as a story for popular reading it possesses grave faults. Its pages are too full of classic quotations and references; and there is such a constant, labored, almost forced display of erudition."[44] Ironically, the *Godey's* review gets at the heart of Evans's purpose. Granted, the references are constant and usually labored, but Evans, as both the novel and her letters reveal, was actively trying to expand the mind of the audience *Godey's* cultivated:

middle-class women. Her method, while slighted by *Godey's*, struck a chord with readers.

Indeed, the initial and continuing popularity of the novel suggests that many readers, unlike the critics, were not put off by its allusions and references; indeed, such displays seemed to enhance the instructive potential of reading. A Virginian reader, Ethel W. Hewitte, responding to her local paper's call for letters on favorite books, characterized *St. Elmo* as a kind of cognitive tool. Hewitte stressed the challenge of the text, noting that "To read 'St. Elmo' and appreciate it requires much thought." For her, such a challenge was a natural rationale for reading itself: "To enjoy reading, one must read books in which the characters are just a little above the ordinary characters in everyday life; else reading would not be a recreation." [45] In a similar vein, a Tennessee reader, when asked why she enjoyed novels such as *St. Elmo*, replied: "I want something worth my while, that will teach me something—like St. Elmo."[46] And what could readers learn from *St. Elmo*? John Ruskin's theory of art.

In a set piece late in the novel, Edna and one of her charges, Felix, gaze up at Fredric Church's "Heart of the Andes." Edna prompts him to connect the painting to "something of which we often speak (265)." Felix thinks for a moment and then "Slowly but accurately . . . repeated the eloquent tribute to 'Mountain Glory,' from the fourth volume of 'Modern Painters'" (265). This exchange continues for three pages, presenting readers with a wealth of references and information. From Church's painting, the conversation turns to Ruskin, Keats, the English Romantic poet Thomas Campbell, and finally ends with a short disquisition on language and pictorial perspective. While it is difficult to believe that people would actually speak in this manner (a common—and valid—complaint of Evans's critics) this kind of pedantic conversation, a fictionalized treatise on art history, is the kind of instruction that many readers found so appealing.[47]

This appeal speaks to a larger cultural movement: a burgeoning interest in reading as a cultural marker, an index of middle-class (and those who aspired to it) status. Louise Stevenson, in *The Victorian Homefront: American Thought and Culture 1860–1880*, notes that "athough only a tiny number of Americans, less than 2 percent, went to college, most middle-class families informally pursued education as a lifelong endeavor . . . To be middle-class was to be literate."[48] Barbara Sicherman moves the argument from literacy into material culture, claiming that books themselves functioned as a cultural marker: "Books—reading them, talking about them, sometimes owning them—became a marker of middle-class status, for some perhaps the critical marker."[49] This anxiety about class is suggested in the dismissive remarks from the Tennessean reader. She derides the culture around her—it is a "waste" of her "time"—and turns instead to a novel that portrays a different life, one filled with books, arcane references to classic subjects and authors, and intellectual conversation.[50] For many readers, *St. Elmo*, as an instrument of self-improvement, embodied an idealized middle-class life.

The 1867 comments of a middle-class Southern reader, Anna Cook, speak to this interest in higher literacy. In her diary Cook writes, "I have been reading Miss Evans [*sic*] last work St. Elmo . . . [and] found the book deeply interesting, and think it calculated to do good, by its tone of exalted female heroism. I feel so deep a desire to improve my talents and acquire useful information I have resumed the study of my latin [*sic*]."[51] What's interesting here is Cook's focus on *St. Elmo* as instructive and inspirational. She is not immune to Romantic conventions: she had previously noted her affection for Byron, and after reading Susan Warner's *Wide, Wide World* and *Queechy* writes, "If I could find a strong man yet that loved me with this depth of a passionate nature and perfectly understood me I could rest with quiet confidence."[52] Yet the character St. Elmo, colored in the very Bryonic hues she seems to desire, isn't even mentioned; instead, it is a desire for the pursuit of knowledge, a desire to improve herself and follow a more rigorous course of study in Latin that holds her interest. These comments show that the didacticism Evans felt was central to her writing—a didacticism grounded in religion—made the erudition displayed in the novel *attractive* to readers. Instead of turning them away from the work, as the reviewer from *Godey's* suggested, it lured them in.

This desire to inculcate knowledge—a scholarly didacticism—marks one of the differences between Evans and the domestic novelists with whom she is often associated. Maria Cummins, in a letter to her mother regarding proofs from her novel *El Fureidîs* (1860), notes a very particular change she would like to make: "The only thing I would alter is what I now feel was an affectation on my part—the word *Mitéra* [which Cummins uses as a substitute for mother] . . . Seeing it in print I feel afraid it will be incomprehensible to the general reader."[53] For Evans, a word like "*Mitéra*" would be central to her mission of enlightenment and instruction. Instead of an "affectation," such diction is part of her style, and for some an attraction.

In Evans's case, this effect on readers is not merely conjecture. The writer Isabella Maud Rittenhouse, after reading Evans's later novel, *Vashti* (1869), reports in an 1881 diary entry that "I suppose it did me good for it kept me running to the Dictionary or to an encyclopedia to see who Joubert is, or where the 'cheerless temple of Hestia' stands or stood, or to find out what 'a wan Alcestis and 'a desperate Cassandra he had seen at Rome' indicated."[54] Rittenhouse makes it clear that even readers like her, who balked at the implausibility of Evans's fiction fell prey to her mission: education.

And it was not only female readers who succumbed to the lure of encyclopedias engendered by Evans's fiction. The advertising executive Ernest Elmo Calkins (note his middle name) recalls that as a child, *St.*

*Elmo*'s "erudite and recondite allusions stimulated [my] curiosity, and for several years afterward [I] made a game of the research necessary to find out what the author was talking about."[55] In one of many self-referential nods, the novel itself acknowledges its didactic impulse: Edna wonders if her readers

> [w]ill . . . thank me for my high opinion of their culture, in assuming that it will be quite as plain to them as to me? If there should accidentally be an allusion to classical or scientific literature, which they do not understand at the first hasty, careless, novel-reading glance, will they inform themselves, and then appreciate my reason for employing it, and thank me for the hint? (333)

The answer, as suggested by Hewitte, Cook, Rittenhouse, and Calkins, is yes. These individual readers represent part of a wider sphere of undocumented influence. An 1894 commentator acknowledges the criticism of Evans's work as "pedantic," but like Evans's herself sees an educative bent in her work: "it is well established that Mrs. Wilson's books have in many instances stimulated her young readers to study history, mythology and the sciences, from which she so frequently draws her illustrations."[56]

Interestingly, while Evans's erudition runs on dual tracks—self-improvement and religion—her audience seems to ride only one of the trains—self-improvement. There is no indication from the diaries and comments on Evans's work that the readers disputed or ignored her religious message; and while the public comments on the novel often acknowledge religiosity, the personal comments in diaries are silent on this subject. This silence speaks directly to my argument: the deep faith exhibited in the novel, by the narrator and the characters, is a given. The faith allows the more controversial erudition to be pulled into sharper focus. While a seemingly puzzling omission, it follows Roger Chartier's understanding of "reading [as] a creative practice, which invents singular meanings and significations that are not reducible to the intentions of authors of texts or producers of books."[57] Thus it is not the religiosity of the novel that bears notice: it is the intellectualism. Yet without the overlay of religion—without the holy imprimatur—Edna and Evans's status as a inculcators of knowledge would be weakened. By marrying two of the most potent cultural forces, religion and self-improvement, Evans creates a venue through which woman's intellect becomes central: to do otherwise, she suggests, is to veer off Christ's path.

Evans's confluence of intellect and religion helps explain the marriage plot in the novel, which often perplexes modern critics.[58] Early in the novel Edna refuses a proposal from Gordon Leigh, a wealthy and desirable bachelor, because, as their tutor Rev. Hammond informs him,

> intellectually she is your superior. She feels this, and will not marry one to whose mind her own does not bow in reverence. To rule the man she

> married would make her miserable, and she could only find happiness in being ruled by an intellect to which she looked up admiringly. (123)

Here the stereotypical roles are reversed; instead of the supposedly superior masculine intellect ruling the roost and making marriage decisions, the woman is in control. Granted, Edna's later marriage to St. Elmo fulfills the cultural duty of submission set out in the novel, investing her acquiescence to him with a religious dimension. But readers can also draw a more subversive message from Edna's and St. Elmo's courtship and marriage; yes, bow to men—and others—who are your superior, but if you cannot find such a man, then you are free, as Edna was, to pursue your intellect. Unlike her readers, Edna is trapped in the confines of the genre and, from the first pages of the novel, is destined to first attract, then repel, then finally yield.

This shift, from an emphasis on religion and domestic concerns to an emphasis on the intellectual "capacity" of women is part of a larger movement in the culture. It led a young Tennessee woman, in an 1891 survey, to remark on the change in women's lives from an insistence on marriage to an embrace of independence, an independence fostered by the intellect. She told an interviewer that "thanks to the public schools" a woman can "secure an education and by the force of her intellect command an honorable position in the best society." Illustrating the prescient nature of Evans's narrative, she suggests that marriage can be postponed if a woman does not meet "a man who is her equal in mental culture." More radically, she asserts that a man may not be "more able to take care of her than she is to take care of herself."[59] Some twenty years after *St. Elmo*'s publication, Edna's goal of emancipation is complete. According to this young woman, education has freed women from the inevitability of the altar and enabled them to live independently.

Perhaps Evans herself sympathized with the idea of a female mind unencumbered by marriage. One early twentieth-century historian states that Evans's original goal was to leave Edna unmarried "but in deference to the critical judgment of her aunt she amended the plot."[60] Coming secondhand from a friend of Evans, the remark cannot be substantiated, but it speaks to the tension in a novel featuring a strong willed and intellectual character acquiescing so readily to the silencing of her voice. Once Evans opened the floodgates of knowledge and brought erudition into the domestic fold, women were free to shrug off the religion used to smuggle it in, and begin their slow rise to intellectual independence.

As the decades edged into the new century, interest in the religiosity of Evans's work waned and her intellectualism became more prominent. A 1902 review of Evans recognized her as "a pioneer in the demand for the higher education of women"—without the usual nod to her faith or devotion.[61] This change marks the novel as a transitional text, like Louisa May Alcott's *Little Women,* which also features an intelligent and independent female character who makes her way in the world as a writer yet marries at the story's end. Both novels have one foot pointing to the conservatism of conventional domestic fiction, while the other points in a distinctly more liberal direction. At the end of the novel, while Edna will no longer write, she retains her prodigious learning.[62] The popularity and commentary on the novel show that many nineteenth-century readers sought the example of a strong-willed and intelligent heroine such as Edna; she offered a positive role model amidst a culture that often suppressed women's desire for learning.

Instead of focusing on the repressive aspects of the novel, modern scholars can imitate these earlier readers. A reader reception approach can lead critics away from a reflexively suspicious interpretation to a more open one. Such an interpretation celebrates the transformative nature of reading, where a person is changed by a text and moved to action. While Evans may not approve of the final results of these actions—woman's suffrage, feminism—for many readers, Edna's sacred erudition sparked a desire for further intellectual study, a desire that effectively transforms religion from a force of oppression to a force of liberation.

This use of religion as a liberative force, and paradoxically a source of secular enlightenment, became a hallmark of the later nineteenth century. The Chautauqua movement, like *St. Elmo*, joined fervent Protestantism with an aggressively intellectual mission. Combining scholarship with religiosity, the movement offered extensive reading lists, reading groups, meetings, lectures—in short, the entire panoply of intellectual self-improvement—under the banner of religion. In language echoing Evans, one of the founders of Chautauqua, John Vincent, makes this connection clear, stating that the movement was based on the belief that

> all knowledge, religious or secular, is sacred to him who reverently surrenders himself to God, that he may become like God, according to the divinely appointed processes for building character. And he has a right to all attainments and enjoyments in the realm of knowledge, for the possession of which he has capacity and opportunity. Science, travel, literature, the works of art, the glories of nature—all things are his who is one with God.[63]

Expanding from its 1874 roots as an institute for training Sunday School teachers, the enrollment in the Chautauqua Literary and Scientific Circle, which offered four-year correspondence courses modeled on a college curriculum, grew to 250,000 in 1900.[64] Its popularity suggests that Evans's marriage of intellect with high religious and moral purpose found a welcome audience in nineteenth century America. Those who participated in the Chautauqua curriculum use words denoting growth, advancement, achievement (in other words, the discourse of emotional and intellectual satisfaction) to describe the programs, all of which mirror the comments of readers of *St. Elmo*. An early history of Chautauqua recounts the story of two young women mired in a Calvinist "monasticism" whose "broken spirits revolted from a religion of happiness." After enrolling in and graduating from a Chautauquan reading course, "they were literally born anew." Intellectual study had "awakened their entire being and brought them into a new world."[65] Both the cause (scholarship) and effect (personal growth) link the Chautauquan Circle to the ideals espoused in *St. Elmo;* in both, religion served as the vehicle for a decidedly secular mission: intellectual well-being.

This mission, according to a 1902 column in *Bookman* recalling the "best sellers" of the nineteenth century, is central to *St. Elmo*'s success. The writer focuses on how the novel's "lofty ideals" had "done much to brighten the lives of many hundreds of thousands of readers."[66] The use of a text as consolation, a refuge amidst the storms of life, while common to readers, is anathema to critics. The forensic nature of a reader reception approach can recapture and focus such enthusiasms, transforming them from a blank chorus of "thumbs up" to a map of the popular mind. By examining the responses of period readers and critics to the novel, particularly her grounding of its heroine in Christianity and its embrace of intellectualism for women, *St. Elmo*'s power as both a work of popular fiction and as an agent of change emerges. Applying a historical reading to the text reveals the importance of religion in the transformation of women's education; it helped transform the feminine pursuit of knowledge from a cultural poison to an elixir deemed safe for domestic consumption.

## BIBLIOGRAPHY

"Advertisement." *New York Times*. November 20, 1898: 8.

Baym, Nina. *Woman's Fiction: A Guide to Novels by and About Women in America, 1820–1870*. Ithaca, New York: Cornell University Press, 1978.

Beecher, Catherine and Harriet Beecher Stowe. *The American Woman's Home or, Principles of Domestic Science*. 1st ed. 1869. Hartford, Connecticut: Harriet Beecher Stowe Center, 1996.

Bledstein, Burton J. "Introduction: Storytellers to the Middle Class." In *The Middling Sorts: Explorations in the History of the American Middle Class*, edited by Burton J. Bledstein and Robert D. Johnston, 1–30. New York: Routledge, 2001.

"Books that Girls Like." *The Boston Sunday Globe*. December 2, 1894. 14.

Boyd, Anne E. *Writings for Immortality: Women and the Emergence of High Literary Culture in America*. Baltimore, Maryland: The Johns Hopkins University Press, 2004.

Brown, Herbert Ross. *The Sentimental Novel in America 1789–1860*. Durham, NC: Duke University Press, 1940.

Brown, Matthew P. "The Thick Style: Steady Sellers, Textual Aesthetics, and Early Modern Devotional Reading." *PMLA*. 121 (2006): 67–86.

C. Jim. "The Most Read Books." June 7, 2011. Accessed August 8, 2011.http://whatmiddletownread.wordpress.com/2011/06/07/the-most-read-books/

Calkins, Earnest Elmo. *Louder Please! The Autobiography of a Deaf Man*. Whitefish, Montana: Kessinger Publishing, LLC, 2006.

Chartier, Roger. "Texts, Printings, Readings." In *The New Cultural History*, edited by Lynn Hunt, 156–74. Berkeley: University of California Press, 1989.

"Chronicle and Comment." *The Bookman; a Review of Books and Life*. September (1902): 1–16. Accessed November 4, 2009. American Periodicals Series Online.
Clarke, Edward. *Sex in Education; or, a Fair Chance for Girls*. Boston: James Osgood & Company, 1875.
Cook, Anna Maria Green. *The Journal of a Milledgeville Girl 1861–1867*. Edited by James C. Bonner. University of Georgia Press, 1964.
Douglas, Ann. *The Feminization of American Culture*. New York: Alfred A. Knopf, 1978.
*St. Elmo, or Saved at Last*. Edited by Diane Roberts. Tuscaloosa, Alabama: University of Alabama Press, 1992.
Fidler, William Perry. *Augusta Evans Wilson 1835–1909: A Biography*. Birmingham: University of Alabama Press, 1951.
Fox-Genovese, Elizabeth. "Religion, Meaning, and Identity in Women's Writing." *Common Knowledge*. 14 (2008): 16–28.
"God's Plan of Your Life." *The Ladies' Repository*. April (1865): 205.
Graham, Adeline and Julia Graham. *Adeline & Julia: Growing Up in Michigan and on the Kansas Frontier: Diaries from 19th-Century America*. Edited by Janet L. Coryell and Robert C. Myers. East Lansing: Michigan State University Press, 2000.
Green, Harvey. The Light of the Home: An Intimate View of the Lives of Women in Victorian America. New York: Pantheon Books, 1983.
Harris, Susan K. *19th-Century American Women's Novels: Interpretative Strategies*. New York: Cambridge University Press, 1990.
Hewitte, Ethel W. "My Favorite Novel, and Why." *The Times Dispatch*. October 4, 1908: 8. Newspaper Archive (accessed August 17, 2011).
Holmes, Emma. *The Diary of Miss Emma Holmes: 1861–1866*. Edited by John F. Marszalek. Baton Rouge, LA: LSU University Press, 1979.
Hubbell, Jay. *The South in American literature, 1607–1900*. Durham, North Carolina: Duke University Press, 1973.
Hurlbut, Jesse Lyman. *The Story of Chautauqua*. New York: G. P. Putnam's Sons, 1921.
"J." "St. Elmo." *Galveston Daily News*. February 7, 1897. 1.
Jackson, Gregory S. "'What Would Jesus Do?': Practical Christianity, Social Gospel Realism, and the Homiletic Novel." *PMLA* 121 (2006): 641–61.
Jacobs, Heidi L. M. "Maria Susanna Cummins's London Letters: April 1860." *Legacy* 19 (2002): 241–54.
Jauss, Hans Robert. *Toward an Aesthetic of Reception*. Minneapolis: University of Minnesota Press, 1982.
Kelley, Mary. *Private Woman, Public Stage: Literary Domesticity in Nineteenth Century America*. New York: Oxford University Press, 1984.
Knight, Lucian Lamar. *Georgia's Landmarks, Memorials, and Legends*. Volume I. Atlanta, Ga. Self-published Byrd Print. Co., State Printers. 1914.
"Literary Notices." *Godey's Lady's Book and Magazine*. March (1867): 284.
L. S. M., review of *Woman and Her Needs*, by Mrs. E. Oakes Smith, *De Bow's Southern and Western Review*. September 1852. 267–91. *Google Books*. Accessed November 12, 2009.
McClelland, Averil. *The Education of Women in America: A Guide to Theory, Teaching, and Research*. New York: Garland, 1992.
"Miss Evans' New Novel." *New York Times*. January 5, 1867: 2.
Mitchell, Silas Weir. *Wear and Tear, or, Hints for the Overworked*. Philadelphia: J. B. Lippincott & Co., 1871.
Moss, Elizabeth. *Domestic Novelists in the Old South: Defenders of Southern Culture*. Baton Rouge: Louisiana State University Press, 1992. Print.
Mystery. "Cacoethes Scribendi." *Scott's Monthly Magazine*. April (1867). 347–53.
Pattee, Fred. *The Feminine Fifties*. New York : D. Appleton-Century Co., 1940.
Porter, Noah. *Books and Reading or What Books Shall I Read and How Shall I Read Them?* New York: Charles Scribner's Sons, 1882.
P. S. R. "ART. IV.—MISS EVANS—ST. ELMO." DeBow's Review, Devoted to the Restoration of the Southern States. March (1867): 268+.

"Religion, the Basis of Society." *McGuffey's New Fifth Eclectic Reader: Selected and Original Exercises For Schools*. Cincinnati: Wilson, Hinkle & Co., 1866.

"Review 1." *The Dial; a Semi-Monthly Journal of Literary Criticism, Discussion, and Information*. November 16, (1902): 334.

Rittenhouse, Isabella Maud. *Maud*. Edited by Richard L. Strout. New York, Macmillan Co., 1939.

Roberts, Diane. Introduction to *St. Elmo. Or, Saved at Last*, by Augusta Jane Evans, v-xxiii. Tuscaloosa, Alabama: University of Alabama Press, 1992.

Rutherford, Mildred Lewis. *A Hand-Book of American Literature from Early Colonial to Living Writers*. Atlanta: The Franklin Printing and Publishing Company, 1894. *Google Books*. Accessed June 2, 2011.

Scott, John C. "The Chautauqua Movement: Revolution in Popular Higher Education." *The Journal of Higher Education*. 70, no. 4 (July–August 1999): 389–412. http://www.jstor.org/stable/2649308.

Sedgwick, Eve Kosofsky. "Introduction: Queerer Than Fiction." *Studies in the Novel*. 28 (1996): 277–80. Accessed October 3, 2011, Academic Search Premier, (9612174258).

—. "Paranoid Reading and Reparative Reading, Or, You're So Paranoid, You Probably Think This Essay Is About You," *Touching Feeling: Affect, Pedagogy, Performativity*. Durham, NC: Duke University Press, 2003.

Sicherman, Barbara. "Reading and Middle-Class Identity in Victorian America: Cultural Consumption, Conspicuous and Otherwise." In *Reading Acts: U.S. Readers' Interactions with Literature, 1800–1950*, edited by Barbara Ryan and Amy M. Thomas, 137–60. Knoxville: University of Tennessee Press, 2002.

Smith, Erin A. "'What Would Jesus Do?': The Social Gospel and the Literary Marketplace." *Book History*. 10 (2007): 193–222.

Sofer, Naomi. *Making the "America of Art": Cultural Nationalism and Nineteenth-Century Women Writers*. Columbus, Ohio: Ohio State University Press, 2005.

Stevenson, Louise L. *The Victorian Homefront: American Thought and Culture 1860–1880*. New York: Twayne Publishers, 1991.

Tillett, Wilbur. "Southern Womanhood as Affected by the War." *The Century Illustrated Monthly*. November (1891): 9–16.

Titcomb, Timothy. *Titcomb's Letters to Young People Single and Married*. New York: Charles Scribner & Co., 1868.

Tompkins, Jane. *Sensational Designs: The Cultural Work of American Fiction 1790–1860*. New York: Oxford, 1985

Tracey, Karen. *Plots and Proposals: American Women's. Fiction, 1850–1890*. Chicago: University of Illinois Press, 2000.

Vincent, John. *The Chautauqua Movement*. Boston: Chautauqua Press, 1886.

Wayne, Tiffany K. *Woman's Roles in Nineteenth Century America*. Westport, Connecticut: Greenwood Press, 2007.

Webb, Charles Henry. *St. Twel'mo*. 1867. Reprinted in *Travesty*. Boston: William F. Gill and Company, 1875. 111–74.

Wilson, Augusta Jane Evans. *A Southern Woman of Letters: The Correspondence of Augusta Jane Evans Wilson*, edited by Rebecca Grant Sexton. Columbia, South Carolina: University of South Carolina Press, 2002.

Wolf, Maryanne. *Proust and the Squid: the Story and Science of the Reading Brain*. New York: HarperCollins, 2007.

## NOTES

1. Quoted in Harvey Green, *The Light of the Home: An Intimate View of the Lives of Women in Victorian America* (New York: Pantheon Books, 1983), 56; "God's Plan of Your Life," *The Ladies' Repository*, April 1865, 205; "Religion, the Basis of Society," *McGuffey's New Fifth Eclectic Reader: Selected and Original Exercises For Schools* (Cincinnati: Wilson, Hinkle & Co., 1866), 306; Catherine Beecher and Harriet Beecher Stowe,

*The American Woman's Home or, Principles of Domestic Science* (Hartford, Connecticut: Harriet Beecher Stowe Center, 1996), 19.

2. For a concise summary of the typical domestic narrative, see Nina Baym *Woman's Fiction: A Guide to Novels by and about Women in America, 1820–1870* (Ithaca, New York: Cornell University Press, 1978), 10–11.

3. Elizabeth Fox-Genovese, "Religion, Meaning, and Identity in Women's Writing," *Common Knowledge* 14 (2008): 25.

4. The term *readers* throughout this chapter is broadly defined, encompassing both "professional" readers—critics and authors—and "non-professional" readers—everyone else. This definition is grounded in Maryanne Wolf's definition of an "Expert" reader, which acknowledges that a sophisticated interpretation and understanding of a text is not limited to those who publish. *Proust and the Squid: the Story and Science of the Reading Brain*, (New York: HarperCollins, 2007), 143.

5. Diane Roberts, introduction to *St. Elmo. Or, Saved at Last*, by Augusta Jane Evans (Tuscaloosa, Alabama: University of Alabama Press, 1992), xii, xviii.

6. P. S. R., "ART. IV.—MISS EVANS—ST. ELMO," *DeBow's Review, Devoted to the Restoration of the Southern States*, March 1867, 268.

7. Mary Kelley, *Private Woman, Public Stage: Literary Domesticity in Nineteenth Century America* (New York: Oxford University Press, 1984), 25.

8. "Books that Girls Like," *The Boston Sunday Globe*, December 2, 1894: 14; C. Jim, "The Most Read Books." June 7, 2011. http://whatmiddletownread.wordpress.com/2011/06/07/the-most-read-books, accessed August 8, 2011; "Advertisement," *New York Times* November 20, 1898: 8.

9. William Perry Fidler, *Augusta Evans Wilson 1835–1909: A Biography* (Birmingham: University of Alabama Press, 1951), 129. He also notes that *St. Elmo*'s insertion into the material culture of America, with steamboats, towns, etc., named after the central characters is another extratextual indication of the novel's popularity, 125.

10. And unlike Edward Casusabon in George Eliot's later *Middlemarch*, Edna completes her task.

11. Augusta Jane Evans Wilson, *A Southern Woman of Letters: The Correspondence of Augusta Jane Evans Wilson*, ed. Rebecca Grant Sexton (Columbia, South Carolina: University of South Carolina Press, 2002), 2. Letter to Rachel Lyons.

12. Ibid., 18.

13. It is important here to clarify that for Evans, intelligence and the intellect meant an encyclopedic knowledge of philosophy, history, religion, and literature, not a self-questioning, philosophic turn of mind. This, in part, explains her ability to advance what would seem like a progressive agenda, education for women, yet publically and privately reject any notion of woman's rights or suffrage.

14. Ann Douglas, *The Feminization of American Culture* (New York: Alfred A. Knopf, 1978), 9.

15. Ibid., 62.

16. Mystery, "Cacoethes Scribendi," *Scott's Monthly Magazine*, April 1867: 347.

17. Kelley, *Private*, 106.

18. Anne E. Boyd, *Writings for Immortality: Women and the Emergence of High Literary Culture in America* (Baltimore, Maryland: The Johns Hopkins University Press, 2004), 81–82.

19. Naomi Sofer, in her insightful study *Making the "America of Art": Cultural Nationalism and Nineteenth-Century Women Writers* (Columbus, Ohio: Ohio State University Press, 2005), recognizes and explores what she labels Evans's "religious aesthetic program for national cultural development" (65). While addressing similar issues, Sofer's work differs markedly in approach: unlike my own which examines contemporary responses to her work, she relies almost exclusively on Evans's letters, essays, and fiction.

20. J., "St. Elmo," *Galveston Daily News*, February 7, 1897: 1.

21. Ibid., 1.

22. Elizabeth Moss addresses this tension between Southern feminine mores and the ideals put forth by writers: "their fictions provided female readers with means and motivation to transcend the bounds of culturally prescribed womanhood but at the same time articulated grave doubts as to southern femininity's potential for rehabilitation" in her survey of Southern domestic fiction *Domestic Novelists in the Old South: Defenders of Southern Culture,* (Baton Rouge: Louisiana State University Press, 1992), 2–3.

23. Eve Kosofsky Sedgwick, "Introduction: Queerer Than Fiction," *Studies in the Novel* 28 (1996): 278, 279. Accessed October 3, 2011, Academic Search Premier, (9612174258). A fuller discussion of reparative criticism can be found in Sedgwick's "Paranoid Reading and Reparative Reading, Or, You're So Paranoid, You Probably Think This Essay Is About You," *Touching Feeling: Affect, Pedagogy, Performativity* (Durham, NC: Duke University Press, 2003), 123–51.

24. Hans Robert Jauss, *Toward an Aesthetic of Reception,* (Minneapolis: University of Minnesota Press, 1982), 19.

25. Ibid., 20.

26. Timothy Titcomb, *Titcomb's Letters to Young People Single and Married* (New York: Charles Scribner & Co., 1868), 164.

27. Noah Porter, *Books and Reading or What Books Shall I Read and How Shall I Read Them?* (New York: Charles Scribner's Sons, 1882), 114.

28. Ibid., 115.

29. See Baym, *Woman's Fiction,* 41–44, and Jane Tompkins *Sensational Designs: The Cultural Work of American Fiction 1790–1860* (New York: Oxford, 1985), 149–60 for succinct overviews of the influence of religion on domestic fiction.

30. Wilson, *A Southern* 21–22.

31. Ibid., 135.

32. L. S. M., review of *Woman and Her Needs,* by Mrs. E. Oakes Smith, *De Bow's Southern and Western Review,* September 1852: 272, *Google Books.* Accessed November 12, 2009.

33. Edward Clarke. *Sex in Education; or, a Fair Chance for Girls.* (Boston: James Osgood & Company, 1875), 39.

34. Averil McClelland reports the slow shift in high schools from more practical concerns— teaching and child care—to college prep by the end of the century in *The Education of Women in America: A Guide to Theory, Teaching, and Research* (New York: Garland, 1992), 128. See Tiffany K. Wayne's *Woman's Roles in Nineteenth Century America* (Westport, Connecticut: Greenwood Press, 2007), 71–98, for a brief overview of woman's education in nineteenth-century America.

35. Adeline and Julia Graham, *Adeline & Julia: Growing Up in Michigan and on the Kansas Frontier: Diaries from 19th-Century America,* ed. Janet L. Coryell and Robert C. Myers (East Lansing: Michigan State University Press, 2000), 108, 95.

36. Consider the claims of the influential health writer Silas Weir Mitchell in *Wear and Tear, or, Hints for the Overworked.* (Philadelphia: J. B. Lippincott & Co. 1871), 37; he cautioned that too much study overtasks "the brain[s]" of women, often leading them to "[break] down with weak eyes, headaches, [or] neuralgias." This is a claim Adeline rejects.

37. Graham, *Adeline,* 112.

38. P. S. R., "ART," 268.

39. Habakkuk also includes an injunction that probably was not lost on Evans: "Write the vision, and make it plain upon tables" (Habakkuk 2:2), a command fulfilled as the novel unfolds.

40. Erin A. Smith, "'What Would Jesus Do?': The Social Gospel and the Literary Marketplace." *Book History.* 10 (2007): 194.

41. See also Gregory S. Jackson's categorization of Social Gospel novels as "homiletic," which he defines as "aim[ing] to facilitate private devotion, strengthen moral autonomy, and foster social engagement through particular acts of reading" in "'What Would Jesus Do?': Practical Christianity, Social Gospel Realism, and the Homiletic

Novel." *PMLA* 121 (2006): 642. The same caveats concerning Wilson's conservatism apply here as well.

42. J, "St. Elmo," 1.

43. "Miss Evans' New Novel," *New York Times*, January 5, 1867: 2.

44. "Literary Notices," *Godey's Lady's Book and Magazine*, March 1867: 284.

45. Ethel W. Hewitte, "My Favorite Novel, and Why," *The Times Dispatch*, October 4, 1908: 8. Newspaper Archive. Accessed August 17, 2011.

46. Quoted in Jay Hubbell, *The South in American literature, 1607–1900* (Durham, North Carolina: Duke University Press, 1973), 615.

47. Of course, the obverse was true for some readers. Instead of being impressed by the display of erudition in Evans's fiction, Emma Holmes, a young member of the "southern elite" (xvi), dismissed it. Discussing Evans's 1864 novel *Macaria*, she writes that "I like the book very much but think she has certainly tried to display all her learning in a small space & has only shown herself thoroughly pedantic." In *The Diary of Miss Emma Holmes: 1861–1866*, edited by John F. Marszalek, (Baton Rouge, LA: LSU University Press, 1979), 370. Like many reviewers of *St. Elmo*, for Holmes, Evans lays it on too thickly.

48. Louise L. Stevenson, *The Victorian Homefront: American Thought and Culture 1860–1880* (New York: Twayne Publishers, 1991), xxv.

49. See also Burton Bledstein's "Introduction: Storytellers to the Middle Class," in *The Middling Sorts: Explorations in the History of the American Middle Class*, edited by Burton J. Bledstein and Robert D. Johnston,1–30 (New York: Routledge, 2001).

50. Hubbell, *The South*, 615.

51. Anna Maria Green Cook, *The Journal of a Milledgeville Girl 1861–1867*, edited by James C. Bonner (University of Georgia Press, 1964), 111.

52. Ibid., 32–33, 37–38

53. Heidi L. M. Jacobs, "Maria Susanna Cummins's London Letters: April 1860," *Legacy* 19 (2002), 249.

54. Isabella Maud Rittenhouse, *Maud*, ed. Richard L. Strout (New York, Macmillan Co., 1939), 26.

55. Earnest Elmo Calkins, *Louder Please! The Autobiography of a Deaf Man* (Whitefish, Montana: Kessinger Publishing, LLC. 2006), 38.

56. Mildred Lewis Rutherford, *A Hand-Book of American Literature from Early Colonial to Living Writers* (Atlanta: The Franklin Printing and Publishing Company, 1894), 582–83, *Google Books*. Accessed June 2, 2011.

57. Roger Chartier, "Texts, Printings, Readings," *The New Cultural History*, ed. Lynn Hunt (Berkeley: University of California Press, 1989), 156.

58. See Kelly, *Private Women Public Stage*; Fox-Genovese, "Religion," and Karen Tracey's *Plots and Proposals: American Women's Fiction, 1850–1890*, (Chicago: University of Illinois Press, 2000) for alternate readings of the ending.

59. Quoted in Wilbur Fisk Tillett, "Southern Womanhood as Affected by the War," *The Century Illustrated Monthly*, November 1891: 11.

60. Lucian Lamar Knight, *Georgia's Landmarks, Memorials, and Legends*, (Atlanta, Ga. Self-published Byrd Print. Co., State Printers, 1914), 235.

61. "Review 1," *The Dial; a Semi-Monthly Journal of Literary Criticism, Discussion, and Information*, November 16, 1902: 334.

62. The consequences of suppressing a mind will have to wait till Charlotte Perkins Gilman's 1892 "The Yellow Wallpaper."

63. John Vincent, *The Chautauqua Movement* (Boston: Chautauqua Press, 1886), 13.

64. John C. Scott, "The Chautauqua Movement: Revolution in Popular Higher Education," *The Journal of Higher Education* 70 (July–August 1999): 396. http://www.jstor.org/stable/2649308.

65. Jesse Lyman Hurlbut, *The Story of Chautauqua* (New York: G. P. Putnam's Sons, 1921), 220.

66. "Chronicle and Comment," *The Bookman; A Review of Books and Life*, September 1902: 12, Accessed November 4, 2009. American Periodicals Series Online.

# NINE

# Milton's "L'Allegro" and "Il Penseroso"

## *Prophetic Joy Anticipated*

Daniel O'Day

The seventeenth century in England was a time of collective fascination with the concept of melancholy. In Shakespeare's *Much Ado About Nothing*, Don John nearly destroys the lives of those about him, with little or no explanation save his melancholia. Malvolio the malcontent does his utmost to shift the mood of *Twelfth Night* from celebratory to somber, but he is fortunately exiled from the scene, albeit with more than a touch of cruelty. And Hamlet's brooding uncovers a vile truth while at the same time setting the stage for multiple deaths. In 1621, when Robert Burton published the first edition of *The Anatomy of Melancholy*, a rambling and extensive treatise, he explored the myriad forms of melancholy he had researched, in predominantly scholarly seclusion, from ancient texts and more contemporary examples. Adopting the persona of Democritus Junior, he claimed to supplement the writings of Democritus, the "laughing philosopher" of ancient Greece, and to provide examples of as well as commentary on the sometimes tragic, sometimes simply bizarre manifestations of this condition.[1]

Four years later, John Donne delivered a spiritually optimistic sermon to his St. Paul's Cathedral congregation on the same subject, urging its members to move beyond melancholy and to embrace joy. His words suggest a full awareness of the very real ways in which melancholy had come to dominate the contemporary psyche:[2]

> God hath accompanied, and complicated almost all our bodily diseases of these times, with an extraordinary sadnesse, a predominant melancholy, a faintnesse of heart, a chearlesnesse, a joylesnesse of spirit, and therefore I returne often to this endeavor of raising your hearts, dilating your hearts with a holy Joy, Joy in the holy Ghost, for *Vnder the shadow of his wings,* you may, you should *rejoyce.*
>
> If you looke upon this world in a Map, you find two Hemisphears, two half worlds. If you crush heaven into a Map, you may find two Hemisphears too, two half Heavens; Halfe will be Joy, and halfe will be Glory; for in these two, the joy of heaven, and the glory of heaven, is all heaven represented unto us. And as of those two Hemisphears of the world, the first hath been knowne long before, but the other, (that of America, which is the richer in treasure) God reserved for later Discoveries; So though he reserve that Hemisphear of heaven, which is the Glory thereof, to the Resurrection, yet the other Hemisphear, the Joy of heaven, God opens to our Discovery, and delivers for our Habitation even whilst we dwell in this world.[3]

Donne envisions a solution to this perceived crisis. Urging his flock to consider carefully the meaning of joy, he in his role as priest introduces a metaphor from the literature of exploration, a subtle comparison, borrowed from his poetry, between the richness of far away America and the glory of God's kingdom, both distant but nonetheless reachable for those committed to moving in faith beyond the immediate and the known.

Although not meant to persuade a congregation, the two companion poems, "L'Allegro" and "Il Penseroso," which the poet John Milton wrote in his mid-twenties, provide a framework for his own response to this ongoing philosophical, psychological, and religious conversation. The nature of melancholy is among the many interrelated issues with which he wrestles as a young man contemplating his future. Whether focused on matters of chastity, mortality (particularly the death of someone young), his choice of a career, the image of himself that he wishes to project, or early attitudes toward the body politic and the church, Milton is continually engaged in precocious thought about relationships with his God and his fellow man. Although we are not entirely certain of their exact date, "L'Allegro" and "Il Penseroso" appear to have been composed somewhere between the latter stages of his undergraduate experience at Cambridge (circa 1628) and 1635, the year when he takes up residence at Horton, in Buckinghamshire.[4] According to Hughes, they probably follow his twenty-first birthday poem "On the Morning of Christ's Nativity" (1629) in which he considers what the Incarnation means for him.[5] They are placed very near his Sonnet VII "How Soon Hath Time," which verses reflect the pressures associated with choosing a profession, and in all likelihood precede *A Mask Performed at Ludlow Castle,* better known as *Comus,* presented in 1634 and dealing with the very personal question of celibacy. Falling as they do somewhere in the middle of this sequence, the poems focus especially on Milton's youthful visions of who he is and how he hopes, even expects, to flourish.

"L'Allegro and "Il Penseroso" are a young writer's contribution to contemporary dialogue about the popular subject of melancholy. But in a more important sense the theme serves as a framing device for Milton's speculative contemplation about his artistic and spiritual growth and about his own visionary definition of well-being. Establishing a contrast between mirth ("L'Allegro") on the one hand and melancholy ("Il Penseroso") on the other, Milton takes serious note of melancholy's numerous and varied implications. He specifically emphasizes the distinction between the Galenic black melancholy of madness as described in "L'Allegro's" opening lines and the creative melancholy of "Il Penseroso's" considerably more pensive, yet joyful conclusion. As Babb and Miller both remind us, black melancholy acquires its name from the assumption that an overabundance of black bile has been its cause, whereas the more positive form of melancholy bespeaks the presence of black bile in moderation.[6] Galen, the ancient Greek physician was primarily concerned with melancholy as madness, whereas Aristotle was more interested in positive melancholy as a special attribute of the ancient Greek thinkers and heroes.[7] Milton draws upon these distinctions with particular emphasis on Aristotle's theory and the ways it manifests itself in Christian thought. For him, creative melancholy is a joyous condition that he hopes will characterize his more mature years, resulting in poetic as well as religious inspiration.

It is, however, the idea of contrasts and the balancing as well as reconciliation of those contrasts that lies at the heart of Milton's understanding of what it means to flourish. As he interprets it, progression toward a more exalted state does not necessarily mean the abandonment or negation of one interest and replacement of it by another. On the contrary, it suggests that acceptance and appreciation of the manifold aspects of each person's life are what nourish but also define individual talent and the individual himself. Such appreciation and acceptance are, for Milton, essential to a state of well-being, which he characterizes as spiritual and artistic wholeness.

An overarching theme of Milton's early poetry, and one that manifests itself prominently in "L'Allegro" and "Il Penseroso," is the balance he seeks to establish between his extensive interest in the classics and a firmly grounded belief in the Christian God. Early in his teens he began formal education at the prestigious St. Paul's School, associated with London's Cathedral, where he would have been required with increasing frequency to translate specific passages from English into Latin. By the time he entered Christ's College, Cambridge, in 1625, he was well equipped to compose his own verses as well as prose presentations in Latin, often as a response to university requirements. His familiarity with classical authors was extensive, as was his immersion not only in the

Bible itself but also in the writings of the Church Fathers. Interest in the relationship between these two traditions was shared, of course, by contemporary churchmen, scholars, and artists, but it was also deeply personal, reflecting Milton's own literary intentions and religious faith.

"The Nativity Ode" is a prime example of Milton's concern with this balance, and as such it sheds light on the ways in which "L'Allegro" and "Il Penseroso" interact with each other. However, in this poem about the birth of the Christ child, he depicts Christianity as supplanting the classical world. In doing so Milton suggests that he too will cast classical interests aside so that God may in some small measure be embodied in his art and his actions. One imagines the young man composing this poem early of some December morning in 1629, pondering the mysteries of the Incarnation, not to mention his own coming of age. The poet (and surely the narrative voice is meant to be Milton's) begins by calling on *his* "Heav'nly Muse," (a quasi-Christian source of inspiration as opposed to one of the muses of classical poetry) for assistance in writing verse worthy of presentation to the newly born Christ.[8] Then, shifting perspective and imagining that he himself is part of the Nativity scene, he describes its peaceful setting, emphasizing the musical harmonies of celestial spheres that complement the infant's arrival. These musical references, soon to be echoed in "Il Penseroso," give way temporarily to the cacophony that will ultimately accompany Christ's battle with evil and to the sounds of classical figures, some of them gods, fleeing "the dreaded Infant's hand" (222). The classical world, notwithstanding the richness and beauty of its allusions, is firmly replaced by God incarnate, who, in the final stanza's shift of mood, sleeps guarded by "Angels . . . in order serviceable" (244). Despite Milton's knowledge of and love for things Greek and Roman, an overwhelming commitment to the Christian God characterizes the poem's orderly and peaceful conclusion. The poet identifies so closely with this serene tableau that the incarnation becomes a genuine and personal reality, as Milton joyfully accepts the presence of God within himself. Like Aquinas, whose theology ultimately bridges the classical and the Christian, the twenty-one year old Milton has begun to consider the nature of "perfect happiness," how he himself will define it and how it is to be achieved.[9]

Preliminary answers to these questions are but dimly apparent in the half light of Bethlehem's stable, but they have been raised and as such become a primary consideration of "L'Allegro" and "Il Penseroso." The questions gain in relevance if one recognizes that classical images, particularly in the form of pastoral allusions, abound in the former, while the movement in "Il Penseroso" progresses ever upward through more Christian manifestations of the pastoral and merges with climactic sounds of the church organ as an acoustical setting for Christian meditation. Yet, despite an obvious contrast between the two perspectives, they are considerably more connected to one another in these two companion poems than in "The Nativity Ode." Not surprisingly the connectedness evolves in part from Milton's rich appreciation of the pastoral tradition itself, with its classical focus on the songs of shepherds and its Christian emphasis on Christ as the protector of his flock, a focus he will treat more extensively in "Lycidas." This appreciation is complemented by an obvious imagistic fascination with and love for the English landscape.

Structurally the contrasts between "L'Allegro" and "Il Penseroso" reflect the Prolusion, an academic exercise and form of debate in which Cambridge undergraduates would first be required to argue one side of a question and then, with a reversal of roles, the opposite point of view. For example, one of Milton's early Prolusions has him addressing the question, "Whether day or night is the more excellent" (Prolusion I). Another (Prolusion VII) raises the question, "Whether learning makes men happier than does ignorance."[10] Were they couched in prose, "L'Allegro" and "Il Penseroso" could almost pass as just this sort of academic debate. "L'Allegro," lighthearted and full or laughter, opts for mirth and jollity, as opposed to the state of mind and action proposed in "Il Penseroso," with its emphasis on quiet contemplation, serious scholarship, and the ways both pave the path to the holiest of connections with God. Like the Prolusions, these poems are rhetorically argued and replete with intellectual reference. But they echo the Prolusions in yet another way: both engage subtly and often playfully with an audience sufficiently well versed to recognize the classical and Christian allusions but also aware that the concepts under consideration concern the speaker in very personal not to mention interpersonal ways.[11]

In the opening lines of "L'Allegro," the speaker banishes the more frightening manifestations of melancholy, namely madness:

> Hence loathed Melancholy
> Of Cerberus and blackest midnight born,
> In Stygian Cave forlorn
> 'Mongst horrid shapes and shrieks, and sights unholy,
> Find out some uncouth cell,
> Where brooding darkness spreads his jealous wings,
> And the night-Raven sings;
> There under Ebon shades, and low-brow'd Rocks,
> As ragged as thy Locks,
> In dark Cimmerian desert ever dwell. (1–10)

In its place he conjures up Euphrosyne, daughter of Venus and Bacchus, symbol of mirth, and one of the three graces.[12] It is she who sets the mood for the next 143 lines, all of them rhymed couplets more regular and more cheerful than lines in the brief introduction. Milton asks if he may spend time with her accompanied by "Jest," "youthful Jollity," and the "Mountain Nymph, sweet Liberty," as they visit scenes of laughter mixed with "unreproved pleasures free." And visit he does, though in his imagination, natural landscapes peopled with pastoral characters telling pastoral stories, and embraced at every step by music, whether it be the Cock ringing "Mattins," "jocund rebecs," or the "soft Lydian airs," in which Milton asks to be "lapped." At the poem's conclusion he becomes more specific about the kind of music he means—something resembling the strains of Orpheus when he "half-regain'd" his Eurydice from Hades. Here Milton takes us back to the poem's opening lines clarifying the primary function of Mirth as he sees it—namely, to draw one forth from melancholy as manifested in hellish madness and set the afflicted soul on the right path to a cure. David Miller in his article "From Delusion to Illumination: A Larger Structure for 'L'Allegro' and 'Il Penseroso'" notes that the activities described in "L'Allegro" were perceived by both Galen and Burton as possible cures for melancholy when it assumed this particular form.[13] The poem's final couplet, "These delights if thou canst give, / Mirth with thee I mean to live," (151–52) is a charming commitment, to mirth as a condition, but at the same time a tentative one. Given this inference, it is not surprising that in the introductory verse paragraph to "Il Penseroso" the poet does an about face, dismissing as "vain deluding joys" the scenes just discussed, calling them "the brood of folly without father bred," "fancies fond," and "the fickle pensioners of *Morpheus'* train."

Milton quickly follows up with an explanation introducing the reader to a more positive take on melancholy, the form that he associates with divine inspiration and the gift of creativity. He has moved from a description of country pleasures and is about to embark on a discussion of something more profound—the nature of what he perceives as true joy.[14] The poems have now established three clearly defined sets of contrasts: the distinctions between mirth and melancholy, between the two extremes associated *with* melancholy (madness and contemplative religious creativity), and between worldly happiness and the joyous state of mind, as well as soul, which, as he will ultimately explain, leads to unity with God. Milton hails the Melancholy of "Il Penseroso" as a "Goddess, sage and holy . . . Whose Saintly visage is too bright / To hit the Sense of human sight." Here again, he concentrates on lineage, depicting her as the daughter of Saturn and Vesta's incestuous union, Vesta being Saturn's daughter as well.[15] Unashamedly mixing the classical and the Christian, he slips into a vision of her as a "pensive Nun," her soul transfixed in ecstatic gaze. Like her counterpart, Euphrosyne, Milton next imagines her in the company of others—Peace, Quiet, "Spare Fast," "retired Leisure," and the "Cherub Contemplation," all described in musical context, but with harmonies of a different kind—in this case the music of "the Muses in a ring" . . . who "Round about Jove's Altar sing." We are welcomed into Melancholy's landscape by the song of the nightingale, listening to which the poet fancies himself on solitary walks through the trees as the bird's singing merges into the "Even-song" of a woodland

"Chantress." Ever so gradually the scene shifts to some high tower where he scans the heavens to unfold the spirit of Plato, imagines himself reading Greek tragedies or the poetry of Chaucer, and finally falls into a half sleep, breathed upon by "th' unseen Genius of the Wood." In a Miltonic version of the dream play, we find ourselves mysteriously privy to a climactic Christian moment framed by a prayerful sound and light scenario of "Cloisters," "antic Pillars," translucent church windows, a "pealing Organ," and a "full voic'd Choir" leading in just a few lines to the poem's conclusion. It is here that the poet imagines himself dissolved "into ecstasies" by the music. And this music is an essential part of what he hopes will characterize an almost monastic old age, where he may know the heavens but also the secrets of the earth, as he puts it, "Till old experience do attain / To something like Prophetic strain." The final couplet, "These pleasures Melancholy give, / And I with thee will choose to live" indicate that "Il Penseroso's" themes, particularly those relating to prophetic joy, are the final message of the pairing and win the debate. In comparison with "Mirth with thee I *mean* to live," *choose* indicates uncompromising conviction. Melancholy has the last word, and there is no directly spoken rebuttal from Mirth to counter the argument.

At the same time, there is another very important dimension to the relationship between these two poems. As Brooks, Hardy, and others have pointed out, virtually every reference, every image in "Il Penseroso" echoes some image, word, phrase, or inference in "L'Allegro."[16] The parallels are manifold and omnipresent. "L'Allegro's" Euphrosyne is replaced by the figure of Melancholy in "Il Penseroso," with Milton intent on telling us about the parentage of each as well as the allegorical figures in their company. A lark and a cock of the first poem's morning landscape become the nightingale of the second. The pastoral scenes through which the youthful poet walks grow much more somber as the midnight bell resounds in the ear of "Il Penseroso's" older more serious man. "Soft Lydian airs" give way to the booming polyphonic music of the church organ. The comic genre is replaced by the tragic. The mythological Orpheus, whose role is climactic in "L'Allegro," appears again but as a considerably less important figure in the context of ideals associated with Christian melancholy.[17] And the "fickle pensioners of *Morpheus'* train" transform themselves into "Il Penseroso's" dreamlike state verging on inspiration. Suffice it to say, these are by no means all of the parallels established throughout. There are a great many more, suggesting that in addition to debate, in addition to linear progression from worldly to more spiritual perspectives, the two poems are meant to echo and reflect one another—and in significant ways. Prolusions, of course, if successfully developed, should anticipate and even mirror the opponent's argument. But the mirroring here is somewhat more complex. We are introduced to Melancholy at the beginning of "L'Allegro" only to return to a different form of it at the end of "Il Penseroso." If we consider the two pieces as one argument instead of two that oppose one another, the progression of that one argument, while in a sense linear, is in fact circular, emphasizing that while the two aspects of melancholy are at opposite ends of the spectrum, they are at the same time closely intertwined.

These three structural emphases—linear progression, debate, and, for want of a better term, circular reflection—play against one another almost in the manner of contrapuntal melodies. Georg Frederic Handel and his librettist Charles Jennens seem in part to have recognized a contrapuntal pattern when they set the two poems to music in early 1740, juxtaposing clusters of lines from one poem with parallel clusters from the other and employing this structure from beginning to end. Their primary emphasis was, however, on the contrast in moods—so much so, in fact, that Jennens insisted on adding a separate movement entitled *Il Moderato,* the purpose of which was to establish a middle ground between what he perceived as the extremes of mirth and melancholy.[18] But stunning as the music is, it recognizes only one part of the picture, giving less than adequate attention to the complexity of Milton's thought and to his culminating lines about "old experience" attaining "to something like prophetic strain." If one looks at them more closely, these two poems are in large measure vehicles for consideration of the word *prophecy,* its meaning, and as far as Milton is concerned, its religious and artistic implications for himself. The concept of prophecy is therefore key to an understanding of the complex relationship between the two paired works and to Milton's own perception of well-being as a unique combination of the spiritual and the artistic.

Lest we attribute Milton's aspirations to prophecy as verging on arrogance, it is important to remember that many writers in the early church, the Middle Ages and Milton's own time were thinking along similar lines. As William Kerrigan reminds us, a number of Milton's contemporaries, among them John Donne and Thomas Hobbes, emphasize the prophetic responsibilities of the preacher as well as the links between prophecy and poetry.[19] Kerrigan quotes the following well-chosen passage from *Leviathan,* noting that even though Hobbes did not support the Puritan cause, he nevertheless reflected ideas about the nature of prophecy that shed light on Milton's convictions:

> The name of PROPHET, signifieth in Scripture sometimes Prolocutor; that is, he that speaketh from God to Man, or from man to God: And sometimes Praedictor, or a foreteller of things to come: And sometimes one that speaketh incoherently, as men that are distracted. It is most frequently used in the sense of speaking from God to the people. So Moses, Samuel, Elijah, Jeremiah and others were Prophets. And in this sense the High Priest was a Prophet, for he only went into the Sanctum Sanctorum, to enquire of God; and was to declare his answer to the people . . . Also they that in Christian congregations taught the people are said to prophecy . . . For Prophecy . . . signifieth . . . praising

God in Psalmes, and Holy Songs. And in this signification it is, that the Poets of the Heathen, that composed Hymnes and other sorts of Poems in the honor of their God, were called *VATES* (Prophets) as is well enough known by all that are versed in the Books of the Gentiles, and as is evident where St. Paul saith of the Cretans, that a Prophet of their owne said, they were Liars; not that St. Paul held their Poets for Prophets, but acknowledgeth that the word Prophet was commonly used to signifie them that celebrated the honour of God in Verse.[20]

With his climactic emphasis on prophecy in "Il Penseroso," Milton echoes a number of Hobbes's ideas. He is fully conscious of the classical tradition in which diviners were perceived as privy to the will and intent of the gods.[21] Herbrechtsmeier and Sheppard list several manifestations of this kind of prophecy, most prominently ecstatic pronouncements, among them those at Delphi, suggesting "possession by the deity."[22] At the conclusion of "Il Penseroso" Milton longs to be dissolved "into ecstasies," but ecstasies of quite a different kind:

There let the pealing Organ blow
To the full voic'd Choir below
In Service high and Anthems clear,
As May with sweetness, through mine ear,
Dissolve me into ecstasies,
And bring all Heav'n before mine eyes. (161–65)

He has previously alluded to ecstatic classical oracles in *The Nativity Ode* but has described their displacement at the moment of Christ's birth, characterizing them as suddenly "dumb" ("The Nativity Ode," 173). The ecstasies imagined in "Il Penseroso" are far from oracular in the classical sense and bespeak none of the frenzied noise associated with Greek or Mesopotamian prophecy. Instead they are associated with music as a metaphor for celestial harmonies, and ecstasy as something inspired by, if not closely identified with, harmonic music itself.[23] Milton's sense of ecstasy is also closely linked with poetic tradition, classical and Judeo-Christian prophets frequently expressing themselves, as Hobbes makes clear, in verse form.

Milton's "At a Solemn Music," written in 1633, casts further light on his unique understanding of musical harmony as part of the ecstatic condition. In this poem, allusions to ecstasy are merely indirect, the primary emphasis being fallen man's inability to connect with the harmonies of heaven. But in the short space of twenty-eight lines, Milton's sense of music as spiritual symbol *and* as a vehicle for poetic expression becomes clear:

Blest pair of *Sirens*, pledges of Heav'n's joy,
Sphere-born harmonious Sisters, Voice and Verse,
Wed your divine sounds, and mixt power employ
Dead things with inbreath'd sense able to pierce,

And to our high-rais'd fantasy present
That undisturbed Song of pure concent,
Aye sung before the sapphire-color'd throne
To him that sits thereon,
With Saintly shout and solemn Jubilee,
Where the bright Seraphim in burning row
Their loud uplifted Angel-trumpets blow,
And the Cherubic host in thousand choirs
Touch their immortal Harps of golden wires,
With those just Spirits that wear victorious Palms,
Hymns devout and holy Psalms
Singing everlastingly;
That we on Earth with undiscording voice
May rightly answer that melodious noise;
As once we did, till disproportion'd sin
Jarr'd against nature's chime, and with harsh din
Broke the fair music that all creatures made
To their great Lord, whose love their motion sway'd
In perfect Diapason, whilst they stood
In first disobedience and their state of good.
O may we soon again renew that Song,
And keep in tune with Heav'n, till God ere long
To his celestial consort us unite,
To live with him, and sing in endless morn of light.

As a poet, Milton's challenge will be the joining together of voice and verse, the sung and the spoken word. In "Il Penseroso" he anticipates that his own unique form of prophetic ecstasy, the result of music, will enable him to bring the marriage about. But at the same time this ecstasy will be consistent with the "Peaceful hermitage, / The Hairy Gown and Mossy Cell / Where I may sit and rightly spell / Of every Star that Heav'n doth shew, / And every Herb that sips the dew" ("Il Penseroso", 169–72). His descriptions of music and ecstasy are ultimately framed in silence, solitude, and, contemplation, all *generated* by sounds, which inspire a vision appearing before his spiritual eyes. Said vision mirrors Milton's earlier bow to "divinest Melancholy / Whose Saintly visage is too bright / To hit the sense of human sight" (12–14). Just as the vision will be spiritual, so too will the sounds be directed to the soul. And as Kester Svendsen observes, there will be a perfect correspondence between Milton's inner harmony, the harmonies he has perceived in nature, and the harmonies that characterize all spheres surrounding the earth.[24]

Given Milton's age when he writes about prophecy and his awareness of prophecy as a concept generating continued theological debate, he searches for his own personal definition of this term as well, one that reflects a combination of classical, Hebraic, and Christian traditions but also fits with his own talents and aspirations as a poet, who through his writings serves a prophetic if not priestly function. At the heart of these traditions lies a basic but very important question: To what degree should the individual ego be part of the prophetic process? Moores, focusing on the ecstatic, argues that "in all cases self and the world are radically transformed in a moment of intense positive emotion."[25] Milton wrestles with this question, realizing on the one hand that humility is an essential element of prophetic interpretation, but on the other that humility must be balanced with what he perceives as his own very special intellectual and poetic gifts. False prophets notwithstanding, ancient pagan prophecy is to some degree associated in his mind with ecstatic frenzy and a minimum of personal ego, the prophetic interpreter simply experiencing possession by the deity and then engaging in divination.[26] By contrast, however, "Il Penseroso," and the poems surrounding it, suggest that Milton is more interested in the kind of biblical prophecy that is best achieved through an ecstatic process of active and thoughtful engagement with poetic ideas.

This perspective on prophecy is also closely tied to the images of Melancholy and Saturn that he introduces at the beginning of "Il Penseroso." Erwin Panofsky in his important two-volume book, *Albrecht Durer*, explains how the association between Melancholy and Saturn developed over a period of years, building on the ideas of Aristotle and later those of the Florentine Neoplatonists. Panofsky paraphrases Aristotle on those who experience melancholy, saying that they are "by nature"

> as opposed to the downright insane—marked by a peculiar excitability which either over-stimulates or cripples their thoughts and emotions and may, if not controlled, cause raving madness or imbecility; they walk, as it were, on a narrow ridge between two abysses. But they walk, just for this reason way above the level of ordinary mortals.[27]

He goes on to show how Neoplatonists extended this idea and made it "a scientific basis for Plato's theory of 'divine frenzy,'" or to paraphrase the concept one step further, divine inspiration, the melancholy person being therefore superior in an intellectual and/or artistic sense to others and at the same time divinely connected.[28] The Neoplatonists also exalted Saturn, the forebear though defeated leader of the Olympians, simply because he was the progenitor, the creator of all that the Olympians merely governed. As Panofsky puts it, Neoplatonists "hailed (Saturn) as their celestial patron just as they reconciled themselves to melancholy as their terrestrial condition."[29] In wishing to be identified with Melancholy and Saturn, Milton is no doubt pondering the idea of prophecy as a balance between divine inspiration and innate creativity, more precisely artistic creativity, since the figure of Melancholy gradually over time became more and more associated with the arts.[30]

Perhaps most important of all, Milton implies in both poems that he is concerned with prophecy as a way of understanding the relationship between time and eternity. His attitudes regarding time are particularly well summarized in his sonnet, "How Soon Hath Time," written in 1631:

> How soon hath Time, the subtle thief of youth,
> Stol'n on his wing my three and twentieth year!
> My hasting days fly on with full career,
> But my late spring no bud or blossom show'th.
> Perhaps my semblance might deceive the truth,
> That I to manhood am arriv'd so near,
> And inward ripeness doth much less appear,
> That some more timely-happy spirits endu'th.
> Yet be it less or more, or soon or slow,
> It shall be still in strictest measure ev'n
> To that same lot, however mean or high,
> Toward which Time leads me, and the will of Heav'n;
> All is, if I have grace to use it so,
> As ever in my great task-Master's eye.

The poet's concern that at the age of twenty-three he has not yet written anything worthy of note implies a frustration that gives way to something more than a hope that God will work things according to a different time schedule. Frustrated by his own youthful appearance that belies advancing years, he expresses impatience with time itself as well as his inability to keep pace. But the frustration of quatrains one and two is brought to tentative resolution in lines 10 through 14, where he acknowledges the need for acceptance of Heaven's will. Milton must have the grace to accept it, but paradoxically *that* grace must be the product of a higher grace, proceeding from God himself. Only then can he understand the reality of eternity as opposed to the artificiality of mortal time. Metaphorically speaking, withdrawal from the world, as it is described in "Il Penseroso," suggests the need for a spiritual atmosphere in which such acceptance can flourish, acceptance being an essential part of the prophetic experience. Ironically the prophet must also strive to achieve this end, fully conscious of the ways different aspects of the personal life (in Milton's case youthful jollity *and* serious contemplation) not only parallel and/or contrast with one another but also are part of the same seamless tapestry. The latter cannot exist without the former because every aspect of contemplative solitude is both patterned on *and* developed out of more lighthearted attitudes and desires.

Awareness of such connections not only facilitates a clearer understanding of the self, but also lays the foundation for loss of self and for what Milton, fully recognizing his own talents, perceives as his life's work and anticipates as his own unique state of well-being. This prophetic focus in the final lines of "Il Penseroso" therefore explains the poem's structural relationship with "L'Allegro." In addition to assuming the form of a debate, the two poems move in linear progression from youth to maturity, with Milton presumably looking toward what he expects to become. But even more important, given the parallels between youth and old age as well as between the classical and Christian perspectives included in both works, extremes and apparent opposites are blended into one timeless, joyous whole. The young Milton is not entirely sure whether or how he will be able to transform this three quarters of a vision into reality. With his maturing sense of irony, he could also be wondering whether such serious aspirations will ultimately be subject to circumstance and compromise. But if he manages to achieve what he is setting out to do, his efforts will have been dependent upon acknowledgement, as opposed to rejection, of "old experience," and upon the exercise of free will. He therefore presses forward, with a hope for divine inspiration, but also with the conviction that if he is to flourish, he must actively *choose* to follow the path that is beginning to materialize before him.

Edward Tayler, in his fine book, *Milton's Poetry,* notes that for Augustine, "Time exists as the order of change and becoming, even as the medium in which the soul seeks salvation; but Eternity exists as the realm of God, of true Being that subsists without contingency or change."[31] Tayler goes on to explain the ways in which Protestantism embraced the idea of types, interpreting the words and actions of the Old Testament as prefigurings of the life and teachings of Christ. Tayler quotes the following passage, a paraphrase from Augustine, which, by the time of the Renaissance, had become thoroughly familiar to theologians:

> The Old Testament is the occultation, or hiding of the new, and the new is the manifestation of the old. For what is delivered and taught in figures, types, and prophecies of the old, the same . . . be taught in the new, but much more fully.[32]

The idea of typology, which focuses on time as an important element of prophecy, is very much a part not only of Milton's earlier works but of his subsequent major works as well. In *Paradise Regained,* Christ, who resists temptation, is seen as the new Adam. In *Paradise Lost* the seeds of redemption are already present in the disobedience of our first parents. At the poem's conclusion Adam is shown the evils that he and his descendents will encounter once the expulsion from the Garden has taken place, but he also watches as the Angel presents him with a kind of pageant, outlining the major events of the Old Testament and culminating in the life, death, resurrection, and ascension of Christ. The latter is not only viewed in the context of the former but is also implicit in every stage of its development. However, the fallen reader understands the pageant as historical development, and Adam and Eve, who have just been withdrawn from a state in which God's time is the only familiar condition, must accommodate themselves to this totally new way of thinking. In the company of generations to follow, they (and we with Milton as our guide) must also attempt to regain an understanding of what has been forgotten.

*Paradise Lost*, published some thirty plus years after Milton's completion of "L'Allegro" and "Il Penseroso," focuses in myriad ways on the primary emphases of these two poems. And typology is implied in the epic's opening lines:

> Of Man's First Disobedience, and the Fruit
> Of that Forbidden Tree, whose mortal taste
> Brought Death into the World, and all our woe,
> With loss of *Eden*, till one greater Man
> Restore us, and regain the blissful Seat,
> Sing Heav'nly Muse, that on the secret top
> Of *Oreb* or of *Sinai*, didst inspire
> That Shepherd, who first taught the chosen Seed,
> In the Beginning how the Heav'ns and Earth
> Rose out of *Chaos*; (Book I, 1–10)

Milton will undertake a new version of the original Genesis story related, according to legend, by the earliest of prophets, the shepherd of Sinai, Moses himself.[33] And just as the focus of that new story will be the replacement of the Old Adam by Christ, the New Adam, so too will Milton attempt to stand in the shoes of his prophetic forbear, both becoming in a very real sense one and the same. The Milton who here invokes the Muse of epic poetry does so with mature humility, with the voice of someone who has endured, and with the firm belief that, for him, this muse is indeed the Holy Spirit. His tone, harking back to "L'Allegro" and "Il Penseroso," is still anticipatory, and justifiably so because of the enormous task before him. It is also more realistic, bespeaking the wisdom that accompanies experience and acknowledging that ideal states of well-being, while something to strive for, invariably remain just beyond our horizons. But there is joy in recognition that he is now at last prepared to assume a prophetic role of consequence, and that based on his understanding of the story's timelessness, he is finally in a position to undertake this "advent'rous Song, / That with no middle flight intends to soar / Above the *Aonian* Mount, while it pursues / Things unattempted yet in Prose or Rhyme" (Book I, 13–16).

A deeper sense of what this preparation has entailed is implied in a passage from *An Apology for Smectymnuus*, which Milton wrote a decade after his completion of "L'Allegro" and "Il Penseroso":

> And long it was not after, when I was confirmed in this opinion, that he who would not be frustrate of his hope to write well hereafter in laudable things, ought himself to be a true poem, that is, a composition and pattern of the best and honorablest things—not presuming to sing high praises of heroic men and famous cities, unless he have in himself the experience and the practice of all that which is praiseworthy.[34]

His vision of the contemplative life, as spelled out in the final lines of "Il Penseroso," never quite touches on the importance of prophetic virtue.

However, during the intervening years, Milton has grown to realize that the prophet, in order to become an interpreter of God's word and to engage fully in the timelessness of his providence, must prove himself worthy. This important dimension of prophecy is emphasized in the next seven lines of the Invocation to *Paradise Lost*:

> And chiefly Thou O Spirit, that dost prefer
> Before all Temples th'upright heart and pure,
> Instruct me, for Thou know'st; Thou from the first
> Wast present, and with mighty wings outspread
> Dove-like satst brooding on the vast Abyss
> And mad'st it pregnant: What in me is dark
> Illumine, what is low raise and support. (Book I, 17–23)

Milton is not so much declaring himself worthy (his allusion to the darkness of his own understanding will recur frequently throughout the poem) but praying that he will be sufficiently so in order to embark on the great literary adventure of his life and faithfully to stay the course. In "Il Penseroso" he hoped the sounds of the organ and choir would "dissolve" him "into ecstasies," but here his vision is deeper and more all embracing, reflecting the kind of humble self-awareness that so often results from experience itself. For, as he implies in the Invocation's final lines, only genuine humility and submission to divine guidance, well-being more wisely comprehended, will enable him to "assert Eternal Providence, / And justify the ways of God to men."

## BIBLIOGRAPHY


Abrams, M. H., ed. *The Norton Anthology of English Literature,* Seventh Edition, Vol. I. New York: Norton, 2000.

Babb, Lawrence. "The Background of 'Il Penseroso.'" *Studies in Philology* 37 (1940): 257–73.

Bok, Sissela. *Exploring Happiness: From Aristotle to Brain Science.* New Haven: Yale University Press, 2010.

Brooks, Cleanth and John Edward Hardy. *Poems of Mr. John Milton: The 1645 Edition with Essays in Analysis.* New York: Harcourt Brace, 1951.

Donne, John. *John Donne's Sermons on the Psalms & Gospels.* Edited by Evelyn M. Simpson. Berkeley: University of California Press, 1963.

Herbrechtsmeier, William E. and Gerald T. Sheppard. "Prophecy: An Overview." In *The Encyclopedia of Religion,* Second Edition, Volume 11, edited by Lindsay Jones et al., 7423–28. Detroit: Thomson Gale, 2005.

Hicks, Anthony. Notes accompanying Musical Heritage Society C.D. recording of Handel's "L'Allegro, il Penseroso ed. il Moderato." London: Hyperion Records, 1999.

Hobbes, Thomas. *Leviathan.* Edited with an Introduction by C.B. Macpherson. Hamondsworth: Penguin, 1978.

Kerrigan, William Wallace, "Milton and the Drama of Prophecy." PhD diss., Columbia University, 1971.

Milton, John. *John Milton, Complete Poems and Major Prose.* Edited by Merritt Y. Hughes. Indianapolis: Odyssey Press, 1957.

Miller, David M. "From Delusion to Illumination: A Larger Structure for *L'Allegro – Il Penseroso.*" *Publications of the Modern Language Association* 86, Number 1 (January 1971): 32–39.

Moores, Donald J, ed. *Wild Poets of Ecstasy: An Anthology of Ecstatic Verse.* Nevada City: Pelican Pond, 2011.

Panofsky, Erwin. *Albrecht Durer,* Volume I. Princeton: Princeton University Press, 1945.

Parker, William Riley. *Milton, A Biography.* Second Edition. Edited by Gordon Campbell. Oxford: Clarendon Press, 1996.

Potkay, Adam. *The Story of Joy: From the Bible to Late Romanticism.* Cambridge: Cambridge University Press, 2007.

Seilhamer, Frank H. *Prophets and Prophecy: Seven Key Messengers.* Philadelphia: Fortress Press, 1977.

Svendsen, Kester. "Milton's L'ALLEGRO and IL PENSEROSO." *Explicator* 8.7 (1950): 49.

Tayler, Edward W. *Milton's Poetry: Its Development in Time.* Pittsburgh: Duquesne University Press, 1979.

Tillyard, E.M.W. "Milton: *L'ALLEGRO* AND *IL PENSEROSO.*" *The English Association,* Pamphlet No. 82 (1932).

## NOTES

1. M. H. Abrams et al., ed. *The Norton Anthology of English Literature,* Seventh Edition, Volume I (New York: Norton, 2000), 1560–1561. See also Sissela Bok, *Exploring Happiness: From Aristotle to Brain Science* (New Haven, CT: Yale University Press, 2010), 108–10.

2. Adam Potkay, *The Story of Joy: From the Bible to Late Romanticism* (New York: Cambridge University Press, 2007), 84–85.

3. Cited in Potkay, 84–85. Full quotation taken from John Donne, *John Donne's Sermons on the Psalms & Gospels,* ed. Evelyn M. Simpson (Berkeley: University of California Press, 1963), Sermon 4, 111–12.

4. Merritt Y. Hughes, Introduction to "L'Allegro" and "Il Penseroso" in *John Milton, Complete Poems and Major Prose,* ed. Merritt Y. Hughes (Indianapolis: The Odyssey Press, 1957), 67–68. See also William Riley Parker, *Milton, A Biography,* Second Edition, ed. Gordon Campbell (Oxford: Clarendon Press, 1996), 98.

5. Hughes, 42, 67–68. "On the Morning of Christ's Nativity" subsequently referred to as "The Nativity Ode."

6. Lawrence Babb, "The Background of 'Il Penseroso,'" *Studies in Philology* 37 (1940): 257–73. David M. Miller, "From Delusion to Illumination: A Larger Structure for *L'Allegro–Il Penseroso,*" *Publications of the Modern Language Association* 86.1 (1971): 32–39.

7. Babb, 260–61.

8. This and all subsequent Milton quotations are taken from John Milton, *John Milton, Complete Poems and Major Prose,* ed. Merritt Hughes (Indianapolis: The Odyssey Press, 1957).

9. See Bok's discussion of Aquinas, *Summa Theologica* in *Exploring Happiness,* 71.

10. Hughes, 68.

11. E.M.W. Tillyard, "Milton: *L'Allegro* and *Il Penseroso,*" *The English Association* 82 (1932): 8–9.

12. Hughes, footnote, 68.

13. Miller, 34.

14. Potkay sheds light on this condition when he says that "Augustine imagines the saints as a group of (almost) disembodied individuals, each absorbed by an intellectual joy he or she shares, as though alone with God." *The Story of Joy,* 45.

15. Hughes, footnote, 72.

16. Cleanth Brooks and John Edward Hardy, *Poems of Mr. John Milton: The 1645 Edition with Essays in Analysis* (New York: Harcourt, Brace, 1951), 136–138.
17. Miller, 34.
18. Anthony Hicks, Notes accompanying Musical Heritage Society C.D. recording of Handel's "L'Allegro, il Penseroso ed. il Moderato." (London: Hyperion Records, 1999), 6.
19. William Wallace Kerrigan, "Milton and the Drama of Prophecy" (Ph.D. diss., Columbia University, 1971), 122–29.
20. Thomas Hobbes, "Of a Christian Commonwealth," *Leviathan,* ed. with Introduction by C.B. Macpherson (Hammondsworth: Penguin, 1978), 456–57. Quoted in Kerrigan, 126.
21. William E. Herbrechtsmeier and Gerald T. Sheppard, "Prophecy: An Overview." In *The Encyclopedia of Religion,* Second Edition, Volume 11, ed. Lindsay Jones, et al. (Detroit: Thomson Gale, 2005), 7423.
22. Ibid., 7424.
23. With regard to the musical references in this poem Potkay says the following: "Ecstasy is not widely applauded before the Romantic era. Only then does it become a (semi) secularized aesthetic and erotic category. In England, the process begins with Milton's *Il Penseroso,* a meditative, reclusive speaker whom a chapel choir and organ 'dissolve[s] . . . into ecstasies.' Music will thereafter be the centerpiece of English and later German ecstasy . . ." *The Story of Joy*, 28.
24. Kester Svendsen, "Milton's L'Allegro and Il Penseroso," *Explicator* 8.7 (1950): Item 49.
25. D. J. Moores, Introduction to *Wild Poets of Ecstasy: An Anthology of Ecstatic Verse,* ed. D.J. Moores (Nevada City: Pelican Pond, 2011), 9.
26. Herbrechtsmeier and Sheppard, 7423–28.
27. Erwin Panofsky, *Albrecht Durer,* Volume I (Princeton: Princeton University Press, 1945), 165.
28. Ibid.
29. Ibid., 167.
30. Ibid., 170.
31. Edward W. Tayler, *Milton's Poetry: Its Development in Time* (Pittsburgh: Duquesne University Press, 1979), 16.
32. Qtd. in Tayler, *Milton's Poetry: Its Development in Time*, 28.
33. Merritt Hughes, footnote, 211. See also Frank H. Seilhhamer, *Prophets and Prophecy: Seven Key Messengers* (Philadelphia: Fortress Press, 1977), 8–17.
34. Merritt Hughes, 694.

# TEN

# On Becoming Neighbor Rosicky

## *Willa Cather, William James, and the Constructs of Well-Being*

Christine E. Kephart

Among the most anthologized and best loved of Willa Cather's short fiction, "Neighbor Rosicky," first published in 1930, returns to the Nebraska prairie of *O Pioneers!* (1912), the novel Cather considered her first real success.[1] In this gently measured story, Czech farmer Anton Rosicky's primary concern is the welfare of his family. He fears that his oldest son, Rudolph, will abandon the farming life for the city, thus also abandoning the values Rosicky has tried to instill in his children, and that Rudolph's wife Polly, an American girl raised in the town, will similarly be unwilling to settle into prairie life; he reflects what Cather lamented in a 1921 interview: "All the farmer's sons and daughters seem to want to get into the professions where they think they may find a soft place. 'I'm sure not going to work the way the old man did,' seems to be the slogan of the day."[2] Rosicky's apprehension stems from his own experience with city life, where he could find no soft place, and it is made all the more urgent because, as Cather tells us in the ironic first sentence, he has a heart condition from which we know he will die. With a plot of little action and mostly reflection, consisting primarily of Rosicky's thoughts and narratives as he retells and relives the difficult life events that have brought him to this place and time, Cather directs our focus to the way the good-hearted Rosicky holds his son and daughter-in-law in the embrace of family and farm.

A simply beautiful and slow-paced narrative of sympathy, contentment, and affirmation, "Neighbor Rosicky" reads like a sequel to Cather's novel *My Antonia* (1918) and contains a poignant reminiscence of Cather's father.[3] At the time she wrote and published "Rosicky," first serialized in 1930 and then collected in *Obscure Destinies* in 1932, her father had died and her aging mother was failing, the impact of which "turned her mind to family and friends [and the Nebraska] of her youth."[4] Lest we fear treading too close to the edge of intentional fallacy, we recall other fiction that brought Cather a comparable sense of comfort. In a letter about *Death Comes for the Archbishop* (1927), she explains, "Writing this book . . . was like a happy vacation from life, a return to childhood, to early memories."[5] Concurrent with "Neighbor Rosicky," *Shadows on the Rock* (1931) brought similar consolation, Cather's mother having died just before the novel was published; Cather later recalls that "she would always be grateful to *Shadows on the Rock* for carrying her over a hard stretch of her life."[6] In this light, certainly the familial love that suffuses "Neighbor Rosicky" and the sympathy with which Cather crafts her title character and his family read as a convincing narrative of personal affirmation.

At its core, the elderly Rosicky, a quiet hero for the well-being of his family and community, struggles with the stories that have defined him, including stories of suffering and loss as well as memories of early self-destructive tendencies, events that bring him to a decisive point: continue in a senseless oblivion or figure out what a meaningful life is and how to attain it. Cather's narrative explores the concept and constructs of the latter, of well-being and Rosicky's journey toward it. In fact, Rosicky addresses William James's question, from *Varieties of Religious Experience*, "What is human life's chief concern?" And, in James's words, Cather and Rosicky answer simply, as we all do, "It is happiness" (78).

James asks the same question that Aristotle examines in his *Nichomachean Ethics*, aligning his philosophy of happiness with the classical tradition of eudaimonia, not a trite, saccharin, smiley-faced happiness, not a feeling, but rather a concept that encompasses well-being, resilience, and the human capacity to flourish. In brief, Aristotle asserts in the *Ethics* that all undertakings aim at happiness. Defined as an activity, happiness means living and doing well, as having a virtuous *daimon*, or spirit, the achievement of which is the highest human good. Happiness may involve, naturally, positive experiences of affirmation and love, but it may also grow out of adverse experiences and suffering, in which case something transformative occurs to pull one from adversity into a new sense of self and well-being. This concept, moreover, has an individual focus, but it extends as well to one's larger political community, however that may be defined. Yet, how one comes to achieve this new, or renewed, state, and even to flourish, is elusive. Aristotle wonders if happiness occurs by chance, by divine intervention, or by practice and training.[7]

Understanding and actualizing happiness, all agree, is neither simple nor universal. James knows it: "How to gain, how to keep, how to recover happiness, is in fact for most men at all times the secret motive of all they do, and of all they are willing to endure" (VRE 78). Through Rosicky, Willa Cather, with a knowing look toward William James, explores the path to eudaimonia; in so doing she reveals a deep understanding of elements of and means by which we may achieve well-being and contentedness,[8] exemplified through the interconnected values of heightened consciousness, the acknowledgment of human suffering, the necessity of human agency, and the thoughtful narrative arrangement of one's life.

## "A DEEPER KIND OF CONSCIOUS BEING": ROSICKY'S TWICE-BORN PATH TO WELL-BEING

In *Varieties of Religious Experience,* James distinguishes between the once-born and the twice-born religious soul. The once-born, or healthy-minded, religious person, is an optimist. For him, "the world is a sort of rectilinear or one-storied affair, whose accounts are kept in one denomination, whose parts have just the values which naturally they appear to have, and of which a simple algebraic sum of pluses and minuses will give the total worth. Happiness and peace consist in living on the plus side of the account" (166). Although James admires and recognizes degrees of experience within the once-born, classifying Whitman and Emerson as healthy minded, he nonetheless somewhat suspiciously describes the once-born as "passionately flinging themselves upon their sense of the goodness of life, in spite of the hardships of their own condition, and in spite of the sinister theologies into which they may be born" (79); the soul of the healthy minded, he advises, "is of the sky-blue tint, whose affinities are rather with flowers and birds and all enchanting innocencies than with dark human passions" (80). Darker human passions and challenges lie instead with the twice-born.

The twice-born is a more complex soul for whom "the world is a double-storied mystery" (VRE 166). Counting himself among their number, James explains that the life of the twice-born begins in inner conflict, in battling demons, even in depression or melancholy, but it ends in a rebirth. As opposed to the healthy-minded religious person, the sick soul, or divided self, struggles with these demons and does not begin in the assumption, as some healthy minded do, that the world is composed, even its darker elements, of "innocencies." James defines the psychology of the twice-born as one based in "a certain discordancy or heterogeneity in the native temperament of the subject, an incompletely unified moral and intellectual constitution" (167). For this soul, "Peace cannot be reached by the simple addition of pluses and elimination of minuses from life. . . . There are two lives, the natural and the spiritual, and we must lose the one before we can participate in the other" (166–67).

James, allowing that such a rebirth, or conversion, is not exclusive to the religious-minded, writes:

> For example, the new birth may be away from religion into incredulity; or it may be from moral scrupulosity into freedom and license; or it may be produced by the irruption into the individual's life of some new stimulus or passion, such as love, ambition, cupidity, revenge, or patriotic devotion. In all these instances we have precisely the same psychological form of event—a firmness, stability, and equilibrium succeeding a period of storm and stress and inconsistency. In . . . non-religious cases the new man may also be born either gradually or suddenly. (VRE 176)

In conversion, the twice-born go through a "process . . . of redemption, not of mere reversion to natural health, and the sufferer, when saved, is saved by what seems to him a second birth, a deeper kind of conscious being than he could enjoy before" (157). The second birth, then, brings new awareness to this soul who finally realizes what had been the cause of the suffering—be it melancholia or another serious brand of storm and stress—and who then, ideally, accomplishes "the sense that all is ultimately well with one, the peace, the harmony, the *willingness to be*, even though the outer conditions should remain the same" (248). In the circle of the twice-born reside Tolstoy and John Bunyan, two writers important to Cather,[9] and, as Cather might have it, here we find too a source for understanding Rosicky as Cather's secular twice-born soul looking to construct a eudaimonic life.

On first meeting Rosicky, he almost seems to be one of James's sky-blue optimists. He has a heart condition, but, Cather writes, "He did not look like a sick man" (4). Doctor Ed Burleigh, the country physician who examines Rosicky at the opening of the story, observes that "Rosicky's face . . . suggested a contented disposition and a reflective quality that was gay rather than grave" (4–5). But in the experience of the twice-born soul, life, "the double-storied mystery," is complex, James tells us; and, as James biographer Robert Richardson reminds us, "the sick soul is not, in many cases, changed by conversion into happy healthy-mindedness."[10] He is unlikely to become a sky-blue optimist; he is more likely, as Rosicky illustrates, to continue grappling with the challenges that have at once shamed him and defined his path to becoming the deeply feeling and conscious being that we find in Cather's hero. Indeed, we soon learn that behind Rosicky's visage—or belied by it—is the story of man who was "sick," signaling the Jamesian sick soul, but who has been reborn into the deeper consciousness of the twice-born;[11] we read in him the narrative of one who has achieved the eudaimonic life, having emerged from a stormy period into firmness and stability, even love and flourishing, having recognized the virtuous daimon within.

Rosicky's rebirth into the virtuous life begins in the linking of hardship with generosity. His Czech mother dies when he is a boy, leaving young Anton to the care of his grandparents in the country, where "he formed those ties with the earth and the farm animals and growing things which are never made at all unless they are made early" (NR 32). At age eighteen, homeless, speaking no English and in need of a way to make a living in the Cheapside district of London, Rosicky takes a position as an apprentice with a "wretchedly poor" German tailor and his wife (26). As the name Cheapside suggests, Rosicky and the tailor's family were always hungry, always dirty, and their clothes, ironically, threadbare. He spent two years there—"The only part of his youth he didn't like to remember. . . ." (26). The death of his parents notwithstanding, this experience offers Rosicky his first real knowledge of instability and the absence of joy. Daily he lived in a mere corner of the Lifschnitz dwelling in Cheapside, sleeping on an "old horsehair sofa, with a feather quilt to wrap himself in. The other corner was rented to a wretched, dirty boy, who was studying the violin . . . Rosicky was dirty, too. There was no way to be anything else"; and there was no way to escape the "bugs in the place, and multitudes of fleas" (43–44). Although he would prefer not to remember this period in his later years, reliving it, whether through private reflection or by sharing it with his family, serves to remind Rosicky at all times—and to remind readers—of the details and moments he has had to struggle through in order to become "a deeper kind of conscious being."

Linked to this image, examples of simple generosity balance the hardship and begin to trigger in Rosicky a need to tap into his inner reserves of resilience. Lifschnitz, the tailor who takes on Rosicky and provides him shelter, "didn't much need an apprentice, but he was sorry for the boy and took him in for no wages but his keep and what he could pick up" (NR 43). To the eighteen-year old immigrant Rosicky looking to satisfy basic human needs, Lifschnitz is an immediate answer to an immediate need; for the elderly Rosicky recounting the story in retrospect, the tailor's charity is an early example of compassion and generosity in the face of acute hardship. Lifschnitz's other boarder, the violin student who increases the discomfort in their living quarters, is too, like the young Rosicky, the recipient of the tailor's generosity.

In another Cheapside episode, Rosicky experiences a low moral point leading to, conversely and necessarily, a state of higher consciousness and virtue. Driven by keen hunger, he recalls, Rosicky eats the Christmas goose that Mrs. Lifschnitz had prepared for her poor family and boarders, the one meal of the year that would be plentiful and fully nourishing. Burdened with guilt and shame at his transgressive behavior, he wanders the streets of London looking for a solution to replace the meal and finds himself peering into the Christmas warmth of a German restaurant. In a Dickensian moment, he begs help of Czech-speaking diners leaving the restaurant; they offer their sympathy and money with which Rosicky not only restores the Christmas goose but also supplements it with a grander feast. The family, forgetting about the goose, receives the feast as a miracle. But the miraculous here is the outcome for Rosicky. By humbling himself to right his wrong—in short, by doing well—his virtuous action is greeted by an answering action of generosity. Now having twice benefitted from the kindness of strangers, to borrow a phrase (thrice, really, since the Czech diners will also ensure Rosicky's passage out of Cheapside to new opportunities in New York), Rosicky learns a rich lesson from this Cheapside period: the possibility of compassionate responsibility in the face of physical discomfort and privation. An early example of living and doing well through the selflessness of others, themselves outsiders because of poverty or immigrant otherness, the generosity of Lifschnitz and Rosicky's Czech compatriots forms an early stage of Rosicky's gradual process out of stormy inconsistency toward equilibrium, as James would explain it, toward a deeper consciousness of purpose, toward an understanding of well-being. His own clarity, too, of the right- and wrongness of his behavior, even when justified by near starvation, reveals his innate sense of virtue.

The deeper kind of consciousness that Neighbor Rosicky realizes results, too, from recognizing and facing down inner demons in his twenties and thirties. On leaving Cheapside at age twenty, he moves to New York where he works again as a tailor and boards in the home of an Austrian furniture maker. There for many years, "he had what he would call a happy home life" (28). The opposite of the Cheapside experience, "It was a fine life; for the first five years or so it satisfied him completely. He was never hungry or cold or dirty, and everything amused him: a fire, a dogfight, a parade, a storm, a ferry ride. He thought New York the finest, richest, friendliest city in the world" (NR 28). He also made money, although he was not given to saving it. "But as the years passed, all alike, he began to get a little restless" and "he got to drinking. He was likely to drink too much of a Saturday night" (29). In short, he becomes an alcoholic.

Rosicky is not Cather's first alcoholic, but he is unusual in that he overcomes his dissipation. The heavy drinker Frank Shabata in *O Pioneers!*, one of the many Bohemian immigrant farmers on Cather's Nebraskan prairie, neither takes to the land, like his more successful neighbors the Bergsons, nor to people, preferring a jealous, angry, and resentful stance, even toward his beautiful and loving wife Marie. The deterioration of the Shabata marriage eventually steers Marie to the fateful embrace of Emil Bergson. Frank, in a drunken rage, comes upon "their dark figures on the grass, in the shadow of the mulberry tree" (262) and kills them with "his murderous 405 Winchester" (261). Frank is never able to find a fulfilling path, never able to realize the spiritual rebirth of the twice-born: his alcoholism begins in unhappiness and ends in tragedy.

The alcoholics in Cather's *The Song of the Lark* (1915), the music professor Wunsch and Spanish Johnny, displaced immigrants both, are similarly incapable of conversion. Studying alcoholism and the artist in *The Song of the Lark*, Charmion Gustke[12] suggests that Wunsch drinks to escape a feeling of homelessness and artistic failure (68), whereas Spanish Johnny's "alcoholism feeds his art and is primitive in its demand for recognition" (66–67). Gustke also considers them "caught within the double-bind of alcoholism and immigration" (69), as Frank Shabata undoubtedly is. In these cases, the disease of alcoholism hinders progress toward the virtuous life, resulting instead in spiritual stagnation at best, in death at worst. Yet somehow Anton Rosicky, a man with a similar profile as Cather's earlier alcoholic characters, avoids their fate. Trying to understand why he drinks so much in New York, "to figure out what ailed him," Rosicky finally learns that he does so "to get a temporary illusion of freedom and wide horizons" (30), that is, to escape the imprisoning walls and stagnation of the city,[13] elements that, he instinctually knows, obstruct and counter well-being. He also seems to know the value of temperance, or moderation, and to call on wisdom to change his behavior, in contrast to Cather's other drinkers, sick souls who do not get well for various reasons.

In portraying Rosicky as an alcoholic, Cather borrows from and plays specifically on James's depiction of the twice-born Tolstoy. One of Cather's enduring favorites was *Anna Karenina*. She never wavered in her love of the novel or of Tolstoy's early works, but she did criticize Tolstoy's later work as social reform instead of art. In 1896 she objected to the "moral purpose" of Tolstoy's late fiction saying, "Now that he lives like a recluse and makes pea soup for Russian peasants he writes some of the most wearisome stuff that is published."[14] Still, despite his late works of social reform, asceticism, and Marxist concerns, like *The Death of Ivan Ilyich*, she would write in a 1936 letter that Tolstoy nonetheless always seemed to care more for the condition of the human mind than the economic conditions under which we live; for this she continued to admire Tolstoy[15] and this is the very philosophy that she expresses through Rosicky. Like Tolstoy, Rosicky learns that "he had been living wrongly and must change," to borrow James's words (VRE 185);[16] both men "had drunk too deeply of the cup of bitterness ever to forget its taste, and their redemption is into a universe two stories deep" (VRE 187). Cather enjoys a pun here, for Rosicky, an alcoholic, has indeed drunk too deeply. She further clearly and playfully transposes the reference to James's description of Tolstoy: her alcoholic Rosicky, in James's words regarding Tolstoy's experience, certainly becomes "flat sober" and "dead" through alcoholism; Rosicky finally realizes that, again to James, "Things were meaningless whose meaning had always been self-evident" (VRE

152–53). In accepting his addiction and learning to understand its source, Rosicky thus makes another move toward "conversion" out of the instability of what had for a long time seemed "a fine life." As occurs in the conversion process of the twice-born, "one idea replaces another as the focal point of our minds," in Richardson's paraphrase,[17] and so Rosicky begins to investigate a new life for himself, one that leaves far behind the Cheapside poverty, one that frees him from his current city imprisonment and the vices that made it (un)endurable.[18]

Further connecting Rosicky's growth toward eudaimonia with James's understanding of Tolstoy and the right kind of life, Cather borrows an image from James. The twice-born Russian writer, James remarks,

> was one of those primitive oaks of men to whom the superfluities and insincerities, the cupidities, complications, and cruelties of our polite civilization are profoundly unsatisfying, and for whom the eternal veracities lie with more natural and animal things. His crisis was the getting of his soul in order, the discovery of its genuine habitat and vocation, the escape from falsehoods into what for him were ways of truth. (VRE 186)

Echoing James, Rosicky is "a very simple man. He was like a tree that has not many roots, but one tap-root that goes down deep" (NR 32); like Tolstoy, Rosicky also discovers his "genuine habitat and vocation," which is, as it happens, literally "with more natural and animal things" on the farm. James and Cather's shared arboreal image grows from a long tradition of tree symbolism that connects to well-being and eudaimonia. In its basic and ancient representation, a tree signifies the life of the cosmos, the roots, trunk and foliage representing the process and dimensions of life, and in its continuity, generation, regeneration, and immortality. Its verticality speaks to the growth trend, a symbolically rich visual image of growth stretching skyward to link worlds, as in the Christian tradition in which trees connect earth and heaven. Of course, in Christian mythology, the tree also conjures the image of the cross, the so-called Tree of Life.

Tolstoy applies the image of the cross to the end of *The Death of Ivan Ilyich*, one of his later stories that, to reiterate, Cather protested for its moral agenda and relative lack of art. A painful narrative about learning to live the right kind of life, the story ends with the stark image of Ilyich dying, like Christ, on the cross. This ending represents the austere and ascetic Christian morality that Tolstoy promotes at this stage of his proselytizing and writing; it is an equally austere message of the right kind of life that Ivan Ilyich comes to understand and to be converted to through his physical suffering. Unlike Ilyich, Rosicky is a secular hero and generally a less-suffering one, but he shares with Ilyich the need to understand and achieve the right kind of life. Tolstoy's depiction of Ilyich in his

Christ-like death, moreover, finds some parallel in Rosicky. Susan J. Rosowski likens Rosicky to Christ, "who . . . changes the world by inspiring others to love," suggesting that "Neighbor Rosicky" is a narrative about the "sacred power of love."[19] Additionally, Rosicky's stories read like Jesus's parables; in this way, they are unlike Tolstoy's *Ivan Ilyich*, which is clearly a lesson, but one delivered in an unrelenting punishing tone, and one in which the protagonist, Ilyich, remains disconnected from the humanity around him. Rosicky's parables, on the other hand, are warmly delivered and intended to impart vicarious lessons about well-being, about the instability, as James would phrase it, and absence of joy that results when the human condition is unprivileged. Relating the Cheapside episode of his life to his children, for example, has a particularly profound impact on Polly who, after hearing it, "thought [she and Rudolph] might have his family come over for supper on New Year's Eve." When he learns this, Rosicky's "heart leaped for joy" (NR 56–57).

Another scene, not one of Rosicky's recollections or retellings, but an episode that happens in the current chronology of "Neighbor Rosicky," also reads like a parable. In the Parable of the Thistle, as we might call it, old Rosicky attempts to help his son and daughter-in-law by weeding their property, by *rooting out* undesirable thistle that might "take the alfalfa" (62). The idea of rooting out weeds echoes themes in several of Jesus's parables, including those of the Sower, of the Wheat and the Weeds, of the Mustard Seed, all of which use agricultural metaphors to teach good and evil. The Parable of the Thistle similarly offers a lesson, specifically to Polly and Rudolph, not about religious values but about the roots of suffering and flourishing, from a farmer who would know.

The images of trees and roots recall another salient iteration of the growth metaphor in James. In *Varieties*, James delivers one of his most quotable and oft-quoted sayings in italicized emphasis: "The *roots* of a man's virtue are inaccessible to us": "By their fruits shall ye know them, not by their roots" (VRE 20). Richardson astutely observes, "For a man who thought less of roots than of fruits," James offers extensive examples and lists of the sources for many concepts presented in *Varieties*.[20] This point is not lost on Cather who has it both ways in "Neighbor Rosicky." Aligning herself with her philosophic predecessor's approach in *Varieties*, she makes Rosicky's twice-born roots accessible to us and to his children. Rosicky is rooted in his early experiences in Cheapside and New York, experiences at the heart of his well-being, experiences intended to be the roots of his children's future. His roots are also, of course, Cather's. She was raised with the Bible and *Pilgrim's Progress*, steeped in the Christian imagery and concepts that helped shape her fiction, and clearly her fiction is rooted in James, a source that goes beyond "Neighbor Rosicky."

Like Christ, from whom the Christian fruits of love and generosity come, like trees, like James and Cather, we are to know Rosicky by his fruits as well, all of which comprise a world of flourishing images: the farm; the family of six well-fed children who will likely carry on the farming tradition; the many scenes incorporating food in all of its detail and appetite-whetting aromas; the child that Polly and Rudolph are expecting; the philosophy of goodness and contentedness that Rosicky imparts to his family in his privileging of people over money and material things. These are the fruits of stability, of consistency, of goodness. Now when he thinks of the conditions in which he had lived his city days, ways that continue to make him feel "very bad in de heart" (NR 53), Rosicky walks to the barn to give his horses a treat: "It was his way of expressing what he felt" (61). This tree of a man with one deep taproot, a tree of figurative and literal life to his family, expresses himself in the most natural and nourishing way possible, by feeding his family and his farm.

## CASH-VALUE EXPERIENCE: ROSICKY'S PRAGMATIC APPROACH TO EUDAIMONIA

Not only does Rosicky have the roots, fruits, and qualities of the twice-born who has been reborn into the virtuous life, he also figures in the process as a Jamesian pragmatist. James's doctrine of pragmatism, which he summarizes as "a *doctrine of action* in the widest sense, the study of all human powers and means,"[21] is found in the "Philosophy" chapter of *Varieties* and developed more fully in *Pragmatism: A New Name for Some Old Ways of Thinking* (as well as in other lectures and texts that repeat and sometimes refine the ideas therein).

In "Philosophy," James considers the "Science of Religions" in the light of physical science and lived experience. By way of analogy, he writes, "Yet as the science of optics has to be fed in the first instance, and continually verified later, by facts experienced by seeing persons; so the science of religions would depend for its original material on facts of personal experience, and would have to square itself with personal experience through all its critical reconstructions. It could never get away from concrete life, or work in a conceptual vacuum" (VRE 456). Earlier in the same chapter, reflecting specifically on the theological underpinnings of Christianity, he asks how theological concepts like the indivisibility and immateriality of God "can make any definite connection with our life? And if they severally call for no distinctive adaptations of our conduct, what vital difference can it possibly make to a man's religion whether they be true or false?" (445). In a later passage, he offers a concise summary of pragmatism, writing simply that "the true is what works well" (458).

In *Pragmatism* (1909),[22] James repeats this point with emphasis: "*If theological ideas prove to have a value for concrete life, they will be true, for pragmatism, in the sense of being good for so much. For how much more they are true, will depend entirely on their relations to the other truths that also have to be acknowledged*" (73). The pragmatic approach allows one to be a humanist, another term for pragmatism used by James's younger colleague F.C.S. Schiller, who preferred the term *humanism* to *pragmatism*. Approving Schiller's nomenclature, James explains that "to an unascertainable extent our truths are man-made products. . . ."; "Human motives sharpen all our questions, human satisfactions lurk in all our answers, all our formulas have a human twist" (242). In short, "you can't weed out the human contribution" (254).

Pragmatism also grounds truth in lived experience and usefulness. James asserts:

> Pragmatism . . . asks its usual question. "Grant an idea or belief to be true," it says, "what concrete difference will its being true make in any one's actual life? How will the truth be realized? What experiences will be different from those which would obtain from if the belief were false? What, in short, is the truth's cash-value in experiential terms?" (P 200)

He adds later, "On pragmatic principles we cannot reject any hypothesis if consequences to life flow from it" (273). These are the very principles at work in Rosicky, a Jamesian pragmatist concerning himself with the human world on experiential terms in order to effect his own flourishing.

For one thing, Rosicky is a "worldly" man in the sense that he has indeed experienced the world, as his travel and city stories reveal; but he is also of this world, bound to the earth in thought and deed, the tree with "one tap-root that goes down deep." Cather neither imbues Rosicky with religious sentiment nor situates his growth from suffering to the eudaimonic life within religion. One story in particular illustrates this aspect of Rosicky's character. Mary Rosicky, Anton's wife, recounts the story of a Fourth of July when Rosicky learns that because of drought his forty acres of corn have been destroyed. Without telling his family the dreadful news, not even his wife, Rosicky arranges a dinner and takes his sons for a splash in "the horse tank down by the windmill" (NR 47). A Methodist preacher stopping by to invite the Rosicky family "to meet at the schoolhouse that night to pray for rain" is greeted by a naked Rosicky; "the preacher," embarrassed, "acted like he ain't never seen a naked man before" (48). This moment spotlights the difference between Rosicky's actions and the beliefs of the preacher. If truth is what works, as James tells us, then prayer for Rosicky is not truth. After all, how will prayer revive the crop or compensate for the lost value of it? What indeed is the cash-value, or usefulness, of prayer in this case? Rosicky's answer to the preacher comes in his nakedness, a humorous but forceful reminder that Rosicky, like the preacher, is human and thus vulnerable to slings and arrows as well as capable of acting. The true, then, is what he gains by experience, that of his early years in the city and his unexpected response to the drought that focuses on the human condition of his family rather than on the crop that is lost. Although the truth for Rosicky is not prayer, he would not, as neither James nor Cather would, deny the preacher his prayer because consequences to life likely flow from prayer to the preacher. But for Rosicky, to paraphrase James's question in *Varieties*, what difference in this case can prayer make in human experiential terms? And what consequences to life will flow from it as opposed to those that flow from Rosicky's privileging of love and his demonstration of generosity in the face of economic plight, a lesson he first learned, we remember, from the poor Cheapside tailor Lifschnitz. We also see, and Rosicky knows, that by his own action and choices he has gotten to this point in his life. As the agent of his own well-being, he has lived a doctrine of action leading to a deep sense of well-being.

As a result of his unusual approach to life, one in which monetary gain is secondary, Rosicky perplexes the larger farming community. Neighbors wonder why the Rosicky family "didn't get on faster" despite their industriousness, why they were comfortable simply being out of debt. Doctor Ed reflects, "Maybe . . . people as generous and warm-hearted and affectionate as the Rosickys never got ahead much; maybe you couldn't enjoy your life and put it in the bank, too" (NR 14-15). Maybe we hear William James again asking, "What, in short, is the truth's cash-value in experiential terms?" Doctor Ed, who diagnoses this good-hearted man with a bad heart, understands the answer. He will carry it with him as he doctors other neighbors in the country, effectively treating others with Rosicky's medicine: the pragmatic approach to well-being and emotional health. Rosicky, through Doctor Ed, thereby also fulfills a core value of eudaimonia: that the virtuous person act and live well within his political community, that he be a good neighbor, as Neighbor Rosicky certainly is.

As if to underscore the experiential component in her pragmatist, Cather emphasizes Rosicky's hands. Doctor Ed, worrying over Rosicky's physical health, wishes he were not diagnosing Rosicky, this man with the knowing eye and "such a warm brown hand" (NR 8). A tailor for many years before becoming a farmer, Rosicky continues to mend and stitch for his family; the "thickened nail of his right thumb told the story of his past" (21), but he figuratively stitches his stories together for his family's benefit, effectively, he hopes, tailoring their future. And certainly we know that to accomplish change in his city days he has done what comes to hand, by his own means and methods, not by miracle or prayer. Moreover, Rosicky intends to hand on, so to speak, the first-hand lessons he has learned so that the next generation need not suffer as he has done.

Polly, his daughter-in-law about whose fulfillment with a country life Rosicky is unsure and concerned, is especially aware of Rosicky's hands. When he has his first heart attack at her home, she nurses him through the attack, signaling an epiphany that Rosicky has hoped to inspire. For

Polly, it is a forceful realization: she now contemplates him and his lessons in the context of her life, recognizing that he "had a special gift for loving people" (NR 66) that was apparent in, among other things, his hands. She then holds his hand in her own, a beautiful image suggesting human understanding, a human bond, the linking of the generations, and a new branching from the tree of well-being. "Polly remembered that hour long afterwards; it had been like an awakening to her. It seemed to her that she had never learned so much about life from anything as from old Rosicky's hand. It brought her to herself; it communicated some direct and untranslatable message" (67). As James might explain it, "such a tingling and trembling of unrecovered associations is the penumbra of recognition that may surround any experience and make it seem familiar."[23]

In Polly's awakening we also hear a Jamesian idea of perception that is directly linked to eudaimonia. As James explains it in *Varieties*, "the practically real world for each one of us, the effective world of the individual, is the compound world, the physical facts and emotional values in indistinguishable combination" (151). In this poignant instance of "indistinguishable combination," Polly "sat holding [Rosicky's] warm, broad, flexible, brown hand," a hand "so alive and quick and light in its communications," a hand with "a great deal of generosity" in it (NR 66–67). Rosowski reasons that "Polly's awakening completes the ironic reversal begun in the story's opening exchange: Rosicky dies of a 'bad' heart, content in having seen into Polly's good one. His last thoughts are an extended play upon the meanings of 'heart,' by now used exclusively for the capacity to love."[24] His actions, the work of his hands and heart, have been motivated by and focused on love of others, that is, his family and concern for their future well being, not to mention the impact this "neighbor" might make on the greater community. Finally, this heart-sick man, in having become a man with a deeper consciousness through his twice-born experiences has also effected a transformative experience for Polly.

Complementing the power of Rosicky's hands to communicate the message of eudaimonia to Polly is an energy signaled by his "twinkling" features, especially his eyes. From the moment we meet him, Rosicky's voice and smile twinkle (NR 7, 10); his eyes twinkle and flutter (21, 64); they are "funny bright eyes," eyes that "gleam" (37, 65), in contrast to "the look in the eyes of a dishonest and crafty man, of a scheming and rapacious woman" (59), the kind of eyes Rosicky meets on his journey to becoming twice-born. Rosicky is not the first of Cather's characters whose eyes twinkle and gleam. In *Shadows on the Rock*, several characters are notable for the unique twinkling of their eyes: the apothecary Auclair, his daughter Cécile, Pierre Charron and Blinker. In Auclair's eyes gleams a clear message (the *clair* of his name meaning *clear*) of, among other things, optimism as he thinks of grandchildren in his future.[25] Blinker, whose name is telling, blinks a cross-eyed message about his tortured history, but his blinking also marks him as a figure "of revelation and transfiguration" in terms of Gothic luminosity.[26] Similarly, in her paralleling of Rosicky to Christ, Rosowski imagines Rosicky's twinkling as a halo effect around him—James and Cather might use the word *penumbra,* a term they share[27] —an indication that Rosicky is a revelatory figure who can effect transformation. Indeed, we learn through Polly that he does, that he "had a special gift for loving people like an ear for music or an eye for colour. It was quiet, unobtrusive; it was merely there. You saw it in his eyes—perhaps that was why they were merry" (NR 66). This *thereness* in Rosicky's eyes is another formulation of Cather's concept of "the thing not named," the theory that

> whatever is felt upon the page without being specifically named there—that, one might say, is created. It is the inexplicable presence of the thing not named, of the overtone divined by the ear but not heard by it, the verbal mood, the emotional aura of the fact or the thing or the deed, that gives high quality to the novel or the drama, as well as to poetry itself.[28]

James explains it this way: "Philosophy lives in words, but truth and fact well up into our lives in ways that exceed verbal formulation. There is in the living act of perception always something that glimmers and twinkles and will not be caught, and for which reflection comes too late" (VRE 456–57). Through Rosicky's twinkling eyes, Cather winks a nod to James with whom she collaborates in communicating the pragmatic experience of constructing the good life, a lesson Rosicky wordlessly imparts to Polly. The glimmering may be ineffable, but its message is nonetheless true, *there.*

Rosicky's twinkling eyes are, moreover, triangular in shape (NR 4), "three-cornered eyes" (24), like the symbolic Eye of Providence. Depicting an eye centered within a triangle, apex pointing skyward and rays emanating from the eye, the Eye of Providence is traditionally considered the symbol of a benevolent, all-seeing, all-knowing god; with his secular eye of providence, Cather once again links Rosicky to Christian myth. His providential position is underlined when with twinkling eyes he looks up at "frosty winter stars" (41), an associative link to the navigational North Star. He clearly sees himself playing a benevolent and guiding role for his family, telling Polly, "I'm goin' to look out fur you" (37). For her, the truth of Rosicky's experiences is her guide; or as James explains it, "To copy a reality is, indeed, one very important way of agreeing with it, but it is far from being essential. The essential thing is the process of being guided. Any idea that helps us to *deal,* whether practically or intellectually, with either the reality or its belongings, that doesn't entangle our progress in frustrations, that *fits,* in fact, and adapts our life to the reality's whole setting will agree sufficiently to meet the requirement. It will hold true of that reality" (P 213). Polly now knows through Rosicky that

> true ideas lead us into useful verbal and conceptual quarters as well as directly up to sensible termini. They lead to consistency, stability and flowing human intercourse. They lead away from eccentricity and isolation, from foiled and barren thinking. . . . and eventually, all true processes must lead to the face of directly verifying sensible experience *somewhere*, which somebody's ideas have copied. (P 215)

Rosicky hopes his sons will also copy his ideas, experience them vicariously, so that they "could get through the world without ever knowing much about the cruelty of human beings" (NR 60).

## IDEAS THAT WORK: THREADING TOGETHER THE EUDAIMONIC LIFE

Finally, the frame-story approach with which Cather constructs this narrative of well-being finds philosophical footing in James. Evelyn I. Funda has usefully diagrammed "Neighbor Rosicky" to show a pattern of "companion" stories that structure Rosicky's life as he relates it to others or in private reflection.[29] Beginning with the opening line foretelling Rosicky's death from heart attack, "Neighbor Rosicky" proceeds in a symmetrical pattern of past and present companion tales, creating a zigzag timeline that connects and contrasts stories of, for instance, poverty and plenty, vice and virtue.[30] The meta structure of the narrative asks us to consider the ways by which Cather, through Rosicky the tailor, patterns, stitches, fits together the stories to construct the process of coming to the good life—the stories he tells, those he keeps to himself and the episodes that occur in the timeframe of "Neighbor Rosicky."[31] Cather also employs multiple narrators and a fluid sense of time that often blurs the chronology of the episodes.

"A literary pragmatist, Cather was drawn to ideas that *worked*,"[32] and for piecing together this story, and likely much of her fiction as Merrill Maguire Skaggs has revealed, James's ideas worked.[33] Instructive here is James's concept of the linking of experiences. As he explains in the chapter "The One and the Many" from *Pragmatism*, a chapter that explores "whether the world is at bottom one great fact or many little facts,"[34] James examines how lines of influence come together to form a unified world. He writes, "Human efforts are daily unifying the world more and more in definite systematic ways. . . . The result is innumerable little hangings-together of the world's parts within the larger hangings-together, little worlds, not only of discourse but of operation, within the wider universe";

> everything that exists is influenced in *some* way by something else, if you can only pick the way out rightly. Loosely speaking, and in general, it may be said that all things cohere and adhere to each other somehow, and that the universe exists practically in reticulated or concatenated forms which make of it a continuous or 'integrated affair.' (P 136–37)

In "Neighbor Rosicky," Willa Cather illustrates how little hangings-together arrange into a life. Parables, lived experience, reflections, people, and images become juxtaposed and re-presented in multiple combinations, threaded together by nouns, adjectives, and grammatical rules; these very lines of influence comprise the hangings-together that create this universal story of human warmth and goodness.[35] We respond because, as Cather, James, and we know, our own lives are likewise constructed—by the episodes that make our histories, by our rewriting of those episodes in memory and recollection, by the way we make the pieces hang together in the arrangement of the narrative we want to present. Through "Neighbor Rosicky," Cather makes us more conscious of the value of the purposeful, meaningful design of a life as exemplified in Rosicky's fruitful and conscious narrative.

Cather closes "Neighbor Rosicky" with a final contemplation on the meaning of Rosicky's life, and a final emphatic nod to James, in the image of the graveyard.[36] We first hear Rosicky musing on the graveyard early in the story, just after he learns of his heart condition:

> It was a nice graveyard, Rosicky reflected, sort of snug and homelike, not cramped or mournful,—a big sweep all round it. A man could lie down in the long grass and see the complete arch of the sky over him, hear the wagons go by . . . It was a comfort to think that he would never have to go farther than the edge of his own hayfield. The snow, falling over his barnyard and the graveyard, seemed to draw things together like. And they were all old neighbors in the graveyard, most of them friends. (18–19)

Doctor Ed's reflection of the same scene, in the closing passage of the story, sounds a similar note of completion and comfort:

> A sudden hush had fallen on his soul. Everything here seemed strangely moving and significant, though signifying what, he did not know . . . For the first time it struck Doctor Ed that this was really a beautiful graveyard . . . This was open and free, this little square of long grass which the wind for ever stirred. Nothing but the sky overhead, and the many-coloured fields running on until they met that sky . . . Nothing could be more undeathlike than this place. (70–71)

Both passages merge farm and graveyard, sky and earth, life and death. Perhaps Cather offers us here an Emersonian circling, but Skaggs reasons, "Completing a life's circle may be a once-born Emersonian goal, for Emerson found the circle the most basic image of the universe . . . ; but completed circles are likely to menace twice-born, file-gnawing Jamesians. James prefers ragged edges to completeness."[37] Cather, on the other hand, prefers things her way. She will have the roots *and* the fruits, and in the close of "Neighbor Rosicky" she again thinks of James, of the concept of unity or happiness, if not circling, that results from the conversion of the divided sick self. The evocative graveyard is a lovely testament to Rosicky who, in the course of searching for and achieving the eudaimonic life, has emerged out of the discord of the sick-soul into "the smooth waters of inner unity and peace" and of "enduring happiness" (VRE 175), conjured in the hush Doctor Ed experiences at the graveyard; Rosicky dies in, in James's words, "a state of assurance" (247), having reached "the positive ideal which he [has longed] to compass" (209). The closing scene draws the completed arc of Rosicky's life of well-being accomplished through his Jamesian pragmatism and twice-born experiences. Finally, Doctor Ed thinks, as do we, "Rosicky's life seemed to him complete and beautiful" (NR 71): complete, beautiful—a fitting end to the virtuous life.

## BIBLIOGRAPHY


Aristotle. *Nichomachean Ethics*. Translated by Robert C. Bartlett and Susan D. Collins. Chicago and London: University of Chicago Press, 2011. Kindle edition.

Bohlke, L. Brent, ed. *Willa Cather in Person: Interviews, Speeches, and Letters*. Lincoln: University of Nebraska Press, 1986.

Cather, Willa. "My First Novels [There Were Two]." In *Willa Cather on Writing*, 91–97. Foreword by Stephen Tennant. Lincoln: University of Nebraska Press, 1988.

———. "Neighbor Rosicky." In *Obscure Destinies*. 1930. New York: Vintage Books, 1974.

———. "The Novel Démeublé." In *Willa Cather on Writing*, 35–43. Foreword by Stephen Tennant. Lincoln: University of Nebraska Press, 1988.

———. "On *Death Comes for the Archbishop*." In *Willa Cather on Writing*, 3–13. Foreword by Stephen Tennant. Lincoln: University of Nebraska Press, 1988.

———. *O Pioneers!* 1913. Boston: Houghton Mifflin, 1941.

Funda, Evelyn I. "'Neighbor Rosicky': Ever-Widening Time." *Nebraska English Journal* 37.1 (1991): 51–62.

Gustke, Charmion. "Somewhere Between Temperance and Prohibition: The Wandering Alcoholics in *The Song of the Lark*." *Willa Cather Newsletter and Review* 54.2 (2010): 65–69.

James, William. *Pragmatism: A New Name for Some Old Ways of Thinking*. New York: Longmans, Green, and Co., 1909.

———. *The Varieties of Religious Experience*. 1902. Edited by Martin E. Marty. New York: Penguin, 1982.

Kephart, Christine E. *The Catherian Cathedral: Gothic Cathedral Iconography in Willa Cather's Fiction*. Madison, NJ: Fairleigh Dickinson University Press, 2012.

Richardson, Robert D. *William James: In the Maelstrom of American Modernism*. Boston and New York: Houghton Mifflin, 2006.

Robinson, Phyllis C. *Willa: The Life of Willa Cather*. New York: Doubleday, 1983.

Rosowski, Susan. "Obscure Destinies: Unalterable Realities." In *The Voyage Perilous: Willa Cather's Romanticism*, 189–204. Lincoln: University of Nebraska Press, 1986.

Skaggs, Merrill Maguire. "*Death Comes for the Archbishop*: Willa Cather's Varieties of Religious Experience." In *Willa Cather and the Culture of Belief*. Edited by John J. Murphy. Provo, Utah: Brigham Young University Press, 2002.

———. "Willa Cather's Radical Empiricism." *Willa Cather Newsletter and Review* 47.1 (2003): 15–19.

———. "William James and the Walls for Unfurnished Fictions." *Willa Cather Newsletter and Review* 46.1 (2002): 8–12.

Slote, Bernice, ed. *The Kingdom of Art: Willa Cather's First Principles and Critical Statements, 1893–1896*. Lincoln: University of Nebraska Press, 1966.

Urgo, Joseph R. "Cather's Secular Humanism: Writing Anacoluthon and Shooting Out into the Eternities." *Cather Studies* 7 (2007): 186–202.

Woodress, James. *Willa Cather: A Literary Life*. Lincoln: University of Nebraska Press, 1987.

## NOTES

References to the primary works of Willa Cather and William James are abbreviated as follows:

NR: "Neighbor Rosicky"

P: *Pragmatism: A New Name for Some Old Ways of Thinking*

VRE: *Varieties of Religious Experience*

1. See Cather's essay "My First Novels [There Were Two]," in which she calls *O Pioneers!* a more satisfying book for her to write than her other "first" novel, *Alexander's Bridge*. She writes about the former: "Here there was no arranging or 'inventing'; everything was spontaneous and took its own place, right or wrong"; in contrast, *Alexander's Bridge* is "unnecessary and superficial" (92).

2. L. Brent Bohlke, ed. *Willa Cather in Person: Interviews, Speeches, and Letters*. (Lincoln: University of Nebraska Press, 1986), 48.

3. James Woodress, *Willa Cather: A Literary Life* (Lincoln: University of Nebraska Press, 1987), 438; and Susan J. Rosowski, "*Obscure Destinies*" (In *The Voyage Perilous: Willa Cather's Romanticism*, Lincoln: University of Nebraska Press, 1986) 189.

4. Woodress, 438.

5. Willa Cather, "On *Death Comes for the Archbishop*," 11.

6. Phyllis C. Robinson, *Willa: The Life of Willa Cather* (New York: Doubleday, 1983), 258.

7. Aristotle, *Nichomachean Ethics*, Book 1, Chapter 8, Kindle edition, 2011

8. Merrill Skaggs's expert scholarship into the impact of James on Cather's fiction has definitively confirmed the association of the two icons of American literature and thought; indeed, Skaggs's efforts have begun revealing the extensive presence of James in Cather's work and has thus opened up to Cather studies a mine of possibility, both in Cather's borrowing of concepts and even specific words and phrases. See Skaggs's "*Death Comes for the Archbishop*: Willa Cather's Varieties of Religious Experience," "Willa Cather's Radical Empiricism," and "William James and the Walls for Unfurnished Fictions" for an understanding of Cather's borrowing of James's most culturally influential works.

9. The influence of Tolstoy on Cather, through James's lens and otherwise, will become clear in this essay. As for Bunyan, Cather scholars will recognize the value to Cather of Bunyan's presence in James's twice-born order. Along with the Bible, Bunyan is one of the earliest and most enduring influences on her imagination; her fiction is peppered with references to *Pilgrim's Progress*.

10. Robert D. Richardson, *William James: In the Maelstrom of American Modernism* (Boston and New York: Houghton Mifflin, 2006), 403.

11. For a more enlightening discussion of the once-born/twice-born binary in Cather's *Death Comes for the Archbishop*, see Skaggs's "*Death Comes for the Archbishop*: Willa Cather's Varieties of Religious Experience."

12. See Gustke's article "Somewhere Between Temperance and Prohibition: The Wandering Alcoholics in *The Song of the Lark*" for an insightful look at the role of alcoholics in relation to art and artists in Cather.

13. "Binary-loving James" (Skaggs's "Cather's Varieties of Religious Experience, 105) would appreciate this classic city-country opposition.

14. Quoted in Bernice Slote, ed., *The Kingdom of Art: Willa Cather's First Principles and Critical Statements* (Lincoln: University of Nebraska Press, 1966), 378.

15. Woodress, 477–78.

16. In *Varieties*, James cites Tolstoy's *Confession*.

17. Richardson, 405.

18. Bill Wilson, founder of Alcoholics Anonymous, acknowledged the influence of *Varieties of Religious Experience* on the principles of AA, especially the conversion experience. He wrote to Carl Jung "that in founding AA he had done little more than make 'conversion experiences— nearly every variety reported by James—available on an almost wholesale basis'" (in Richardson, *Maelstrom*, 405). Interestingly, AA was founded in 1935. Cather was onto something: *Obscure Destinies*, the collection of stories in which "Neighbor Rosicky" is included, was published in 1932 after first appearing in *The Women's Home Companion* in 1930. Frank Shabata, Wunsch, and Spanish Johnny, of course, come even earlier; see Gustke who contextualizes Wunsch and Spanish Johnny in the era of Prohibition.

19. Rosowski, 191–92.

20. Richardson, 397.

21. Quoted in Richardson, 491.

22. See Richardson's excellent summary of the Pragmatism lectures and the principles therein, 491–97.

23. This quotation is from James's *Psychology* and is quoted in Skaggs's "Williams James and the Walls for Unfurnished Fictions," 12, which discusses the influence of James's *Psychology* on Cather's thought and fiction; regarding this James passage, Skaggs remarks on the parallel concept in Cather's "démeublé" theory.

24. Rosowski, 193.

25. Christine E. Kephart, *The Catherian Cathedral: Gothic Cathedral Iconography in Willa Cather's Fiction* (Madison, NJ: Fairleigh Dickinson University Press, 2012), 98.

26. Ibid., 99.

27. Skaggs, "Unfurnished Fictions," 11.

28. Cather, "The Novel Démeublé," 41–42.

29. Funda, " 'Neighbor Rosicky': Ever-Widening Time," 52–54.

30. Ibid.

31. Augusta, in *The Professor's House* (1925), another of Cather's tailors, patterns and sews dresses for the St. Peter women. These patterns often intermingle with the professor's notes for his nonfiction volumes, suggesting the foundational material of stories and the often unexpected ways by which storytelling begins before being linked and formed into narrative. Augusta's sewing and patterning crosses with and interrelates to the patterns, organization, and ideas of Professor St. Peter's academic scholarship, and all work in the larger context of Cather's design and arrangement of novel elements in terms of medieval philosophy and Gothic cathedral imagery (Kephart, *Catherian Cathedral*, 62–63).

32. Joseph R. Urgo, *Cather's Secular Humanism*, 189; Urgo's article draws on James's *Pragmatism*.

33. Skaggs writes that Cather "would later reproduce in her fiction literally dozens of [the] images and ideas" from the first three chapters of James's *Psychology: The Briefer Course* (Skaggs, "Unfurnished Fictions," 8). This is proving true for many of James's works.

34. Richardson, 445.

35. It is difficult to choose from among James's many passages expressing similar ideas. The entirety of the following passage, which builds on the sentence "you can't weed out the human contribution," used earlier in this essay, could also work here and it is one in which James employs the metaphor of grammar: "You see how naturally one comes to the humanistic principle: you can't weed out the human contribution. Our nouns and adjectives are all humanized heirlooms, and in the theories we build them into, the inner order and arrangement is wholly dictated by human considerations, intellectual consistency being one of them. Mathematics and logic themselves are fermenting with human rearrangements; physics, astronomy and biology follow massive cues of preference. We plunge forward into the field of fresh experience with the beliefs our ancestors and we have made already; these determine what we notice; what we notice determines what we do; what we do again determines what we experience; so from one thing to another, altho the stubborn fact remains that there *is* a sensible flux, what is *true of it* seems from first to last to be largely a matter of our own creation." *Pragmatism*, 254–55.

36. Skaggs "bluntly" asserts that "Cather remains more 'exciting' (a James word) to read than James does because she trusted and then applied his ideas to her prose as he did not. Had he realized, as she did, what it might mean for a reader's quick comprehension and long retention to associate objects together instead of ideas, and had he then provided his texts with juxtaposed things as she did hers, he might still be taught in as wide a variety of classes . . . as she is" (Skaggs, "Unfurnished Fictions," 10).

37. Skaggs, "Cather's Varieties of Religious Experience," 119.

# ELEVEN

# The Career of Joy in the Twentieth Century

Adam Potkay

## I. HOW JOY GOT A BAD REPUTATION

Sullied in the strength-through-joy histrionics of Nazi Germany and the Soviet empire, "joy" still retains a sarcastic ring, especially to European ears. Nazis appropriated the term for the *kraft durch freude* ("strength through joy") fellowship of the German Worker's Front and the automobile named after it, the *Kdf-wagen,* later known as the Volkswagen.[1] The postwar novel *House of Dolls,* published under the concentration-camp pseudonym "Ka-tzetnik 135633," contains an account of the "Labor via Joy" camp where women prisoners are divided into a "labor division" of half-starved workers and a "joy division" of well-fed, forcibly sterilized sex slaves.[2] ("Joy Division" later became the witheringly ironic name of a Manchester post-punk band in 1978; the band's legendary career, capped by the single "Love Will Tear Us Apart (Again)," came to a premature end when lead singer Ian Curtis committed suicide in May 1980.) Compulsory "joy," a Nazi ideal, also became a part of the sloganeering of the Soviet republics. At the dawn of the "Prague Spring" of 1967, Milan Kundera managed to take his revenge upon this joy in his first novel, *The Joke* (Žert). Its protagonist, Ludvik, recalls University life in "the first year after February 1948" (the month in which a coup d'état transformed Czechoslovakia into a communist state and Soviet satellite): "Not only was I unencumbered with inner sorrows, I was blessed with a considerable sense of fun. And even so I can't say I wore the joyous physiognomy of the times: my sense of fun was too frivolous. No, the joy in vogue was devoid of irony and practical jokes; it was, as I have said, of a highly serious variety, the self-proclaimed historical optimism of the victorious class, a solemn and ascetic joy—in short, Joy with a capital J."[3]

Ludvik protests against a "Joy" that joy can be invoked (politically, aesthetically) for morally dubious (or worse) purposes, or with dubious effects. What propagandists have all too readily understood is that "joy" can be used as a kind of shorthand for what one should approve, and approve in an ardent manner. In this light, even Schiller's "To Joy" or the congregational hymn "Joy to the World" bespeaks an imperative or prescriptive joy, not simply some description of a joyful state. Joy, most basically, is an emotional response that ratifies something—often something that comes as a surprise—as a good; its opposite is grief or dejection. For this reason Aristotle, who had much to say about the proper regulation of all the passions, stressed the educational and civic importance of joy and grief. That which bonds citizens is "finding joy in the same things." Reading Aristotle's line from the vantage of twentieth-century fascist and totalitarian ideologies is a bit chilling.

That chill comes from the knowledge, painfully clear in the wake of Nazism, that people can rejoice in, or be manipulated to rejoice in, hideous actions and attitudes. Aesthetic education can involve moral degradation, or at least not eliminate moral idiocy. That Beethoven's setting of Schiller can incite ultraviolence as readily as "world feeling" is a theme of Anthony Burgess's 1962 novel, *A Clockwork Orange*, and its 1971 film adaptation by Stanley Kubrick.[4] The novel's first-person narrator, the criminal thug Alex DeLarge, recalls raping two young girls to "the lovely Ninth": "the male human goloss [voice] coming in and telling them all to be joyful, and then the lovely blissful tune all about Joy being a glorious spark of heaven, and then I felt the old tigers leap in me and then I leapt on these two young ptitsas"; after the rape, he fell asleep "with the old Joy Joy Joy Joy crashing and howling away."[5] Alex later becomes, as Gail Hart puts it, "a disabled or incapacitated criminally violent thug" after "a regime of drug-supported aversion therapy that brings him to the point where he feels mortally nauseated whenever his natural inclinations to violence manifest themselves"[6] ; he is also conditioned to feel nausea whenever he hears symphonic music (Burgess's novel) or, in Kubrick's film, specifically Beethoven's Ninth, the soundtrack to the violent films—including German war films—he is compelled to watch.

Probably for the best, "joy" has not been rehabilitated as a term of European politics or what we might loosely call public religion, despite the 1972 selection of Beethoven's *freudenmelodie* (the "Ode to Joy" melody without words) as the official anthem of the European Union. Europeans take their heritage of official joy-talk with a very large grain of salt—and rightly so, given the brutal history of top-down, nationalist or imperialist joy. Let us be duly skeptical of propagandistic "joy," especially when the promise of communal wholeness depends on sacrificial scapegoats, as it almost always does: for example, the symbolic "Jews" in John's Gospel or, more virulently, flesh-and-blood Jews (and Slavs and gypsies and homosexuals) in Nazi ideology.

In the United States, government at all levels—federal, state, local—inculcate and celebrate not joy but "freedom." Thus, when the American Leonard Bernstein conducted the Ninth Symphony in Berlin in 1989, a central event in the celebration of the destruction of the Berlin Wall, it seemed only natural that he should follow the nineteenth-century French habit of replacing Schiller's *freude* with *freiheit*, turning the chorus to joy into one to "freedom." Freedom is, after all, what American civic religion enshrines, and Bernstein's flourish belonged to a heady moment, with the fall of the Soviet Empire, when it seemed that the world might swiftly become America writ large. The September 2001 terrorist attack on the World Trade Center, followed by the war in Iraq, put a damper on this type of liberal-democratic millennialism.

It is not the government but rather corporate advertisers who mass-market joy in the United States. My preferred dishwashing liquid, for example, has as its registered trademark "Joy." ("Joy" is also the brand name of a floral eau de toilette created by Jean Patou in 1930.) "Joy," a Procter & Gamble product that allows me to clean my dishes cheaply and efficiently, is the instrumental cause of a mild pleasure in my life; it does not, however, occasion joy. Randall Jarrell's 1965 poem "Next Day" features a woman speaker "moving from Cheer to Joy, from Joy to All" down a supermarket aisle, her own identity gradually erased by affluent suburban life: such satire may seem facile, with an edge of misogyny that, in satires on consumption, hasn't disappeared (it persists through *American Beauty*).[7] But it does raise the interesting question of why soap products are marketed as they are. It might be that the executives and admen who affixed "joy" to a dishwashing liquid were really trying to retail small joys (the fulfillment of clean plates), but it's hard to imagine them doing so without parodying some more exalted notion of joy with a sneer at those who don't get the joke. Sugary carbonated beverages are also sold as, or in lieu of, emotional fulfillment. In my time I've seen "the joy of Pepsi" slogan eclipse an earlier Coke jingle that involved "teaching the world to sing in perfect harmony" by buying it a Coke, because Coke's "the real thing." Why soda in particular should be marketed as the means of world salvation I am at a loss to account. I suspect the very absurdity of the proposition—the thing that nobody needs transubstantiated into the one thing, "the real thing," that everyone needs—recommends it to admen as a sign of their own cynical, magical powers.

Across the board admen offer comfort and belonging as well as self-esteem and prestige: people may notice you in particular if you drive a new Jaguar (high-end advertising), but all people will come together, communally or at least tribally, through buying the same sodas, beers, cigarettes, and soap products (low-end advertising). The roots of this two-pronged American advertising scheme lie, I suspect, in earlier British efforts to sell both prestige and belonging, efforts that, significantly, involved "joy." According to the Oxford English Dictionary, the breezy French phrase "*joie de vivre*" was introduced into English in 1901 and rather quickly became a piece of newsman slang and advert slogan: in 1907, the Westminster Gazette hyped "the new *joie de vivre* of motoring" (a prestige activity) and the Observer, in 1930, touted "the *joie de vivre* of Blackpool Beach" (a site of social recreation).

"Joy," as it became a (suspect) phrase of adverts and politics, didn't fare well in the high culture of later nineteenth- and twentieth-century England and America. The passion terms in general fell out of favor, as did the more or less coherent and universalizing psychology they provided writers from Aquinas to the Romantics. In dialectical opposition to the mass mind of consumerist culture arose the unique, unduplicable minds portrayed in high bourgeois art. Literary realism—I'm thinking particularly of novels by William Dean Howells and Henry James[8] —tends to avoid the representation of discrete emotions, the "classic eleven" schematized by Aquinas (love, desire, joy, hatred, avoidance, sorrow, hope, despair, audacity, fear, anger). For Howells, and especially for James, emotion becomes difficult to label precisely because it becomes highly customized, contoured to individuals and their distinctive points of view. Emotional consciousness, or the conscious negotiation of emotionality, is portrayed in relation to a character's deeply individualized and fluid vision of his or her place in the world. In practice, forms of social self-consciousness predominate—embarrassment and anxiety—alongside jealousy and what we might call love, although expressions of love are rare. Isabel Archer's inner landscape, three to four years into her marriage, strikes me as characteristic of realist preoccupations: she feels, in general, "refined embarrassment"; she feels, "to-day," when "there was nothing clear . . . a confusion of regrets, a complication of fears" (*The Portrait of a Lady* Chapter 40). James's depiction of positive emotional states often relies on the deconstruction of established emotion terms, as in his paradoxical transformation of "ecstasy" (the soul's flight from body and identity) into something acutely self-conscious and social in Gilbert Osmond: "The elation of success, which surely now flamed high in Osmond, emitted meanwhile very little smoke for so brilliant a blaze. Contentment, on his part, took no vulgar form; excitement, in the most self-conscious of men, was a kind of ecstasy of self-control" (Chapter 35).[9]

Of course, the stress of transformation on the traditional language of the emotions does not always appear so strikingly as it does in James. Still, it is to some degree present in Wilde (in Dorian's "rose-coloured joy," for example) and in Yeats's Nietzschean "tragic joy." For psychology to be fully sounded, passions needed to be complicated, idiosyncratic associations explored, paradoxical connections traced. Thus Ivor Gurney, in a June 21, 1916, letter written during a brief respite from front-line fighting in France, fantasized of the "revenge of Joy" he would one day have on life, and one wonders of this striking locution whether it is more to the benefit of revenge or the disadvantage of joy.[10] Nonetheless, Gurney's capitalized view of "Joy" already seems something of a relic in the modernist poetic landscape then emerging with Imagism, Vorticism, Pound, and Eliot. The last sclerotic gasp of a late Romantic lexicon of personified "joy" may be Walter de la Mare's poem "Joy" in a 1940 issue of the *Atlantic Monthly*.[11] Modernists eschewed the term because of its affiliations with the "passéists" (as Pound might say); rejecting emotion terms in general as stiffly rhetorical or theatrical (e.g., "O Joy!"), modernist poets—like realist novelists before them—sought to explore more subtle and fluid feelings and ambient moods.[12]

The post-war literary mood may be described in a number of ways, but joyful is not one of them. Gurney never got his "revenge of joy" on life: in the summer of 1917, he was the victim of a poison gas attack that left him periodically delusional for the rest of his life; he died in 1937, after fifteen years of confinement in mental hospitals. In 1922, Eliot published his postwar monument to shattered ideals, *The Waste Land*, in which the words "die," "dying," "death," or "dead" appear eighteen times (in several languages) and "joy" (or "bliss" or "happiness") not at all. What kept Eliot's romance of death, decay, and sterility alive—so to speak—for much of the twentieth century was the series of atrocities that continued more or less unabated from August 1914 onward and that would by mid-century leave tens of millions dead from warfare, deportation, extermination, and disease. Statistics of death led, among Western intellectuals, to a love of death, as if to turn death into a fetish was a way of taming its scandalous power. "We are in love, at least in our literature, with the fantasy of death": so spoke Lionel Trilling in 1950, on the centenary of the death of William Wordsworth. Wordsworth's acute and varied perception of the "sentiment of being"—his sense of wonder at his own existence and that of other creatures—contrasts, Trilling maintained, with Eliot's influential disdain for common life. Trilling summarized the intellectual climate of his day: "We imagine, with nothing in between, the dull not-being of life, the intense not-being of death; but we do not imagine being—we do not imagine that it can be a joy."[13]

The "we" for whom Trilling spoke have now passed or are passing away. Western civilization did not end, as some then feared in might, in the Cold War era, and neither did joy in its religious or Romantic varieties. Indeed, imaginings of joy, which never really went away, have gained new visibility, particularly in America.

## II. JOY IN OUR TIME, OR THE ROAD TO NOWHERE

What has become, in left-leaning academic circles, the more or less accepted view of later twentieth-century Western culture is set forth in the grand synthesis of Fredric Jameson's *Postmodernism*: we inhabit a dystopia of mass media, multiscreen distraction. Times Square or Disneyland are concentrated examples of the postmodern condition. Simulacra/simulation is squeezing out authentic objects or experiences. This attenuation of life is set in motion by the dispersed power of postnational, postindustrial capital. The only joys Jameson admits into this world are what he calls the "joyous intensities" felt in relation to glossy material things.[14] What Jameson ignores, however, are the spiritual strivings of American, and even of avowedly postmodern, life. To draw one from many possible examples: in Don DeLillo's *timor mortis* campus novel, *White Noise* (1985), the protagonist Jack Gladney (the Chair of "Hitler Studies" at a small liberal arts college) desperately wants to believe in "something, somewhere, large and redoubtable enough to justify . . . [children's] shining reliance and implicit belief." As Jack thinks this, the sleeping child he observes whispers from his dream, "Toyota Celica," the echoed voice of a TV car advertisement. Yet Jack's desire for cosmic meaning persists despite, or through, its frustration by a world of simulacra.[15] Spiritual quests or orientations, as John A. McClure has recently shown, inform a wide range of contemporary novelists, both those that are canonically postmodern (Thomas Pynchon and Ishmael Reed as well as Don DeLillo) and those typically but unfairly excluded from the category, including Toni Morrison, Leslie Marmon Silko, and Latin American "magic realists." Indeed, McClure makes a strong case for seeing the postmodern as the "post-secular."[16]

Of course, in most quarters of America belief in a super-sensual world never went away, and neither did the religious joy with which this book's historical survey began. Indeed, Christian joy is on the ascendant, for better or for worse. Thus Rev. Richard John Neuhaus, a conservative Catholic who has built bridges with evangelical Protestants, nonetheless complains of three aspects of contemporary evangelical culture: "the overly confident claims to being born again, *the forced happiness and joy*, the awful music."[17] Joy also features prominently, as we've seen, in the post-Christian Book of Mormon and Church of Jesus Christ of Latter-Day Saints. Buddhist traditions have extended to curious westerners the promise of what seem quite spectacular joys, rendered here as varying grades of "rapture" or "happiness": "*Minor happiness* is only able to raise the hairs on the body. . . . *Showering happiness* breaks over the body again and again like waves on the seashore. *Uplifting happiness* can be powerful enough to levitate the body and make it spring up in the air. . . . But when *pervading (rapturous) happiness* arises, the whole body is completely pervaded, like a filled bladder, like a rock cavern invaded by a huge inundation."[18] The lure of joy has led a growing number to medieval traditions of Jewish mysticism, with Kabbalah Centers (again for better or worse) spreading across the country. Within Judaism, joy persists at the ideal heart of Hasidic communities: as the Yiddish writer Isaac Bashevis Singer writes through the voice of his character Reb Leyzer: "The real truth is this: The whole world is joy. Heaven is a festival all year long. Of all lies, the greatest falsehood is melancholy."[19]

Given this American spiritual context, let me return to the Blakean question with which I began my book: in what gardens are joys growing now? Set aside purely personal joys—discoveries, homecomings, and the rounding accidents of one's own life. Where will we find active sites of interpersonal or collective joys? By my lights, they're to be found especially in *religion* and in *music*—especially in so far as those two are the same thing, religion found in the spirit of music and music in the spirit of religion. Music and (or as) religion relate to the present moment and/or the eternity of the force (call it life, Nature, the Dionysian, Will, the Holy Spirit, God) that rolls through the moment. Music and religion—we might add sports and games, too, and to some degree all fine arts—exist and may take us to a separate world within the world, apart together with co-communicants, mutually withdrawn for joyful replenishment from the realm of practical necessity and day-to-day affairs, in touch with something immanent in that realm.[20]

The joys in which I trust are joys "on the road to nowhere": that is to say, joys that are non- or antiteleological; that aren't founded on an expectation of some radical change of or departure from the only place or planet we know; joys that aren't yoked to some master narrative of progress or growth. It's these joys, and these joys alone, that may lead us to the "nowhere" of Thomas More's Greek neologism, *utopia* (Greek, *ou*, not, no + *topos*, place).[21] Joys in the here and now of life, aiming at no definite destination and conscious of the conditions of our lease on earth, are the only utopian joys we can fairly claim. I distrust sacred teleology for the same reason that I reject the secular teleology of Hegelian or Marxist theory: both not only sacrifice the present to the future but also tend to justify terrible sacrifices in the present—of the natural world, which will die anyway, says the apocalypticist; of undesirable types or peoples who impede the march of history or triumph of the Party, says the revolutionist.

I distrust ateleological doctrines of progress, too, specifically our capitalist faith in infinite material improvement through unlimited economic growth. During the 1990s Francis Fukuyama declared history at a Hegelian end with liberal democracy and market capitalism triumphant over all; the U.S. stock market soared toward heaven; and any evils incidental to global capitalism (e.g., sweatshop labor in Asia, the destruction of world ecosystems) might be seen as subordinate to and ultimately curable by the providential march of commerce, a species of faith Clifford

Geertz has tartly dubbed "economicist theodicy."[22] This faith currently seems poised to destroy our planet through overpopulation, depletion of natural resources, degradation of ozone and environment—all the ills that should be readily apparent to anyone not blinded by a faith that Jesus Christ is coming back soon, or a too-optimistic belief that the imminent terra-forming of Mars will in due course usher in the interplanetary federation of the *Star Wars* film series. To look around oneself, here where we are and not where some may think we're headed, is to see that unlimited growth in the annual consumption of energy and materials cannot, in a limited planet, be sustained forever. Population reduction and a steady-state economy is, realistically, our only path for staying where we already are.[23]

Joy on the road to nowhere may be joy in the planet, its ecosystems, its myriad sentient creatures (including asses and idiots) and the very fact of their sentience—we find this in the "Green Romanticism" that stems from Thomson and Wordsworth and extends to Hoyt Axton's "joy to the fishes in the deep blue sea" and Sharon Olds's litany of marine life in her poem "Outdoor Shower": "Then feel them going: / salp, chitin, diatom, dulse, the / blind ones of the ocean," with whom we share "the simple fields of God, liquid and solid."[24]

Joy on the road to nowhere may be erotic joy (*joi*), especially if we think of it not as "the unsatisfied desire more desirable than any other satisfaction" but rather, as it often appears in the troubadour lyrics, the prolonged desire more desirable than any immediate gratification. As such, *joi* may become the means of redeeming eros, now so often reduced to an impatience for climax. *Joi* may be another name for the "libidinal morality" that Herbert Marcuse found in Freud: "Is there perhaps a 'natural' self-restraint in Eros so that its genuine gratification would call for delay, detour, and arrest?"[25] Indeed there is, he thought, and he castigates the mass culture of advanced industrial society for inculcating immediate gratifications—especially those of a partial and localized sexuality—at the expense of an erotics of life, in which "the environment from which the individual could obtain pleasure . . . as [from] an extended zone of the body" would be as broad and lush as possible.[26]

Joy on the road to nowhere may still be found in the Enlightenment formulation of ethical joy, the joy of performing virtuous or generous deeds, or bearing witness to events that add to the sum of general communal or human happiness. Such joys are, I'd like to think, a common part of our lives; in the United States we pay annual tribute to the ideal of ethical joy in the ritual Christmas-time television broadcasts of Frank Capra's 1946 film *It's a Wonderful Life*. The film's climactic image of a small-town community pulling together to save the virtuous George Bailey (Jimmy Stewart) from unmerited financial disaster affords a lesson in ethical joy, the viewer participating vicariously in a community in which individuals share each other's joy and grief. The other day, in my own relatively small town in Virginia, I saw a license plate, "Joy 05" (was it the fifth "Joy" plate in Virginia?) with a license-plate holder inscribed, "Practice random acts of kindness." Assuming that the driver theorized joy as the consequence rather than the motive of those acts, he or she would be a true heir of Shaftesbury's.

Alternatively, joy on the road to nowhere may be tragic joy, the affirmation of human values despite and through suffering and annihilation, evils natural and moral, such as we find in Wagner, Nietzsche, and Yeats—or, for a more recent example, in Ridley Scott's popular film *Thelma and Louise* (1991). The name "Thelma" is of uncertain derivation, but it's pretty to think it comes from the Greek *thelēma*, "will," Scott's film representing the rise of will in the once-passive housewife Thelma (Geena Davis) through her friendship with the more assertive Louise (Susan Sarandon). Finally, for its audience, the film evokes the Dionysian-tragic joy of seeing its heroes crushed and subsumed by the indestructible universal will. Thelma and Louise, driving off a cliff together, joyously end the film on the road to nowhere—their car filmed in a slow motion arc in the air, accompanied by triumphant soundtrack music that cheers them on (a chorus of women, against a drum and synth soundtrack, intone something that sounds like "and we fly away"). Tragic joy involves precisely this upward arc of facing death down. What it evades, as Scott's film does, is death itself—car-crash, explosion, incineration, waste. Beyond its false glamorization of dying as an act unconnected to death, tragic joy is not without other ethical dangers: defeatism or facile martyrdom, on the one hand (are Thelma and Louise, finally, free from these faults?) and on the other, reveling in the prospect of destruction (is Ridley Scott free from this, or are we?). Thelma and Louise, who up the road have killed a (bad) man, turn their backs on the possibility of social forgiveness and redemption figured by the sympathetic detective (Harvey Keitel) who chases their car during its suicide sprint. Like Tristan and Isolde, their glory lies in renouncing the day world, valuing their bond of love beyond their ties to life.

With Marcuse, I can imagine a world in which death wouldn't be celebrated as an existential category. Freud's death instinct veers us away from tension or pain; if we could overcome the pains superadded by an unjust society (of the type that *Thelma and Louise* depicts broadly in its Texan world of sexist husbands, predatory cowboys, and boorish truckers) then the death drive might converge with the pleasure principle and come to rest in a fulfilled present.[27] Tragedy and Christian religion have inverse orientations toward death: the tragic actor dominates through love the fate or conditions that crush her; the religious acolyte submits to fate or circumstance through hope in the Sabbath of eternity. Death is either the wall against which to flex one's strength or the door to a place where rest and pleasure come together. But doesn't life itself, under conditions one might imagine into being, offer ample opportunities for both exertion and rest?

Joy on the road to nowhere may be religious joy, but religious joy centered on the here and now, especially the here and now permeated with the eternal (or call it heavenly) spirit of music. With the increasing democratization of religion in Britain and especially the Americas, church service and field revival alike supplemented the speaking voice of the orator with the coalescing power of melody and rhythm. From the congregational hymns of Isaac Watts through the carnival songs of Brazilian Catholic/Candomble religion to the twentieth-century Christian campfire song "I've got joy, joy, joy deep down in my heart," music has proved a motive to earthly joy that is more than a metaphor for heavenly blessedness.[28]

In twentieth-century America, music flows through religion, at its Dionysian best, and music may become its own religion. Wagner was the first art-composer to view music as a religious experience independent of any formal religion, hearing in the *freudenmelodie* "the chorale of the new communion," and turning his own darkened opera house in Bayreuth into a new kind of church, committed to a religio-aesthetic spectacle that would engross the mind and senses. The rock group Led Zeppelin, in titling its 1973 album *Houses of the Holy*, alluded to arena-rock as a new religion—one, we might note, that drew upon both European operatic tradition and African-American traditions of gospel, soul, blues, and (hybridized) rock 'n' roll. Ideally one should hear music live, as a congregant or audience, rather than through one's home stereo, as an aesthete. The analogue and now digital reproduction of music connects us to, but also separates us from, joy in the moment, the joy of what Harry Smith labeled "social music" in his multiple-album set, *Anthology of American Folk Music* (1952). Like Coleridge in his poems of vicarious joy, the at-home listener to music created for a church, stage, or otherwise communal context "contemplates with lively joy the joy she cannot share."

In the spectrum of social music, gospel and soul shade into music conventionally irreligious but a religion unto itself, especially psychedelic and neo-psychedelic rock, disco, punk, post-punk, hardcore, techno, "sampledelia," rave culture. Sinatra at the Paramount Theatre in 1942 and the Beatles at Shea Stadium in 1965 inspired a maenadic abandon that first gave pop music the credence of the religious revival, but the rock/dance experiences I'm thinking of here are less centered on hierarchical star/fan relationships than shared as collective rituals, situations in which everybody (or nobody) is a star, in which the barriers between audience and band are permeable, in which "the scene" is more than the music.[29] Readers may recall reading about if not being part of the Electric Kool-Aid Acid Test or the Exploding Plastic Inevitable in the 1960s; think, too, of Grateful Dead or Phish concerts; Parliament-Funkadelic shows; disco in the Studio 54 or later Limelight era; the Ramones at CBGBs;

mosh pits at hardcore shows; the rave scene that thrived, particularly in Britain, in the 1990s. The club drug Ecstasy—its very name the culmination of the Romantic association of ecstasy with music—served as the chemical catalyst for losing one's individual ego in repetitive music's hypnotic flow and the Dionysian fervor of the crowd. The drug apparently facilitates a group regression into the pre-Oedipal libidinal uncertainty of ego or body boundaries.[30]

Describing the rave scene from the inside, Simon Reynolds hoisted the credo of an earlier British rock critic: "We must make of joy once more a crime against the state." Awash in developing varieties of "house" or techno dance-music (electronic, percussive, nonverbal), the rave "was the Dionysian paroxysm programmed and looped for eternity." Reynolds concedes that it's hard to describe the raves he experienced—"a culture that is fundamentally amnesiac and nonverbal"—though in attempting to do so he often employs analogies drawn from religion: "the dance floor was a fervent congregation of 'space-age Baptists'"; a pioneering techno DJ is like a "shaman, a techno-mystic who developed a science of total sound in order to create spiritual experiences for his followers."[31] Still, Reynolds' quandary is an interesting one: it's hard to tell stories about the rave. As such, does the rave fit into the story of joy? The joy of the rave, of raw rock 'n' roll, of gospel and soul, is joy in the body (even if it's the soul that's singing) or in the current of the "one" that underlies the illusion of individuation—and as such it doesn't, existentially, have much of a story to tell. As joy passing into ecstasy, it's where the story ends. Stories need the Apollonian (characterization, form); they need unsatisfied individual desire; they quite often need—to recur to the troubadour's term—*joi*.

## III. JOY IN AMERICAN BEAUTY

The best story of joy in recent years, to my mind, is the capstone American film of the 1990s, the Academy-Award sweeper *American Beauty* (1999, director Sam Mendes, screenplay Alan Ball). Its central protagonist, Lester Burnham, follows a trajectory through most of the nonreligious joys touched upon in my book: released at the film's end from the *joi* of unsatisfied desire he experiences several minutes of ethical happiness; although these turn out to be the last minutes of his life, he experiences in a sort of afterlife or Nietzschean "eternal recurrence" an intense joy in the mundane—in, as he puts it, "every single moment of my stupid little life"—and particularly in the beauty of nature, humanity, and the work of human hands.

*American Beauty* might have been titled, by analogy with well-known Jane Austen novels, *Joy and Joylessness*. A *New York Times* ad for the film's original theatrical run features a key snippet of the film's dialogue, set above the head of an elegant middle-aged woman (the character Carolyn Burnham, played by Annette Bening) as she looks up in profile into the eyes of her husband (Lester Burnham, played by Kevin Spacey) with just a touch too much cold determination for the classic romantic still that this would otherwise be: "Joyless? I am not joyless! There happens to be a lot about me that you don't know, mister smarty man. There is plenty of joy in my life." This is Carolyn's retort to her husband's accusation that she has indeed become joyless, and one may well ponder the assumptions behind such an accusation. It could only come into play among people with a lingering Protestant sense that it's a *duty* as well as a great gift to have joy in one's life. Despite the conspicuous absence of Christian practice in the affluent white suburb the Burnhams inhabit, it is nonetheless a place still haunted by the specter of joylessness unleashed by Luther and English Protestant writers, including Spenser and Donne.

And despite Carolyn's retort, there is no joy in her real estate-brokering and adulterous life. She has attractive possessions, in particular a $4,000 living room sofa upholstered in Italian silk and a silver Mercedes-Benz-ML320 SUV in which she listens, alternately, to motivational tapes and to Bobby Darrin's song "Don't Rain on my Parade." She has a liaison with her town's self-advertised "King" of real estate, Buddy Kane (Peter Gallagher), whose mantra for getting ahead—"in order to be successful one must project an image of success"—makes her dewy-eyed. Their one scene of motel sex revs on a mutual narcissism of the most embarrassing sort, with dialogue such as "You like getting' nailed by the King?" and "Oh yes I love it, fuck me your majesty!" It's painfully clear to the viewer if not to Carolyn herself that, as her husband Lester tells her, property, pleasure, and self-empowerment do not add up to joy.[32] Joy is about feeling not so alone, and Carolyn Burnham is utterly alone.

Carolyn's quest for empowerment leads her, at Buddy's prompting, to frequent a firing range; she then starts carrying a pistol in her car's glove compartment. Her covert gun helps her to maintain a sense of control over her psychologically threatening husband, Lester. Lester comes to challenge the commodious life she inhabits by quitting his desk job—he worked, significantly, in advertising, the profession that sucked the blood from "joy." He threatens her control of their shared home by chafing against her exclusive selection of the family's dinnertime music: she favors the sort of "cocktail lounge music" (instrumental, easy-listening) designed to placate an environment; he reverts to listening to the rock music he loved as a teenager. The next time he rides in his car he's listening to the Guess Who's "American Woman" (1970), a song protesting U.S. materialism and militarism. Indeed, Lester resumes much of his teenage routine, including weight lifting, beer drinking, pot smoking, and—for a job—fast-food burger flipping.

He also, though this is one feature of his new life Carolyn doesn't know, fantasizes about a self-styled teenage temptress, Angela (Mena

Suvari). Angela is his daughter's high school friend and, after the prize roses Carolyn cultivates in her front garden, the second possible "American Beauty" of the film's title. (The "American Beauty" conceit of woman-as-native rose goes back at least to the David/Evans/Altman song "American Beauty Rose," recorded by Frank Sinatra in 1961). Through Angela, Lester imagines joy as a unifying experience, a two-in-oneness that he no longer hopes for in his marriage. The only eroticism we glimpse in the Burnham's master bedroom suite comes in two scenes of Lester masturbating, once in the shower and once in his bed with his wife beside him. Masturbation is the film's symbol of pleasure without joy, an immediate gratification less desirable than the phantasm of union.

Lester imagines Angela into being, picturing her for us (via Conrad Hall's cinematography) in spectacular baths, endless vistas, of red rose petals. She is the Stella to his Astrophil, the Laura to his Petrarch—or, to think of Otto Preminger's 1944 film *Laura*, the Laura to his Mark Macpherson. Lester's unsatisfied and ultimately unsatisfiable desire to enter into and lose himself in his idealized beloved is what the troubadours termed *joi*. *Joi* is the first aspect of joy that Lester Burnham recovers in reverting to that dimension of time rather than space that is "high school"; we may note that there's something gamely male-adolescent in troubadour desire—its voyeurism, its deliciously unfulfilled erotic dreaming. Recall the Everly Brother's pop hit of 1958: "Whenever I want you all I have to do is dre-e-e-e-eam: dream, dream, dream."

And yet the language of joy is a paradoxical one: as Lester Burnham will discover in the course of *American Beauty*, it's better to have loved and lost than never to have lost at all. Lester's long-desired opportunity for sexual contact with Angela arrives, and as she lies back nervously on a sofa, shedding her former bravado about sex, she says to Lester, "This is my first time…I'm sorry…I should tell you in case you wondered why I wasn't—better." The pathos of the scene triggers Lester's realization that the idealized, sexual-Edenic world in which he had placed her and in which she willingly moved ("high school," as both had misread it) is an illusion and valuable, if at all, as a means of unmooring desire from mundane reality. Lester realizes that to penetrate Angela would be to "de-flower" her, and thus to lose the joy of the ideal or "angelic"—the next type of "American Beauty" to which the film's title refers. Lester had, perhaps, been reviewing American Romanticism: as Emerson wrote in his essay "Love," "In the actual world—the painful kingdom of time and place—dwell care, and canker, and fear. With thought, with the ideal, is immortal hilarity, the rose of joy." Dickinson, in turn, wrote of "maddest Joy": "Within its reach, though yet ungrasped / Desire's perfect Goal— / No nearer—lest the Actual— / Should disenthrall thy Soul—" (poem #1430).

In the end, Lester comes to see the actual Angela as an anxious young woman in need of comforting, and along with this basic (yet earned) ethical insight he realizes that he's a father, too, tenderly recollecting his daughter Jane, whose existence he had too long neglected. Lester, in short, extricates himself from the narrative of *joi* which, when pursued beyond play, typically ends in death—of self and/or of the beloved, in a manner either real or figurative. Unfortunately for Lester, his neighbor, Marine Corps Colonel Frank Fitts (Chris Cooper), a profoundly repressed homosexual who has harbored and briefly expressed a physical desire for him, has no comparable luck in recognizing *joi* for what it is, and so turns the aggression spawned by *eros* against Lester, whom he shoots in the back of the head. The character of Colonel Fitts betrays the film's naturalism and plays on "suburban gothic" clichés, the repressed homosexual next door as son-beating martinet and crypto-Nazi; and yet as a figure who embodies the Aristotelian or National Socialist imperative that all men find joy in the same thing, the Colonel fits in very well. By killing Lester, he both wreaks vengeance on a man who turned away his advances, and eliminates all trace of his temporary inability to conform.

Fortunately for Lester, what in the hour of his death replaces his fifteen-minutes of *eudaimonia* is a lesson about a still more basic joy of being, seeing one's relation to the wider circles that radiate outward from one's own egocentric sphere. The new circle Lester draws upon dying comprehends the beauty of (American) life itself, or at least select and benign images from it: this is a sanitized and sentimental version of the eternal recurrence, one lacking (no doubt for commercial purposes) the astringency of Nietzsche's thought experiment or Yeats's therapeutic self-analysis. In the film's closing montage, images of Lester's life unfold before both him and us in all their surprising beauty: a September sky, the sheen of a sixties car, Carolyn in the gayety of younger years, his daughter Jane. Accompanying these images Lester speaks to us, posthumously: "I guess I could be pretty pissed off at what's happened to me, but it's hard to stay mad when there's so much beauty in the world. . . . My heart fills up like a balloon that's about to burst, and then I remember to relax and stop trying to hold onto it, and then it flows through me like rain. And I can't feel anything but gratitude for every single moment of my stupid little life." The film's final shot is a levitating aerial view of the tree-lined town where he's lived, which from above looks much more pleasing, compositionally, than it ever had before.

Lester appears to have been inspired in his final flight by his friend Ricky Fitts (Wes Bentley), the colonel's dope-smoking and dope-dealing teenage son, and the film's Romantic visionary. Ricky keeps a videotape diary of all the things that happen in their suburban neighborhood, an investigation into the intense beauty of the mundane: the plain girl who lives next door, Lester's daughter Jane (Thora Birch), who eventually finds her soul mate in Ricky; a dead bird on the grass, which he films "because it's beautiful"; and what he calls "the most beautiful thing I've ever filmed," a white plastic bag blowing in circles in front of a red brick wall, among a few dead leaves, within the electrical air currents that precede a snow storm. Ricky screens his film of the bag in the air for Jane, commenting "That's the day I realized there was this entire life behind things, and this incredibly benevolent force that wanted me to know that there was no reason to be afraid, ever. . . . Sometimes there's so much beauty in the world I feel like I can't take it and my heart's just going to cave in." Ricky's film points the moral that, as in Wordsworth's "Tintern Abbey," we owe to "forms of beauty" the intuition of a spiritual, connective force that "impels / All thinking things, all objects of all thought, / And rolls through all things." For Wordsworth as for Ricky, apprehending this motion and spirit in "the joy of elevated thoughts" renders one impervious though not oblivious to the evils of the world, so that

> neither evil tongues,
> Rash judgments, nor the sneers of selfish men,
> Nor greetings where no kindness is, nor all
> The dreary intercourse of daily life,
> Shall e'er prevail against us, or disturb
> Our cheerful faith that all which we behold
> Is full of blessings.

Lester Burnham recalls the image of Ricky's animate bag as his life passes before him, and in his posthumous address to us he echoes Ricky's neo-Wordsworthian words to Jane.

In death, Lester has seen through, he tells us, to something more—although precisely what that is he cannot tell us, given the ineffability of joy. The film's last lines belong to Lester's disembodied voice: "You have no idea what I'm talking about, I'm sure. But don't worry— [screen goes black]—you will someday." The ideal viewer of *American Beauty* will find comfort and joy not only in Lester's moral breakthrough but also in his speaking to us from beyond death, from some type of posthumous existence, some more permanent interweaving in the benevolent system of things—a space that's not evidently religious, but that certainly is post-secular. Lester beholds again, this time with aesthetic distance, his own life and that of his family and community, a recurrence that "stretches on forever like an ocean of time." This immortality is not an escape from his mortal life but rather a sustained reunion with and blessing of it. His vantage point is the space, I would suggest, in which new joys are growing in America.

## BIBLIOGRAPHY

Altieri, Charles. *Painterly Abstraction in Modernist American Poetry: The Contemporaneity of Modernism*. New York: Cambridge University Press, 1989.

Burgess, Anthony. *A Clockwork Orange*. New York: Penguin Books, 2000.

Cetinsky, Karol. *House of Dolls*. Translated by Moshe M. Kohn. New York: Simon and Schuster, 1955.

Cowdery, Ray. *Your KdF-Wagen*. New York: Victory WW Two Publishing Limited, 2002.
De la Mare, Walter. "Joy." *Atlantic Monthly*, January 1940.
DeLillio, Don. *White Noise*. New York: Viking Penguin, 1985.
Epstein, Mark. *Thoughts without a Thinker: Psychotherapy from a Buddhist Perspective*. New York: Basic Books, 1995.
Geetz, Clifford. Review of *Creative Destruction: How Globalization Is Changing the World's Cultures*, by Tyler Cowen. *The New Republic*. (February 17, 2003).
Geller, Jacklyn. *Here Comes the Bride: Women, Weddings, and the Marriage Mystique*. New York: Four Walls, Eight Windows, 2001.
Goodstein, Laurie. "How the Evangelicals and Catholics Joined Forces." *New York Times*, May 30, 2004.
Grant, Lindsey. "The New American Century?" *Negative Population Growth, Inc. Forum*, 2004.
Gurney, Ivor. *Collected Letters*. Edited by R. K. R. Thornton. Machester: Carcanet Press, 1991.
Hart, Gail Kathleen. *Friedrich Schiller: Crime, Aesthetics, and the Poetics of Punishment*. Newark: University of Delaware Press, 2005.
Huizinga, J. *Homo Ludens: A Study of the Play Element in Culture*. Boston: Beacon Press, 1955.
James, Fredric. *Postmodernism, or, The Cultural Logic of Late Capitalism*. Durham: Duke University Press, 1991.
James, Henry. *The Portrait of a Lady*. Edited by Fred B. Millet. New York: Modern Library, 1951.
Jarrell, Randall. *The Complete Works*. New York: Farrar, Strauss, and Giroux, 1981.
Knight, Arthur. "Star Dances: African-American Constructions of Stardom, 1925–1960." In *Classic Hollywood, Classic Whiteness*, edited by Daniel Bernardi, 386–414. Minneapolis: University of Minnesota Press, 2001.
Kundera, Milan. *The Joke*. New York: Harper Collins Publishers, 1992.
Landes, Ruth. *City of Women*. New York: Macmillian, 1947.
Mann, Donald. "An Essay on a Sustainable Economy." *Negative Population Growth, Inc. Forum*, 1999.
Marcuse, Herbert. *Eros and Civilization: A Philosophical Inquiry into Freud*. Boston: Beacon Press, 1966.
———. *One-Dimensional Man: Studies in the Ideology of Advanced Industrial Society*. Boston: Beacon Press, 1964.
McLure, John A. "Postmodern/Post-Secular: Contemporary Fiction and Spirituality." *Modern Fiction Studies* 41.1 (1995): 143–44.
Olds, Sharon. *Blood, Tin, Straw*. New York: Alfred A. Knopf, 1999.
Reynolds, Simon. *Blissed Out: The Raptures of Rock*. London: Serpent's Tail, 1990.
———. *Generation Ecstasy: Into the World of Techno and Rave Culture*. New York: Routledge, 1999.
Singer, Isaac Bashevis. "Androgynous." *The New Yorker*, September 29, 2003.
Sullum, Jacob. *Saying Yes: In Defense of Drug Use*. New York: Tarcher/Putnam, 2003.
Trilling, Lionel. "Wordsworth and the Rabbis." In *The Opposing Self*. New York: Viking, 1955.

## NOTES

1. The "KdF-Wagen" was first advertised in a 1939 pamphlet, stamped with the Nazi swastika, published by Volkwagenwerk, Berlin. For a facsimile reprint with English translation by Ray Cowdery, see *Your KdF-Wagen*.

2. "Ka-tzetnik" served as the pseudonym for the Polish-born Israeli novelist Karol Cetinsky; written in Hebrew, *House of Dolls* was translated into English by Moshe M. Kohn (1955).

3. Kundera, *The Joke*, p. 23. Cf. the complaint of the Cuban novelist Reinaldo Arenas that during Castro's regime in the late 1960s "the joy of life had been lost": "One of the most nefarious characteristics of tyrannies is that they take everything too seriously and destroy all sense of humor. . . . By taking away their (the Cubans') laughter, the Revolution took away from them their deepest sense of the nature of things" (*Before Night Falls*: 229, 239). Compare also the Romanian writer Norman Manea, whose collection of four novellas of life under Ceauşescu is aptly titled *Bonheur Obligatoire* (translated into English as *Compulsory Happiness*).

4. I am indebted to the fine analysis of Burgess's novel and Kubrick's film in Gail K. Hart, *Friedrich Schiller*, 144–59.

5. *A Clockwork Orange*, 46–47.

6. Hart, 146–47.

7. Jarrell, *Complete Poems*, 279–80.

8. And I am greatly assisted in my thinking by my colleague Melanie Dawson, whose knowledge of literary realism far exceeds my own, and who graciously corresponded with me on this topic.

9. Henry James, *The Portrait of a Lady*, ed. Fred B. Millet (New York: Modern Library, 1951), 2 volumes in one, (2) 78–79.

10. Gurney writes: "It is sweet to think what a revenge of Joy I will have on Life for all this. For all this grey petty monotony, I will gather all the over-strength of spirit so hardly earned and force it, coax it, lead it to the service of Joy forever" (*Collected Letters*, ed. R. K. R. Thornton (Manchester: Carcanet Press, 1991), 97).

11. De la Mare's poem (in *The Atlantic* 165, January 1940) tells a familiar story of joy's connection to grief, beginning with "This little smiling Boy / Stretched out his hands to me/ Saying his name was Joy; / Saying all things that seem/ Beautiful, wise and true / Never need fade when he/ Drenches them through and through/ With witchery"; in the second stanza the speaker seeks out this boy named joy and finds him at night weeping "like the nightingale."

12. See Charles Altieri, *Painterly Abstraction in Modernist American Poetry: The Contemporaneity of Modernism* (New York: Cambridge University Press, 1989).

13. Trilling, "Wordsworth and the Rabbis." In *The Opposing Self*, 104–32 (New York: Viking, 1955); 120, 129.

14. Jameson, *Postmodernism, or, The Cultural Logic of Late Capitalism* (Durham: Duke University Press, 1991), 6, 26–29.

15. Don DeLillo, *White Noise* (New York: Viking Penguin, 1985), 148–49.

16. McLure writes: "In suggesting that many postmodern texts are shot through with and even shaped by spiritual concerns, I mean several things: that they make room in the worlds they project for magic, miracle, metaphysical systems of retribution and restoration; that they explore fundamental issues of conduct in ways that honor, interrogate, and revise religious categories and prescriptions; that their political analyses and prescriptions are intermittently but powerfully framed in terms of magical or religious conceptions of power. But I mean as well, that their assaults on realism, their ontological playfulness, and their experiments in the sublime represent a complex and variously inflected reaffirmation of premodern ontologies—constructions of reality that portray the quotidian world as but one dimension of a multidimensional cosmos, or as hosting a world of spirits" ("Postmodern/Post-Secular: Contemporary Fiction and Spirituality," *Modern Fiction Studies* 41.1 (Spring 1995): 143–44).

17. Quoted in Laurie Goodstein, "How the Evangelicals and Catholics Joined Forces," *New York Times* Sunday, Week in Review, May 30, 2004: 4. Emphasis mine.

18. Quoted from the 4th-century Sri Lankan Buddhist, Buddhaghosa, in Mark Epstein, *Thoughts without a Thinker: Psychotherapy from a Buddhist Perspective* (New York: Basic Books, 1995), 132.

19. Singer speaks here through the voice of his character Reb Leyzer Walden, a Polish Hasid from the eighteenth or nineteenth century, and chief narrator of the story "Androgynous," trans. Joseph Sherman, *The New Yorker*, September 29, 2003: 100. "Androgynous" was originally published in Yiddish in 1975.

20. J. Huizinga saw "play"—which he saw as being "apart together" with others, intensely absorbed "outside and above the necessities and seriousness of everyday life"—as the anthropological root of religion (*Homo Ludens: A Study of the Play Element in Culture* (Boston: Beacon Press, 1955), 12, 26). I see religion (optimally), along with music (which one "plays"), as a concentration of the joy that adheres in play, without play's competitiveness (agon) and agony.

21. My thinking about joy on the "road to nowhere" is indebted to Simon Reynolds, *Blissed Out: The Raptures of Rock* (London: Serpent's Tail, 1990), 126, 138.

22. Geertz, reviewing Tyler Cowen's *Creative Destruction: How Globalization is Changing the World's Cultures* for *The New Republic*, February 17, 2003, 27.

23. My thoughts on sustainable economy are indebted to the publications of Negative Population Growth, esp. Donald Mann, "An Essay on a Sustainable Economy," *NPG Forum* 1999, and Lindsey Grant, "The New American Century?," *NPG Forum* May 2004.

24. Sharon Olds, *Blood, Tin, Straw*, 54.

25. Herbert Marcuse, *Eros and Civilization: A Philosophical Inquiry into Freud* (Boston: Beacon Press, 1966), 226–28.

26. Marcuse, *One-Dimensional Man: Studies in the Ideology of Advanced Industrial Society* (Boston: Beacon Press, 1964), 73.

27. Marcuse, *Eros and Civilization*, 235.

28. On the syncretism of Catholic and "Candomble" (Yoruba for 'mysteries' or 'ritual') religion in mid-twentieth-century Bahia, Brazil—and the spirit of music that drives its rituals of spirit-possession—see Ruth Landes, *City of Women* (New York: Macmillan, 1947).

29. On the African-American context of the "star turn" and its relation to the communal circle, see Arthur Knight, "Star Dances: African-American Constructions of Stardom, 1925–1960." In *Classic Hollywood, Classic Whiteness*, edited by Daniel Bernardi (Minneapolis: University of Minnesota Press, 2001), 386–414.

30. Ecstasy is the street name for the synthetic psychoactive drug MDMA, developed in 1912 by the German pharmaceutical company Merck as an appetite suppressant. It is characterized in both medical and popular literature as a "hug drug" capable of breaking down emotional barriers; while lowering sexual inhibitions, it also commonly causes impotence. See the summary of literature on Ecstasy in Jacob Sullum, *Saying Yes: In Defense of Drug Use* (New York: Tarcher/Putnam, 2003), 168–91.

31. Simon Reynolds, *Generation Ecstasy: Into the World of Techno and Rave Culture* (New York: Routledge, 1999), 4–5, 9, 35.

32. Jacklyn Geller, within an extended reading of *American Beauty* as a satire on the mass-marketed ideal of marriage as a perpetual honeymoon, is especially keen about Carolyn Burnham: "She has inhaled the philosophy of America's new age corporate gurus who urge their clients to succeed through focused cheeriness." In *Here Comes the Bride: Women, Weddings, and the Marriage Mystique* (New York: Four Walls, Eight Windows, 2001), 361.

# Index

# About the Contributors

**James Pawelski** (coeditor) is a senior scholar at the University of Pennsylvania, where he serves as the founding director of the Master of Applied Positive Psychology (MAPP) Program, the world's first degree program in positive psychology, and as a Special Advisor to the Positive Psychology Steering Committee. He is the founding Executive Director of the International Positive Psychology Association (IPPA) and a charter member of the Board of Directors of that organization. In addition to publishing numerous peer-reviewed articles in philosophy, he has authored *The Dynamic Individualism of William James* (2007). He is also a contributor to and section editor of *The Oxford Handbook of Happiness* (2011). James is currently coediting (with Moores, Potkay, Mason, Wolfson, and Engell) a collection of poems on human flourishing—*Human Flourishing: An Anthology of Eudaimonic Poetry.*

Contact: pawelski@psych.upenn.edu

**D.J. Moores** (coeditor) is assistant professor of English and program coordinator at Kean University. He is the author of numerous scholarly articles and conference papers, as well as three critical books: *Mystical Discourse in Wordsworth and Whitman* (2006), *The Dark Enlightenment: Jung, Romanticism & the Repressed Other* (2010), and *The Ecstatic Poetic Tradition: An Aesthetics of Ecstasy* (forthcoming). In addition to compiling and editing *Wild Poets of Ecstasy: An Anthology of Ecstatic Verse* (2011), he is also currently collaborating (with Pawelski, Potkay, Mason, Wolfson, and Engell) on another edited volume—*Human Flourishing: An Anthology of Eudaimonic Poetry.*

Contact: dmoores@kean.edu

**Charles Altieri** (contributor) is professor of English at the University of California–Berkeley, where he also occupies the Rachael Anderson Stageberg Chair. He is a distinguished, influential scholar and the author of the following books: The Art of Modern American Poetry , The Particulars of Rapture: An Aesthetics of the Affects ; Postmodernism Now: Essays on Contemporaneity in the Arts ; Subjective Agency: A Theory of First-Person Expressivity and Its Social Implications ; Canons and Consequences ; Painterly Abstraction in Modernist American Poetry: The Contemporaneity of Modernism ; Self and Sensibility in Contemporary American Poetry ; Act and Quality: A Theory of Literary Meaning ; Enlarging the Temple: New Directions in American Poetry of the 1960s ; and Bibliography of Modern and Contemporary Anglo-American Poetry.

**Paola Baseotto** (contributor) is adjunct professor of English at Insubria University. Her published works include numerous scholarly articles and three books: *"Disdeining life, desiring leaue to die": Spenser and the Psychology of Despair*; *Language to Language*; and *Fighting for God, Queen and Country: Spenser and the Morality of Violence*. As a specialist in the interplay of Renaissance theological and medical discourses, she has presented papers at international conferences throughout Europe and has taught seminars at Princeton University and Loyola University (Chicago).

**David Bordelon** (contributor) is associate professor of English at Ocean County College. A specialist in print culture and reader reception/response theory, he is the author of numerous articles and book chapters and is currently working on a monograph, *Charles Dickens and Nineteenth Century America: The Great Actuality of the Current Imagination*.

**John Briggs** (contributor) is distinguished professor of English at the University of California–Riverside. In addition to numerous articles, he is the author of *Lincoln's Speeches Reconsidered*. He has also written *Francis Bacon and the Rhetoric of Nature*, which earned him the Thomas J. Wilson award for the "best first book" published at Harvard University Press in 1988.

**James Engell** (contributor) is Gurney Professor of English and professor of comparative literature at Harvard University. A distinguished and influential scholar in the fields of Romanticism and eighteenth-century studies, he has authored or edited the following books: *Saving Higher Education in the Age of Money*; *The Committed Word: Literature and Public Values*; *Coleridge: The Early Family Letters* (editor); *Forming the Critical Mind*; *The Creative Imagination*; and *Coleridge's Biographia Literaria* (coeditor), among others.

**Amanpal Garcha** (contributor) is associate professor in the English department at Ohio State University and the author of *From Sketch to Novel: The Development of Victorian Fiction* (2009).

**Christine E. Kephart** (contributor) is director of the Writing Center and Tutoring Resources at Ocean County College in New Jersey, and she also teaches literature and theory at Kean University. In addition to conference papers and journal articles, she has recently published *The Catherian Cathedral: Gothic Cathedral Iconography in Willa Cather's Fiction*.

**Erin Lafford** (contributor) is completing graduate work in Victorian Literature in the School of English and Scottish Language and Literature at the University of Glasgow. She is the author of journal articles on Elizabeth Bishop and Gerard Manley Hopkins (*Literature and Theology*) and William Blake's *Milton* (*Literature Compass*).

**Emma Mason** (contributor) is a reader in the department of English and comparative literary studies at the University of Warwick. A prominent Romanticist in the United Kingdom, she is the author of *The Cambridge Introduction to Wordsworth*; *Women Poets of the Nineteenth Century*; and, with Mark Knight, *Nineteenth Century Religion and Literature*. She is coeditor of *The Oxford Handbook of the Reception History of the Bible* and *The Blackwell Companion to the Bible in English Literature* and the editor of *Elizabeth Jennings: The Collected Poems*.

**Daniel O'Day** (contributor) is professor of English and chair of the English department at Kean University, where he has also served as Director of the Developmental Studies and General Education Programs. His recent scholarship has focused on the novels and short stories of Elizabeth Bowen, Edith Somerville, and Martin Ross, on the theme of reconciliation in Shakespearean comedy, and on the poetry of John Milton. In addition to authoring numerous conference papers and articles, he has also written *Quest for Childhood: A Critical Study of Henry Vaughan and Thomas Traherne*.

**Adam Potkay** (contributor) is Professor of English and William R. Kenan Professor of Humanities at the College of William and Mary. He is the author of *The Story of Joy: From the Bible to Late Romanticism*, which won the Harry Levin Prize, the American Comparative Literature Association's award for the best book in literary history and literary criticism. He has written two additional books—*The Passion for Happiness: Samuel Johnson and David Hume* and *The Fate of Eloquence in the Age of Hume*—and edited two others: *Henry Fielding: The History of the Adventures of Joseph Andrews* and *Black Atlantic Writers of the 18th Century: Living the New Exodus in England and the Americas*. Adam is also currently in press with *Wordsworth's Ethics* (The Johns Hopkins University Press).

**Michael West** (contributor) is professor of English at the University of Pittsburgh. He is the author of numerous scholarly articles as well as *Transcendental Wordplay: America's Romantic Punsters and the Search for the Language of Nature*, which won Phi Beta Kappa's Christian Gauss Prize for the best book of literary scholarship and criticism in 2000.

Contact: mikewest@pitt.edu